The Christmas Almanack

Gerard & Patricia Del Re

RANDOM HOUSE
REFERENCE
NEW YORK

The Christmas Almanack, 2nd edition

Copyright (c) 1979, 2004 by Gerard and Patricia Del Re

All rights reserved under International and Pan-American Copyright Conventions. Published in the United States by Random House Reference, an imprint of The Random House Information Group, a division of Random House, Inc., New York and simultaneously in Canada by Random House of Canada Limited, Toronto. No part of this book may be reproduced in any form or by any means, electronic or mechanical, including photocopying, recording, or by any information storage and retrieval system, without the written permission of the publisher. All inquiries should be addressed to Random House Reference, Random House Information Group, 1745 Broadway, New York, NY 10019.

RANDOM HOUSE is a registered trademark of Random House, Inc.

An earlier edition of this work was published in 1979 by Doubleday, a division of Random House, Inc.

Please address inquiries about electronic licensing of reference products for use on a network, in software or on CD-ROM to the Subsidiary Rights Department, Random House Reference, fax 212-572-6003.

This book is available for special discounts for bulk purchases for sales promotions or premiums. Special editions, including personalized covers, excerpts of existing books, and corporate imprints, can be created in large quantities for special needs. For more information, write to Random House, Inc., Special Markets/ Premium Sales, 1745 Broadway, MD 6-2, New York, NY, 10019 or e-mail specialmarkets@ randomhouse.com.

All biblical quotations throughout this volume are taken from the King James Version (KJV).

Grateful acknowledgement is made to Gene Pritsker for the carol sheet music and Cheryl McWard for select recipes.

Visit the Random House Web site: www.randomhouse.com

Interior design by Nora Rosansky

Library of Congress Cataloging-in-Publication Data is available.

0 9 8 7 6 5 4 3 2 1
ISBN: 0-375-72078-2

With love to Richard S. Lane and Barbara Zena Wallace

For Tom and Thomasina Dougherty

"I WILL HONOR CHRISTMAS IN MY HEART
AND TRY TO KEEP IT ALL THE YEAR."

 Ebeneezer Scrooge
A Christmas Carol
1843

Contents

Christmas on the Table

✤Dinners✤

✤Breads✤

✤Desserts✤

Introduction

Classic Christmas books are like sweet Christmas memories. They are rarely forgotten, but nestle in the mind and heart for long winter naps, only to be reopened each year in anticipation of the Christmas season. *The Christmas Almanack* was conceived with that very notion in mind. We hope that this book will become a classic holiday companion—something to pull off your bookshelf to read and enjoy each Christmas season.

This new edition of *The Christmas Almanack* not only brings the book up to date, but also encompasses an unprecedented scope of yuletide observances including films, sheet music, literature, food, and a diverse collection of cultural traditions. From around the world and across the centuries, *The Christmas Almanack* rings in Christmas with all its sounds and splendor. Whether you're reading about Handel's *Messiah,* or Mass of the Rooster, the Sugarplum Fairy or sugarplum recipes, Pantomimes or Père Noel, each page is brimming with facts and knowledge to command your attention and fulfill all your Christmas dreams, now and for years to come.

Merry Christmas!

Christmas in the Bible

Many of us are familiar with the biblical Christmas story. In fact, most of us would say we know the story backwards and forwards. For most of us, what we know about Christmas has come not from the biblical story but from paintings, music, stories, Christmas cards, television specials, and movies. Hollywood has probably affected our idea of Christmas more than the Bible ever has. Here is the original Christmas story, as written in the King James Bible.

Luke 2:1-20

And it came to pass in those days, that there went out a decree from Caesar Augustus, that all the world should be taxed. 2 (And this taxing was first made when Cyrenius was governor of Syria.) 3 And all went to be taxed, every one into his own city. 4 And Joseph also went up from Galilee, out of the city of Nazareth, into Judaea, unto the city of David, which is called Bethlehem; (because he was of the house and lineage of David:) 5 To be taxed with Mary his espoused wife, being great with child. 6 And so it was, that, while they were there, the days were accomplished that she should be delivered. 7 And she brought forth her firstborn son, and wrapped him in swaddling clothes, and laid him in a manger; because there was no room for them in the inn. 8 And there were in the same country shepherds abiding in the field, keeping watch over their flock by night. 9 And, lo, the angel of the Lord came upon them, and the glory of the Lord shone round about them: and they were sore afraid. 10 And the angel said unto them, Fear not: for, behold, I bring you good tidings of great joy, which shall be to all people. 11 For unto you is born this day in the city of David a Saviour, which is Christ the Lord. 12 And this shall be a sign unto you; Ye shall find the babe wrapped in swaddling clothes, lying in a manger. 13

And suddenly there was with the angel a multitude of the heavenly host praising God, and saying, 14 Glory to God in the highest, and on earth peace, good will toward men. 15 And it came to pass, as the angels were gone away from them into heaven, the shepherds said one to another, Let us now go even unto Bethlehem, and see this thing which is come to pass, which the Lord hath made known unto us. 16 And they came with haste, and found Mary, and Joseph, and the babe lying in a manger. 17 And when they had seen it, they made known abroad the saying which was told them concerning this child. 18 And all they that heard it wondered at those things which were told them by the shepherds. 19 But Mary kept all these things, and pondered them in her heart. 20 And the shepherds returned, glorifying and praising God for all the things that they had heard and seen, as it was told unto them.

Matthew 2:1-23

1Now when Jesus was born in Bethlehem of Judaea in the days of Herod the king, behold, there came wise men from the east to Jerusalem, 2 Saying, Where is he that is born King of the Jews? for we have seen his star in the east, and are come to worship him. 3 When Herod the king had heard these things, he was troubled, and all Jerusalem with him. 4 And when he had gathered all the chief priests and scribes of the people together, he demanded of them where Christ should be born. 5 And they said unto him, In Bethlehem of Judaea: for thus it is written by the prophet, 6 And thou Bethlehem, in the land of Juda, art not the least among the princes of Juda: for out of thee shall come a Governor, that shall rule my people Israel. 7 Then Herod, when he had privily called the wise men, inquired of them diligently what time the star appeared. 8 And he sent them to Bethlehem, and said, Go and search diligently for the young child; and when ye have found him, bring me word again, that I may come and worship him also. 9 When they had heard the king, they departed; and, lo, the star, which they saw in the east, when before them, till it came and stood over where the young child was. 10 When they saw the star, they rejoiced with exceeding great joy. 11 And when they were come into the house, they saw the young child with Mary his mother, and fell down, and worshipped him: and when they had opened their treasures, they presented unto him gifts; gold, and frankincense, and myrrh. 12 And being warned of God in a dream that they should not return to Herod, they departed into their own country another way. 13 And when they were departed, behold, the angel of the Lord appeareth to Joseph in a dream, saying, Arise, and take the young child and his mother, and flee into Egypt, and be thou there until I bring thee word: for Herod will seek the young child to destroy him. 14 When he arose, he took the young child and his mother by night, and departed into Egypt: 15 And was there until the death of Herod: that it might be fulfilled which was spoken of the Lord by the prophet, saying, Out of Egypt have I called my son. 16 Then Herod, when he saw that he was mocked of the wise men, was exceeding wroth, and sent forth, and slew all the children that were in Bethlehem, and in all the coasts thereof, from two years old and under, according to the time which he had diligently inquired of the wise men. 17 Then was fulfilled that which was spoken by Jeremy the prophet, saying, 18 In Rama was there a voice heard, lamentation, and weeping, and great mourning, Rachel weeping for her children, and would not be comforted, because they are not. 19 But when Herod was dead, behold, an angel of the Lord appeareth in a dream to Joseph in Egypt, 20 Saying, Arise, and take the young child and his mother, and go into the land of Israel... 22 But when he heard that Archelaus did reign in Judaea in the room of his father Herod, he was afraid to go thither: notwithstanding, being warned of

God in a dream, he turned aside into the parts of Galilee: 23 And he came and dwelt in a city called Nazareth: that it might be fulfilled which was spoken by the prophets, He shall be called a Nazarene.

Christmas Myths

The following details about the Christmas story are not documented in the Bible, or at least not in the way that everyone knows them. They inspire the imagination and succeed in making Jesus' birth more real to us, but they probably never happened.

The Journey to Bethlehem

In popular myth, the journey from Nazareth to Bethlehem has Mary seated on a donkey. In fact, no donkey is mentioned in the Bible, although it may have existed. As for the hardship of the journey, undoubtedly all travel in that time was difficult, but this trip was not to be unique for Joseph and Mary. Bethlehem is just five miles from Jerusalem and, according to Luke 2:41, Jesus' "parents went to Jerusalem every year at the feast of the passover." Thus the trip was to be an annual pilgrimage for them.

The phrase "great with child" conjures up in the modern mind an image of Mary being near the time of delivery. In fact, this King James translation is just a seventeenth-century euphemism for "pregnant," with no indication of how far along that pregnancy might be. There is no hint as to how long Mary and Joseph were at Bethlehem before the birth took place. People assume it was within the first night or two because there was no room at the inn, but such a situation might have arisen at any time, and the Bible does not give an answer.

The Stable

No stable is mentioned in the texts of Matthew and Luke. The word translated as "manger" may mean either "stable" or "stall." A stall could be either in a stable or outdoors. Moreover, an inn of the time does not fit our modern conception of a main building with individual rooms and a stable out back. An inn could often be a large, one-roomed structure where the travelers slept elevated on cots or platforms, and the animals were in the same room on the floor. Thus a manger might be indoors, on a different level from the sleeping facilities but in the same room. We really can't say where Christ was born.

Popular tradition once made the stable a cave. Thus, when Constantine became Christian and sought the birthplace of Jesus, he decided on a series of caves near Bethlehem. In keeping with the general trend of adapting the pagan to the Christian, he tore down a temple to Adonis and erected the Church of the Nativity on the same spot, over the cave where he believed Jesus was born.

The Animals

There is no mention of the friendly animals that popular art and fiction have depicted clustered around the manger, emanating warmth and adoration. However, since a manger was for the feeding or housing of such animals, it is probably safe to assume that animals were around somewhere. The image of the King of Heaven humbling Himself to be surrounded by the beasts of the field has proved to be enduring as well as inspiring. Countless legends tell how all animals kneel in adoration on Christmas Eve at midnight, just as their ancestors did in the original stable, and how the animals can also speak at that time.

Several medieval carols and pageants presented the charming story of the animals seeking to worship the newborn king with their own voices. Each response is cleverly suited to the "language" of each animal. The rooster crows out, "Christus natus est," Latin for "Christ is born." "Ubi?" "Where?" muses the taciturn ox. The excitable sheep bleat out, "Bethlehem!" "Hihamus" or "eamus," brays the donkey, "let's go." And a young calf replies, "Volo!" "I'm going!"

The Angels' Song

The song of the angels— and on earth peace, good will toward men—is a blessing to biblical scholars, since its exact translation has given them gainful employment for centuries and shows no sign of letting up. "Peace toward men of good will" is just as correct a translation of Luke's ambiguous Greek. The examination of fine details of grammar, usage, and prosody and textual comparisons have not produced a definitive answer on who should expect God's peace and good will, all men or only those who have tried to deserve them.

The Three Wise Men

Matthew does not tell us how many Wise Men there were, nor who they were and where they came from. Tradition finally settled on three since three gifts are mentioned, but as late as the third century there were paintings of four Wise Men, and earlier there had been as many as a dozen.

The word that Matthew uses for the Wise Men is magoi. This word was applied to a multitude of practitioners of the occult arts. Fortunetellers, astronomers, augurers, and general magicians were all referred to as magi. One widely held theory is that the Magi of the Bible were priests of Zoroaster from Persia. Their functions in this religion would have included the interpretation of signs and astrology. Babylonia and Arabia are also very possible sources for the magicians we call the Wise Men.

The idea of the Wise Men as kings (as in "We Three Kings of Orient Are") does not appear in the Gospels but was added in popular tradition later. This idea probably arose from application of Psalm 72:10-11: "...the kings of Sheba and Seba shall offer gifts. Yea, all kings shall fall down before him."

Whatever their origin and status, the Magi caught the popular imagination with their exotic and mysterious story. The early Church paid far more attention to them than to the prosaic shepherds. In the Roman catacombs, the Magi appear in paintings at least two centuries earlier than the shepherds, and far more prominently. It was not until the Protestants arose to decry the adoration of relics and the elaborate symbolism accorded the Magi that the simple shepherds who did not bear such a "taint" were elevated to the major position in nativity scenes that they now occupy.

With the intense interest that the early Church had in them, it is natural that the Magi should begin to acquire names and homes and characteristics. Numerous traditions arose with such tongue-twisting names as Yazdegerd, Hormizdah, and Perozadh, Kings of Persia, Saba, Sheba, or, less specifically, "the East." The sixth century marks the first appearance in a Greek manuscript, which is known only from a later Latin translation, of the names Balthasar, Melchior, and Gaspar or Caspar. Each was a king and each was assigned a kingdom and a particular royal gift. Balthasar, a black King of Ethiopia and forty years old, brought myrrh in a gold-mounted horn. Melchior, also forty or sometimes older, King of Arabia, brought a casket of gold in the form of a shrine. Gaspar was King

of Tarsus and a beardless youth of twenty when he brought frankincense in a jar or censer. Thus the Magi represented people of all races and all ages kneeling in adoration.

The gifts of the Wise Men have been taken symbolically to mean many different things, but the general symbolic value of each is clear. Gold was the purest material and therefore worthy of a king. Incense was used in the worship of a god, carrying prayers upward with its sweet scent. Myrrh was a balm for physical suffering. Thus, it has been suggested, Jesus was being worshiped as king, god, and great physician, or sacrifice. The gifts may also suggest what each Christian must offer up to God: virtue, prayer, and suffering.

The time allowed for the Wise Men's journey is not specified in the Gospels. As nothing says whether the star arose at Jesus' birth or before it, there is really no way of telling when they set out. Popular tradition varies from twelve days to two years and puts their arrival on January 6, Epiphany, although no one thinks twice of Christmas manger scenes that show them arriving a few minutes after the shepherds, who came from just down the road.

However long that first trip to Bethlehem, the Wise Men's journeys were far from ended. The cathedral at Cologne, Germany, contains a shrine that is said to hold the still-uncorrupt remains of the Three Kings. These bodies were once taken to Constantinople either by Empress Helena, mother of Constantine, in the third century, or by Emperor Zeno in the fifth century. After the First Crusade, they turned up in Milan and then were moved to Cologne by the emperor Frederick Barbarossa. In 1903 the cardinal of Cologne returned some of the relics to the cardinal of Milan.

The Star of Bethlehem

The Star of Bethlehem appears in pictures as a great shining light that would have created astonishment in anyone seeing it. But Matthew does not indicate that anyone besides the Magi paid it any notice. Herod asks them when they first saw it as though it had not been seen or particularly noticed in Jerusalem. Yet it must have been something that would have special meaning to trained observers of the skies such as the Wise Men. Three major theories have been put forward as natural explanations of the star:

1. The star may have been a nova. A nova is a star that explodes, becoming suddenly very bright where it may have been dim before, and remaining highly visible, sometimes even during the day, for weeks at a time. Astronomers in many parts of the world, however, had been keeping records since long before this time, and none indicated a nova occurring in the last few years B.C. or the first few years A.D.

2. The star may have been a comet. A comet is a celestial body that appears as a bright head trailing a luminous tail of gases and particles. It has the advantage over a star as a candidate for the Star of Bethlehem in that it moves and could conceivably seem to lead the Wise Men. By stretching our dates somewhat, it is possible to put Halley's comet, which returns about every seventy-seven years, into approximately the right place. It would have appeared in 12 B.C. in the constellation Leo, which might be interpreted symbolically as the Lion of Judah. But comets were known to the people of the time as comets, not as stars, and they were more often thought to presage catastrophes than joyous occasions.

3. The most popular theory is that the star may have been a planetary conjunction. An ordinary conjunction occurs whenever two planets are

passing each other at their closest point as viewed from the earth. This happens as often as every twenty years or so, depending upon the specific planets. Much rarer is a conjunction of three planets. The great astronomer Kepler saw such a conjunction of Mars, Jupiter, and Saturn in October of A.D. 1604. His calculations showed that there is such a conjunction every 805 years. This would mean that one occurred in the range of time when we think Jesus was born—in the year 7-6 B.C.—and appearing most brightly in the months of May-June, September-October, and December of 7 B.C. This would result in a particularly bright star or pattern of stars that might be noticed by anyone, but would have special significance for an astrologer.

These are the scientific explanations put forward to account for the star. Most Christians are satisfied with the simple words of Matthew: "... and, lo, the star, which they saw in the east, went before them, till it came and stood over where the young child was. When they saw the star, they rejoiced with exceeding great joy."

Christmas on the Calendar

Jesus' Birthday

We celebrate Christmas as the birthday of Jesus Christ, even though scholars tell us there is no hard evidence that indicates on what date Jesus was born. In fact, there is no certainty even about the year.

Luke does give certain clues to the year. The appearance of the angel to Elisabeth, the future mother of John the Baptist, happened "in the days of Herod," and we know that Herod, the king of Judaea, died in March or April of 4 B.C. (The abbreviation B.C. stands for "before Christ" and was only established as an approximation of when Christ was born.)

Luke also tells us that shortly before Jesus' birth "there went out a decree from Caesar Augustus, that all the world should be taxed," and that this happened when Cyrenius was governor of Syria. Records show that the only census taking place during the governorship of Quirinius (the accepted modern spelling of Cyrenius) took place in 7-6 B.C. This would be two years before the death of Herod. Since Matthew says Herod ordered the massacre of all male children in Bethlehem under two years of age in an attempt to kill the Messiah, it would appear that Jesus was probably approaching two years of age before Herod died, meaning that Jesus was born in 6 B.C.

The year 6 B.C. would also accord roughly with Luke's statement that Jesus was about thirty years of age in "the fifteenth year of the reign of Tiberius Caesar" (Luke 3:1, 23), which would have been A.D. 27-28.

The earliest reference to Christmas being celebrated on December 25 appears in Antioch in the middle of the second century. As the Christian Church was still a persecuted minority, no official determination was made until the fourth century, when the Roman emperor Constantine embraced Christianity, thereby ensuring Christianity's eventual domination of Western culture. According to the Philocalian Calendar, a Roman almanac of the year 336, December 25 was the date for the Nativity Feast, indicating popular acceptance of that date. In 350 December 25 was officially delared as Christmas Day by Pope Julius I.

By the fifth century, Christmas had become so important in the Church calendar that it was considered to be the beginning of the ecclesiastical year. The start of the Church calendar was later moved back to include Advent, the season of preparation for the coming of Christ. In 529 the Emperor Justinian made December 25 a civic holiday, thereby prohibiting any work on that day. The Council of Tours in 567 established the period of Advent as a time of fasting before Christmas and proclaimed the twelve days from Christmas to Epiphany a sacred, festive season.

Winter Solstice Celebrations That Preceded Christmas

As Christians celebrated Christmas year after year and century after century, they borrowed, adopted, or simply carried over elements of other midwinter celebrations. The time of the winter solstice has always been an important season in mythology. The winter solstice often fell around December 25 on the Julian calendar. At this time, in the northern hemisphere, the sun is at its lowest ebb and the promise of spring is buried in cold and snow. It is the time when the forces of chaos that stand against the return of light and life must once again be defeated by the gods. People once believed that at the low point of the solstice they must resort to ritual, ceremony, and celebration help the gods overcome the dark. Throughout the world, the winter solstice has been a time of great festivity.

In Mesopotamia there was a year's-end celebration called Zagmuk. A criminal was set up as a mock king and eventually executed as a scapegoat for the people's sins of the previous year. In the Mesopotamian creation myth, the great god Marduk had subdued the monsters of chaos before the world began, but their restraints were loosened with the dying of the sun, and they had to be conquered again at the end of each year. To help their god, the Mesopotamians made a wooden image of these monsters and burned in a great bonfire. It may well be that this wooden image traveled a circuitous route over the course of hundreds of years to become the Yule log of northern celebrations.

Persia and Babylonia also had winter solstice festivals, called Sacaea. Slaves and masters exchanged places. Two criminals were chosen: one was set free; one was treated as a king and then executed.

In Greek mythology, Zeus overthrew Kronos and the Titans at this time of year to establish his own reign. In Roman mythology, Zeus was called Jupiter, and Kronos became Saturn. According to legend, Saturn once escaped defeat by Jupiter and reigned during a time of great peace and prosperity known ever afterward as the Golden Age. Goodness and plenty were available for all and all men were equal. But the Golden Age did not last. Saturn was forced out again by Jupiter. In his temple at Rome, the feet of Saturn were bound in chains all year long as a symbol of his defeat, except for one brief period. This was the Saturnalia, the celebration of the return of the Golden Age.

The Saturnalia ran from December 17 to 24 and was followed shortly by the kalends, which was also a great celebration for early Christians. All businesses were closed except those that provided food or entertainment. Slaves were made equal to masters or even given a higher rank than them. Gambling, drinking, and feasting were encouraged. People exchanged

gifts, called strenae, from the vegetation goddess Strenia, whom it was important to honor at midwinter. Originally these gifts were merely twigs from her sacred grove, but they later became fruits or cakes and finally small figures and more elaborate gifts. Men dressed as women or in the hides of animals and caroused in the streets. Candles and lamps were used to frighten the spirits of darkness, which were powerful at this time of year. At its most decadent and barbaric, Saturnalia may have been the excuse among Roman soldiers in the East for human sacrifice. This, however, was the extreme. Generally, Saturnalia was a boisterous, noisy revel meant both to celebrate the Golden Age and to help overcome the forces that threaten the earth at the sun's ebb.

Why December 25?

At the same time as the the kalends celebration, the Romans enacted rituals of a much older celebration that glorified the ancient Persian deity, Mithra, the god of light. At this point in the calendar, immediately following the winter solstice, the days were lengthening little by little.

Mithra, a figure spoken of in the Zend-Avesta, or sacred Zoroastrian scriptures, was born out of a rock on December 25. Rome was famous for its flirtations with strange gods and cults, and in the third century the emperor Aurelian established the festival of Dies Invicti Solis, the Day of the Invincible Sun, on December 25. Mithra was an embodiment of the sun, so this period of its rebirth was a major day in Mithraism, which at that time was Rome's latest official religion. It is believed that the emperor Constantine adhered to Mithraism up to the time of his conversion to Christianity in A.D. 312. He was instrumental in seeing that the major feast of his old religion was carried over to his new faith. The new celebration became known as Christ Mass.

Early Christians were familiar with the symbolic identification of Christ with the Sun, as in Malachi 4:2: "But unto you that fear my name shall the Sun of righteousness arise with healing in his wings." It was easy to replace the Invincible Sun symbolically with this new Sun of Righteousness, and most of the festivities were carried over whole into the new religion.

Yule

As the Christian faith was carried into northern Europe, two important pagan festivals celebrated by the Germanic and Celtic peoples found their way into the celebration of Christmas.

In December, ten to twelve days were set aside for celebrating a holiday known as Julmond. The origins of the word Jul, which became our familiar "Yule" and "Yuletide" remain shrouded in mystery. It may relate to the Germanic word iul or giul, which means "a turning wheel." This would relate to the turning of the seasons or the rising of the wheel-shaped disc of the sun. More likely, it derives from the word geola, which means "feast" and was sometimes used to mean the whole month of December.

In the celebration of Jul, wheat was worshiped, and its products, bread and liquor distilled from the grains of the field, were exchanged as gifts and heavily imbibed. In midwinter, the idea of rebirth and fertility was tremendously important. In the snows of winter, the evergreen was a symbol of the life that would return in the spring, so evergreens were used for decoration. The boar, which was the symbol of Frey, a god of regeneration, was killed and eaten. Light was important in dispelling the growing darkness of the solstice, so a Yule log was lighted with the remains of the previous year's log.

This was the background that the Christian missionaries found as they moved north, starting in the fifth century. It was very much like Rome with its pre-Christian, and, as before, the local customs were swallowed up into the practice of the new faith. The various saints' days festivities throughout November and December took on the aspects of the harvest feasts, and Christmas was observed throughout Europe with feasting and presents , a celebration, full of evergreens, light, and noise. As many customs lost their religious function, they passed into the realm of superstition, becoming good luck traditions and eventually merely enjoyable customs without rationale. For example, the mistletoe is no longer worshiped, but has become an excuse for rather nonreligious activities.

Christmas Festivities at Their Peak

The celebration of Christmas as feast reached its heights in medieval England. The twelve days of Christmas were a time to call the court together and indulge in unequaled revelry. Kings and bishops vied to outdo each other in the splendor of their retinue's apparel, the elaborateness of their entertainments, the pageantry of their tournaments, and the groaning bounty of their banquet tables. One course of such a banquet, a Christmas pie, was described as being 9 feet in diameter, weighing 165 pounds, and containing 2 bushels of flour, 20 pounds of butter, 4 geese, 2 rabbits, 4 wild ducks, 2 woodcocks, 6 snipes, 4 partridges, 2 neats' tongues, 2 curlews, 6 pigeons, and 7 blackbirds. At one Christmas Henry III had 600 oxen slaughtered, not to mention the game and fish or the veritable oceans of wine needed to ease the passage of such a herd down the throats of king and court.

Christmas also became the time for all good nobles and merchants to show their loyalty to their king by making him splendid gifts. There was an understanding as to how much each should give, and cash was considered an appropriate present. In the mid-thirteenth century, when the merchant class was stubborn about doing its share, Henry III closed the shops for two weeks until the merchants agreed to come up with the stipulated two thousand pounds.

Gambling was very popular at Christmas in medieval and Renaissance England. It was considered a quiet sport and therefore more suitable in fashionable circles than some of the rowdier entertainments that were popular among the common people. Edward IV actually passed an act restricting card play to the twelve days of Christmas. It is said that Queen Elizabeth I's indulgent nobles gave her loaded dice to play with so that she would always win.

By the sixteenth century, the celebration of Christmas had become a boisterous affair. Bands of mummers, dressed like beasts and women as in the days of Saturnalia, begged money and caroused, even invading churches to disrupt services with their merriment.

The Backlash Against Christmas

Inevitably, there were reactions against what Christmas had become. Since the earliest days of the Church, the religious had inveighed against the way Christ's birthday was celebrated. There was even great controversy over whether His birthday should be celebrated at all. As early as A.D. 245, the Church father Origen was proclaiming it heathenish to celebrate Christ's birthday as if He were merely a temporal ruler when His spiritual nature should be the main concern. This view was echoed throughout the centuries, but found strong widespread advocacy only with the rise of Protestantism. To these serious-minded, sober clerics, the celebration of Christmas flew in the face of all they believed. Drunken revelry on Christmas! It was merely an excuse to continue the customs of pagan Saturnalia. The Protestants found their own quieter ways of celebrating, in calm and meditation. The strict Puritans refused to celebrate at all, saying that no celebration should be more important than the Sabbath. The Pilgrims in Massachusetts made a point of working on Christmas as on any other day.

This made little difference to the world at large until the Puritans came to power in England, beheading King Charles I and establishing Oliver Cromwell as Lord Protector of the country.

On June 3, 1647, Parliament established punishments for observing Christmas and certain other holidays. This policy was reaffirmed in 1652 with these words:

RESOLVED BY THE PARLIAMENT

That no Observation shall be had of the Five and twentieth day of December commonly called Christmas-Day; nor any Solemnity used or exercised in Churches upon the Day in respect thereof.

The town criers passed through the streets ringing their bells and shouting, "No Christmas! No Christmas!" For those who celebrated Christmas quietly in their churches, this caused a good deal of soul-searching and some martyrlike acts of courage. For the common people, however, it provided a new form of Christmas entertainment: the riot.

Christmas Under the Puritans

from a historical account

Upon Wednesday, Decem. 22, the Cryer of Canterbury by the appointment of Master Major [Mayor] openly proclaimed that Christmas day, and all other Superstitious Festivals should be put downe, and that a Market should be kept upon Christmas day. Which not being observed (but very ill taken by the Country) the towne was thereby unserved with provision, and trading very much hindered; which occasioned great discontent among the people, causing them to rise in a Rebellious way.

The Major being slighted, and his Commands observed only of a few who opened their Shops, to the number of 12 at the most: They were commanded by the multitude to shut up again, but refusing to obey, their ware was thrown up and down, and they, at last forced to shut in.

The Major and his assistants used their best endeavours to qualifie this tumult, but the fire being once kindled, was not easily quenched. The Sheriffe laying hold of a fellow, was stoutly resisted; which the Major perceiving, took a Cudgell and strook the man; who, being no puny, pulled up his courage, and knockt down the Major, whereby his Cloak was much torne and durty, beside the hurt he received. The Major thereupon made strict Proclamation for keeping the Peace and that every man depart to his own house. The multitude hollowing thereat, in disorderly manner; the Alderman and Constables caught two or three of the rout, and sent them to Jayle, but they soon broke loose, and jeered Master Alderman.

Soon after, issued forth the Commanders of the Rabble, with an addition of Souldiers, into the high street, and brought with them two Foot-balls, whereby their company increased. Which the Major and Aldermen perceiving took what prisoners they had got, and would have carried them to the Jayle. But the multitude following after to the King's Bench, were opposed by Captain Bridg, who was straight knoct down, and had his head broke in two places, not being able to withstand the multitude, who, getting betwixt him and the Jayle, rescued their fellows, and beat the Major and Aldermen into their houses, and then cried Conquest. (From *Brand's Popular Antiquities,* New Edition, 1905, Vol. I)

Christmas Restored

In 1647, ten thousand men from Canterbury and the surrounding area gathered and passed their own resolution that "if they could not have their Christmas day, they would have the King back on his throne again." Eventually the monarchy was restored in 1660. Christmas regained its official acceptance. As the court had less and less real power and as the middle class rose, Christmas became more a celebration of the people and less an excuse for royal display. The middle class had its own versions of the Christmas feast, and the popular dramatic forms of the pantomime and the St. George play replaced the royal masque as the primary form of Christmas entertainment.

America was later in recovering from the Puritan influence than England. Christmas was outlawed in New England until the middle of the nineteenth century. In 1856 Christmas Day was still an ordinary workday in Boston, and failure to report to a job was grounds for dismissal. Classes were held in Boston public schools as late as 1870. It was probably the influence of immigrants from Germany and Ireland that finally convinced the Yankees that Christmas could be a harmless, pleasant, and even religious festivity. The first state to declare Christmas a legal holiday was Alabama in 1836. The last was Oklahoma in 1890.

The Christmas Season

We may think we know what we mean by the Christmas season, but every country has a slightly different idea of it. The Catholic Church's reckoning of the whole season stretches from Advent, four Sundays before Christmas, to Candlemas on February 2.

Most countries start festivities or preparations from two to three weeks before Christmas (often St. Nicholas' Day) and end on Epiphany, January 6. The following are some of the notable exceptions:

- Armenia confuses the whole question. The Armenian Church celebrates Christmas on January 6 in deference to the old Julian calendar. Thus their whole season starts about the time the rest of the world's celebrations are ending.

- In Iran, Christmas is preceded by a partial fast that lasts the entire month of December to Christmas Day.

- Holland starts Christmas on the last Saturday of November, when St. Nicholas arrives by boat, and finished on the second day of Christmas, December 26.

- Spain begins festivities on December 8 with the Feast of the Immaculate Conception and doesn't let up until Epiphany.

- Sweden stretches the season for a whole month, from St. Lucia's Day on December 13 to January 13.

- The United States is one of the biggest exceptions to the rule. Our Christmas starts with Santa's arrival at the big Thanksgiving parades and stretches through New Year's or, sometimes, January 6. That makes for a lot of shopping days.

It Happened on Christmas

--[800]-- Pope Leo III crowns Charles the Great (Charlemagne) Roman Emperor

--[1066]-- William the Conqueror crowned King of England

--[1223]-- St. Francis of Assisi assembles 1st Nativity scene (Greccio, Italy)

--[1492]-- Columbus' ship Santa Maria lands in Dominican Republic

--[1745]-- Treaty of Dresden gives much of Silesia to the Prussians, ending Austria's Second Silesian War

--[1758]-- Haley's comet first sighted by Johann Georg Palitzsch

--[1776]-- Washington crosses the Delaware river to surprise/defeat 1,400 Hessian soldiers

--[1831]-- Louisiana and Arkansas are first U.S. states to observe Christmas as a holiday

--[1868]-- President Andrew Johnson grants unconditional pardon to all persons involved in Southern rebellion (Civil War)

--[1901]-- Boers surprise attack British in the Battle at Tweefontein Orange

--[1914]-- Legendary unofficial "Christmas truce" between British and German troops during World War I

--[1926]-- Yoshihito, 123rd emperor of Japan, dies and is succeeded by Hirohito

-◦[1931]◦- New York City's Metropolitan Opera broadcasts an entire opera over radio

-◦[1939]◦- Montgomery Ward introduces Rudolph, the 9th reindeer

-◦[1941]◦- Japan announces surrender of British-Canadian garrison at Hong Kong

-◦[1942]◦- Russian artillery tanks battle with German armies at Stalingrad

-◦[1947]◦- Taiwan passes Human Rights laws

-◦[1953]◦- Avalanche of lava from Ruapehu volcano in New Zealand kills 150

-◦[1962]◦- USSR performs nuclear tests at Novaya Zemlya, USSR

-◦[1974]◦- Cyclone Tracy devastates city of Darwin, Australia

-◦[1976]◦- Egyptian SS Patria sinks in Red Sea, about 100 killed

-◦[1979]◦- USSR transports army to invade Afghanistan

-◦[1983]◦- First live telecast of Christmas parade at Walt Disney World in Orlando, Florida

-◦[1989]◦- Japanese scientists achieve -271.8 degrees C, the coldest temperature ever recorded

-◦[1991]◦- Mikhail Gorbachev formally resigns as President of USSR

-◦[1997]◦- For first time, U.S. box office movie revenues pass $6 billion

Christmas Traditions From Around the World

The joys of Christmas burst forth in celebrations as varied and colorful as the people who celebrate. A hundred languages sing the happiness of Christ's coming around the ceppo, the crèche, the bonfire, or the Christmas tree. In a thousand different ways, the people of the earth join their hearts in the great communion of humankind that only this season can bring. There are traditions as old as Bethlehem to remind us of all that has gone before; there are constantly newborn customs as fresh and spontaneous as the wonder of a child's first Christmas. Let us look at some of the celebrations from around the world so that we can learn new forms of joy.

Abbot of Unreason

In the Middle Ages the Abbot of Unreason performed the same functions as the Lord of Misrule except that he was dressed in clerical robes. He was particularly popular in Scotland. He would supervise the mumming and merrymaking in courts and in large households. As with most of the medieval Christmas festivities, he tended to get out of hand and turn into a rather sacrilegious character. For that reason he was banned in England by Act of Parliament in 1555. However, it was not until the time of the Commonwealth and the ban on all Christmas festivities in both England and Scotland that he really disappeared, and as the Scottish never fully resumed their Christmas celebrations, he never returned.

Advent Calendar

The Advent calendar originated in Germany and Scandinavia, but it has now become very popular in America as well. Sometimes the Advent calendar is the picture of a house with windows that can be opened to reveal the tiny pictures behind them. Other times it is a picture of a typical Christmas scene or snowscape with perforated areas that can be removed or opened, again to reveal the pictures behind. There is one window or flap for each day of Advent, the season before Christmas, or, sometimes, one for each day of December leading up to Christmas. Each day, the children are allowed to reveal one picture. If there are several children in the family, the privilege rotates from one to another, usually with much confusion, since everyone wants it to be his or her day each time. The pictures thus revealed are of toys or Christmas scenes or anything else appropriate to the season. The last and largest picture is revealed on December 25. It is traditionally the nativity scene, which gives meaning to all the joy and fun that the other pictures represent. Some contemporary Advent calendars reveal a candy or other small treat in a pocket behind each flap.

Advent Wreath

The Advent wreath is of Lutheran origin, but its sense of joyous anticipation has made it popular with many other religious groups in England and America. It is an evergreen wreath with four candles set in holders attached to it. Beginning four Sundays before Christmas, on the first Sunday of Advent, one candle is lit each week as a symbol of the light that will come into the world with the birth of Jesus. On the last Sunday before Christmas, all four are lit to give a radiance to the church altar or the dining room table, wherever one wises to set up the wreath. In some countries,

Advent candles are similarly burned each week, but without being set in a wreath.

Ale Posset

A traditional hot drink of Yorkshire, England, ale posset consists of milk curdled with ale, beer, and wine, and very often spiced. It was the final beverage taken by families of old Yorkshire on Christmas Eve. As part of the annual ritual, each family member at this time would take sip or "sup" for good luck.

Armenia

Christmas is celebrated in Armenia on January 19. This is caused by two factors. First, the early Armenian Church rejected the idea of December 25 as Christmas and clung to the earlier notion that Christ's birthday should be celebrated on the same day as his baptism, January 6. Second, when Pope Gregory XIII created his calendar to correct the mistakes in the earlier Julian calendar, the Armenian Church rejected it for religious purposes. Therefore, the thirteen days' difference between Gregorian and Julian in this century makes their January 6 the same day as our January 19.

The Armenians prepare for Christmas with a fast. They eat no animal food for a week and no food at all on the last day before Christmas. The fast is broken only after the Christmas Eve service, when they return home to a dinner of rice pilaf. The children then go onto the roofs with handkerchiefs and sing carols. Adults fill up the handkerchiefs with presents of raisins or fried wheat or sometimes money. There are also morning services on Christmas Day.

Asalto

Traditional Christmas fun in Puerto Rico begins on Christmas Night, when the streets are invaded by merrymakers, very often in the middle of the night when all sane people are asleep. This *asalto,* or invasion, begins with much shouting and laughing and leads to the singing of the traditional light, joyous carols known as *aguinaldos.* These songs appeal to the host's sense of generosity, and the appeal is seldom in vain. The host climbs out of bed and acknowledges his cheerful guests, often as many as thirty people, by opening his home to them. Singing and feasting takes place, and in an hour or so the happy host joins his guests as they hurry off to invade someone else's peace and quiet.

Australia

Australia was settled by the British, so Australian Christmas customs are the descendants of the traditional British Christmas. But as the climate is the reverse of that of the mother country, there are no sleigh rides, Yule logs, or any of the other snug comforts against the cold. The main articles of decoration are the Christmas bell and the Christmas bush, and after the hearty afternoon feast, supper may be a picnic in the countryside or at the beach. Swimsuits are perfectly ordinary attire for the Christmas weather.

One tradition that is purely Australian began in 1937. On Christmas Eve, radio announcer Norman Banks saw a lonely old woman listening to Christmas carols on the radio while a lone candle burned forlornly in the window. Thinking about how to make the world brighter for such people at that time of year made the words "Carols by Candlelight" spring into his head, along with an idea. The next Christmas Eve he broadcast a great carol sing by all who wanted to join in, from the Alexandra Gardens along the banks of Melbourne's main river. Carols by Candlelight became a joyous annual tradition and was eventually broadcast in many other countries around the world. Each year, more than 30,000 people gather to sing carols and join hands at midnight for "Auld Lang Syne." It is a great showing of community and Christmas spirit unequaled anywhere else in the world.

Austria

Christmas in Austria is a very musical time. Many of the world's greatest carols, including "Silent Night," have come to us from Austria, and they can be heard everywhere throughout the country as Christmas approaches.

December 6 is the day when St. Nicholas and his grotesque assistant, Krampus, may pay a visit, just as the Wise Men are often on hand for January 6. But the gifts are brought on Christmas Eve by the Christkind, or Christ Child. Sometimes the Christkind will even help to decorate the Christmas tree before the big Christmas Eve supper, which will probably feature carp as a main course. Dinner on Christmas Day will be roast goose with all the trimmings.

A curious figure named Sylvester still lurks in Austrian Christmas season tradition, most especially on New Year's Eve. He is old and bearded and ugly, and he hides in the shadows wearing a wreath of mistletoe. If a young beauty is unfortunate enough to linger too long beneath the magic pine bough, Sylvester is liable to leap out and kiss her vigorously. His rights are severely limited, however, as he is banished with the arrival of the New Year; and besides, if one knows who it is lurking behind the false whiskers, it is not necessarily an unpleasant experience at all.

Babouschka

Babouschka is the traditional Christmas gift-giver in Russia. Even under the Communist regime which didn't acknowledge Christmas, the tradition of Babouschka was upheld in a quiet way. She is something between a witch and an old woman, her name meaning simply "grandmother." Legend says she refused shelter to Mary and Joseph and misdirected the Wise Men on their way to Bethlehem. To atone for these sins, she was condemned to wander the earth on Epiphany Eve, looking for the Christ Child but never finding him, and dropping off presents for good little boys and girls on her way.

Bambino

Bambino is the Italian word for baby, but at Christmastime it is used specifically to refer to the representations of the baby Jesus that are placed in the countless manger scenes in homes and churches all over Italy. The most famous Bambino is one dating from medieval times in the Church of Santa Maria in Aracoeli in Rome. It is brought to the crib every year at Christmas with elaborate ceremonies, and children preach sermons before it. Offerings are sent to the church from all over the world for candies to be placed at the manger in which it lies. It is credited with a number of miracles.

One famous story concerns a woman who feigned sickness in order to be left alone with the miraculous image. She replaced it with a false image and stole the real one. None of the priests knew of the exchange, but that night there was a great ringing of bells and hammering at the main door of the church. When the priests hurried to open it, they found no one there except the image of the Christ Child, which had come home of its own accord.

Befana

Befana is a female Santa Claus to Italian children and is very active at Christmastime in that country, particularly on January 6, the Feast of the Epiphany. In fact, her name is probably just a popular corruption of the word *Epiphany*. The legend has it that Befana, a very old and decrepit woman, refused to interrupt her household duties and avail herself of an invitation extended to her by the Magi to accompany them on their journey to Bethlehem to find the Christ Child. She was too busy sweeping the floor! In some versions, they needed a guide in their search and asked Befana to help them find the way, but she refused to help them, or even misdirected them. The part of the legend that seems universal is that toward dawn, when the Magi had been gone for some time, Befana had a change of heart and went out to search for them, but was unable to find the Three Kings. Through the centuries, this old woman, carrying gifts in her apron, searches for the caravan of the Wise Men. Her gifts eventually go to good little boys and girls. She also happened to have some bags of ashes for those who weren't quite so good during the year.

In Italy, January 6 is also called Befana Day, and Befana fairs are held all over the country, notably in Rome. Whistles and earthenware images of Befana are traditionally sold at them.

Belgium

In Belgium, St. Nicholas pays two visits to each house. On December 4 he comes to check the behavior of each child, to find out who's been naughty or nice. Then on December 6 he returns with just rewards for all, either presents or switches, which he leaves in the shoes or small baskets that have been placed inside near the doorway. Just to get on his good side, there are also snacks of hay, water, and carrots left for his horse or donkey.

Christmas Day itself is reserved for religious celebrations, although Nativity plays sponsored by the churches are a well-loved institution. These are often performed in sixteenth-century costumes, which would have been modern dress when the tradition began. In some villages, three virtuous men are chosen to portray the three Wise Men and go throughout the town, caroling at each door and receiving small gifts of food that are eaten on the spot.

Bells

The ringing of bells at Christmastime is a holdover from pagan midwinter celebrations. When the earth was cold and the sun was dying, evil spirits were very powerful. One of the ways to drive them off was by making a great deal of noise. As making a great deal of noise was also rather fun, the noisemaking ceremonies were entered into with much good will. Bells were a very useful part of this, since you could play a bell and shout or sing at the same time.

Today, church bells ring throughout the world on Christmas Eve, not to drive away the evil spirits, but to welcome in the spirit of Christmas with a joyful noise. In Scandinavia, bells signal the end of work and the beginning of festivity. In England the tolling of the devil's knell welcomes the birth of Christ. In Italy and Spain it signals the Midnight Mass. In America no sidewalk Santa could hope to function without a hand bell to brighten the sounds of the city with its joyous tinkle. And we all join in lustily to sing "Jingle Bells," while we think of sleigh bells and dashing horses and being bundled under warm furs—a treat which almost none of us have actually experienced but which we all remember vividly in our collective Christmas memory.

Belsnickel

Belsnickel, or Pelznickle, is another name for Knecht Rupprecht to the Pennsylvania Dutch. He is one of the frightening companions of St. Nicholas who is there to see to it that the children who have been bad don't get off lightly. He used to be portrayed by a man wearing a sheet and a mask. Now whole groups of children will dress up in costumes and go "belsnickling," parading through the street to parties at friends' houses.

Berchta

Berchta, or Frau Freen, or Budelfrau, as she is variously known in German folklore, is a frightening old woman who watches out for laziness at Christmastime. She appears in the Tyrolean Alps during the twelve days of Christmas, chastising young women who leave unspun thread at their spinning wheels. She has nothing really to do with Christmas. Her concern is for household duties and seeing to it that they don't get neglected at the approach of the holidays by casting bad-luck spells on lazy females. She was probably invented by someone who never had to undergo the drudgery of keeping a house, presumably a man.

Birds' Christmas Tree

This is a custom throughout the Scandinavian countries at Christmastime and is in keeping with the general tendency to try to share the festivities with all animal and even plant life so that the coming year will be a prosperous one. A sheaf of wheat or some other grain, or even just seeds and bread, is placed on a pole and set up outside where the birds are known to congregate. This is done on either Christmas Eve or Christmas Day. The sight and sound of the outdoor festivity at the birds' Christmas tree can add greatly to the zest and warmth of the indoor celebration.

Black Peter

To the medieval Dutch, *Black Peter* was another name for the devil. Somewhere along the way, he was subdued by St. Nicholas and forced to be his servant. This is how he appears now in Dutch folklore, following behind St. Nicholas and carrying the bag of presents. At St. Nicholas' commands, he drops the gifts down the chimneys and into the children's shoes, thereby saving the saint the difficulty and dirtiness of making the trip down the flue himself, *à la* Santa Claus. Curiously, Black Peter dresses in sixteenth-century Spanish clothes. Holland was then under the control of Spain and understandably didn't like it; hence this Dutch version of the devil dressed in Spanish clothes. Today Black Peter carries a bag into which he can pop any children who have been irretrievably bad and carry them off to Spain, which seems a rather mild punishment.

Blowing in the Yule

Blowing the Yule is one of the delightfully noisy traditions of Christmas. This custom probably originated in pagan times when noise was thought to

drive off evil spirits. It is today found in areas of Germany and the Scandinavian countries. A group of musicians take their instruments to the belfry of the local church and lustily play four Christmas carols, one in each direction of the compass. They finish with a joyful peal of the bells, which announces that Christmas has arrived.

Boar's Head

The association of the boar's head with Christmas feasting probably dates back to pagan times when the Germanic god Frey, who cared for the fertility of the herds, was symbolized by a boar. Therefore, at mid-winter, a boar would be sacrificed to the god to ensure many new calves and lambs in the spring. This sacrifice was carried over into Christmas tradition as a nonreligious custom.

A much more amusing explanation of the origin of this traditional Christmas dish concerns a student at Queen's College, Oxford, in England. He was walking in the nearby forest of Shotover reading a volume of Aristotle when he was charged by a boar. Having found Aristotle's philosophies hard to swallow himself, he cried out *"Graecum est"* (roughly, "It's Greek to me") and crammed the book down the boar's throat, choking him to death. As he was a poor student, he couldn't afford to lose his textbook, so he cut off the boar's head to get it back. Not wanting to waste anything, he took the head back to his college, where it was roasted and eaten with great festivity. No indication was given in this story of what happened to the rest of the boar.

Whatever its origin, the boar's head was an important part of the medieval English Christmas feast. It took more than a week to properly skin, soak, salt, preserve, prepare, and cook—not to mention the problems of hunting it down in the first place, since the wild boar was a very dangerous animal. The boar's head was brought into the banquet in a procession of cooks, huntsmen and servants, all elaborately dressed to provide as much spectacle as possible. While bringing it in, they would sing the "Boar's Head Carol," which is one of the earliest extant English carols, having appeared in a book printed in 1521. It is partly in Latin as well as English:

> The boar's head in hand bear I,
> Bedecked with bays and rosemary;
> And I pray you, my masters, my berry,

> Quot estis in convivio: [Who are in such good spirits:
> Caput apri defero,   I bear the head of the boar,
> Reddens laudes Domino.   Giving praise to the Lord.]

The ceremony of the bringing in of the boar's head began to die out as early as the thirteenth century, as the wild boar began to become extinct in the British Isles. There are still some places, however, that preserve the custom as a deliberately quaint Christmas tradition, with the one change that a suckling pig must make do for the hard-to-get boar. One such place is Queen's College, Oxford, where a poor student may have started the whole thing with a well-placed tome of indigestible philosophy.

Bonus

A Christmas bonus is the gift given by a business firm to its employees at Christmastime. It probably had its origin in the same tradition as the English Boxing Day, when tradesmen were tipped for good service as an incentive to continue to perform well. Sometimes, the Christmas bonus is some kind of merchandise, such as a turkey or ham for the traditional Christmas dinner. More often, it is a sum of money, which may be determined on the basis of a percentage of the company's profits or the number of years of the employee's service. The Christmas bonus began as a freewill gift, but with the increased influence of the labor movement and the rising costs of Christmas festivities, the bonus has become a contractually agreed-upon necessity with some governmental regulation and taxation. The amount of the bonus is hammered out at the negotiating table, the IRS gets its share, and what's left is usually spent before it's received, but the recognition of service at Christmastime is still a nice idea.

Boxing Day

Boxing Day, December 26, is a legal holiday in England and has nothing to do with prizefighting. The custom of boxing derives from the opening of alms boxes in church on December 26, the Feast of St. Stephen, to distribute the collected money to the poor who have not enjoyed as nice a Christmas as those who are better off. The idea was picked up by apprentices and assistants, who would take a Christmas box around to their employer's customers, asking for tips in return for their service during the year. Eventually children picked up the practice, making it a sort of "trick or treat."

Boy Bishop

One of the most curious figures of the medieval Christmas celebrations was the Boy Bishop. Most churches and cathedrals at that time had a choir school affiliated with them to provide altar boys and the boys' choirs that were extremely popular throughout the Middle Ages. The custom may have begun as early as the tenth century, but definitely by the twelfth century Boy Bishops were being elected in most European countries. A boy elected from among the choristers would be invested with the powers of a bishop on St. Nicholas' Day, December 6. He would then serve until the Feast of the Holy Innocents on December 28. He took up offerings, blessed the people, preached, and led the services except, probably, for the actual saying of the Mass. He wore elaborate and extremely expensive vestments, which were provided by the Church and which, because of their size, were not usable for any other function during the year. He was extremely popular with the people who gave more attention to this young bishop who entertained them than they might have to a more adult one.

The ceremonies involving the Boy Bishop became more and more elaborate. In a Spanish church, one investment was described thus: "A chorister being placed with some solemnity upon a platform, there descended from the vaulting of the ceiling a cloud, which, stopping midway, opened. Two angels within it carried a miter, which, in their descent, they placed upon the head of the boy."

Anyone who has seen a herd of six-year-olds troop to the front of a modern-day church and attempt to get through one verse of "Jingle Bells" knows that children can be a very charming and not at all sacrilegious part of Christmas festivities. Unfortunately the Boy Bishop, who was probably just as innocent to begin with, did not remain so. His term of office became an excuse for more boisterous forms of entertainment and he became more closely linked with the Lord of Misrule as a leader of revels with dancing and feasting and singing. His services became, in some instances, a parody of the traditional church service and sometimes included indecent songs and jokes.

The Church outlawed the practice of electing a Boy Bishop. It took a good while for it to die out, though, as it was an extremely popular form of entertainment. In England, it was not until 1542, when Henry VIII forbade the practice in the English Church, that the Boy Bishop was really done for. Yet some private groups still celebrated in a modified form, and vestiges remain today in Italy, where children will preach sermons at Christmas before the image of the infant Jesus in the manger.

Brazil

Brazilian Christmas falls at the beginning of their summer season. No sleigh rides for them. It is a time for boating, picnicking, and other summer festivities. The red and green of Christmas decorations are provided not by midwinter holly but by eucalyptus leaves and brilliant red flowers of many sorts.

The *pesebre,* or manger scene, is important, but there is also a Christmas tree decorated with candles. On Christmas Eve the *cena,* or meal, is set out before the family goes to Midnight Mass so that the Holy Family can have some of it if they wish while everyone is out. A popular menu includes turkey, fish, and champagne. Before going to bed, the children set out their shoes for Papa Noël. On Christmas morning, the children fix breakfast, then get their presents from their shoes and look for other gifts that are hidden around the house. Christmas evening can be spent outdoors in the balmy weather and is a great time for fireworks.

Buzebergt

Buzebergt is another unpleasant old woman who is connected with Epiphany. She comes to the Bavarian regions of Germany. Unlike Befana and Babouschka, she does not bring gifts but has a surprise of a different sort for those who cross her path. She carries a pot of starch instead of a bag of goodies or an apronful of presents, and she smears this starch on anyone she can catch.

Candle

Light was an important part of the pagan midwinter festivities, since this was the time when the sun ceased to wane and began to grow stronger and brighter. In imitation, candles and bonfires helped to drive away the forces of cold and darkness. Wax tapers also were given as gifts at the Roman festival of Saturnalia. To the Christian community, the lighting of candles took on the additional symbolic significance of Jesus as the Light of the World. Christmas candles are made in all shapes, colors, and sizes and are very often manufactured with such Christmassy scents as balsam and evergreen. Very often candles are displayed as Christmas motifs on Christmas cards and seals. In 1962 the U.S. Post Office issued its first Christmas stamp, which showed a Christmas wreath and a pair of candles. The beautiful idea of Christmas candles shining from home windows is a custom still practiced in Europe, particularly on Christmas Eve; for, who knows, the stranger who is given light and comfort by the candle in the darkness might be Mary seeking shelter from the night. In Ireland during the years of suppression, the late seventeenth through ninteenth century, Catholics placed candles in the windows of certain homes so priests would know where to celebrate the Midnight Mass. In Sweden St. Lucy appears wearing a crown of candles. In Victorian England tradesmen made annual Christmas gifts of candles to their loyal customers. Thirty thousand candles lend their glow to the Australian custom of Carols by Candlelight. In many parts of the world, the Advent candles or the candles of the Advent wreath reflect the dawning season and remind us of the coming of the Light. And it was the addition of lighted candles to the old paradise tree that marked the birth of our most beloved tradition, the Christmas tree. The Christmas candle, with its brightness, sacredness, and sense of well-being, is an indispensable part of the Christmas season.

Candlemas

Candlemas is the celebration of the ritual purification of Mary, which, as required by Jewish law, took place forty days after the birth of her child. Candlemas is thus February 2. The first celebration of this day took place in the late seventh or early eighth centuries under Pope Sergius I. Later in the century, the custom of blessing the candles that were carried in processions gave the day its popular name of Candlemas.

In many countries, Candlemas has been looked upon as the end of the Christmas season, probably since the purification of Mary would be looked upon as the last chapter in the story of Christ's birth. This was the day when the decorations would be taken down and stored away for another year. The Christmas plants would be burned with the remnants of the Yule log (always holding back the one piece to light next year's log) and the ashes spread over gardens and fields to ensure a good harvest. The Yule log for the next year would be chosen then. Candlemas was also a good day for weather forecasting. If it was a sunny day, there would be forty more days of cold and snow. This belief has carried over into American tradition: February 2 is Groundhog Day.

Card

The immediate predecessors of Christmas cards were called Christmas pieces. These were elaborate colored sheets of paper with biblical scenes or pictures of nature at the head and around the borders. In the middle, schoolchildren would put their best sample of penmanship to show their parents how diligent their studies had been. Usually they expressed a wish for happy holidays or promises to be good or something else of dubious sincerity designed to put the parents in a good mood when gift-giving time came.

Two things made the advent of the Christmas card an inevitability. One was the creation of the "penny post" by the British postal system, in 1840. This made it possible and relatively inexpensive to correspond with larger number of friends. The other was the great increase in printing in the early nineteenth century due to the invention of the steam press. Printers could turn out more and more and were looking for markets to exploit. The Christmas piece was already an important source of income; the Christmas card would be a landslide.

The first Christmas card was probably designed by John Calcott Horsley at the suggestion of and for his friend Sir Henry Cole in 1846. The card depicted three panels: in the center one was a family enjoying wine; on either side were shown acts of charity, the feeding and clothing of the poor; beneath it all was the sentiment "A Merry Christmas and a Happy New Year to You." The center panel caused a stir and drew much heated criticism because one of the family members offering the toast was a child enjoying his first sip of wine. Temperance adherents accused the creator of the Christmas card of condoning excessive drinking and fostering the moral corruption of children. Nevertheless, a thousand copies of the card were printed and sold for a shilling each.

It is impossible to say definitely that the Horsley-Cole card was the first

Christmas card, although it is generally accepted as such. In 1844 W. A. Dobson sent out hand-painted cards to friends rather than Christmas letters. As these were not printed, they are not considered in the running. In the same year, the Rev. Edward Bradley lithographed cards to his friends, again not a printing process for mass production and not sold to the general public. The one card that may possibly lay claim to being older than the Horsley-Cole card was designed by William Egley. This card carries a very clear date-for the first three figures. The last figure is obscure, so the date may be either 1842 or 1849. If it is the former, then William Egley is the Father of the Christmas Card; if the latter, he is just another imitator.

Louis Prang, a German-born printer in Roxbury, Massachusetts, printed his first American cards in 1875. Even more important than his printing was the fact that he did more than anyone else to popularize the cards by instituting nationwide contests for the best Christmas designs, which were awarded cash prizes.

Today Christmas cards are one of the greatest nuisances and greatest pleasures of Christmastime. More than 3.5 billion Christmas cards are purchased each year in the United States and Britain. Many families send reports of what they've done during the year, so you catch up on the doings of old friends. Pictures may let you see how big the kids are getting. And a display of cards around the Christmas tree, or on the table or on the wall, is one of the very loveliest of Christmas decorations, for every card both brightens the room and reminds you of a friend who is there in spirit.

Ceppo

The Italian *ceppo* is closely related to the Christmas pyramid of northern Europe, but has never been replaced by the Christmas tree as its northern equivalent has been. The *ceppo* is a pyramid-shaped framework with several shelves which is decorated all over with greenery, ribbons, candles, and other Christmas ornaments. On it shelves sit gifts and sweets and sometimes the *presepio,* or manger scene. Often it will have a motor in its base so that it will revolve like a merry-go-round.

Cert

Cert is a demon in Czech Christmas lore. He accompanies Svaty Mikalas (St. Nichola when he descends from heaven on a golden cord on December 6 to give gifts to the children. A good angel makes up the third member of the extremely mixed company. Cert is dressed in black garments and carries a whip and chains as symbols of the punishment for naughty boys and girls.

Chile

Chile's gift-bringer is called Viego Pascuero, or Old Man Christmas. He strongly resembles Santa Claus and likewise travels on a sleigh drawn by reindeer. However, as chimneys are less than roomy in this warm clime, he contents himself with climbing in a window.

As in all of Latin America, the manger scene is the center of festivities. Following the midnight Mass of the Rooster, the Christmas Eve meal often includes *azuela de ave,* a chicken soup filled with potatoes, onions and corn on the cob; and *pan de pasqua,* a Christmas bread filled with candied fruit.

China

In China, Christmas is called Cheng Dan Jieh, the Holy Birth Festival. China has been exposed to Western influences, including Christianity, for only about four hundred years. Less than one per cent of the population is

Christian. Yet these Christian Chinese celebrate Christmas joyfully with customs that they have adapted from the missionaries who brought them the word. They have the Christmas tree, which they call the Tree of Light, and hang up stockings for presents. These gifts are brought by their version of Santa Claus, whom they call Lam Khoong-Khoong (Nice Old Father) or Dun Che Lao Ran (Christmas Old Man). Festive paper lanterns are hung for decorations, and fireworks, which were invented in China, are an important part of the revelry.

Christkind

Christkind (or Christkindli or Christkindlein) means Christ Child in German, and originally it applied to the Holy Infant, who was thought to bring the gifts on Christmas Eve. Gradually it evolved, however, into the name given a sort of angelic helper who brought the presents instead of the baby Jesus. Christkind is a veiled, radiant figure who wears a sparkling, jeweled crown, carries a tiny Christmas tree or a wand, wears a flowing white robe, and has golden wings. Often a window is left open for it to enter by. It lets the household know that it has been there by ringing a bell when the presents are all in place beneath the tree. The Christkind is looked for each year in certain areas of Switzerland, Austria, and Germany and in America's Pennsylvania Dutch country. Just as its appearance and gender have changed over the years, its name has been changed into more of a real name, Kris Kringle. In America, this name has been incorrectly picked up as just another name for Santa Claus. Thus we wrongly think of Kris Kringle as being male, when actually, it is an angelic being, Christkind cannot be said to have any gender at all.

恭祝聖誕並賀新禧

Christmas Greetings

C.M.B.

These are the initials of the three Wise Men, Caspar, Melchior, and Balthazar. They are written over front doors of homes in Poland, the Czech Republic, and Sweden by the Stair Boys on their Epiphany Day visits. Along with the initials, three crosses are drawn. According to tradition, homes marked with these holy symbols will experience only good fortune throughout the year.

Costa Rica

Bright tropical flowers highlight Costa Rican decorations for Christmas. Special trips are made to gather the wild orchids that bloom in the jungle areas. The manger scene is called a *portal* and is decorated with these brilliant flowers and colorful fresh fruit. Wreaths are very popular, not of holly, but of cypress leaves and red coffee berries.

The supper after Midnight Mass will consist of tamales and other local dishes. Children used to leave their shoes out for the Christ Child to fill, but more and more Santa Claus is relieving Him of this pleasant task as American influence continues to gain in strength.

Cradle Rocking

This was a charming custom emphasizing the humanity of the Christ Child. It originated in Germany at the Midnight Mass of Christmas Eve. A manger scene would be set up in the church, and the celebrant and altar boys would rock the cradle of the Holy Infant. Lullaby-like carols would be sung at the same time to help the infant Jesus sleep. With the Protestant Reformation and its forbidding of images in church, this practice began to die out, but even now there are some vestiges of it left.

Czech Republic

In 1992 Czechoslovakia's legislature adopted a constitutional amendment that called for the formation of two separate countries: the Czech Republic and Slovakia. Since then, the two countries have adopted varying customs and beliefs. Upon gaining their independence, many Czechs reverted to some of the ancient traditions practiced by their ancestors, including their celebration of Christmas.

Several of the Czech Republic's Christmas traditions pertain to the themes of life and death, which is especially visible during the Christmas Eve dinner. During the meal, no one is allowed to leave the table as it is believed to mean that he or she will not be present for future Christmases to come. As a result, all the dishes are prepared and placed on the table before anyone is seated so that no one will have to get up before the meal is finished. A similar belief is that the flame of the candles on the table should not be allowed to go out for fear of a death in the upcoming year. A traditional Christmas Eve dinner includes sauerkraut soup, potato salad, carp, and a vast assortment of fruits and nuts. Honey is also a big part of the Christmas celebration. Customarily the mother makes a cross with honey on the forehead of each member of the family as protection against evil, then everyone dips a Christmas Eve waffle into the honey and eats it along with garlic. The honey represents goodness and health, while the garlic is intended to ward off the evils of sickness.

Later in the evening, the family may attend Midnight Mass. The music will most often include the well-known *Czech Christmas Mass* (1796), composed by Jan Jakub Ryba, as well as some traditional Czech carols. It is believed that St. Nicholas climbs down from heaven on a golden rope. On Christmas Eve the children place their shoes on the window sill before going to bed; good children receive gifts in their shoes, while bad children will only find coal.

Perhaps the most interesting Czech tradition is the Christmas tree which hangs from a ceiling beam. The decorations are typically home-made with paper and straw. In addition to candles, food such as honey pastries, walnuts, apples and pine cones are also often used.

Denmark

Christmas is an especially jolly time in Denmark, where the national sense of humor gets free play at this time of year. Notices appear in the paper three months in advance advising that it is almost the deadline for Christmas packages to Tasmania, Fiji, the Aleutians, and many of those other locales which are sure to be on everyone's mailing lists. The Folketeatret in Copenhagen goes through its annual soul-searching and finally announces that this year's Christmas program will be called *Christmas in Nøddebo Rectory*—a great surprise to everyone, as this program has been given at this theater only every year since 1888. And Christmas is the time when the Nisser can run amok. A Julnisse (plural, nisser) is a mischievous elf who lives in the lofts of old farmhouses and concerns himself with playing practical jokes on one and all. He wears gray homespun with a red bonnet, long red stockings, and white clogs. He must be left a bowl of rice pudding on Christmas Eve or his jokes will indeed be terrible. If he is properly placated, however, he can be very friendly and will watch over the livestock throughout the year. He is closely associated with the household cat, and there are even those who attribute the disappearance of the Christmas Eve rice pudding to the cat itself rather than to the Nisse, but these are people without proper Christmas spirit.

The big Christmas Eve dinner starts off with rice pudding sprinkled with cinnamon, with a magic almond hidden in it. The child getting the almond in his or her portion will win a surprise, usually a marzipan animal or some other goodie. The main course is roast goose stuffed with apples and prunes, with red cabbage and small caramel-browned potatoes. For dessert there is an astonishing variety of Danish pastries and baked goods.

As Greenland is a Danish possession, that has become the popular home for Santa Claus. Letters written to Santa Claus, Greenland, are answered by the Danish Tourist Association.

A famous Danish Christmas tradition is the Christmas plate. This may have started long ago when the wealthier Danes gave plates of cookies and fruit to their servants for Christmas presents. As the plates would be of a higher quality than anything those servants would have, they would be collected and kept separate from the day-to-day china. The collection of Christmas plates became fashionable, and special plates were issued for the occasion. Today, two leading manufacturers issue different designs each Christmas, often featuring that delightful Christmas symbol the Julnisse.

Dipping in the Kettle

In memory of an ancient famine, the family gathers in Swedish kitchens on Christmas Eve before the midday meal. A great pot is filled with a broth made of the drippings of pork, sausage, and corned beef. Each family member dips a piece of dark bread on a fork into the broth until the bread is thoroughly saturated and then eats it. This *doppa i grytan,* "dipping in the kettle," is necessary for good luck and a coming year of plenty.

Ecuador

Christmas Day in Ecuador is a day of colorful procession as the Indians who live and work in the highlands and mountains dress in their finest and ride their brightly arrayed llamas down to the ranches where their employers live. They bring gifts of fruit and produce, which they lay before the image of the Christ Child in the *pesebre,* or manger scene, which is set up in the ranch house. Children, too, bring their gifts and make pretty speeches to the Holy Infant, asking blessings for their family and their animals. Then there is a fiesta with much singing and dancing outdoors. The owner of the ranch distributes gifts to all his employees and their families. The huge meal will consist of roast lamb, baked potatoes, and brown sugar bread. There is always entirely too much to eat, so that the processions that wend their way into the mountains at the end of the day are as heavily laden with leftovers as they were with offerings in the morning.

Eisteddfod

In Wales at Christmastime, a Christmas poem is designated each year to be set to music. Choirs all over the country vie for the honor of having their music chosen to be the official Christmas carol. These choirs come together in the marketplaces of every size village and town to sing their version as well as the official carols from many years past. This combination of carol singing and contest is called an *eisteddfod*. There is also a National Eisteddfod, held every year since 1860, which determines the final selection and also has contests in drama, prose, and poetry. The custom of choosing a national carol was begun sometime in the tenth century.

England

Ever since Dickens sparked the revival of interest in the old-fashioned Christmas, England has been second to none in the enthusiasm and variety of its Christmas celebrations. Many customs are its own, but many others from all over the world have found their way into the heart and hearth of the English Christmas.

Father Christmas reigns in the place of Santa Claus or Saint Nicholas, although his dimensions, joviality, and dress make him hard to distinguish from his American cousin. Letters are sent to him by children who want to be sure he has got their order straight. These letters are not mailed, though; they are thrown into the fireplace. If they go up the chimney, the wish will be granted; if not, one's wish goes ungranted. This uses up a good deal of paper, but does save on postage to the North Pole. Stockings are hung by the chimney or at the foot of the child's bed to receive small presents, which are opened Christmas morning.

The Christmas tree has occupied a central position in the festivities ever since Prince Albert brought it from his native Germany in the mid-nineteenth century. However, it has never completely replaced the combination of greenery and mistletoe called the kissing bough, probably because it is very awkward to try to kiss under a Christmas tree.

Such venerable customs as the bringing in of the Yule log and the boar's head are not commonplace today, although the ceremonies do still survive in some institutions such as the universities. In the countryside, you can still find some Christmas mummers, amateurs who perform plays of St. George at the drop of a hat, and waits still carol their way through the village streets. In a place in Yorkshire, the tolling of the devil's knell takes place every Christmas Eve. The church bell is rung once for every year since Christ's birth, with the last stroke timed exactly for midnight.

Christmas has always been a time of feasting for the English. Once it was good old English roast beef (Sir Loin, as it was dubbed in the Middle Ages) that held pride of place. But now that unlikely bird from America, the turkey, has conquered the British as it has so many countries and occupies the place of honor at most Christmas dinner tables. Dessert, however, is still British: mince pies and flaming plum pudding (called Christmas pudding). Mince pies contain no minced meat and plum pudding has no plums, but the English would never let mere fact stand in the way of tradition.

In Trafalgar Square in the heart of London, a great Christmas tree is set up each year. During World War II, King Haakon of Norway was forced into exile in Britain when the Germans occupied his country. Each year during the war, Norwegian forces would smuggle a tree through the German coast patrols at great risk so that the king could celebrate Christmas before a tree from his beloved homeland. Since the war, Norway has expressed its gratitude to the British people for their help by continuing to send a tree that can be shared by all. Thus the giant tree in Trafalgar Square stands as a symbol both of the child who brought such love with Him into the world and of the love that can exist between people. It is sad that it so often requires great hardship to discover that love.

Father Christmas

Although he is the English equivalent of Santa Claus, Father Christmas is rather different from our jolly old elf and even further removed from the original ascetic and holy St. Nicholas. Father Christmas developed from several pagan predecessors. The Roman Saturnalia celebrated the brief return each year of the Golden Age when the god Saturn returned to rule over Italy. Saturn was a giant who came bearing good food and wine, joy and revelry, and equality of all people. When carried into the northern regions of Europe, Saturn was probably combined with the wild figure of Odin and his raging host of spirits who would sweep across the land during the winter. Thus Father Christmas was never a Christian religious figure, but symbolized rather the arrival of those secular pleasures that came from elsewhere than the Christian tradition. He was always portrayed as a giant, wearing a scarlet or green robe lined with fur; crowned with holly, ivy, or mistletoe; and carrying the Yule log and a bowl of Christmas punch. The Ghost of Christmas Present in Dickens' *Christmas Carol* is probably meant to be Father Christmas: "The walls and ceiling were so hung with living green, that it looked a perfect grove, from every part of which, bright gleaming berries glistened. The crisp leaves of holly, mistletoe, and ivy reflected back the light, as if so many little mirrors had been scattered there; and such a mighty blaze went roaring up the chimney. . . . Heaped up upon the floor, to form a kind of throne, were turkeys, geese, game, poultry, brawn, great joints of meat, sucking-pigs, long wreaths of sausages, mince-pies, plum-puddings, barrels of oysters, red-hot chestnuts, cherry-cheeked apples, juicy oranges, luscious pears, immense twelfth-cakes, and seething bowls of punch, that made the chamber dim with their delicious steam. In easy state upon this couch, there sat a jolly Giant, glorious to see; who bore a glowing torch, in shape not unlike Plenty's horn. . . . It was clothed in one simple deep green robe or mantle, bordered with white fur. This garment hung so loosely on the figure, that its capacious breast was bare, as if disdaining to be warded or concealed by any artifice. Its feet, observable beneath the ample folds of the garment, were also bare; and on its head it wore no other covering than a holly wreath set here and there with shining icicles. Its dark brown curls were long and free: free as its genial face, its sparkling eye, its open hand, its cheery voice, its unconstrained demeanour, and its joyful air. Girded round its middle was an antique scabbard; but no sword was in it, and the ancient sheath was eaten up with rust."

Fête des Rois

The Feast of the Kings is the name given by the French to January 6, Epiphany, in honor of the Wise Men. It is, traditionally, a day for dining out for French families, unlike Christmas, which is a day of feasting at home. It is also the day when tradespeople are rewarded with gifts of money for loyal service, much like the English Boxing Day.

First-footing

In some areas of the world, such as Scotland, first-footing takes place at the New Year, but in much of rural England it happens on Christmas Day. The first-footer is the first person to enter the house and is said to "let in Christmas." In some areas, he is professionally hired to be sure that all is done properly, because there are many superstitions involved in this custom. He carries an evergreen twig, comes in at the front door, passes through the house, and exits at the rear. He may be given salt or bread or some other small gift as a symbol of hospitality. He should have dark hair, but not red hair, as that is the color associated with Judas Iscariot. To let a woman in first is thought to be disastrous.

And what does a successful first-footing accomplish? This carol, which is sung in some areas where the first-footers move in a group, gives us the answer:

> I wish you a merry Christmas
> And a happy New Year;
> A pocket full of money
> And a cellar full of beer,
> And a great fat pig
> To last you all the year.

France

The center of French Christmas celebration is the *crèche,* or manger scene. Every home will have its own nativity setting featuring the tiny clay figures called *santons,* "little saints." These brightly colored images are made by local craftsmen throughout the year and are sold at great Christmas fairs at Marseilles and Aix in the South of France where the tradition is strongest. The manger scene, which was created by St. Francis in Italy in 1223 or 1224, was brought to France by Pope John XXII in 1316 when the papacy was moved to Avignon in southern France. About 1800, Italian vendors brought some of the *santi belli* which were popular in Italy and which quickly caught on in France. Soon local figures began to make their appearance at the manger side, since the people were less concerned with historical accuracy than with expressing in their own way their adoration of the Christ Child. Thus it became a perfectly normal sight to see the town mayor between the ox and the ass; a knife grinder arriving with the Magi, and a gypsy, the town crier, a hunter, or a gardener being serenaded by the angels' song, all carefully detailed in clay.

The Christmas tree has never gained general acceptance in France. The Yule log was once important, but now it is remembered mostly by the shape it gives to a cake, the *bûche de Noël,* which is traditionally baked at Christmastime.

After Midnight Mass on Christmas Eve comes the *réveillon,* the late supper that is the culinary high point of the season. As might be expected in a country where every region has its own high standard of native cuisine, the menu varies widely. In Alsace, goose is the main dish, and in Brittany, buckwheat cakes with sour cream; Burgundy feasts on turkey and chestnuts, while Paris revels in oysters and pâté de foie gras. After dinner, the children see to it that their shoes are set out by the fireside for presents, which are brought by Père Noël (Father Christmas) or le Petit Noël (Little Christmas, the Christ Child). Once the shoes were the traditional sabots, wooden peasant shoes, but now almost anything will serve. Adults don't exchange presents until New Year's. Puppet shows and nativity plays are popular forms of entertainment on Christmas Day and provide a good place to send the children after they have eaten, broken, or gotten bored with whatever Père Noël brought them.

Frumenty

Traditionally, frumenty was the first food eaten on Christmas morning in many areas of England. It was made of wheat slowly stewed in milk and served with raisins, sugar, and spices.

Germany

So much of our modern Christmas originated in Germany that to understand the German Christmas fully, you must read this whole book and that might begin to give you the idea. To summarize it briefly, the German Christmas is a tremendously important time to each person and family. Preparations are made for weeks. Advent wreaths, candles, and calendars set the mood. St. Nicholas' Day, December 6, although not actually celebrated by most people, marks the real beginning of the season. Although the crib is often found in German homes, frequently in beautifully carved wood, the tree is the center of attention. The custom began in Germany, and every German home must have a tree. Usually it is the mother who trims the tree on Christmas Eve. No one else is allowed in until it is finished, usually about 6:00 P.M. on Christmas Eve. Church services are held Christmas Eve, and many famous Christmas carols dating back as far as Martin Luther are sung. It is the Christkind who brings the presents, accompanied by one of its many devilish companions, Knecht Rupprecht, Pelznickle, Ru-Klas, or one of the other monstrous playmates created by this nation, which is known for its fairy tales. The highlight of the Christmas food is the cookies. There are dozens of different German Christmas cookies, shaped like or stamped with familiar holiday designs. Edible trees and tiny baked brown gnomes fill the warm kitchens for a week before the festivities, but disappear afterward like a flash to turn into happy smiles and round tummies.

Gift

Gift-giving at the winter solstice goes back to the Roman festival of Saturnalia and Kalends. At first the gifts consisted simply of twigs from a sacred grove as good luck emblems. That soon escalated, however, and food, candles, statues of gods, and small pieces of jewelry became the standard gifts. These presents were called *strenae* and survive still in France, where gifts called *étrennes* are exchanged in January. To the early Church, gift-giving at this time was a pagan holdover and therefore severely frowned upon. However, the people would not part with it, and some justification was found in the gift-giving of the Magi and later figures such as St. Nicholas. So by the Middle Ages, gift-giving was accepted. This was especially true in the courts of kings, where a formal exchange of gifts was often very carefully regulated as to the correct amount to be spent. Today, gift-giving is such an important part of our festivities that the whole year's budget has to be carefully planned to allow for the expense, often with the help of a Christmas club, and retail firms count on December as their biggest sales month of the year. That's a far step from passing out a few evergreen twigs for good luck.

Grandfather Frost

Russia has several legendary figures who brought fights at Christmas time. Father Christmas or Kolyáda came on Christmas Eve, while Babouschka came on Epiphany Eve. During the officially atheist Communist regime, these semireligious characters were not tolerated. In their place Grandfather Frost appeared, a figure who brought presents on the nonreligious holiday of New Year's. He is an old man dressed in winter furs like Santa Claus, or sometimes in bishop's robe like St. Nicholas, although he was not allowed any religious function.

Great Supper

This is the name given to the meal taken after Midnight Mass in many parts of France. It is a banquet consisting of thirteen different foods, many of them rich desserts. The number thirteen is symbolic of Christ and his twelve Apostles.

Greece

Easter is a more important feast day than Christmas for the Greeks. Christmas is a more a time of religious observance. Still, there are some customs associated specifically with Christmas.

As December is a time of storms in the seas around Greece, St. Nicholas is important not as a bringer of gifts but as the patron of sailors. Thinking ahead to the rough seas to come, many seamen are especially religious on December 6, the feast day of the good saint who stilled the waters.

At dawn on Christmas, the children go from house to house singing carols called *kalanda* and accompanying themselves on tiny metal triangles and clay drums. The pig that has been fattening since harvest-time is slaughtered for the main course at Christmas dinner, although in some areas chicken is also enjoyed. A special loaf of *christopsomo,* or Christbread, has been baked for the occasion. It is decorated elaborately with frosting, usually in some way that indicates the family occupation, such as a plow for a farmer. In some areas, it is traditional to give the first slice to a beggar; others put an olive sprig into the loaf, decorate it with dried figs, apples, and oranges, and don't eat it until Epiphany. Another loaf is often baked for the livestock in the shape of a harness or something similar and crumbled into their food to bring good luck in the coming year.

A great log called the *skarkantzalos* is often burned during the entire twelve days of Christmas. This is not just for Christmas cheer, but specifically to frighten away the Kallikantzaroi, the evil spirits that slip down the chimney at Christmastime and cause all sorts of devilment.

Greek Cross Day

An important part of the Christmas festivities in the Eastern Church takes place on January 6, the day long considered Christ's birthday before the final acceptance of December 25. On this day, which is known as Greek Cross Day, the Blessing of the Waters takes place when a crucifix is dipped into the sea, lake, or river by the local priest. The practice dates back to the second century and is connected by many with Christ's first miracle, when He changed the water into the wine at the wedding at Cana. Others believe the Blessing of the Waters has its origins in Christ's baptism, which is said to have taken place on January 6. Whatever its origin, the blessed water, called "Baptismal Water," is taken home by the faithful, who believe its application will cure spiritual and bodily ailments. In some areas, the crucifix is thrown into the water and young men of the parish plunge in to retrieve it. The one who brings up the cross from the water receives special blessings and gifts and is hailed as a hero for the day. The Blessing of the Waters is common in the Greek, Syrian, and Coptic churches and is also carried out in Greek and Russian communities all over the world, including American cities such as Tarpon Springs, Florida.

Guatemala

For nine days before Christmas, *posada* processions pass through the streets of Guatemala. The beat of drums and the crackle of fireworks provide lively accompaniment as the people carry figures of Mary and Joseph to a friend's house and sing a carol asking for lodging for the Holy Family. After ritual questions and answers, the doors are opened and Mary and Joseph are taken to the *nacimiento,* or manger scene, where they will remain until the next night, when they will once again go out seeking shelter. Everyone who accompanied the figures on their quest makes a great party with punch and hot tamales and dancing once the goal is accomplished. On Christmas Eve, the figure of the Christ Child is added to the *nacimiento* at the last of the nine houses to receive the Holy Family. This is the signal for the biggest party of all, and the house selected had better be a large one, since everyone who was involved over the last nine days will show up on this night.

The Christmas tree has joined the *nacimiento* as a popular Christmas ornament because of the large German population in Guatemala. Gifts are left under the tree on Christmas morning by the Christ Child for the children. Parents and adults do not exchange gifts until New Year's Day. As in all of Latin America, Midnight Mass on Christmas Eve follows the *posada* and is in turn followed by a full supper.

Hans Trapp

In many areas of Germany, Hans Trapp is the demon who accompanies Christkind on its gift-giving rounds. He has a blackened face and wears a bearskin. He often arrives first and threatens the children with a stick until the Christkind arrives and banishes him.

Heaven

In Finland, a heaven is a type of Christmas ornament. It is not one that is hung on the tree, however; it is hung in the center of the dining room ceiling. It is made up of brightly colored paper stars, paper baubles, little silver bells, flags, and other ornaments that will reflect the candlelight to form a festive setting for the Christmas banqueting.

Holland

To the Dutch, St. Nicholas' Day is the time of greatest revelry in the Christmas season. Even the chilly, drizzly weather of December can do nothing to dampen their spirits.

Much as Santa first appears in America at Thanksgiving parades, St. Nicholas comes to the Netherlands on the last Saturday of November. No flying sleigh for him—he arrives by steamer. As he comes into the port of Amsterdam (and his double into the harbor towns), all business and traffic stop as the people pour out to greet him. He disembarks with his servant Black Peter and riding his white horse. He is dressed in traditional bishop's robes while Black Peter wears picturesque sixteenth-century Spanish attire. They are greeted by the mayor and lead a great parade through the streets to the royal palace. Here all the royal children are waiting and must give accounts of their behavior over the past year, just as all Dutch children must do. After the princes and princesses have proved their worth, the parade continues to a major hotel, where St. Nicholas will establish his headquarters for the season.

December 5, St. Nicholas' Eve, is when the presents are exchanged. The presents are called "surprises" because they are disguised as much as possible to make the final discovery more delightful. A small gift may be wrapped inside a huge box, or hidden inside a vegetable, or sunk in a pudding. A large gift may lurk in the cellar with clues to its location elaborately gift-wrapped. All surprises must be accompanied by a bit of verse.

It would cause quite a shock in our Senate, but it is no surprise to the Dutch if a distinguished legislator rises in Parliament on St. Nicholas' Eve and addresses his colleagues in verse. His respondents compound the fun by answering him in rhyme. All are lighthearted when St. Nicholas comes.

On Christmas itself, there are no presents. There are church services both Christmas Eve and morning and a big dinner in the evening. The Christmas tree is the center of the home celebration, which consists of carols and storytelling in the afternoon. December 26 is also a holiday, called Second Christmas Day, and is a time to take it easy and probably go out to eat.

Holly

Holly is a familiar green shrub, usually thought of as having red berries and dark glossy green leaves with thorny tips, although there are many other varieties whose leaves and berries may vary in color. The bright colors of the holly made it a natural symbol of rebirth and life in the winter whiteness of northern Europe. In late December the Teutonic peoples traditionally placed holly and other evergreens around the interior of dwellings to ward off winter bad weather and unwanted spirits. Holly flourishes in almost any kind of soil and extreme temperatures, but does not do well in the shade. The berries are poisonous to human beings.

Traditionally in England, the prickly holly is called "he" and the non-prickly "she." Which type of holly is first brought into the house at Christmas determines who will rule the household for the coming year.

Hunting the Wren

This odd and somewhat violent custom is common only in the more rural areas of England and Ireland. It may have had its origins in the ancient custom of sacrificing an animal as a symbol of the death and rebirth of the old year. The wren is widely called the "King of the Birds," and it is normally illegal to kill one, which may be what makes it appropriate for this sacrifice the day after Christmas.

After the bird was killed by the village boys on the morning of St. Stephen's Day, it would be placed on a pole or on a bundle of evergreens and carried from house to house. Traditional carols were sung, such as:

> The Wren, the Wren, the King of All Birds,
> St. Stephen's Day was caught in the furze,
> Although he is small, his family is great,
> Open up, lady, and give us a "trate."

OR,

> We hunted the wren for Robin the Bobbin,
> We hunted the wren for Jack of the Can,
> We hunted the wren for Robin the Bobbin,
> We hunted the wren for everyone.

The owner of the home thus serenaded would give a treat to the carolers and would received a feather in return for good luck. Today, happily, a stuffed wren or one made out of straw has largely replaced the real thing.

India

Although the population of India is overwhelmingly Hindu and Muslim, Christmas Day is still a national holiday. Traditions vary according to region: Christians in the plains often decorate banana or mango trees, while the urban regions have adopted more western images in their decorations, including traditional Christmas trees topped with stars, tinsel, and colorful streamers, as well as Santa Claus appearances in shops and department stores. The church buildings are decorated with colorful flowers, candles, paper ornaments, and toys. The Christmas morning services begin at around 4 or 5 o'clock in the morning, and are traditionally followed by fireworks displays. Giving *baksheesh,* or charitable handouts, to the impoverished people of the country is also customary this time of the year.

Iran

In Iran, Christmas is called the "Little Feast," reflecting its secondary importance to Easter, which is called the "Big Feast." The whole month of December leading up to Christmas is a period of fasting during which no meat, eggs, milk, or cheese may be eaten. This lasts until after the Communion at Christmas Day Mass. Then the day is given over to feasting. There is no exchanging of presents, but this is considered an appropriate time to give the children new clothes, just as Easter is the time for a new outfit in America.

Ireland

To the Irish, Christmas is a time for religious celebration rather than revelry. Most houses have a manger scene, and there are few Christmas trees.

The best-known Irish Christmas custom is that of putting a candle in the window, often decorated with some greenery, on Christmas Eve. The idea is to help light the way of the Holy Family or any other poor travelers out on such a night. After the evening meal, the table is also set with bread and milk and the door left unlatched as a symbol of the hospitality that the family is offering to Mary and Joseph and the little one to come.

One festive tradition that remains is the pudding that caps the meal. Three puddings are made early in December, one each for Christmas, New Year's, and Twelfth Night. The day after Christmas, St. Stephen's Day, brings the rowdy old custom of hunting the wren, when boys go from door to door with a wren on a stick (usually, today, the wren is not a real one), singing the traditional song and begging for treats.

Israel

Christmas comes three times each year to the village of Bethlehem. The Western Church celebrates on December 25. The Russian Orthodox Church celebrates on December 25, too, but it is December 25 by the old Julian calendar, which means that it comes on January 7 by our reckoning. The Armenian Church celebrates on January 6 by the old Julian calendar, which means January 19 to us. What makes it even more confusing is that Epiphany is celebrated twelve days after Christmas by the Western and Eastern churches, so while the Russian Orthodox are welcoming Christmas, the Roman Catholics are celebrating Epiphany. All of this overlaps and comes together in the Church of the Nativity.

The Church of the Nativity was built in the sixth century by the Emperor Justinian on the ruins of the original church built by the Emperor Constantine and his mother, St. Helena. That church, in its turn, had been built to replace a temple to the Greek god Adonis. All of these structures were built in Bethlehem over a series of caves that were considered to be the location of Christ's birth. The church was almost destroyed in 614 by Persian invaders, but they were stopped by a mural of the Magi that showed the Kings in Persian dress, since that was assumed to be their home country.

The Church of the Nativity does not belong to any one religious group, but is carefully administered and looked after by a combination of bodies. The rights and responsibilities of each group are carefully spelled out and watched over by civil authorities to prevent conflict. Certain areas are allotted to each group. For instance, in the Grotto of the Nativity, the traditional spot of Jesus' birth, the Catholics control the manger set up there while the Greeks and Armenians split the altar and are strictly limited as to what pictures or vessels they may place on it.

In the nineteenth century, the French were pushing the interests of the Roman Catholics in the church; the Russians were on the side of the Eastern Church. There was considerable conflict between them. Then the star marking the exact location of this original manger disappeared. This unfortunate incident caused accusations and counteraccusations and was finally one of the contributing causes of the Crimean War. A new star was finally placed in the Grotto-by the Turkish Sultan, of all people. This fourteen-pointed silver star stands there still. The floor around it is marked in Latin, *Hic De Virgine Maria Jesus Christus Natus Est,* "Here of the Virgin Mary, Jesus Christ was born."

Christmas Eve festivities traditionally begin at Shepherds' Field, where the shepherds heard the song of the angles. Here again, rivalry is apparent, as there are three different Shepherds' Fields, one Greek Orthodox, one Roman Catholic, and one controlled by the YMCA. The Greek field dates from the fourth century and so may have a prior claim, but the YMCA field features a carol sing in the early evening.

The only Protestant service is an Anglican one, which takes place in the Greek monastery attached to the church. Even the Catholic services are not in the church itself but in one of the attached buildings. They begin about 10:30 P.M., under the supervision of the Patriarch of Jerusalem, and last until two in the morning, when a procession carries the image of the Christ Child to the Grotto to be laid in the manger. There it will remain until just after the Greek Christmas Eve service on January 6, when it will be removed as part of the Catholic Epiphany service.

There is room for only a few hundred people at the invitation-only service, but Manger Square outside the church is decorated and the service is broadcast on a large television screen on the wall of the police station. Thousands of people crowd into the square to be close to the great mystery of this night.

Italy

Italy was the birthplace of the manger scene, which is still the primary clement of Italian Christmas decoration. Craftsmen called *figurari* make the world-famous figures called *pastori* that enliven the Italian manger scene or *presepio*, found in every home and church. Special care is taken with the Bambino, the figure of the infant Jesus. A particularly famous Bambino is displayed each year at the Church of Santa Maria in Aracoeli in Rome. It is said to have performed miracles and to have come home by itself when it was kidnapped. Children often stand before the manger scene in the church and preach sermons, which they have been carefully taught by their parents, complete with gestures and declamatory style. This custom, symbolic of the child who came to show the world the truth, is strongly reminiscent of the medieval custom of preaching by the Boy

Bishop without the sacrilegious excesses of that custom.

There used to be a very charming tradition in Italy and Sicily, but it has fallen into neglect. Ten days before Christmas the *pifferari*, shepherds from the Calabrian region, would come to Rome and play their bagpipes, the *zampogne*, before the many shrines to the Virgin both in the streets and in private homes. Similarly, the local shepherds would come to Naples and Sicily. Although they had no songs for him, they would also be sure to stop in at carpenters' shops to pay their respects to Joseph.

The main Christmas meals vary from region to region in Italy, but a general menu would feature *capitone*, roasted, baked, or fried female eel for the meatless Christmas Eve supper, the *pranzo della vigilia*; Christmas dinner might consist of *tortellini, a capon*, and a variety of home-baked cakes. On Christmas Eve the children present their parents with their Christmas letter, consisting of best wishes and promises to be good printed in their best hand on ornate stationery and strongly reminiscent of the English Christmas piece, which may have been the forerunner of the Christmas card.

Gift-giving is saved for Epiphany. On January 6 it is Befana, the old woman who foolishly refused to help the Wise Men, who brings gifts or bags of ashes or the children.

Jack Horner Pie

Obviously, this is named for the Christmas or mince pie from which the famous nursery rhyme character abstracted a plum. The term applies to a type of Christmas gift in modern England. It is a container in the shape of a pie, although it is not to be eaten. Its actual function is to contain a variety of small gifts and goodies, like a grab bag.

Jamaica

Jamaican Christmas festivities reached their height in the late eighteenth and early nineteenth centuries with feasts and processions featuring strolling singers and performers. In this century, the celebration came under more regulation so that performers had to be licensed. This has added to a general decline, although all the customs can still be found in various parts of the island.

The women were called "set-girls," because they worked together in a set of a specific number. They danced to the accompaniment of gourd rattles, fifes, triangles, and tambourines. The men were called "actor boys" or "koo-koo boys." They wore masks and elaborate headdress and would sometimes perform plays or skits. The name *koo-koo boys* derived from a song in one of the plays which begged for food. "Koo-koo" was the sound used to imitate the rumbling of an empty stomach.

The most colorful figure in these bright festivities was the John Canoe dancer. He wore a mask, a wig, and a military jacket. On his head was a pasteboard houseboat with puppets of sailors, soldiers, or plantation worker. Often this was of great size, and the most skilled dancer had to be chosen to wear it. The name *John Canoe* is obscure. It may be a corruption of the French *gens inconnu*, which means "unknown people," or it may come from *cornu*, "horned," since early dancers wore animal masks. The origins of all these festivities are lost in antiquity, but they seem to derive equally from African and European customs.

The following description of the lively Jamaican festivities was published in 1874:

> At the Christmas carnival the younger women adorned themselves with all the finery they could procure. . . . Gaily adorned, the damsels paraded the streets in parties, known as the Reds and Blues, or the Yellows and Blues, each seeking to outshine the other. . . .
>
> . . . Their frocks were usually of fine muslin, with satin bodices of the colors named above. In Kingston and Montego Bay, groups of twenty, thirty, or even more, passed through the streets, singing and dancing as they went. Each party had its queen, dressed far more gorgeously than the rest, and selected for much the same reasons as the May Queen of an English village.
>
> Sometimes the "sets" as these companies were termed were all of the same height. Others varied greatly in this respect, but were carefully arranged, the line tapering down from the portly, majestic woman who led the procession, to quite little children in the rear. But every one in the set was dressed exactly alike, even in the most minute particulars, not excepting the parasol and the shoes, the latter frequently of white kid, then costing nine or ten shillings sterling a part. There was another rule from which departure was unknown-blacks and browns never mingled in the same set. The Creole distinction of brown lady, black woman, was in those days of slavery and social distinctions strictly observed; and, except in the smaller towns, different shades of color did not readily mingle.
>
> While these sets were parading in the streets, John Canoe parties also displayed themselves. . . . The different trades and occupations formed separate parties, each with its John Canoe man, or some

quaint device. In some cases a resemblance might be traced to the English mummers of olden time. Now and then these people were dressed up to represent characters they had seen on the stage. Shakespeare was sadly parodied on such occasions. Richard III, for example, after shouting vociferously for a horse, would kill an opponent, who, however, again revived, and performed a sword dance with the monarch.

Bermuda was the home of similar Christmas festivities, as were parts of the American South.

Japan

Similar to China, Christmas is not a national holiday in Japan, as only one to two percent of the population is actually Christian. In recent decades, however, it has become an increasingly popular celebration, especially among younger generations. While Christmas in Japan is a less-celebrated event compared to the Japanese New Year, more and more people have adopted Christmastime festivities, including decorating their homes, exchanging gifts, and enjoying a special meal with loved ones. The traditional Japanese Christmas food is a sponge cake decorated with strawberries and whipped cream. A western influence is particularly noticeable in public spaces such as shops and department stores, which feature artificial Christmas trees, Santa Claus' face in advertisements, and Christmas carols in English. Although Santa Claus is a well-known figure in Japan, his presence is strictly commercial. Traditionally, the Japanese god Hoteiosho is the Christmas gift-bearer in Japanese culture. He is most often depicted as an old man carrying a large sack, and since it is a common belief that he has eyes in the back of his head, Hoteiosho is typically regarded as overseer of appropriate behavior among children.

Julbock

Julbock means Yule goat in Swedish and is the name of one of the popular symbols of Christmas. In pagan times, Thor, the god of thunder, was supposed to ride on a goat. This picturesque means of travel has been adapted in our time to more Christian ends. It is the Julbock, a goat made of straw, who provides transportation for the Jultomten when he makes his rounds on Julafton, Christmas Eve, to deliver presents and get his offering of porridge.

Julebaal

Julebaal is the Danish name for the Christmas fire. The fire is always started with a remnant of last year's Yule log and is meant to dispel any evil spirits that might be lurking about the house.

Julebukk

This is the Norwegian version of trick or treat. It is named for Thor's goat, which was a popular costume in old pagan festivities. Any type of costume is considered appropriate today as the children go door to door after Christmas asking for treats.

Julesvenn

America's worldwide influence has introduced Santa to many countries that did not have a tradition of Christmas gift-giving. Many of these countries adopted Santa Claus without any change. Norway, however, looked back to its national mythology to find a similar figure. They found it in Julesvenn, who used to come during the midwinter festivities of Jul to hide

lucky barley stalks around the house as a symbol of good harvests to come. The timing was right, and slipping into the house to leave happy surprises fitted the image as well, so Julesvenn was a natural to play Santa Claus and bring presents on Christmas Eve.

Julklapp

Julklapp means Christmas box and is a delightful custom in northern Germany, Denmark, and Sweden. There will be a knock or a ring at the door, and a present will be thrown in. The giver hurries away before he or she can be discovered. The present itself attempts to be as mysterious as the giver, since it is wrapped in many layers of paper or several different-sized boxes, or may merely contain directions for finding where the real present is hidden. The longer it takes to determine what the present is and who gave it, the more successful the Julklapp.

Julnisse

A Julnisse is a Danish Christmas elf. One lives in every barn and is attached to the household. He is known for playing practical jokes. Thus, as with the World War II gremlin, which was created as an explanation for inexplicable mechanical failures, any accident around the house can be blamed on the Nisse. He is described as being very small and wearing gray homespun with a red bonnet, long red stockings, and white clogs, although no one but the family cat ever actually sees him. Every Christmas Eve he must be left a bowl of rice pudding to placate him and ensure that he will watch over the family and the farm animals for another year. The Julnisse is as popular in Danish advertising and decoration as Santa Claus is in America.

Jultomten

The Swedish Jultomten is similar to Danish Julnisse in that he is an elf who lives in the hayloft and is a guardian of the household, but he is also the one who brings the Christmas gifts. He sports a red cap and a long white beard and rides in a sleigh pulled by the Julbock when he comes on Christmas Eve to deliver the presents which will be found under the Christmas tree.

Kallikantzaroi

In Greek superstition, the Kallikantzaroi are evil, half-human monsters who, during most of the year, chop away beneath the ground at the tree that supports the earth. At Christmas time, that tree is renewed by the birth of Christ and the enraged demons come to the surface to vent their fury in malicious practical joking. They slip down chimneys and put out the fire in a particularly indelicate manner or ride on people's backs and force them to dance until they are exhausted. There are several ways of guarding against them. One is to keep the *skarkantzalos*, the Christmas log, burning brightly all twelve days of Christmas so they can't get down the chimney. Another is to burn salt or an old shoe, the smell of which will keep them away. Also, the lower jaw of a pig hung behind the door or inside the chimney will keep them out for reasons lost in antiquity. The Kallikantzaroi roam the earth until Epiphany, or Greek Cross Day, when the Blessing of the Waters drives them underground again.

Any child born on Christmas or during the twelve days is in danger of becoming a Kallikantzaroi, in opposition to other national traditions that usually hold a Christmas child to be lucky. In Greece, the baby must be bound in tresses of garlic or straw or have his toenails singed to protect him from his terrible fate. Similarly, in Poland and parts of Germany, folk traditions hold that werewolves are active during the twelve nights of Christmas and that a child born then faces the danger of becoming one.

Kettle

In the United States and Europe, sidewalk Santas use a kettle for receiving donations. The idea is said to have begun at the turn of the century in California, when the Salvation Army used soup kettle from one of its mission kitchens to collect donations for survivors of a shipwreck to buy food and clothing. Today the coins thrown in by the passing throngs are turned into Christmas dinners and happy Christmases for the poor.

Kissing Bough

Until the introduction of the Christmas tree in the middle of the nineteenth century, the kissing bough was the primary piece of decorative greenery in the English Christmas. It was in the shape of a double hoop with streamers going up to a central point, like a Maypole with two circles of garlands. It was made up of evergreen boughs, holly, and ivy and hung with apples and pears or ribbons and ornaments, with lighted candles and a bunch of mistletoe hanging from the center. As its name implies, the woman who "accidentally" wandered under the kissing bough had to pay the ancient penalty and allow herself to be kissed. Other names for this decorative and useful ornament were the kissing ring, the kissing bunch, and the kissing ball. As these names demonstrate, the exact shape may have varied, but what went on under it remained the same.

Klapparbock

The name of this Danish creature means "Goat with Yule gifts." As with the Swedish Julbock, he probably derives from the goat Thor rode on, but unlike his Swedish counterpart, he is not a pleasant character. He is often represented by a man in a goatskin, and his job is to frighten children who have not been quite as good as they should have been.

Klaubauf

Klaubauf is a demonic page who accompanies St. Nicholas on December 5 when he visits Austria on the eve of his name day. Dressed in rags, Klaubauf has a shaggy hide, a coal-black face, goatlike horns, fiery eyes, and a long red tongue. Clanking chains are attached about his feet. He serves as a very effective warning to naughty children.

Knecht Rupprecht

The Christmas demon Knecht Rupprecht first appeared in a play in 1668 and was condemned by the Roman Catholic Church as being a devil in 1680. That did not dim his popularity or notoriety, depending on how you looked at it. Today he still shows up in much of central and northern Europe, especially parts of Germany and Austria. To the Pennsylvania Dutch, he is known as Belsnickel. Other names for the same character are Pelznickle, "Furry Nicholas," and Ru-Klas, "Rough Nicholas." From these names, it is easy to see that he is looked upon as not merely a companion to St. Nicholas, but almost another version of him. There is some speculation that Knecht Rupprecht derives from the pagan god Odin and represents the darker side of St. Nicholas' character, that of the punishment which must be meted out to the wicked. Knecht Rupprecht's job is to examine children in their knowledge of prayers and punish those who are deficient.

Krampus

Another Christmas demon from lower Austria, Krampus, or Grampus, accompanies St. Nicholas on December 6. He carries a rod or whip for children who are badly behaved or who don't know their school lessons. However, Krampus does not get to test his rod, for St. Nicholas intercedes on a child's behalf when the child promises to be good and to study hard.

Krippe

This is the German word for crib and is used to apply to manger scenes set up in church or home. The Krippe has never been as important to the Germans as the Christmas tree, but it was once very popular for the Christmas Eve custom of cradle rocking. Germany has a rich tradition of wood carving and has produced many beautiful examples of hand-carved Krippen.

Kris Kringle

Kris Kringle is a popular corruption of the name of the Christkind, who was originally the Christ Child and later the gift-bringing angelic figure in much of northern Europe. When the Pennsylvania Dutch brought this figure with them to America, it mingled with the notions of other immigrants and became, by the middle of the nineteenth century, a figure very much like Santa Claus, who was himself rather new at the time. The idea that Kris Kringle was just another name for Santa Claus became part of the tradition and was solidified in the popular mind by the movie *Miracle on 34th Street*.

Lamb's Wool

This was one of the traditional hot drinks in the English wassail bowl; it was the toast floating on the top that made it look like lamb's wool. The drink itself was made up of hot ale, sugar, nutmeg, cinnamon, cloves, eggs, and roasted apples.

Lights

One of the greatest sources of danger in the old Christmas celebration was the burning candles on the Christmas tree. They were lovely, but they were a fire hazard of the first order. Often buckets of water were kept standing around the living room to douse the blazes that happened all too easily.

The idea of electric Christmas tree lights first occurred to Ralph E. Morris, an employee of New England Telephone, in 1895. The actual strings of lights had already been manufactured for use in telephone switchboards. Morris looked at the tiny bulbs and had the idea of using them on his tree. When the idea was introduced commercially, it caught on immediately and led to a great proliferation of sizes, shapes, and colors in Christmas tree lights as well as to vastly increased safety.

Lord of Misrule

The Lord of Misrule was the leader of the Christmas revelries in medieval England. In the court, he was appointed by the king or members of the nobility and was in charge of arranging all the feasting, masquing, and mumming to take place during the Twelve Days of Christmas. He was also given very real power in that all, even the king, had to submit to his whims during the period of his reign. Obviously there had to be some exceptions, and a wise Lord of Misrule did not overstep the bounds if he wished to retain the favor he had been shown in being appointed. But within those bounds, he was king of the day.

Among the commoners, the Lord of Misrule presided over less orderly proceedings as the people frolicked through the streets. This description of a fifteenth-century Lord of Misrule in Norfolk, England, calls him by the name King of Christmas, but gives a good picture of his typical doings:

John Adman, a wealthy citizen, made disport with his neighbours and friends, and was crowned King of Christmas. He rode in state through the city, dressed forth in silks and tinsel, and preceded by twelve persons habited as the twelve months of the year. After King Christmas followed Lent, clothed in white garments trimmed with herring skins, on horseback, the horse being decorated with trappings of oyster-shells, being indicative that sadness and a holy time should follow Christmas reveling. In this way they rode through the city, accompanied by numbers in various grotesque dresses, making disport and merriment; some clothed in armour; others, dressed as devils, chased the people, and sorely affrighted the women and children; others wearing skin dresses, and counterfeiting beats, wolves, lions, and other animals, and endeavouring to imitate the animals they represented, in roaring and raving, alarming the cowardly and appalling the stoutest hearts.

The Lord of Misrule and his merry mummers probably derive from ancient Roman times, when dressing up as animals or women or just in fantastic costumes was associated with the Saturnalia. It was also a time when servants were made equal to or even higher than their masters. The Romans also had the Magister Ludi, the Master of the Games, who was appointed to handle all festivities and celebrations on special occasions.

The Lord of Misrule died out after the Restoration of the British kings in 1660 for a number of reasons. He was a very rowdy figure, and the upsurge of Puritan feelings made him very unpopular. He was also no longer welcome to the king. Royalty had thought itself secure until the Commonwealth temporarily abolished the monarchy. Now the king was back in power, but never again would a king be so confident that he could readily give up even the semblance of rule to that madcap monarch, the Lord of Misrule.

Mari Llwyd

Only the Welsh could produce such an unpronounceable-looking name for a Christmas creature. It is a half-man, half-animal fantasy creature whose origin is unknown. It wears a white sheet on decked with such holiday ornaments as bells, Christmas balls, baubles, holly, and tinsel, while a huge headpiece resembling the head of a horse covers the upper torso. Making queer shrill noises, prancing like a hobby horse, dancing, and darting at the children, the Mari Llwyd stirs up laughter and mirth as it parades about the countryside. In former times the head was actually made up of the skull of a horse wired so that the jaws could be worked. Anyone bitten by the Mari Llwyd had to pay a fine.

Mass of the Carols

This Puerto Rican tradition begins each year on December 16. At 5:30 A.M. on that day and each successive day until Christmas Eve, all the people attend the Mass of the Carols. It is so called because of the happy carols that are sung at the mass rather than the usual hymns. Quite frequently, this caroling will be continued after the mass by many people on their way home or to work, helping to carry the joy of the season into everyday life.

Mass of the Rooster

According to tradition, the rooster has crowed only once at midnight, at the moment when Christ was born. Hence, Spanish and Latin American countries call their midnight mass on Christmas Eve Misa del Gallo, the Mass of the Rooster.

Mass of the Shepherds

In honor of the shepherds who first heard the good tidings on the first Christmas, the people of Poland call their Christmas Eve Midnight Mass Pasterka, the Mass of the Shepherds.

Mexico

South of the border, Christmas color is provided by the brilliant red of the Flower of the Holy Night, which we call poinsettia. The Spanish name derives from the time the flower's bright red leaves appear, which is usually around Christmas Eve.

The *posada* is popular in Mexico. For nine days before Christmas, processions go from house to house, or on a smaller scale from room to room within a single house, carrying the images of Joseph and Mary and looking for shelter. Also for days before Christmas, one can see colorful *puestos* in the marketplaces. These are booths set up especially to sell the handicrafts, food, and toys brought down from the mountains by the Indians who have labored all year in preparation for this time.

After the Christ Child has been added to the manger scene on Christmas Eve, it is time for the *piñata*, Mexico's special contribution to the world of Christmas. The *piñata* is an earthenware jar in the shape of an animal, person, or some fantastic figure which is filled with small toys and candy and hung from the ceiling. One child at a time is blindfolded and turned around and given a stick to take a few swings at the hard-to-crack clay figure. When it is finally broken open, everyone scrambles for the goodies that shower down all over the room. At midnight, it is time for the Mass of the Rooster.

Although the children may get small trinkets from the *piñata*, they must wait until Epiphany for their major presents. As in so many Spanish countries, it is the Wise Men who bring the gifts on their day, January 6.

Midnight Mass

In the Roman Catholic Church, the first mass of the Feast of Christmas takes place at midnight, Christmas Eve, that being traditionally the time of

Christ's birth. No one knows for sure when the first Midnight Mass occurred, but it is believed that the custom may go as far back as the early part of the fifth century. Certainly the custom was taken into account in the sixteenth century, when the Council of Trent passed new legislation concerning the hours of masses. Priests are allowed the special privilege of celebrating three masses on Christmas Day. Today, television allows many people to visit some of the famous Midnight Masses without leaving their homes. One such is broadcast from the Church of the Nativity in Bethlehem, the traditional site of Christ's birth. Another comes from St. Peter's Basilica in Rome. In 1975 Pope Paul VI celebrated an unprecedented open-air Midnight Mass before 100,000 people filling St. Peter's Square, which was seen on television by an estimated 330 million viewers in forty-one countries throughout the world.

Many other churches have late services on Christmas Eve, often at 11:00 P.M. rather than midnight. Usually they are candle-lit and feature a great deal of singing of the traditional carols that set the mood for the Christmas celebration to come. The Episcopalian Service of Lessons and Carols is typical of this kind of service. Prophecies of Christ's birth and the Gospel stories are read, interspersed with the singing of ancient carols.

Mince Pie

It seems hard to imagine that a religious controversy could rage over a piece of baked goods, but such was the case with the mince pie. Meat pies become popular in England following the Crusades, when the many eastern spices were introduced to England for the first time by the returning knights. The pies were made of minced bits of venison, pheasant, partridge, peacock, rabbit, apples, sugar, suet, molasses, raisins, currants, and spices in differing combinations. At Christmas a special pie was baked.

The spices and sweetmeats were looked upon as symbolic of the Wise Men's gifts to the Christ Child, so the pie was baked in the rough shape of a manger and an image of the baby Jesus was put on top of it. Later, this image outraged the Puritans, who looked upon it as idolatry. Mince pies were outlawed along with Christmas under the strict Puritan Commonwealth and in the early American New England settlements. All through the seventeenth and eighteenth centuries, the making of mince pies was looked upon as a sign of Roman Catholic leanings. This probably resulted in the change of shape to a normal circular one and the replacement of the Christ Child with spring of greenery.

Today the mince pie has lost its religious nature along with its meat. It is usually made with apples, raising, currants, suet, molasses, lemon peel, spices, sugar, and salt.

Mince pie was also known as "Christmas pie" in medieval England. Thus it is a mince pie that plays an all-important role in a familiar nursery rhyme and the startling story that inspired it.

> Little Jack Horner
> Sat in a corner
> Eating a Christmas pie;
> He put in his thumb
> And pulled out a plum
> And said, "What a good boy am I!"

The real Jack Horner was Thomas Horner, a servant to Richard Whiting, who was a church official at Glastonbury in the time of Henry VIII. That greedy monarch was engaged at the time in seizing as much of the Church's lands as he could get away with. In an effort to appease him, Whiting sent him an unusual Christmas present, a mince pie with the deeds to a dozen rich estates hidden inside it. He hoped that the king would be satisfied and not take any more of his lands. Horner was entrusted with the secret mission. On the way, it is said, he opened the pie and stole one of the deeds for himself. With this "plum" he made his fortune. Little did he know that he would be remembered in a bit of nonsense verse hundreds of years after his death.

Mistletoe

In Norse mythology, Balder was the best loved of all the gods, both by all living creatures and by the gods themselves. But one night he had a dream that indicated danger was approaching. When he told this to his mother, Frigga, she resolved to protect him. She went throughout the world asking and receiving a promise from everything, even the rocks and the trees, that they would not harm Balder. When this was known, it became a great sport to throw deadly objects at Balder, since they would always fall short or turn aside because of their promise. All were happy for Balder's safety except the sly Loki, who was jealous of him. He found out craftily from Frigga that there was one plant so insignificant that she had overlooked it when she was getting the promises: the mistletoe. Taking a sharp sprig of the plant, Loki went to Hoder, Balder's brother, who was blind, and asked why he did not join in the jolly game of throwing objects harmlessly at Balder. Hoder pointed out that he was blind and had nothing to throw. Loki gave him the mistletoe and guided his hand. The dart went straight to Balder's heart and he fell dead. All wept, and Loki was severely punished, but Frigga blessed the plant that had, through no fault of its own, caused Balder's death. She made it a symbol of love and promised to bestow a kiss on all who passed beneath it.

Mistletoe was a holy plant to the ancient Celtic priests called the Druids.

Around the New Year, a priest would cut the mistletoe from the holy oak tree with a golden sickle and catch it in a white cloth, so that it would not touch the ground. It would then be offered in sacrifice to the gods along with two white bulls. There were also ceremonies in which kisses beneath the mistletoe symbolized the ending of old grievances. Sprigs of mistletoe were hung over doors for the same symbolic reasons.

The hanging of mistletoe at Christmas and New Year's was one of many pagan customs carried over into the Christian era, in this case without any specific justification, but simply as a charming custom. The kissing beneath it died out in most areas except England. (Austria has a related custom in which Sylvester kisses anyone beneath the greenery, but this is not specifically mistletoe and only Sylvester is allowed to do it.) The British are known today for their lack of emotional display, but this was not always so. In the sixteenth century, kissing was widespread in England as a form of greeting without requiring close relationship between the kissers. The great continental scholar Erasmus wrote at this time of a visit to England: "Wherever you go, everyone welcomes you with a kiss, and the same on bidding farewell . . . in short, turn where you will, there are kisses, kisses everywhere." It may just be because they were so inclined to kissing anyway that the English preserved the ancient mistletoe tradition when others let it fade.

Mistletoe is a parasitic plant that grown hanging from the limbs of various nonevergreen trees. It has leathery evergreen leaves, yellow-green flowers, and waxy white berries. One old English custom required the plucking of one berry for each girl kissed until the sprig was bare or the man ran out of girls.

The pleasures and harmless frivolity of mistletoe have been delightfully detailed in Dickens' *Pickwick Papers*:

From the center of the ceiling of this kitchen, old Wardle had just

suspended with his own hands a huge branch of mistletoe, and this same branch of mistletoe instantaneously gave rise to a scene of general and most delightful struggling and confusion; in the midst of which, Mr. Pickwick, with a gallantry that would have done honour to a descendant of Lady Tollimglower herself, took the old lady by the hand, led her beneath the mystic branch, and saluted her in all courtesy and decorum. The old lady submitted to this piece of practical politeness with all the dignity which befitted so important and serious a solemnity, but the younger ladies, not being so thoroughly imbued with a superstitious veneration for the custom-or imagining that the value of a salute is very much enhanced if it cost a little trouble to obtain it-screamed and struggled, and ran into corners, and threatened and remonstrated, and did everything but leave the room until some of the less adventurous gentlemen were on the point of desisting when they all at one found it useless to resist any longer and submitted to be kissed with a good grace. Mr. Winkle kissed the young lad with the black eyes, and Mr. Snodgrass kissed Emily, and Mr. Weller, not being particular about the form of being under the mistletoe, kissed Emma and the other female servants just as he caught them. As to the poor relations, they kissed everybody, not even excepting the plainer portions of the young-lady visitors, who, in their excessive confusion, ran right under the mistletoe, as soon as it was hung up, without knowing it! Wardle stood with his back to the fire, surveying the whole scene with the utmost satisfaction; and the fat boy took the opportunity of appropriating to his own use, and summarily devouring, a particularly fine mince-pie that had been carefully put by for somebody else.

Now, the screaming had subsided, and faces were in a glow, and curls in a tangle, and Mr. Pickwick, after kissing the old lady, as before mentioned, was standing under the mistletoe, looking with a very pleased countenance on all that was passing around him, when the young lady with the black eyes, after a little whispering with the other young ladies, made a sudden dart forward and, putting her arm around Mr. Pickwick's neck, saluted him affectionately on the left cheek; and before Mr. Pickwick distinctly knew what was the matter, he was surrounded by the whole body and kissed by every one of them.

It was a pleasant thing to see Mr. Pickwick in the center of the group, now pulled this way, and then that, and first kissed on the chin, and then on the nose, and then on the spectacles, and to hear the peals of laughter which were raised on every side. . . .

Mumming

Mumming is difficult to define exactly since it includes every kind of dressing up and acting out or dancing or performing that people choose to do at Christmastime. The annual Christmas pageant is a form of mummery in our own country.

Mumming can be traced back to the rowdy bands that roamed preChristian Rome at the time of the Saturnalia, dressed as animals or women and carousing in the streets. In the Middle Ages these activities remained popular, sometimes carried on for the entertainment of homeowners who would then be expected to provide a treat, but just as often for the entertainment of only the performer themselves. Sometimes bands would break into church services and disrupt the proceedings with their "geese dancing" (a corruption of "disguise," or "guise" dancing). There were many legends of such sacrilegious revelers who were cursed by a priest and compelled to dance without interruption for a full year until the following Christmas.

In the royal courts, there was usually appointed a Lord of Misrule who governed the mumming. He would set up masques, processions, and other entertainments, as well as leading in spontaneous outbursts. Frequently court personages would disguise themselves and indulge in the unusual license that was allowed the Christmas mummers. Henry VIII himself was known to mask his face, as when, with a band of fellow revelers, he broke into a supper party given by Cardinal Wolsey.

Gradually the official court mumming and the rowdy masquerades of the street died out. But mumming took on a new form as the disguised figures devoted themselves to acting out exotic plays and skits. As these were short performances, they could be done several times a night around a village, in return for the traditional handout. Sometimes the mummers were vagabonds just looking for the money or food; often they were village groups who would perform the same play every year. One of the most widespread Christmas plays was the *Play of St. George*, which existed in many versions, all of them rather naïve to the modern playgoers. Thomas Hardy features this play in his famous novel *The Return of the Native*. The story of the play has nothing to do with Christmas, but as St. George was the patron saint of England, his exploits again the Turks were considered patriotic and a suitable spectacle for Christmas or anytime. Max Beerbohm, in a parody of the style of George Bernard Shaw, described one of these St. George plays:

> Entered, first of all, the English knight, announcing his determination to fight and vanquish the Turkish knight, a vastly superior swordsman, who promptly made mincemeat of him. After the Saracen had celebrated his victory in verse, and proclaimed him-

self the world champion, entered Snt George, who, after some preliminary patriotic flourishes, promptly made mincemeat of the Saracen-to the blank amazement of an audience which included several retired army officers. Snt George, however, saved his face by the usual expedient of the victorious British general, attributing to Providence a result which by no polity stretch of casuistry could have been traced to the operations of his own brain. But here the dramatist was confronted by another difficulty: there being no curtain to ring down, how were the two corpses to be got gracefully rid of? Entered therefore the Physician, and brought them both to life.

Traditionally, after this successful resurrection, a devil would go about with a large frying pan collecting donations. There was obviously very little serious drama here but a very great deal of fun.

America has one very large-scale remnant of mumming in the annual Philadelphia Mummers' Parade. Over a hundred years old, this event still offers a great opportunity for much dressing up, music-making, and satirical reminders of the past year's events.

Nacimiento

As in most of southern Europe, in Spain the manger scene is a more important image of Christmas than the Christmas tree. *Nacimiento* is the Spanish term for a manger scene and is used both in Spain and in most of the Latin American countries. The Magi are very popular in Spain, so they figure prominently in the *nacimiento*. Often in Spanish communities, men dressed as the Three Kings will visit the large outdoor manger scenes during the festivities of Epiphany Eve.

Nativity Scene

St. Francis of Assisi was responsible for the popularization of the nativity scene. It probably existed before him, but only as a decorative element. St. Francis was a very gentle man, known for his love of animals. He wanted to bring home to the people the humanity and humility of the Christ Child. The Church at this time was a very rigid institution, emphasizing that this life was a place of sin and sorrow. St. Francis wanted to add the hope and joy of God's love to this disheartening message. So, in 1223 or 1225, in Greccio, Italy, he constructed a life-sized manger scene with live animals. The gospel was sung around this scene, and this may very well have been the start of caroling, since the church songs of the time were Latin hymns not known for being joyous. The people were charmed and captivated and immediately embraced the nativity scene as a means of making the Christmas message more real.

The nativity scene has always been most important to southern Europe, where the symbol of the first tree amid the winter snows has less meaning because of the warmer climate. The scenes range from the simplest little cutout figures to whole roomfuls or even village squarefuls of elaborately decorated scenery. In the beginning of the eighteenth century, the king of Naples began making his own manger scenes. He was not known for much else, but he was very good at working with his hands. He would carve the figures and his wife would help outfit them. It became very fashionable at the court for the nobility to emulate the king and vie with each other to produce ever more spectacular effects. Very often the stable would be set amid elaborate architectural ruins, which had little to do with biblical times, but offered great opportunity for picturesqueness.

The nativity scene has many names in many countries. In Italy, it is the *presepio*; in France, it is the *crèche*, a name often used in America as well; some areas of Germany have the *Krippe* as well as the tree; The Slovak Republic builds the *jesliky*; Spain and much of Latin America call it a *nacimiento*; Brazil has a *pesebre*; in Costa Rica, it is a *portal*. In all countries, it is a way of bringing home the message that Christ was made a little child and lay lowly in a manger for the sake of humankind.

Noche-Buena

The "Good Night" is the Spanish name for Christmas Eve. Noche-Buena is a time for singing and dancing, both in the streets and around the *nacimiento* at home before it is time to attend the midnight Mass of the Rooster.

North Pole

The North Pole first appeared as Santa's home in the cartoons of Thomas Nast. In 1882 Nast drew a cartoon showing Santa sitting on a box addressed "Christmas Box 1882, St. Nicholas, North Pole." In 1885 another cartoon traced Santa's route on a map, showing him coming home to the North Pole. Nast never gave his reasons for settling on Santa's home territory; presumably he just felt Santa's costume was best suited to a cool climate and he knew that Santa would never do anything by half measures.

Norway

At 4:00 P.M. all work comes to a halt on Christmas Eve in Norway. Everyone bathes and puts on new clothes to greet the season. The largest sheaf of grain is hung out for the birds to make their Christmas merry, too. Christmas dinner begins with rice pudding with a lucky almond hidden in it for someone, and a bowl is also set out for the barn elf so that he will continue to watch over the animals and not turn mischievous. A Christmas pig provides most of the meat dishes.

Traditionally the Norwegians kept the season bright with a Yule log. It literally formed the center of the celebration since it was frequently an entire tree that could only partly fit into the fireplace and so extended well out into the middle of the living room. As it burned, it would be pushed farther and farther into the fire to provide continuous light and warmth through the whole Christmas season. More and more, though, the Christmas tree, introduced from Germany in the 1830s, has taken the place of the Yule log. The celebration may have lost some warmth thereby, but it has gained a great deal in spaciousness.

The worldwide popularity of Santa Claus has caused in recent years the resurrection of an ancient Norse figure called Julesvenn. In ancient times he would come during the feast of Jul to hide lucky barley stalks around the house. Now he comes on Christmas Eve to bring gifts to good children.

After Christmas Day is past, Norwegian children indulge in a custom much like the American trick or treat. It is called Julebukk after the goat that drew the cart of Thor, the god of thunder in Norse mythology. In pre-Christian festivities, Thor's goat was popular as a costume for the Jul festivities. Today children wear costumes and go door to door asking for goodies in a much more innocent version of those ancient revelries.

Old Christmas Day

This is a term still sometimes used in England for January 6, Epiphany. In 1752 Britain finally adopted the Gregorian calendar, which was already current in most other European counties. This calendar was created to correct an error in calculation in the old Julian calendar which was very small, but which over the centuries had accumulated a total error of eleven days. Thus in 1752 September 3 became September 14 in Britain. This caused considerable confusion, especially when it came time for an important holiday such as Christmas. Many people refused to follow the new calendar, but consulted such portents as the famous Glastonbury thorn, which always blossomed on Christmas Eve. When it blossomed on Old Christmas Eve, they followed its example and celebrated by the old calendar. While the calendar is now completely accepted, the old date is still remembered in folklore.

Old Hob

This old English custom is very rare today. Old Hob is a horse who may have had his origin in pre-Christian representations of Odin's eight-footed horse. Like the Welsh Mari Llwyd, the English Old Hob was represented by a horse's head on a pole carried by a man under a sheet. It was accompanied by groups of waifs who sang Christmas ditties and rang hand bells for coins. The Old Hob festivities would begin as early as All Souls' Day, November 2, and usually ended by Boxing Day, December 26. There was similar tradition in northern Germany, where the horse was called Schimmel.

Ornaments

The first Christmas trees had real fruit and flowers as their only ornaments. Cookies, nuts, and other kinds of food were later added. Lighted candles were placed on the trees. All of this was understandably heavy, and it took a sturdy tree to stand up without drooping to the ground. Perhaps as a remedy for this problem, German glass blowers began producing featherweight glass balls to replace the fruit and other heavy ornaments. This was the beginning of the highly specialized industry that today produces the myriad Christmas tree ornaments ranging from simple colored balls and tinsel to elaborate stars and blinking Santa Clauses.

Other countries have some very lovely traditional ornaments. Painted eggshells are a favorite in the Czech Republic. In Sweden, straw figures of animals and little wooden ornaments adorn the tree. The Danish like bells and paper hearts. In Japan, pastel-colored paper fans and delicately cut paper butterflies are popular.

Pantomime

The Christmas Pantomime is to the British what the Christmas show at Radio City Music Hall is to Americans, except that it is found all over, not

just in one place. Pantomimes are presented most often during the twelve days after Christmas and are a treat for the whole family.

The pantomime may have started in the seventeenth century in the form we understand to be pantomime in America, that is, the wordless acting out of a story. But by the early eighteenth century it had come into full flower and refused to be silent. The stories combined as many emotion as possible, serious, comic, and highly adventurous. Elaborate stage transformations were always a main feature.

Today the stories are almost always traditional subjects, such as fairy tales or *Robinson Crusoe,* and exist largely as an excuse to string together a great variety of performers and scenic effects into a giant vaudeville. It is not unusual for a pantomime to include dancers, singers, comedians, acrobats, magicians, and ventriloquists-possibly even swimmers or ice skaters.

Papa Noël

Papa Noël is the Brazilian name for Santa Claus. He comes on Christmas Eve to fill children's shoes with Christmas gifts and sweets.

Pastori

This Italian word for shepherds applies to all the figures made for the *presepio,* the Italian manger scenes. First made in Naples in the eighteenth century, the *pastori* were elaborate figures fashioned out of wood or clay and costumed in silk finery with exquisite detail by the *figurari,* the figure makers. Since the townspeople would worship and celebrate before the *presepio,* it did not seem unreasonable for them to appear as figures in the setting. Thus the mayor, local businessmen, and other townspeople began to appear as carved figures beside the shepherds and Wise Men of the original Christmas. Other popular *pastori* still include animals, birds, bagpipe-playing local shepherds, minstrels, Franciscan monks, angels, and stars.

Père Fouettard

Also known as Père Fouchette, this French Christmas figure takes his name from the French word *fouet,* which means a birch rod. Father Birch Rod comes with Père Noël, Father Christmas, to deal out punishments to those who haven't been good enough to earn a reward from the jolly old man. Père Fouettard carries the birch rod he is named for and also a basket into which irretrievably naughty children can be bundled and carried off.

Père Noël

Père Noël is French for Father Christmas. He is one of the two gift-bringers who come to different areas of France to fill the children's shoes on Christmas Eve. The Christ Child is the other and is called le Petit Noël, "Little Christmas."

Peru

Many Peruvian manger scenes feature the quaintly beautiful figures carved from wood by the Quechua Indians. The techniques they used date back to the sixteenth century, and many of the traditional images and forms of dress also come from that time of the *conquistadores.*

On Christmas Eve, the meal after Midnight Mass features tamales. Christmas Day festivities in Lima, the capital, are highlighted by a bull-fight and a procession with the statue of the Virgin Mary.

Petit Noël

Petit Noël is the name given the Christ Child by the French when he comes in the role of gift-bringer to the children on Christmas Eve. His name means Little Christmas, and he comes to the areas not taken care of by Père Noël, Father Christmas.

Piñata

This is a joyful custom of Mexico and some other areas of Latin America. The *piñata* is a clay or earthenware jar in the shape of an animal or person which is filled with toys, candy, and cookies and suspended from the ceiling. One at a time, children are blindfolded and given a stick. After being turned around until his or her sense of direction is gone, the child is set free to flail wildly in every direction, trying to find the *piñata*. Even if the child hits it, he or she may have trouble cracking the tough jar. When it finally is broken, everyone scrambles for the goodies. To spare the feelings of easily frustrated modern youth, some *piñatas* are now made of easy-to-break papier-mâché.

Plum Pudding

Plum pudding is one of the famous traditional English Christmas dishes. Even for Americans, it conjures up images of a Dickensian Christmas, although most of us have not tasted a plum pudding. That is probably just as well, since this Christmas dish is a bit tricky, and a poorly prepared one is a very hard tradition to swallow.

The first plum puddings were made around 1670. They were a stiffened form of the earlier plum porridge, which was made of similar ingredients but was served semiliquid. Interestingly, plum pudding does not contain any plums. The name may refer to the raisins in it, or to the fact that the ingredients swell during baking. To plum once meant to rise or swell, as we see in the modern to plump. To the early mild porridge or frumenty were added lumps of meat, dried fruits such as raisins and currants, rum and brandy, butter, sugar, eggs, and many spices. These first plum puddings were made in large copper kettles and were prepared several weeks before Christmas. The making of the pudding was attended with much ceremony. The entire household was present and each family member took turns at stirring the thick steaming stew and each made a wish. A coin, a thimble, a button, and a ring were mixed into the pudding. Later when it was eaten, each object would have significance for the finder. The coin would mean wealth, in the new year; the button, bachelorhood; the thimble, spinster-hood; and the ring heralded marriage.

At the Christmas Feast, the pudding came to the table amid great antic-ipation. If eyes could consume, the pudding would have been gone in an instant. The arrival of the plum pudding was the capstone of the Christmas dinner, and there was always room, no matter how full the stomach. What was not eaten was saved, sometimes lasting into mid-January, for the pud-ding was very rich and filling.

Today plum pudding is not made as it once was, but it still requires time and patience. It takes about give or six hours to prepare. This is mainly because all the suet (hard fat from beef or mutton) must dissolve before the flour particles burst. If the fat is not allowed to melt, the pudding will not cook properly, and the results will be a compressed hard pudding, impos-sible to digest. Plum pudding is usually served decorated with holly and with hard sauce on the side.

The champion of all plum puddings was created in the village of Paignton in Devil, England, in 1819. This village had a custom of making a gigantic plum pudding for the entire community once every fifty years. The custom has since been discontinued, but in 1819 the pudding used four hundredweights of flour and 120 pounds each of suet and raising. The finished concoction weighed 900 pounds and had to be pulled by three horses. With great celebration, the pudding was sliced up and served. There was great dismay among the villagers when they discovered that the pudding wasn't properly cooked.

Poinsettia

In Mexican legend, a small boy knelt at the altar of his village church on Christmas Eve. He had nothing to offer the Christ Child on his birthday because he had no money, but his prayers were sincere. A miracle gave him the present that could not be be bought: the first Flower of the Holy Night sprang up at his feet in brilliant red and green homage to the holy birth. Thus was born the flower we know as the poinsettia.

Dr. Joel Roberts Poinsett was the American ambassador to Mexico from 1825 to 1829. His keen interest in botany made him very interested in the Flower of the Holy Night, and he brought it back to his home in South Carolina. It became very popular as a Christmas plant and was named after him.

The red part of the poinsettia is not a flower, but is made up of bracts, inner leaves that are small in most flowers. The actual flowers of the poinsettia are the small yellow buds in the center of the red clusters. Besides the familiar red poinsettia, other varieties can also be found with white and pink flowers, and a yellow variety is found in Guatemala.

There are some areas of our country where the poinsettias are so abundant they turn whole towns into Christmas decorations. The town of Encinitas, California, is known as the Poinsettia Capital of the World because of the superabundance of the flower there. Each Christmas the

Chamber of Commerce organizes special poinsettia tours to view nature's Christmas offering in its most picturesque locales.

Poland

The lucky children of Poland receive presents twice. On St. Nicholas' Day, the good saint himself brings presents. On Christmas Eve, it is the Star Man.

The Star of Bethlehem is the most popular image in the Polish Christmas. It is the first star of Christmas Eve, which marks the end of the Advent fast and ushers in the time of Christmas feasting. The Christmas Eve supper must have an odd number of dishes, from five to thirteen, for luck, and there must be an even number of diners. Empty places are left for absent family members and for the Christ Child. *Oplatki,* small white wafers, are served with the meal. These are symbolic of the Sacred Host that is received at Mass, making the Christmas Eve dinner a secular Communion for the family circle.

After supper the Star Man arrives, attended by the Star Boys. They are dressed fantastically, as Wise Men or animals or other figures from the nativity. The Star Man examines the children in their catechism and rewards them with small presents if they do well, even if they need a bit of coaching. The Star Boys sing carols and are given a treat for their help. After the fun, all go to Pasterka, the midnight Mass of the Shepherds.

Polaznik

This is a custom of the Eastern European Slavic regions that is similar to the English and Scottish first-footing. Polaznik is usually a young man who visits a family at the dawn of Christmas Eve, holding a handful of wheat which he throws over the members of the household before wishing them a

Merry Christmas. After enjoying a large pre-Christmas feast with the family, Polaznik accepts a gift and departs at evening. His visit is looked upon as a sign that the family will enjoy prosperity throughout the coming year.

Posada

The *posada* is a beloved custom of Mexico and other Latin American countries. *Posada* means "inn" in Spanish, and the custom derives from plays that were once performed depicting the wandering of Mary and Joseph looking for shelter. Tradition says their search lasted for nine days. So on December 16 a procession sets out with the figures of Mary and Joseph to find shelter for them. This procession may pass through the streets to prearranged houses, or it may take place entirely inside one house, going from room to room. When the "inn" is reached, there is a ritualistic series of questions and answers to be gone through. One such is called the Litany of Loretto:

> Who knocks at my door, so late in the night?
> We are pilgrims, without shelter, and we want only a place to rest.
> Go somewhere else and disturb me not again.
> But the night is very cold. We have come from afar and we are very tired.
> But who are you? I know you not.
> I am Joseph of Nazareth, a carpenter, and with me is Mary, my wife,
>   who will be the mother of the Son of God.
> Then come into my humble home, and welcome! And may the Lord
>   give shelter to my soul when I leave this world!

The innkeeper always shows himself to be more hospitable than the original one at Bethlehem. When they are allowed to enter, the figures of Mary and Joseph are taken to the manger scene, where they are set among the animals by the crib. This is done for each of eight nights. On the ninth, Christmas Eve, the figure of the Christ Child is also added to the scene. Each evening the *posada* procession finished with singing and dancing.

Presepio

For Italians, the *presepio,* or manger scene, is the absolute center of all festivities. On Christmas Eve, it is set up without the Christ Child, since it is not yet time for his birth. Then on Christmas morning, in a simple ceremony witnessed by the entire family, the mother of the household places the Bambino in the *presepio.* They pray in the presence of this very physical reminder of the real meaning of Christmas.

Puerto Rico

Early in the Christmas season, carolers begin going from house to house or farm to farm. They wear fanciful homemade Magi costumes and sing bright, rhythmic Spanish carols called *aguinaldos* and *villancicos.* They are rewarded with food and drink, and many from each house will join them, so that eventually there are great crowds going singing from place to place. Sometimes, this goes on till dawn.

Nine days before Christmas, the Mass of the Carols begins. This takes place each morning at 5:30 A.M. It is filled with music, and usually the caroling continues on the way to work or home after it is over.

The manger scenes are peopled with *santos,* hand-carved figures that represent some of Puerto Rico's oldest works of art, dating back to the sixteenth century. The tree and Santa Claus are also popular in Puerto Rico, largely because of American influence and that of the large Puerto Rican population which has settled in the United States. Gifts, therefore, arrive on

Christmas morning; but also, following Spanish tradition, on Epiphany. On January 5 in the evening, children leave water, grass, and grain under their beds for the camels of the Wise Men, and the next day they find presents in their place.

Putz

The name *putz* comes from the German *putzen,* which means "to decorate." The *putz* is the Pennsylvania Dutch form of the manger scene. It differs from almost all others in the elaborateness of the winter scene, which includes the stable and the Holy Family as only one element in the whole. The *putz* may take up an entire room and be landscaped with earth, rocks, and water. There may be mill wheels, waterfalls, bridges, fountains, villages, log cabins, and other natural and man-made features.

At Bethlehem, Pennsylvania, which was founded by Moravian missionaries, there is a community putz that is different each year and unveiled only on Christmas Eve. This is an extremely elaborate setting. One year it required 800 pounds of sand, 12 bushels of moss, 64 tree stumps, 40 Christmas trees, 48 angels, 200 animals, 16 lighting effects, 29 lamps, 700 feet of rock and earth, 400 feet of other materials, and several oil paintings.

Pyramid

Before the development of the Christmas tree in the fifteenth or sixteenth century, the Christmas pyramid was the most important decoration to Germany and much of northern Europe. It was a wooden framework in the shape of a pyramid, decorated with greenery and ornaments. Gifts or food, or a manger scene, could be placed on it shelves. As the tree became more popular, more and more of the functions of the pyramid were shifted over to the tree. By the early part of this century, the pyramid was virtually non-existent as a Christmas decoration outside Italy, which imported the idea of the *ceppo* but never took up the Christmas tree.

Red and Green

Red and green are looked upon as the official colors of Christmastime, yet no one can say definitely why that is. The best guess is that they are the colors of the holly. The bright green and red of leaf and berry seen against the cold whiteness of snow would stand as a promise of the winter's end and the spring to come. This promise of life in the midst of death is a fitting symbol for the birth of Christ.

Réveillon

Réveillon is from the same French word that provides a name for one of the Army's most annoying habits, reveille, and means "to awaken." The *réveillon* is the happy meal and celebration that take place in French homes after Christmas Eve Midnight Mass.

Ringing in Christmas

At four in the afternoon of Christmas Eve, all work must stop in Norway so that the Christmas celebrations can begin. Church bells give the signal all across the land, putting an end to work and ringing in Christmas.

Russia

The Russian Orthodox Church still uses the old Julian calendar, so its Christmas celebration falls on January 7, thirteen days behind most other countries. After the 1917 Communist Revolution, Christmas was banned throughout Russia and wasn't openly observed again until the end of the communist regime in 1992. The return to religion also signaled the return to one's roots, as Russian Christians readopted their old traditions, including many customs that had waned well before the Revolution of 1917. Traditionally Russians attend a lengthy Christmas Eve mass. Afterwards, there is often a candlelit procession around the church, led by the church's highest-ranking member. Once the *Krestny Khod* procession completes its circle, the congregation reenters the church to sing some hymns and carols before going home to enjoy a late Christmas Eve feast. The meal is traditionally the end of a several week-long fast. It consists of twelve courses—one to honor each of the twelve apostles—and although fish may be served, other meats are not. The most important dish is a porridge called *kutya.* It is made with berries and whole wheat grains that symbolize hope and immortality, as well as honey and poppy seeds to ensure happiness and success. The *kutya* is eaten from a shared dish to celebrate unity, and some families even throw a spoonful of the porridge up onto the ceiling. It is believed that if the *kutya* sticks to the ceiling, there will be a plentiful harvest in the year to come.

Santa Claus

THE HISTORICAL ST. NICHOLAS

In twenty-first-century America, St. Nicholas is just another name for Santa Claus, bearded, round, and rosy, and dressed in red and white. To most of Europe, he is a thin figure dressed in bishop's robes who comes riding a white horse on St. Nicholas' Day, December 6. What was the real St. Nicholas like?

Unfortunately, very little is known about the real St. Nicholas. Countless legends have grown up around this very popular saint, but very little historical evidence is available. He was born around A.D. 280 in Asia Minor and became bishop of Myra, now Demre, in Turkey. The only definite historical evidence of his life is in the records of the First Council of Nicaea in 325, which was responsible for creating the Nicene Creed, a famous statement of doctrine still widely in use. He was definitely in attendance, although what role he might have played is shrouded in mystery. He probably suffered in the persecution of Christians under the emperor Diocletian, which lasted until about 311, at which time Nicholas would have been about thirty-one. The new emperor Constantine at first tolerated, then encouraged, and finally established Christianity as the state religion. St. Nicholas died about 343.

It was not long after his death that the legends began and the popularity of his cult began to spread. In 1003 Vladimir of Russia came to Constantinople to be baptized and brought back relics and stories of St. Nicholas, who became the patron saint of Russia. It was not much later that the sailors of southern Italy, who also regarded him as their patron, introduced the cult to western Europe. By the height of the Middle Ages, St. Nicholas was probably invoked in prayer more than any other figure except the Virgin Mary and Christ Himself. He was the patron saint of children, students, Russia, bankers, sailors, pawnbrokers, vagabonds, and thieves.

An event that contributed strangely to the growth of St. Nicholas' popularity in Europe was the fact that his body was stolen from Asia Minor and taken to Italy. In 1087, ostensibly to protect the remains from infidels, sailors from Bari in Italy broke into his tomb and carried the body from Myra to their own home. A great basilica, one of the most impressive still in existence, was built to house the saint's new resting place. This new home gave a focus and impetus to the growing cult of St. Nicholas.

Ironically, the church built to house the remains stolen from Myra to protect them from possible desecration by Muslim invaders carries an Islamic message. Skilled Muslim craftsmen from North Africa or the Near East were brought in to help in the construction, and they included disguised Arabic calligraphy as part of a design on the building. It was years before it was realized that the message read "There is no God but Allah, and Mohammed is His Prophet." Church officials decided not to destroy the beauty of the building by effacing the message, and so it remains.

What might have proved a setback to the popularity of St. Nicholas occurred in 1969 when the Roman Catholic Church demoted the saint in its universal calendar of the saints. However, this has had very little effect on celebrations of the saint's day.

The mortal remains of St. Nicholas made their last journey in 1972 when, as a gesture of ecumenicism, the Roman Catholic Church donated some of the relics to the Greek Orthodox Shrine of Saint Nicholas in Flushing, New York. It had taken nine hundred years and a journey to a continent he had never heard of, but at last the mortal remains of the good saint had returned to the Greek Church that he had known in life.

PATRON SAINT OF CHILDREN

St. Nicholas was closely connected with children from the very beginning. Stories relating to his birth are very similar to those of Samuel in the Old Testament. Nicholas' mother, Nonna, had been sterile until the conception of Nicholas, who immediately devoted himself to the service of God, just as did Samuel. He was both physically and religiously precocious. He was said to be able to stand in his bath at an incredibly early age. As an infant, he would observe fast days by refusing his mother's breast until after sunset. Because of these miracles, he was looked upon as an important intercessor both for children and for sterile women.

One of the oldest and most enduring St. Nicholas' stories concerns his role as benefactor of children. It happened after his death, on the eve of his name day, December 6. The people of Myra, where he had been bishop, were celebrating in his memory when pirates from Crete fell upon them. A great deal of booty was seized, and a young boy named Basilios was carried into slavery. He was chosen by the emir of Crete to be his personal cupbearer, and for a year he served in that position. On the eve of the next St. Nicholas' Day, Basilios' parents were in no mood to celebrate with the rest of the town, but as they were devout people they made a quiet celebration at home. Suddenly the dogs began to bark and they rushed to the courtyard to find what the matter was. Had the pirates returned to compete their devastation? Consider their surprise and amazement when there were no pirates, just their son wearing Arab dress and carrying a full goblet of wine. As in all real miracles, they felt as much terror as joy in that first moment. Then Basilios explained that he had just been about to serve his master a cup of wine when a power had lifted him up and carried him off. He had been filled with fear, but then St. Nicholas appeared to him, calmed him, and brought him to his home. St. Nicholas' Day had once again become a cause for rejoicing.

This story took different forms during the centuries to follow, but one element did not change in artwork or story. This touch still brings the miracle home in such a precise way: the full goblet of wine didn't spill a drop during that miraculous, headlong flight across the Mediterranean Sea.

PATRON OF SAILORS

Almost as early as St. Nicholas' protection of children was his patronage of sailors. He decided to make a pilgrimage to Jerusalem and made the trip by boat without letting anyone know who he was. One night on board, he dreamed that the devil was cutting the ropes of the main mast, which he interpreted to mean that a bad storm was brewing. He warned the ship's crew, but also told them that God would protect them, so they shouldn't fear.

The storm blew up quickly, and the ship was out of control. St. Nicholas prayed for their deliverance. One of the sailors climbed to the main mast to tighten the rigging. When he finished, he lost his hold and fell to his death on the deck far below. The storm soon responded to the saint's prayers and lessened. All were grateful for their deliverance, but upset over the death of the sailor. St. Nicholas prayed for him, and suddenly he was restored to life with no injuries at all. St. Nicholas' fame as a healer would later spread wide, but to sailors the saint was always their special protector.

Having a patron involves responsibility as well as benefits. St. Nicholas is no exception. In another story, his visit to the Holy Land was cut short when an angel appeared to tell him to return home with haste. He went to the port and sought for a ship. He finally found one that had just been loaded and whose master agreed for a fee to take him to Patara, his birthplace. But the captain and crew believed that he wouldn't know enough to object when they went first to their home port, which was out of the way. So they set off in the wrong direction. It was not long before a violent storm blew up, and in the heavy seas that it produced the rudder was damaged beyond repair. The storm died as quickly as it had come, and it looked as though they would drift until they died of starvation. But the boat drifted in a very specific direction, and the crew began to hope that they might encounter land somewhere. Indeed, that was what happened and all the sailors were very thankful. When they learned that they had come to land at Patara, the very spot that St. Nicholas had wanted to reach, they were first amazed and then contrite. St. Nicholas forgave them their deception, but cautioned them to be more honest in the future. Thus St. Nicholas not only protected sailors but taught them their responsibilities as well.

PATRON OF STUDENTS AND OTHER VAGABONDS

St. Nicholas probably became the patron saint of students in a roundabout manner: it is more likely that the story relating how he protected three students was created after he had already become the patron of students. It all happened in the Middle Ages. Students did not have a patron, so they probably settled on St. Nicholas since he was already the patron of children and a very popular figure, and as young men they would find him very suitable. Then this story grew up, probably in northern France in the twelfth century.

Three traveling theology students stopped at a roadside inn for the night. While they slept, the less-than-hospitable innkeeper went through their belongings and was delighted to discover a large sum of money. He not only killed the students but, in a nicely melodramatic touch, cut them up, preserved the flesh with salt, and hid it in pickle barrels. St. Nicholas passed that way some time later and sensed was had happened. He miraculously restored the three students to their original forms and brought them back to life.

This story was immensely popular in the Middle Ages. Many pictures show it, and it was the subject of a large number of plays. The scene in which the three students rise up out of the barrels was always a sensation.

As a result of this story, St. Nicholas found himself in unusual company. All travelers began to look to St. Nicholas for protection, including those who might have identified more with the innkeeper than with the students. Vagabonds, thieves, and even murderers took Nicholas as their patron saint. By the time of Shakespeare, such traveling brigands and highwaymen were known as "St. Nicholas clerks" and one of Shakespeare's characters in *Henry IV, Part I* tells of just such a rascal: "I know thou worshippest Saint Nicholas as truly as a man of falsehood may."

PATRON OF CHILDREN

This is the most famous story of St. Nicholas. In his hometown there lived a man with three daughters who had fallen upon particularly hard times. As he could not afford a dowry for any of the three girls, there was no possibility that they would marry, and if they stayed home the whole family would starve. Regretfully, he began to face the necessity of selling his girls into slavery or prostitution—an awful choice, but his only hope in this hard time. St. Nicholas learned of his plight. There is some questions as to Nicholas' background: his family may have been wealthy or middle-class, but they were never poor. The saint, however, never used his money for his own purposes, but only to help others. He resolved to do so in this case. Being a humble man, he did not want any recognition or thanks, so he stole to the house in the dead of night and threw a bag of gold through the window. (In some versions of the story, he throws it down the chimney, thus providing a possible background for Santa Claus' favorite means of dropping in.) The gold saved the eldest girl by providing a dowry so that she could be honorably wed. In the same way, as each girl reached marrying age, St. Nicholas was the guardian angel who secretly provided the means to their happiness. The last time he was discovered by the father, who began to express his extreme gratitude, but St. Nicholas would have none of it. He begged the father to accept the gifts humbly and silently as they were given and to repent of the immoral choice he had almost made. Also, he was asked not to tell the story until after St. Nicholas' death.

PATRON OF PAWNBROKERS

It is easy to see how St. Nicholas became associated with gift-giving and children. It is a little more difficult to see how he also ended up in the company of pawnbrokers. Because Nicholas was the patron saint of sailors, he became very important to merchants who depended for their livelihood on the safe arrival of shipments. He also was known as a protector of oaths and guarantor of financial integrity, largely on the basis of the following story.

Long after St. Nicholas' death, a Christian borrowed a large sum of money from a Jew and swore by St. Nicholas to return it on a certain date. When the date came, the Christian wickedly decided to cheat the moneylender. So he put the exact amount of money into a hollow cane and, in the course of walking to the court where he was to be sued for the money, he asked the Jew to hold his cane for a moment. Then when he came before the court he was able to swear by all that was holy that he had put the exact amount of money into the Jew's hands and that he was being charged twice. The Jew had no choice but to allow himself to be cheated. But St. Nicholas had other ideas. On the way home, the Christian was struck down dead by a runaway cart and his cane split open, revealing the trick. The Jew refused to accept the money under such circumstances, saying that if the saint were as humane as he was supposed to be, he should not let the Christian die. Immediately the Christian was restored to life. He repented his sin and paid the Jew what was owed him. The Jew, in his turn, was so impressed that he converted.

This combination of giving money and protecting oaths on financial matters made St. Nicholas a logical choice for bankers and pawnbrokers. There was also the symbolism from the story of the three dowries of redeeming something of value.

The three bags of gold underwent a metamorphosis. The story was so popular that St. Nicholas was always depicted in paintings with the three bags of gold somewhere about him, even when that was not the story being told. Eventually they were simplified into three gold balls. These gold balls first took on a financial bent when they appeared on the coat of arms of the great Florentine bankers, the Medici family, as a symbol of St. Nicholas. After that they became a common symbol for a pawnbroker's establishment. And that is why three gold balls above the doorway are still the traditional sign for a pawnbroker, although few of us would associate him with the jolly gift-giver St. Nick.

REFORM OF ST. NICHOLAS

The Protestant Reformation raised several problems for St. Nicholas. He had become well established as a gift-bringer and the opener of the

Christmas season on his name day, December 6. With the Reformation, though, it became improper to celebrate anything having to do with Catholic saints. But St. Nicholas was far too popular just to be done away with. Something had to give.

In a few countries, St. Nicholas just changed his name and kept right on going. Thus there developed Father Christmas in England, Weihnachtsmann in Germany, and Père Noël in France. Germany also established the figure of the Christkindlein or Christ Child, who would come with the Pennsylvania Dutch to America, where his name would gradually be corrupted by popular pronunciation until he became Kris Kringle. All these figures were jolly, venerable gift-givers, dressed in clothes appropriate to the season, except for the Christ Child, and even he changed with time so that Kris Kringle looked like all the rest.

At least one country, Holland, did not change the name of St. Nicholas, but did change his religious aspects into purely secular ones. He became just like Father Christmas or Père Noël but kept his old name. When the Dutch settled in New Amsterdam, later to become New York, they brought St. Nicholas with them. But as in so many cases, popular pronunciation had its effect: St. Nicholas became Sinta Claes. The stage was almost set for the arrival of Santa Claus.

SANTA CLAUS AND THE THREE MEN WHO GAVE HIM BIRTH

Although the Dutch brought Sinta Claes with them to the New World in the seventeenth century, Santa Claus was not born until the nineteenth century and was an American, not a Dutch, creation. Having spring from a Puritan beginning, America did not have much to do with saints or Christmas celebration in its earlier years. It was not until after the Revolution that the

Christmas customs of such groups as the Pennsylvania Dutch began to filter out into the general population. And the first great interest in St. Nicholas was stirred up by the writings of Washington Irving.

Irving published a book called *Diedrich Knickerbocker's A History of New York from the Beginning of the World to the End of the Dutch Dynasty.* This was an extremely satirical book, with at least as much fantasy as fact in it. One of the things that Irving did was make St. Nicholas a sort of patron saint for the Dutch and throw him into the story whenever possible, including one appearance as the figurehead of a ship. Fictitious celebrations were included, and St. Nicholas flew about in a wagon to bring children presents. One passage will serve both to show Irving's lively satirical style and to illustrate the picture he drew of St. Nicholas. Oloffe Van Kortlandt, who arrived at a new development named Communipaw too late to get any land, dreams a dream in which St. Nicholas tells the people to settle elsewhere.

And the sage Oloffe dreamed a dream-and lo, the good St. Nicholas came riding over the tops of the trees, in that selfsame wagon wherein he brings his yearly presents to children, and he descended hard by where the heroes of Communipaw had made their late repast. And he lit his pipe by the fire, and sat himself down and smoked; and as he smoked the smoke from his pipe ascended into the air and spread like cloud overhead. And Oloffe bethought him, and he hastened and climbed up to the top of one of the tallest trees, and saw that the smoke spread over a great extent of country-and as he considered it more attentively, he fancied that the great volume of smoke assumed a variety of marvelous forms where in dim obscurity he saw shadowed out palaces and domes and lofty spires, all of which lasted but a moment, and then faded away, until the whole rolled off, and nothing but the green wood were left. And when St. Nicholas had smoked his pipe, he twisted it in his hat-band, and laying his finger beside his nose, gave the astonished Van Kortlandt a very significant look, then mounting his wagon, he returned over the tree-tops and disappeared.

And Van Kortlandt awoke from his sleep greatly instructed, and he aroused his companions, and related to them his dream, and interpreted it, that it was the will of St. Nicholas that they should settle down and build the city here. And that the smoke of the pipe was a type how vast would be the extent of the city; inasmuch as the volumes of its smoke would spread over a wide extent of country. And they all with one voice assented to this interpretation excepting Mynheer Ten Broeck, who declared the meaning to be that it would be a city wherein a little fire would occasion a great smoke, or in other words, a very vaporing little city-both which interpretations have strangely come to pass! . . .

And the people lifted up their voices and blessed the good St. Nicholas, and from that time forth the sage Van Kortlandt was held in more honor than ever, for his great talent at dreaming, and was pronounced a most useful citizen and a right good man-when he was asleep.

One phrase in that passage probably rang a bell for you: "Laying his finger beside his nose, gave . . . a very significant look, then mounting his wagon, he returned over the tree-tops and disappeared." If that sounds suspiciously reminiscent of "And laying his finger aside of his nose,/And giving a nod, up the chimney he rose" there is good reason for it. Irving's book was very popular and was still in current circulation and people's thoughts twenty years later when Dr. Clement Clarke Moore was credited for writing the little poem "A Visit from St. Nicholas." He was the second of the three men most responsible for Santa Claus. His description of the jolly elf solidified Irving's, in whose work, after all, St. Nicholas had not been the central figure. A children's book of the time, *A New Year's Present to the Little Ones from Five to Twelve,* had shown St. Nicholas' sleigh being drawn by one reindeer. That was the first time he had appeared without a wagon and horse. It may have been the idea of snow in winter and St. Nicholas as patron of Russian and other Arctic areas that inspired the sleigh and reindeer. Whatever it was, Moore seized upon it, increased the team to eight reindeer with fanciful names, and froze our image of St. Nick and his coursers until a popular song came along and added the much more prosaic name Rudolph to the crew list.

Moore's poem served in its turn as the inspiration for the man who finally drew a picture of Santa Claus for us. By the 1860s the old Dutch mispronunciation of "St. Nicholas" had gained popular acceptance, and "Santa Claus" had replaced the saint's name as Americans cheerfully mispronounced the Dutch mispronunciation. Santa appeared frequently in children's books, but his appearance varied widely, sometimes tall and thin, sometimes dressed in buckskins. The great political cartoonist Thomas Nast finally popularized a single image of the jolly old elf, based on the description in Moore's poem. He did a whole series of pen-and-ink drawings over a period of years for *Harper's Weekly* which completed the birth of Santa Claus.

The last small touch to our image of Santa Claus came from an unlikely source, the Coca-Cola company. This was his passage from black and white to color. Haddon Sundblom did a series of ads for Coca-Cola beginning in the 1920s which depicted the full-blown Santa we now know with the rosy cheeks that had only been described before in the age of pen and ink. Santa had also grown from the elf size of Moore and Nast to the more-than-human proportions that contribute so much to his jollity.

If Nicholas, the ascetic bishop of fourth-century Asia Manor, could see Santa Claus, he would not know who he was. But it's a safe guess that the saintly patron of children, even if he didn't know who Santa was, would still love him for the joy he brings the world.

Santos

Santos are the hand-carved figures that appear in the Puerto Rican *nacimientos,* or manger scenes, at Christmastime. These figures of wood and clay offer examples of one of the earliest native art forms, dating back to the sixteenth century.

Scotland

Scotland never fully recovered from the Puritan ban on Christmas celebration in the seventeenth century. Even after the Restoration, the innate Scottish Puritanism kept festivities to a minimum. The Scots save most of their energies for Hogmanay, as they call New Year's. Still, there are some customs and observances connected with Christmas. For instance, it is bad luck to let the fire go out on Christmas Eve, since the elves are abroad and only a good, roaring fire will keep them from slipping down the chimney. On Christmas Day itself, it is not unusual to have a bonfire and dance to the sound of bagpipes before settling down to a hearty dinner.

Seals

Christmas seals are the decorative paper stamps sent out each year by the American Lung Association to raise funds. People wishing to use the stamps to close Christmas cards and packages return a contribution for the seals.

Christmas seals were originated by a Danish postmaster, Einar Holboll, in 1903. Since he handled stamps all the time, he had the idea of selling a special decorative stamp at Christmastime and giving the proceeds to a worthy cause. The first seals were printed in 1904 with a portrait of Queen Louise of Denmark. More than four million of these were sold in the Danish Post Office that year.

The European success of Christmas seals led Jacob Riis, a friend of Teddy Roosevelt, to write an article advocating their sale in America. This was the inspiration for Emily Bissell, a Red Cross worker, to introduce Christmas seals for the benefit of the Red Cross in Wilmington, Delaware, in December of 1907. By 1908 the seals were issued coast to coast and were a huge success for a number of charitable organizations. In 1919 the National Tuberculosis Association (now the American Lung Association) became the sole sponsor, and in 1920 the familiar Red Cross symbol was replaced by the double-barred cross, an adaptation of the Lorraine Cross, the emblem of the Eastern branch of the Christian Church since the ninth century.

Shooting in Christmas

This is one of the noisiest of Christmas traditions and is found in parts of Norway. It derives from the old pagan beliefs that noise would drive away evil spirits, which was especially needed at midwinter when the forces of death and cold seemed to have such a strong grip on all of nature. Today young men travel from farm to farm on Christmas Eve, filling the air with gunshot blasts. After the evil spirits have been properly frightened off, the marksmen are rewarded with refreshments for shooting in Christmas.

Shopping Days

Shopping days are the invention of retailers who are concerned that Christmas Day would arrive and we would still have some odd change left in our pockets. Radio, newspapers, and TV all remind us how many shopping days are left until Christmas. There are never enough.

There are two kinds of Christmas shoppers. The first has all of his Christmas shopping done by December 2. He can be recognized by his smug expression and the fact that (like someone who has just quit smoking) he seems unable to carry on a conversation without mentioning at least once that he has finished all his shopping. More often it is the sole topic of conversation. He can also be recognized because very few people will talk to him. The second kind of Christmas shopper does his shopping a little bit later. He can be recognized around the middle of December by his well-intentioned look and his neat appearance; about the twentieth, he has become disheveled and his expression is increasingly haunted. On the twenty-fourth he can be spotted in great flocks inside every store, where he buys any- and everything.

On the day after Christmas, some store or other will always take out an ad saying there are only 364 shopping days to Christmas. No one is amused.

Slovakia

The Slovakian celebration of Christmas is linked with the ancient pagan feast of the winter solstice—a time of the year during which Slovak ancestors believed certain rites would protect their crops, ensure a rich harvest, and bring about happiness and love in the upcoming year. As Christianity spread across Europe, the celebration of Christmas in Slovakia included customs that were influenced by these pagan traditions and myths. The Slovak words for Christmas Eve, *stedry vecer* (or *svati vecer*) literally mean "bountiful eve," which is exemplified in the evening's meal consisting of a wide range of festive dishes (usually twelve different kinds). Traditional dishes include sauerkraut soup with dried mushrooms, fish, peas, homemade bread or wafers dipped in garlic and honey, dried fruits and nuts, as well as an assortment of pastries known as *kolace*. Everyone at the table is expected to have at least a taste of each food in order to be able to enjoy all meals in the year to come. After the meal, the plates are cleared from the

table but food and drinks remain as a token of hospitality for deceased loved ones who may visit after midnight.

The Christmas tree is a prominent element in Slovak Christmas celebrations. The practice of bringing green branches into the home during the winter solstice symbolizes the cycle of new life. Singing carols is also a popular practice, both outside and within the household. Following the Christmas Eve dinner, the streets may fill with carolers and passersby wishing good cheer until the bells ring for Midnight Mass.

Snapdragon

This was once a very popular game played most at Christmas in England. A bowlful of brandy-covered raisins was set ablaze and players snatched the raisins out of the fire and popped them into their mouths before the flames could do too much damage. There was probably very little flavor left in the burned and shriveled raisins, but danger and daring make a great sauce, and snapdragon was popular for many years before dying out.

Spain

The Spanish Christmas season begins December 8 with the feast of the Immaculate Conception, which lasts a week. There is a fascinating custom at this time, which dates back into antiquity, called Los Seises, or The Dance of the Six. While this dance may originally have been performed by six, it is now done by ten boys, who are carefully trained in the tradition. They dance before the altar at the cathedral in Seville in a series of stately poses and movements that symbolize many of the mysteries of the incarnation and birth of Jesus.

As in most of southern Europe, the manger scene, called a *nacimiento,* is more important than the Christmas tree, which is very rare. These scenes are set up both in homes and on a grander scale in village squares. It is a delight for the children to sing and dance before the image of the tiny Christ Child in the family home.

Christmas Eve is called Noche-Buena, the Good Night. There will be singing and dancing in the streets to the sounds of guitars and castanets. At midnight everyone attends the Misa del Gallo, the Mass of the Rooster, so named because of the legend that the only time the rooster has crowed at midnight was the night when Jesus was born. After mass the dinner, or *cena*, is served, usually featuring turkey and the Christmas favorite *turrón*, a candy loaf of roasted almonds in caramel syrup.

Christmas Day is a time for family reunions and exchange of gifts among the adults. The urn of fate is brought out for fun. This is a large bowl with the names of all present in it on slips of paper, which are drawn out two at a time. Officially this is to wish only that the people whose names are so joined will endeavor to be good friends during the coming year, but there is often some finagling of fate to help Cupid do some matchmaking. In some rural areas the Yule log is still part of the festivities.

The Wise Men are very popular in Spain, and it is they who bring presents to the children. On Epiphany Eve, January 5, shoes filled with straw are set out for the camels that carry the Magi. In the morning, of course, the straw has been replaced by presents. Also on Epiphany Eve, it is common for three villagers richly dressed as the Wise Men to pay a visit to the village *nacimiento*, to the delight of the whole village, which gathers to watch them pay homage to the Christ Child.

Stamp

In 1898 Canada instituted its Penny Postal System on Christmas Day. To commemorate the occasion, it issues a stamp with a Christmas motif. Since that time many other countries have printed special postage stamps at Christmastime with either secular or religious themes. These have proved to be very popular, especially in the mailing of Christmas cards, which are made more decorative by the substitution of bright Christmas scenes for stamps with portraits of presidents or monarchs.

The United States issued its first Christmas stamp in 1962. The most popular one ever was produced in 1971. It was a reproduction of the Adoration of the Shepherds by the early Renaissance Italian painter Giorgione. The stamp was the largest printing order in the history of the postage stamp; over a billion copies were printed.

Star Boys

On January 6, the traditional date for the visit of the Wise Men, groups of children in Norway, Sweden, and Poland dress up as the Magi or other biblical figures. Carrying a paper star with a candle inside on a long pole, they go house to house singing carols, performing short plays, or narrating the story of the Three Kings. In return, they are given presents of candy and coins.

Stocking

The custom of hanging up a stocking to receive gifts from Santa Claus probably originates with a variant on the St. Nicholas legend of the three dowry-less girls. In that version, each time that St. Nicholas threw the bag

of gold down the chimney, it landed in a stocking that happened to be hanging up there to dry.

Sugarplums

Sugarplums still exist, although we don't call them that any more. Quite simply, they are round or oval candies made of very rich fruit preserves, cream fillings, and other sweet concoctions, often covered with chocolate. Thus our familiar boxes of Christmas chocolates contain many candies that could be called sugarplums. The name would have died out completely long ago but for its immortalization in two sources, "A Visit from St. Nicholas," where "visions of sugarplums danced" in the children's heads, and the Sugarplum Fairy, a famous dancing character in Tchaikovsky's ballet *The Nutcracker.*

Sweden

The Christmas season lasts a whole month in Sweden, from December 13 to January 13. December 13 is St. Lucia's Day and a very special one for the children. St. Lucia was a young girl who was put to death in Sicily in A.D. 304 for professing Christianity. She is honored in Sweden because legend has it that she brought food to that country during a terrible famine, appearing with her head all circled with light. So before dawn on St. Lucia's Day the eldest daughter of the family dresses herself in a white robe, with a green wreath on her head with lighted candles on it. She wakes her parents by singing the familiar Italian song "Santa Lucia" and brings coffee, buns, and cookies to everyone while they are still in bed. The younger children often wear a conelike hat with a star on top and accompany her on her rounds. There is also an official popular election to choose a Lucia who will preside at the big parade in Stockholm.

Before the midday meal on Christmas Eve, the family gathers in the kitchen for a custom called *doppa i grytan,* "dipping in the kettle." All gather around a pot filled with drippings of pork, sausage, and corned beef and dip dark bread into it, which they eat when it is completely soaked with the drippings. This specifically recalls an ancient famine when there was nothing else to eat, but symbolically it calls to mind all those who are in need and hunger in the midst of thanksgiving and plenty.

The traditional Christmas Eve dinner starts off with smorgasbord with a sip of *akvavit*; then *lutfisk,* a sun-cured cod served in cream sauce, and ham; finally, the traditional rice pudding with an almond in it. The finder of the almond, it is sometimes said, will marry in the next year. No provision is made in this tradition for the already wed or those just out of diapers. Presumably there is some hanky-panky to see to it that the almond ends up in the right serving.

After dinner all gather around the Christmas tree to open the presents. These gifts were brought by the Jultomten, a gnome who lives in the barn, if there is one, and is very similar to the Danish Nisse. He, too, has to have his portion of rice pudding if he is to behave in the coming year. The Julbock is a goat of straw, modeled after Thor's goat, while serves as a steed for the Jultomten in making his rounds. All the presents are accompanied by humorous verses hinting at what the package contains while actually making it as obscure as possible.

On Christmas Day there is a service at five in the morning. After that the day is devoted to rest and to religious observance.

December 26 is called the Second Day of Christmas. The men of the village ride through the streets waking all the people early on this day. It is also a day when extra food is given to the animals.

On January 6, Twelfth Night, the Star Boys come out. These are the children dressed in nativity costumes or other fantastic attire and carrying candle-lit paper stars on poles. They sing from house to house and are given treats.

Christmas finally ends on January 13. When King Canute was king of Sweden a thousand years ago, he decreed that the Christmas feasting should last twenty days. Therefore, instead of ending after twelve days on January 6 (which is actually the thirteenth day if you count both December 25 and January 6), Swedish Christmas lasts another week.

Switzerland

In terms of its traditions, Switzerland is basically four different countries. The language and customs are determined at any given point by who is the closest neighbor in that area. Thus there are predominantly German, French, and Italian areas, as well as the remaining pockets of the Swiss dialect, Romanche. Christmas customs draw upon four distinct traditions and then combine them according to local usage. Gifts may be given on either Christmas Eve or New Year's, and they are brought by the Christkindli or St. Nicholas, or even Father Christmas with his wife, Lucy. Both the manger and the Christmas tree hold sway. Carols drift on the air in four languages. Switzerland has maintained its careful neutrality by absorbing the best of all nations.

Sylvester

Sylvester is a charmingly grotesque custom found in certain parts of Austria. He usually appears on New Year's Eve, although he is associated with Christmas greenery. A standard decoration is a bunch of green pine twigs hung from the ceiling. When a girl passes beneath it, she becomes fair game for Sylvester. He is old and ugly (or wears a mask to that effect) and sports a wreath of mistletoe, and he kisses whoever he can catch under the greenery. At midnight, he is driven out like the old year.

Syria

On Christmas Eve, the outer gates of the homes of Syrian Christians are locked as a reminder of the years of persecution during the Arab conquest of the seventh century when all worship had to be hidden behind closed doors. The whole family gathers in the courtyard with lighted candles, around a pile of wood that will become a bonfire. The youngest son reads the Gospel story of the Nativity, and the father lights the fire. All observe the fire carefully, because the particular way that it spreads through the wood will determine the luck of the household for the coming year. All sing psalms while the fire burns, and when it dies down, they make a wish and jump over the embers. Early on Christmas morning, there is a mass before dawn, and there is a bonfire in the center of the church as well. The image of the Christ Child is carried around the church in a joyous procession.

Syrian children receive their gifts at Epiphany from a very original source, the Smallest Camel of the Wise Men. On their way to see Jesus, the Wise Men traveled in a caravan with many camels. The smallest was exhausted by the long journey but refused to give up, his desire to see the Christ Child was so great. When the infant Jesus saw the faith and resolve of this loving creature, he blessed it with renewed strength and immortality. Every year he comes bearing the gifts for the good boys and girls, who learn the importance of even the most insignificant of us from his example.

Tolling the Devil's Knell

This is an old English custom still practiced in Dewsbury, Yorkshire. A death knell is the ringing of the bells to signify that someone has died. On Christmas Eve the devil's knell must be tolled because, according to folk-lore, the devil died when Christ was born. Therefore the church bell is rung slowly, once for each year since the birth of Christ, with the last ring timed to come exactly at midnight, the traditional moment of Christ's birth.

Tree

ST. BONIFACE AND THE CHRISTMAS TREE

One very popular legend of the origin of the Christmas tree involves the early Christian missionary St. Boniface. In the eighth century he was attempting to win the pagan Germans over to the worship of Christ. One Christmas Eve in the great forest, he was shocked to come upon a ceremony of human sacrifice taking place at the foot of the sacred oak tree of Odin at Geismar. Seizing an ax, he struck one great blow at the tree, which was then toppled by a great wind. The people were awe-struck and won over to Christianity, but they felt lost without the symbol of their giant tree. St. Boniface pointed to a tiny tree that had nestled among the roots of the now fallen oak, and told them to take that as their sign. Christ was a bringer of life "ever green," and the fir tree became his symbol.

THE FIRST CHRISTMAS TREE

Popular legend often attributes to Martin Luther the creation of the first decorated Christmas tree. Walking one night and looking up at the starry sky through the tree branches, he was struck with the idea and hurried home to place candles on the branches of a tree.

The predecessors of the Christmas tree can be seen in the many pagan customs involving tree worship. These especially involved evergreens during the cold of winter when sacrificing to or decorating with greenery was looked upon as a good way to ensure good crops the following year.

The immediate ancestor of the Christmas tree was the paradise tree. In the medieval Church calendar, December 24 was Adam and Eve Day. Many plays would act out the fall of the first two human beings to make clear the meaning of Christ's birth the next day, the coming of the "second Adam," to redeem the failure of the original. A main set piece of this play was the paradise tree, the tree from which Adam and Eve ate against God's command. It being winter, the tree consisted of a fir tree hung with apples. The custom became popular in homes as well as on the stage, and many German households began to set up their own paradise trees on Christmas Eve. In keeping with the legend that trees bloom at midnight on Christmas Eve, paper flowers and other fruits were hung on the trees. Wafers were added as a symbol of the body of Christ, as in the Communion wafer. These wafers gradually were replaced by cookies.

The first reference in print to Christmas trees is a forest ordinance from Ammerschweier in Alsace, Germany, in 1561. This statute says that no burgher "shall have for Christmas more than one bush of more than eight shoes' length." The custom had become so popular that too many trees were being taken from the forest. In 1605 the first description of fully decorated trees came from Strasbourg. "At Christmas they set up fir-trees in the parlors at Strasbourg and hang thereon roses cut out of many-colored paper, apples, wafers, gold-foil, sweets, etc." In 1737 a writer at Wittenberg made the first reference to trees with candles on them. Many of the decorations came from the Christmas pyramid, the wooden structure that probably existed before the Christmas tree. Gradually it became less popular, and decorations were moved over to the tree that took its place. By the end of the eighteenth century, the Christmas tree was to be found everywhere in Germany.

The Christmas tree was known in England as early as 1789, though it did not become generally accepted until the 1840s. At that time the ruling family, which had come from Germany, sometimes had a Christmas tree. Specifically Prince Albert, Queen Victoria's consort, set up a tree in 1844 and started the fad that would later become tradition.

The first Christmas trees in America were probably introduced by Germans also, but under less pleasant circumstances. During the Revolutionary War, Hessians, who were German mercenaries, fought on the British side. These less-than-welcome visitors probably set up the first American Christmas trees.

One of the first Christmas trees set up by an American citizen was in 1847 outside the home of August Imgard in Wooster, Ohio. Americans are quick to realize business opportunities, and so, just four years later, we find record of one Mark Carr, a Catskill farmer, who became the first Christmas tree salesman in New York City. In 1856 Franklin Pierce decorated the first Christmas tree at the White House, and the custom has become a national tradition.

COMMUNITY CHRISTMAS TREES

The idea of a Christmas tree set up out of doors to be decorated and enjoyed by the entire community first occurred in twentieth-century America. Pasadena, California, had the first community tree in 1909. The year 1912 saw New York City's first tree at Madison Square Garden, and also Boston's first on the Common, while 1914 was the first year for a tree in Philadelphia's Independence Square. The first Christmas tree on the White House lawn was set up under Warren G. Harding in the early 1920s. Also in the 1920s, Altadena, California, developed its mile-long stretch of lighted cedars called "Christmas Tree Lane." In 1926 the Nation's Christmas Tree was dedicated. This was the giant sequoia known as the General Grant Tree in Kings Canyon National Park, California. The tree is 40 feet thick at the base, 267 feet tall, and thousands of years old.

Although the community Christmas tree has been largely an American institution, there is one English tree which embodies admirable the combination of Christmas and national spirit that has inspired the many American trees. This is the tree sent to the British people each year by the people of Oslo, Norway, and set up in Trafalgar Square in the heart of London. It is sent in memory of the time during World War II when the Norwegian king was in exile from his German-occupied land. Each year a tree from his own country was brought to him in England, even though smuggling it past the Germans was very dangerous. Since 1947 Norway has thanked Britain for its help with a yearly Christmas tree.

Ukko

Unlikely as it may sound, Ukko is the jolly steed who brings Santa Claus to Finland. He is a goat made of straw, like the Julbock elsewhere in Scandinavia. The Finns don't seem to find anything odd about his name, although it would be difficult for Americans to imagine a sleigh drawn by Dasher, Dancer, Prancer, and Ukko.

United States

Christmas in America embraces almost all of the customs of the entire world. Every ethnic group has its place in our society, and each brings its own customs and traditions. The great diversity of climate across the country also plays a large role in the varying celebrations and festivities; Alaska never has to worry about a white Christmas because it's sure to come, and Christmas Day is just a brief twilight in the midst of the months-long night of the northernmost state. For most people, turkey is the feast, and the presents are placed beneath a Christmas tree. Families try to gather for the holidays, and gifts for children are left behind by Santa Claus on Christmas Eve. While these are some of the most common Christmas traditions celebrated across the United States, they are a myriad of other traditions influenced by America's diverse culture.

In New York City, the Christmas season is a wonderfully bright and decorative one. The annual Macy's Thanksgiving Day Parade kicks off the holiday season with its festive floats and performances, and marks the appearance of the lavish Christmas displays in the department store's front windows. Other stores which are well-known for their festive window treatments include Saks Fifth Avenue, Barneys, and Lord and Taylor. The brilliantly lit Christmas tree in Rockefeller Center has been a popular site to visit for the last seventy years, in addition to the center's seasonal ice-skating rink. The first formal tree lighting took place in 1933 and utilized 700 lights, while today the colossal tree is decorated with more than 30,000 lights and requires five miles of electrical wire. Christmas performances include the *Nutcracker* ballet at Lincoln Center, the Christmas Spectacular featuring New York's famous Rockettes at Radio City Music Hall, and Charles Dickens' *A Christmas Carol* at Madison Square Garden.

The South has an extensive Christmas background. The first American Christmas was celebrated in Florida by Spanish settlers, and the first English Christmas took place at Jamestown, Virginia, in 1607. Captain John Smith wrote: "The extreame winde, rayne, frost and snow caused us to keep Christmas among the salvages where we were never more merry, nor fed on more plenty of good Oysters, Fish, Flesh, Wildfowl and good Bread." In later times, Christmas was a season in the South for riding to the hounds and for great open houses in the plantations and mansions. Today, colonial Williamsburg, Virginia demonstrates each year how Christmas was celebrated in the days of our ancestors, with people in authentic colonial dress and engaging in Christmas rituals of yesteryear. In New Orleans, a month-long Christmas festival takes place in the city's French Quarter; it includes tree lighting, parades, caroling, as well as the selling of handicrafts and foods.

In mid-December, Washington, D.C. hosts the National Christmas Tree Lighting. The event, which takes place on the Ellipse, consists of one large tree symbolizing the nation and smaller ones decorated for each state, and includes caroling and music. Traditionally the president performs the lighting at dusk. In Old Town Alexandria, the annual Scottish Christmas Walk takes place on the first Saturday of December to celebrate the area's Scottish heritage, and includes more than 30,000 visitors.

In Hawaii Santa Claus arrives by boat rather than a reindeer-driven sleigh. *Mele Kalikimaka* means Merry Christmas in Hawaiian. When missionaries and other westerners first brought the customs of Christmas to the Hawaiian islands, the inhabitants had difficulty pronouncing the phrase and changed the words to more easily fit in with the local language. A Christmas dinner in Hawaii might consist of a traditional lu'au, including a pig roasted in an underground pit, various seafood dishes, and sweet steamed rolls filled with chicken or pork called manapua. There is also a less formal celebration known as a *kanikapila* (literally, "to make music"), complete with guitars, ukeleles, and traditional Christmas carols sung in Hawaiian.

In southwestern states, many Christmas customs are derived from Mexican culture such as the children's activity of hitting a *piñata* filled with candies and small gifts.

Caroling is a popular practice in Alaska, where the children wander from house to house carrying a colored star on a long pole as they sing. The songs sung at each home include the Aleut words "*Gristuusaaq suu'uq*," meaning "Christ is born." Everyone joins in on the closing words "*Mnogaya leta*," or "God grant you many years," and afterwards the host typically treats the carolers with doughnuts, cookies, a fish pie called piruk, and sometimes even smoked salmon.

Bethlehem, Pennsylvania was founded on Christmas Eve in 1741 by Moravian missionaries from Germany. Today Bethlehem still boasts the largest Moravian population in the northeast, and their Christmas traditions are steadfastly upheld. Such customs include hanging multi-pointed Christmas stars over doorways, burning a single candle in each window of one's home, and illuminating a huge four-story star of Bethlehem atop South Mountain, which is visible from up to 3 miles away.

In Salt Lake City, Utah, the world-renowned 360-voice Mormon Tabernacle Choir presents the beloved classical music of Christmas in a yearly Christmas concert, while San Francisco's "Sing-it-Yourself Messiah" event has been an annual tradition for the past twenty-five years. Organized by the San Francisco Conservatory of Music, the concert takes place at Davies Symphony Hall in early December, and includes a chorus of more than 3,000 participants singing Handel's 1741 *Messiah*.

Venezuela

The night before Christmas is a lively time in Caracas, because the streets are filled with young people roller-skating their way to a special late mass. A great deal of music and revelry takes place en route, so the Venezuelan Mass of the Rooster is usually a little later than the Midnight Mass in other Latin American countries. After the service, they all roller-skate home to an early breakfast of *hallacas*, meat pies with cornmeal crusts, wrapped in banana leaves and boiled in water.

In Mérida, in the western part of Venezuela, there is a lively custom known as La Paradura del Niño, or the Standing Up of the Christ Child. On the first day of the new year, the Christ Child in the traditional *nacimiento* or manger scene must be stood up in his crib as a symbol of infant's growing maturity. If this is not done, the consequences are delightful. A friend who finds the child lying down will kidnap it and carry it off to his own home, where it is kept in a position of honor. The only way that the original owners can get it back is to throw a *Paradura* party. Godparents are chosen, and there is a procession of friends and family to the hiding place. There the godparents carefully take up the image and bring it back to its home with much caroling and festivity along the way. When it is safely returned to its home (and carefully stood up so the same thing won't happen again), the children offer presents and sing verses of a traditional carol which describe the various gifts. Then there is much dancing and a great deal of refreshments, all provided at the expense of the original malefactors.

Waits

Waits are the old English Christmas carolers. Originally the term applied to the medieval watch men who would patrol the street and call out the hours of the night, together with comments on the weather and sometimes blessings on the householders. Later the term was applied to the official town musicians who played for civic occasions and were hired to play at private parties and weddings. At Christmastime they would walk through the streets playing music on their instruments in return for small treats. By the end of the eighteenth century, most official waits had been abolished and the name was applied to any carolers at Christmastime.

Wales

The Welsh are known as a musical people, both in the making of poetry and in the singing of songs. At no time is it more evident than at Christmas. The best singers of whole towns gather in great *eisteddfods,* or carol sings. Every village has its own choir of trained singers and everyone else joins in. Each year an official set of words is distributed to all the towns, and all vie with each other in producing the best music, which is judged in national competition. The selected music will be sung the following year by all the choirs and will be come part of the great body of carols produced since the custom started in the tenth century.

Christmas is also the time when the Mari Llwyd appears. This grotesque creature, whose origins are lost in antiquity, is played by a man wearing a sheet and carrying a horse's skull or wearing an artificial horse's head. He capers and dances in the streets to the delight of all and tries to bite people with the workable jaw of the horse, in which case they must pay him a small fine.

The main Christmas service is called Plygian and lasts from 4:00 A.M. until the rising of the sun on Christmas morning. Taffy-pulling is a popular way to spend the afternoon.

Wassail

When the cloth was removed, the butler brought in a huge silver vessel or rare and curious workmanship, which he placed before the Squire. Its appearance was hailed with acclamation; being the Wassail Bowl, so renowned in Christmas festivity. The contents had been prepared by the Squire himself; for it was a beverage in the skillful mixture of which he particularly prided himself; alleging that it was too abstruse and complex for the comprehension of an ordinary servant. It was a potation, indeed, that might well make the heart of a toper leap within him; being composed of the richest and raciest wines, highly spiced and sweetened, with roasted apples bobbing about the surface.

Washington Irving, "Bracebridge Hall"

The word *wassail* evolved form the old Anglo-Saxon term *waes hael*, which means "be well" or "hale." The custom originated as a pagan agricultural festival. To help increase the yield of apple orchards, the trees must be saluted in the dead of winter. So at varying times during the twelve days of Christmas, a procession would visit selected trees from the various orchards and either sprinkle the wassail mixture on the roots or break a bottle of it against the trunk as if at a ship's christening. There would be a good luck recitation, such as:

> Here's to thee old apple tree,
> Hats full, sacks full,
> Great bushel bags full,
> Hurrah!

Everyone would make as much noise as possible, partly to frighten evil spirits and partly for the pleasure of making a great deal of noise. This procedure would be repeated until all the major trees had been toasted.

The mixture used on the trees was not exact. It could be mulled ale or cider or wine with apples or eggs in it. Just so, the wassail bowl has never been turned into a recipe, but it usually left to the inspiration of the mixer.

The wassail procession eventually left the orchards and became a sort of progressive Christmas party with caroling. Groups would stroll about the town, singing and being invited in for a glass of punch. This punch bowl became a fixture on Christmas occasions, and can still be detected in the popularity of eggnog and other common punches in modern Christmas festivities.

Aside from the punch bowl, wassailing is primarily known to us today through many familiar carols, such as this one, which may date from the seventeenth century:

Here we come awassailing
Among the leaves so green,
Here we come awand'ring,
So fair to be seen:
Love and joy come to you,
And to you your wassail too,
And God bless you, and send you
A happy New Year,
And God send you
A happy New Year.

Wigilia

Wigilia, the Vigil, is the name given to Christmas Eve in Poland. A fast is observed all day until the first star appears in the sky; then the big supper is served. Straw or hay is placed until the white tablecloth in memory of the stable where Christ was born. Often a sheaf of wheat will stand in each corner of the room, to be taken later into the fields or orchards to feed the bird and bring good luck in the coming year. The food of the supper has been blessed by the village priest, and an empty chair is placed at the table, reserved for the Christ Child who is there in spirit. The evening ends with the midnight Mass of the Shepherds.

Xmas

Xmas is simply an abbreviation of *Christmas.* There are some who have taken offense at the term, considering it a secular attempt to take Christ out of Christmas. That misconception arises out of the modern use of the letter *X* as a means of crossing out unwanted information. The *X* in Xmas, however, is actually the Greek letter *Chi.* Chi is the first letter of Christ's name written in Greek and has always stood in that language as a symbol for Christ without any bad connotations at all. The use of *Xmas* as a simple abbreviation for Christmas dates back to at least the twelfth century and has been in continuous usage ever since.

Yule Log

At the winter solstice, the ancient Mesopotamians made wooden images of the monsters who struggled with the great god Marduk to destroy the world. These images were burned in imitative magic to help the god conquer the evil forces. This practice may be the origin of the Yule log, which came many hundreds of years later.

Whether the Mesopotamian theory is valid or not, it is obvious that light and warmth would be natural sources of comfort in the face of the cold darkness of winter. Thus the burning of bonfires was always an important part of the northern European winter Jul or Yule festivals.

When Yule became Christmas, the Yule log was divested of its religious connotations but of none of its superstitions: The log must be obtained by the family itself, not bought from someone else. It has to be lighted with a piece of last year's log. It must burn continuously for the twelve days of Christmas. If your shadow cast by the light of the Yule log fire seems to be headless, you will die within one year. The log's ashes can cure ailments and avert lightning.

In medieval times, the log for the coming year was selected on Candlemas Day, February 2, and set out of doors in the late spring or summer sun to dry out. In some areas the log had to come from an ash tree and was called the ashen faggot. On other areas it was oak. In medieval England a tenant could eat at his lord's expense for as long as the log he had given his lord kept burning.

With the general disappearance of fireplaces, the Yule log has gradually disappeared, too. Some communities kept the tradition as recently as a century ago on a major scale, but now it survives only very rarely as an archaic spectacle with little real tradition about it. In France the Yule log survives only as the shape of a traditional Christmas cake, the *bûche de Noël*.

la la la

Christmas Music

a

Carols

The word carol probably derives from the Greek work *choros,* which means a dance. Thus the idea of dancing seems to be at the heart of the carol. The early medieval carols were on any subject, religious or nonreligious, even downright unreligious, and were suitable for dancing. They had great popularity among the common people, for whom the plainsong chanting and Latin hymns of the Church held little interest.

It was St. Francis who reconciled the people's love of music with the needs of the Church and may have invented the first Christmas carols as we would call them today. In 1223 or 1224 St. Francis set up the first manger scene at Greccio in central Italy, complete with living animals and statues of the Holy Family. There was also singing of the Gospel message. This was probably done by setting new religious words to the popular carols of the time. Both the manger scene and the carols were a tremendous success, and the thirteenth century saw a great wave of songs at the same time popular and sacred. Some of these songs were specifically composed while many others emerged in the way that folk songs have always developed: by being passed down orally from one generation to another, with changes frequently made along the way.

The greatest of the early carol composers who followed in St. Francis' steps was Jacopone da Todi. He was born into an aristocratic family about four years after St. Francis' death. He was a wealthy lawyer and little given to thoughts of religion or the plight of the poor. But then, at the age of twenty-eight, his life changed. His wife, who was also of the nobility, collapsed and died in the middle of a festive dance. When trying to help her, he discovered that she wore a hair shirt under her splendid robes. The hair shirt, a rough garment worn as a symbol of penitence, haunted him. Da

Todi devoted his life to asceticism and poverty, wandering the roads of Italy and begging. And most important, he sang. His noble background placed him in good stead when it came to composing and writing. His verse was sophisticated, yet it was concerned with humility and poverty. Da Todi sang of the great humanity of the little Christ Child. These carols were famous all over Europe for several centuries.

The popularity of carols in continental Europe continued unabated down to the present time, but in England the rise of the Puritans almost ended the tradition of carols. They were looked upon as frivolous and impious, as was the celebration of Christmas itself was. Even after Puritan rule ended with the Restoration, carols were often overlooked. They were regarded as unsophisticated and unimportant and suffered, even more than most Christmas customs, the general neglect that set in at this time. It was during this period that the Christmas hymn became important. This was a song composed specifically to instruct in doctrine. These songs were often without melody and extremely didactic, sharing none of the natural, joyous impulse that had inspired the earlier carols. Yet even in the midst of this uninspired outpouring, there were some compositions such as "O Come, All Ye Faithful" and "Hark, the Herald Angels Sing" that transcended their limited goals and became true carols.

At the beginning of the nineteenth century, it appeared that the old carols would die out. They existed only in rural regions where they were passed down within families or occasionally printed up as broadsheets for Christmas favors. Several collections of carols were printed by men such as Davies Gilbert and William Sandys. They believed they were recording a form of song that would very soon be extinct, and their collections were instrumental in preserving such songs as "The First Nowell," "God Rest You Merry, Gentlemen" and "I Saw Three Ships." With the new emphasis on Christmas that had sprung largely from the influence of Charles Dickens, the carol was rescued and returned to its former state of popularity.

What is a carol? It is joyous, as was the dance from which it sprang; it is religious, although its religion is usually that of simple people, concerned more with the wonders of that great birth than with doctrine; perhaps most important, it is popular. The great carols endure for centuries, as do the feelings that inspire them.

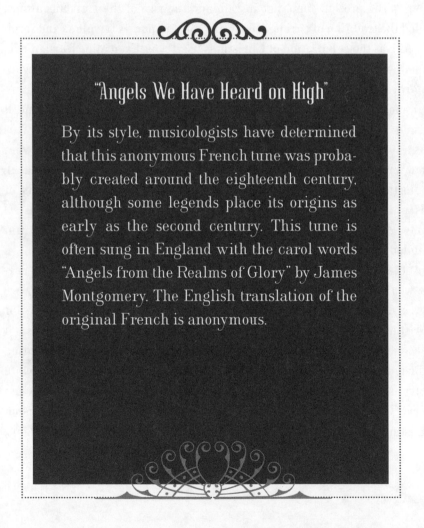

"Angels We Have Heard on High"

By its style, musicologists have determined that this anonymous French tune was probably created around the eighteenth century, although some legends place its origins as early as the second century. This tune is often sung in England with the carol words "Angels from the Realms of Glory" by James Montgomery. The English translation of the original French is anonymous.

Angels We Have Heard on High

French

"Away in a Manger"

There has been a great deal of confusion about this hymn. The words to the first two verses first appeared anonymously in an 1885 American collection of Lutheran hymns. Two years later, James R. Murray, a music editor with a company in Cincinnati, set the text to his own tune and published it in *Dainty Songs for Little Lads and Lasses, for Use in the Kindergarten, School and Home.* No one knows if he was merely mistaken or if he wished to create more interest in the song, but he headed it "Luther's Cradle Hymn (Composed by Martin Luther for his children and still sung by German mothers to their little ones)." Thus, for some sixty years it was universally believed that Martin Luther had written the lullaby. Moreover, some anonymous publisher credited the tune to a "Carl Mueller." No one knows where this name came from, which only added to the confusion. Only in the 1940s was Murray's composition given its correct credit, and the song is still popularly attributed to Martin Luther. A third verse was added sometime before 1892, but again the author is unknown. In Britain, these words are sung to a different tune, which was composed in 1895 by William J. Kirkpatrick, the American composer of "'Tis So Sweet to Trust in Jesus," and "We Have Heard the Joyful Sound."

Luther's Cradle Hymn

"Deck the Halls with Boughs of Holly"

This is one of the most familiar of the purely secular carols of Christmas. It has nothing to do with the birth at Bethlehem, but is concerned entirely with the decorations and festivities attendant upon Christmas and New Year's. The carol is of Welsh origin, but no one has been able to put a definite age to it. It was well known enough by the eighteenth century to appear in a composition by Mozart. The repeated nonsense of "Fa-la-la-la-la" was a very popular feature of medieval ballads and madrigals.

Welsh

"The First Noel"

The author and composer of this great carol are unknown. It is believed to have been written some time before the eighteenth century. The words were first published in Davies Gilbert's *Some Ancient Christmas Carols* in 1823. The tune was first published by William Sandys in his Christmas Carols, Ancient and Modern in 1833.

The First Noel

Moderately

Traditional

"God Rest You Merry, Gentlemen"

This carol is of unknown authorship and probably dates from the sixteenth century or earlier. It was first published in 1846 by E. F. Rimbault, who had collected the tune in the London area. Other tunes have since been found elsewhere, but the one we know today seems most likely to be the original. One of the reasons for its popularity is the general feeling of the tune: it sounds odd and exotic. The word "rest" in the first line is used in the old English sense of "keep": thus, "God keep you merry, gentlemen."

God Rest You Merry, Gentlemen

English

"Good King Wenceslas"

Wenceslas was actually a duke, the ruler of Bohemia in the tenth century, before kings were in fashion. He was murdered by his brother in a court intrigue, but was later canonized because of his good deeds. The story of a page who was kept from freezing by walking in his footsteps was a standard and popular legend by the nineteenth century. The Reverend John Mason Neale, the warden of Sackville College in East Grinstead, Sussex, England, thought this story would make a good carol for St. Stephen's Day, December 26. So he took the anonymous melody from the *Piae Cantiones,* the same Swedish carol collection that gave him the tune and inspiration for "Good Christian Men, Rejoice." As it happened, the tune he chose was not a Christmas carol at all but a carol welcoming the coming of the flowers at springtime. Today, the melody is rarely ever associated with springtime or flowers, but rather King Wenceslas' good will in the cold of winter.

Latin
(16th century)

"Hark! the Herald Angels Sing"

The Reverend Charles Wesley was the brother of John Wesley, the founder of Methodism. Charles Wesley wrote an astonishing total of more than six thousand hymns. In the year 1739 alone, he wrote, among many others, three hymns still loved today: "O for a Thousand Tongues to Sing," "Christ the Lord Is Risen Today," and the beloved Christmas carol "Hark, How All the Welkin Rings." If you aren't familiar with that last one, it's because the first line was changed in 1753 by George Whitefield who published it in a collection as "Hark! the Herald Angels Sing." The carol was originally published in ten four-line stanzas.

"It Came Upon the Midnight Clear"

This is the only widely accepted Christmas carol written by a Unitarian. The Reverend Edmund Hamilton Sears wrote it in 1849 when he was pastor of the Unitarian Church at Wayland, Massachusetts. It was published in 1850 by Uzziah C. Burnap, who adapted the music from a study by composer Richard S. Willis.

The religious background of the author is made clear in that, while the words obviously refer to the angels' song at the birth of Christ, no reference is actually made to that birth or to Christ Himself. The concern is more for the promise of peace than for the actuality of the event. The third stanza is often omitted.

"Jingle Bells"

This is one of the most familiar of all secular carols. It was composed in 1857 by J. Pierpont for a local Boston Sunday school ceremony. It was originally titled "One Horse Open Sleigh," but became better known by the words of its refrain. This carol is unusual in that it is only about wintertime and does not mention Christmas at all.

It Came Upon the Midnight Clear

Richard S. Willis
Edmund H. Sears

James Pierpont

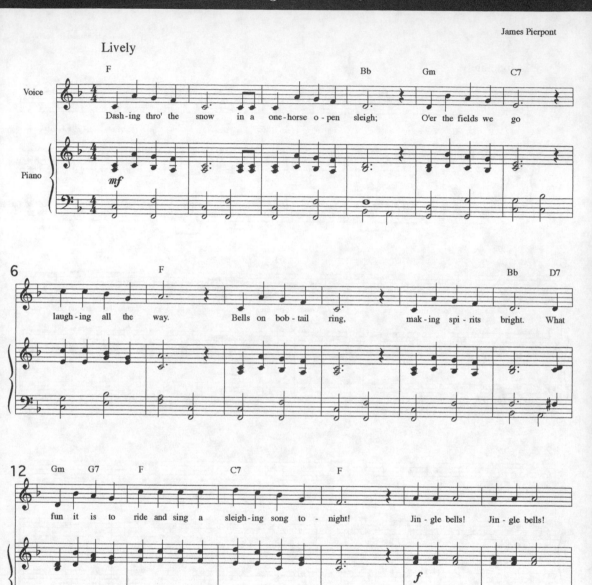

"Joy to the World"

In 1692 Isaac Watts wrote his first hymn. He was eighteen at the time and wrote largely as a protest against the poor doggerel current in Anglican hymnals. When he complained of the low quality of such songs to his father, a deacon, his father suggested that he try to write better ones if he thought he could. Watts instantly produced his already-written hymn. Deacon Watts was impressed and took it to church on Sunday. The hymn was "lined out," that is, read out to the congregation one line at a time so that they could sing it to a familiar hymn tune. The congregation liked it and asked for another for the next week. The same request was repeated and complied with for 222 consecutive Sundays, by which time Watts had created a small revolution in the singing habits of the Anglican Church.

Watts later became an Anglican minister but continued to produce such still-sung hymns as "Alas and Did My Saviour Bleed," "When I Survey the Wondrous Cross," "O God, Our Help in Ages Past," and "Jesus Shall Reign, Where'er the Sun." In 1719, Watts published *The Psalms of David, Imitated*. In this work he put the psalms into modern English verse, allowing for the addition of Christian symbolism and doctrine to the Jewish originals. His reworking of the Ninety-eighth Psalm bears little resemblance to the original but provided the words for one of our most delightful carols, "Joy to the World." Curiously, the song makes no reference to any of the standard images of Christmas, yet its spirit is undeniably that of the best carols. A century later, Watts' words were set to a tune devised by Dr. Lowell Mason from a theme in Handel's *Messiah*.

Joy to the World

Georg Fredrich Handel
Isaac Watts

"O Come, All Ye Faithful"

The origins of this carol were shrouded in mystery for almost two hundred years after it was written. It wasn't until the twentieth century that its original authorship was finally substantiated. It was written around 1742 by an Englishman named John Francis Wade who was living and working at the Roman Catholic center at Douay, France. There was an English university located there that served as a shelter for religious and political refugees from England's internal strife. While making his living as a music copyist, Wade composed the music and the Latin words, "Adeste Fideles." The carol was later brought to England by returning English Catholics. It was first sung at the Portuguese embassy, one of the few strongholds of Catholic culture in England at the time. Because of that, the assumption was made that the carol came from Portugal. The words were not translated for some time, but the tune was used in non-Catholic churches in America with the words "How Firm a Foundation."

In 1841 an Anglican minister named Frederick Oakeley translated the words "Ye Faithful, Approach Ye." He later converted to Catholicism and in 1852 again translated the hymn. This time he produced the words we know as "O Come, All Ye Faithful," translating only the first, seventh, and eight stanzas of Wade's eight-stanza Latin hymn.

This carol seems to break all the rules for proper hymns. Its lines are of unequal lengths and there isn't a rhyme anywhere in it. Yet that has not in any way limited its unflagging popularity.

O Come, All Ye Faithful

Latin Hymn

With motion

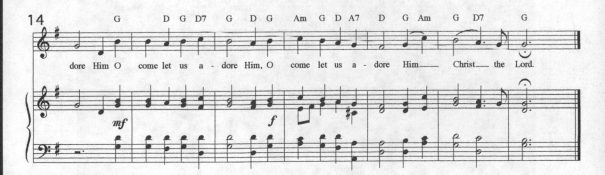

"O Come, O Come, Emmanuel"

This familiar carol most properly belongs to the period of Advent, since it celebrates the expectation of Christ's coming rather than His actual birth. It is based on the "Seven O's," the seven antiphons sung in medieval monasteries at the evening vespers service on the seven nights leading up to Christmas Eve. One was sung each night, and each celebrates a different attribute of the coming Lord. These twelfth-century Latin verses were translated and reduced to five by the nineteenth-century English carol writer John M. Neale, who also wrote "Good King Wenceslas." The tune sung today was adapted by Thomas Helmore from a number of twelfth-century plainsongs. It is these monastic chants which give this carol its particularly ancient favor. To get the full effect, it is necessary to ignore the modern notations that break the melody down into even measures; originally there would have been no such measures—the plainsong would be chanted according to the natural rhythms of the words.

O Come, O Come, Emmanuel

19th Century Plain song

Slowly

O come, O come, Em - man - u - el, and ran - som cap - tive Is - ra -

6

el, that mourns in lone - ly ex - ile here. Un - til the son of God ap - pear. Re -

13

joice! Re - joice! Em - man - u - el shall come to thee, O Is - ra - el.

"O Little Town of Bethlehem"

Phillips Brooks was an Episcopal clergyman with a church in Philadelphia who journeyed to the Holy Land in 1865. On Christmas Eve, he rode on horseback from Jerusalem to Bethlehem. At dusk he stood outside the village, in the Field of the Shepherds, and watched the night stealing through the silent streets. Then he attended the five-hour service at the Church of the Nativity. All of this created a vivid impression on his mind, but it was three years later before he was moved to put pen to paper as he prepared for the Christmas services in his Philadelphia church. He gave the lyrics to his church organist, the local businessman Lewis Redner. He asked him to write a tune for it and jokingly said that if the tune was good enough, he would name it "St. Lewis" after him. Redner was stumped until the night before Brooks wanted the song to be sung by the Sunday school children. Then he awoke during the night with an idea, which he jotted down. The next morning he harmonized it and heard it performed for the first time. It was December 27, 1868. Brooks was delighted with the tune and named it "St. Louis," changing the spelling to spare him embarrassment. It first appeared in the Episcopal Hymnal in 1892, the year before Brook's death, and has gone on to become one of the favorite American carols.

Lewis H. Redner

"O Tannenbaum"

This is one of Germany's very favorite carols. Its origins are completely shrouded in obscurity, having appeared sometime in the Middle Ages. It has never been as popular outside Germany, perhaps because the simplicity of the original words is difficult to translate without their becoming doggerel. The tune of this carol is also used for the Maryland state song, "Maryland, My Maryland." The following is the most familiar traditional English version.

German

Moderately

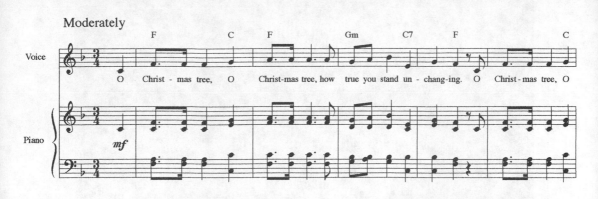

O Christ-mas tree, O Christ-mas tree, how true you stand un - chang-ing. O Christ-mas tree, O

Christ-mas tree, how true you stand un - chang - ing. Your boughs so green in sum-mer-time, re - main so green in

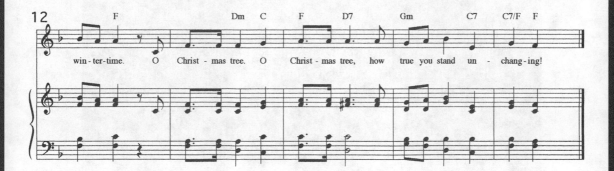

win-ter-time. O Christ - mas tree. O Christ - mas tree, how true you stand un - chang-ing!

"Silent Night"

"Silent Night" is probably the most popular Christmas carol in the world today. Yet probably no other carol was written under such unlikely circumstances and with so many ironic results.

The song was allegedly composed in its entirety on Christmas Eve, 1818. The touching words were composed by Father Josef Mohr, who was the illegitimate son of a seamstress and an army deserter. The Salzach River flowed near the site of the St. Nicholas' Church at Oberndorf, eleven miles northwest of Salzburg, Austria, where Father Mohr was the assistant priest. This closeness of the river had caused rust in the organ so that it could not be played. Faced with the prospect of a Christmas Eve service with no music, Father Mohr sat down and wrote three six-line stanzas of poetry, each beginning "Stille Nacht! Heilige Nacht!" He gave this poem to his organist Franz Grüber and asked him to set it to music that could be sung by the choir and accompanied on a guitar. Grüber's presence was somewhat odd in that he worked as a schoolteacher in Arnsdorf, several miles away, and was also organist for a church there. But he had a stepson play for him there so he could supplement the family income by playing for his friend Mohr in Oberndorf. This was a lucky chance, since what more appropriate place for the best-loved carol to originate than in St. Nicholas' Church?

It took Grüber only a couple of hours to set the words to music and write out the parts. That even left time for a rehearsal with the choir before the midnight service began. The arrangement

was as simple as possible. Mohr sang tenor and Grüber sang bass and accompanied on the guitar. After each stanza was sung in two parts, the choir repeated the last two lines in four-part harmony. As far as Mohr and Grüber knew, they had done no more than get through an awkward situation that night. Neither knew that they had achieved immortality.

In the spring of 1819, a master organ builder came to work on the rusted organ at Oberndorf. No one knows how he came to see or hear the carol. Perhaps Grüber showed it to him along with some of his other compositions to get the response of this man who had seen so much more of the world; perhaps the organ builder just ran across it in the organ loft. Whatever the circumstances, he copied the song and took to singing it on his rounds of the Austrian villages where he worked. It was then acquired from him by two strolling families of folk singers, the Rainers and the Strassers. The two families made it a part of their regular repertory, and although they knew nothing about who had written it, they were instrumental in the spread of the song's popularity. In 1834 the Strassers sang the "Song from Heaven," as they called it, for the king of Prussia. He ordered that it be sung every Christmas Eve by his cathedral choir. The Rainers first brought the song to American in 1839, when it was sung at the Alexander Hamilton Monument in New York City.

By the middle of the nineteenth century the song had gained worldwide popularity, and yet its origin still remained a mystery. It was variously attributed to Joseph or Michael Haydn, Mozart, or even God Himself without the benefit of any intervening composer. In 1854 leading musical authorities received

a letter from the small town of Hallein near Salzburg. The letter was from one Franz Grüber, a schoolteacher, who had the audacity to claim that he had written the tune of the holy song. Granted he did produce a manuscript that seemed authentic, but few authorities wanted to accept such an insignificant source for the world-famous song. Thus the last eight and a half years of Grüber's life were involved in controversy over whether he had written the song or not. Living in small villages as he had, he had not even been aware of the popularity of the song until over thirty years after it had spread around the world.

And what of Mohr, whose words had inspired the song? Sadly, he had always had a drinking problem and was frequently in trouble with the Church authorities. He was transferred twelve times in eight years. His two-year stay at Oberndorf had been the longest time he spent anywhere. Eventually he was sent to the village of Wagrain, where he died of pneumonia in 1848. As he was penniless, his parishioners had to take up a collection to bury him. He was buried on St. Nicholas' Day, and it is unlikely that he ever heard of the "Song from Heaven."

If it had not been for Mohr and the guitar, there would have been no "Silent Night." Ironically, one of the things he was chided for by the Church authorities was bringing the guitar into the church service.

The translation we know today of "Silent Night" first appeared in 1863. The translator was unknown until 1959, when it was determined to have been the Reverend John Freeman Young, who would eventually become the Episcopal bishop of Florida in 1867.

Silent Night

Franz Gruber

"We Three Kings of Orient Are"

This is one of the few modern carols in which both words and music are by a single author. The Reverend John Henry Hopkins, Jr., was Rector of Christ's Church, Williamsport, Pennsylvania, when he wrote it about 1857. It was first published in his very popular work *Carols, Hymns, and Songs,* in 1862. It was the only American carol to appear in *Christmas Carols New and Old,* the English collection by H. R. Bramley and John Stainer that was very influential in bringing about the revival of carol-singing. Hopkins wrote many other hymns and songs, but none ever equaled the popularity of this one. It has always appealed to children because of the dramatic device of assigning each verse to a different king and therefore, often, a different singer. This carol is based more on the legends that grew up around the Wise Men than on the original account in Matthew.

We Three Kings of Orient Are

John Henry Hopkins, Jr.

Moderato

We three Kings of O - ri - ent are, bear - ing gifts we tra - verse a - far,

field and foun - tain, moor and moun - tain, fol - low - ing yon - der star. O_____

star of won - der star of night, star with roy - al beau - ty bright,

west - ward lead - ing still pro - ceed - ing, guide us to thy per - fect light.

"We Wish You a Merry Christmas"

This familiar traditional carol recalls the waits and carolers of old England as they go from door to door singing blessings on the house and asking for some good cheer in return. Numerous versions of this exist with many varying verses, but the author is unknown.

We Wish You a Merry Christmas

Merrily

We wish you a merry Christ-mas, we wish you a mer-ry Christ-mas, we

wish you a mer-ry Christ-mas, and a hap-py new year! Good ti-dings we bring to

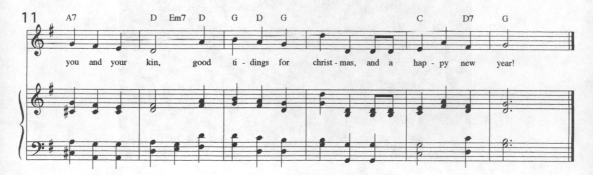

you and your kin, good ti-dings for christ-mas, and a hap-py new year!

"What Child Is This?"

The earliest reference to the haunting folk song "Greensleeves" was in the year 1580. It was so popular and familiar that it is mentioned several times in Shakespeare's *The Merry Wives of Windsor*. The tune has been used for many purposes, including a party song for the Cavaliers during the English Civil War and as a prison lament for Macheath in *The Beggar's Opera*. The original words are still familiar, "Alas, my love, ye do me wrong/To cast me off discourteously," but the Christmas lyrics familiar to Americans were written by the Victorian English hymnist and insurance company executive William Chatterton Dix.

What Child Is This?

Based on Greensleeves
Old English air
W. C. Dix

Classical

Christmas Oratorio

Johann Sebastian Bach composed his *Christmas Oratorio* in 1734. At the time, he was employed as cantor of the Thomasschule of Leipzig, a post he held until his death in 1750. His duties consisted of teaching a class in Latin, training singers and instrumentalists, playing the organ at two churches, and also organizing and directing all musical activities at these churches. As if all that were not enough, he was also responsible for composing all special music and copying out all the parts for singers and instrumentalists. That Bach had time to compose at all is amazing; that he turned out a volume of music almost unequaled in history is astounding; that his music is not just eighteenth-century Muzak but some of the most sublime expressions of the human spirit ever created is beyond belief. During his twenty years at Leipzig, Bach composed some 250 cantatas alone, an average of one a month. Each cantata ran from twelve to forty minutes in length and usually involved a chorus, orchestra, and soloists. Bach composed each work, copied all the parts, taught the performers, and conducted the performance. When asked about his life, Bach replied simply, "I worked hard."

The *Christmas Oratorio* is actually a set of six cantatas composed to be performed one at each of six services between Christmas and Epiphany in 1734-35. The texts are taken mostly from Matthew and Luke, and are appropriate for each of the services.

The six parts tell the story of Joseph and Mary and of Christ's birth, the appearance of the angels to the shepherds, the coming of the shepherds to the manger, the naming of Jesus, the coming of the Wise Men to Herod, and the Magi's visit to Bethlehem. The work is written for orchestra, chorus, and soprano, alto, tenor, and bass soloists. Today it is more frequently performed as a single work than as six separate cantatas.

Bach's music was the culmination of the polyphonic form, the weaving of different melodies together to form a unified whole. But by his time the polyphonic form was considered old-hat and Bach along with it. His music was never fully appreciated in his lifetime; it was too old-fashioned. After his death, the authorities at Leipzig, who had always felt that he neglected his duties as a teacher, resolved that "the school needs a choirmaster and not a music director." His music fell quickly into disuse and survived only as manuscripts in attics and basements. It was Mendelssohn who rediscovered the wonders of J. S. Bach eighty years later when he happened upon a manuscript of the *St. Matthew Passion,* one of the greatest of all choral works, at an auction of a cheese seller's goods. It was being sold as scrap paper.

Hänsel and Gretel

The best-known full-length Christmas opera has nothing to do with Christmas. *Hänsel and Gretel* is traditionally performed at Christmastime, yet Christmas is not even mentioned in it. However, because of its delightful fairy-tale plot, its wonderful gingerbread scenery, and its celebration of childhood, it has become a beautifully appropriate addition to the Christmas season.

Engelbert Humperdinck was a disciple of Richard Wagner. Wagner's operas are known for their heavy (some would say "murky") exploration of German mythology, their elaborate orchestration, and their advanced harmonies. In the hands of Wagner, a musical genius, this blend of the mythological past and the musical future was eminently successful. Very few other composers, however, were able to carry on his tradition or extend it in any way.

Humperdinck had his greatest success through an unlikely means. His sister wrote a little play for her children to perform at home based on the familiar story by the Brothers Grimm of the two children lost in the wood. Humperdinck wrote some little songs for them to sing. It was perhaps the simplicity of this beginning that accounted for the opera's success. Expanding his simple tunes into an opera gave him a core of basic, folklike melody at the heart of the modern Wagnerian harmonic structure of his work. The opera was first performed a few days before Christmas in 1893 at Weimar, Germany. It became tremendously popular in Germany and soon throughout the world. A whole series of fairy-tale operas sprang up in imitation. Fairy tales were easier to relate to than heavy mythology, and the new emphasis on folklike melodies made the works more "hummable."

Hänsel and Gretel is still frequently performed, especially at Christmastime. The New York Metropolitan Opera has presented it more than one hundred

times, and it was the first complete opera broadcast by radio from the stage of the Met, on Christmas Day, 1931.

An interesting note on the cast: the part of Hänsel is written for a mezzo-soprano, that is, a medium-high woman's voice. This may seem odd, since Hänsel is a little boy, but composers have frequently used women's voices to depict young men or boys, presumably to give the feeling of an adolescent sound before the voice has changed. This casting is often balanced in modern productions by the fact that the part of the witch (also written for a mezzo-soprano) is often played by a tenor, to heighten the humor and grotesqueness of the role.

Messiah

On August 22, 1741, George Friedrich Handel began to act strangely. He shut himself into his room, sat at his desk, and almost did not eat or sleep for three weeks while he worked. When his servants tried to get him to eat, he would flare up at them, eyes blazing. If he ate, he continued to work with the hand that didn't hold the bread. He behaved like a madman, and perhaps he was one.

The German-born Handel came to London in 1710 at the age of twenty-five. He immediately became the toast of the town when his opera *Rinaldo* proved to be a big success. Always a prolific composer, he turned out dozens of the popular Italian operas that he aristocratic audience clamored for. But in 1728 disaster struck-in a most unlikely form. A rowdy work called *The Beggar's Opera* was produced in London. A risqué satire on Italian opera and current politics, it contained a score made up of a host of popular tunes of the day (including one from one of Handel's operas) kitted out with new words. It was a smash hit. This was something the common people could enjoy, without having to know Italian or the conventions of the stilted operatic format of the time. Italian opera and its prime composer, Handel, began struggling for life.

One of the steps Handel took to try to regain popularity was the composition of oratorios. The oratorio took on a different form from opera in that the work was not staged, so it did not have to be specifically dramatic and it could be composed in English, which no serious opera of the time could be. He produced fifteen of these in the years leading up to 1741 with varying success. The fickleness of the public was a source of great disappointment to him, and the once-lionized composer found himself being treated as an old-timer. Financially, he was in difficult straits.

When his fit of mad composition came upon him in 1741, he did not even have a commission that he was working on. For all he knew at the time, the new work he was composing might never be performed, but that hardly deterred him. As the days passed without food and rest, Handel was listening to a different, higher voice than that of the public.

A servant found him one day weeping at his desk. He rushed forward to help, but Handel looked up at him with a great light shining through the tears of his eyes. "I did think I did see all Heaven before me, and the great God Himself," he said. He had just completed the "Hallelujah Chorus."

Messiah was completed in twenty-four days, an incredibly short time for a work that takes nearly three hours to perform in its entirety. The completed manuscript was then put aside for the next seven weeks. Finally the Lord Lieutenant of Ireland asked him to visit Dublin and give some charity concerts there. He brought it with him. On April 13, 1742, the first performance of the *Messiah* was given in Dublin.

That first performance had been a tremendous event for the Dublin audience, which had been asked that ladies not wear hoops that evening and gentlemen leave their swords at home in order to accommodate an extra hundred people in the hall. But the *Messiah* was slow catching on in London. It was first performed there in 1743, with much less success than in Dublin. London did not fully accept the *Messiah* until the famous performance at which King George II, moved by the inspiration of the piece, rose at the beginning of the "Hallelujah Chorus." The entire audience stood with him and established a custom that exists to this day of rising in homage to this most sublime and stirring piece of music.

Before his death, annual performances of the *Messiah* had become traditional, with Handel conducting. It was at that time usually performed at Easter. The two centuries since its composition have produced no change in the popularity of the *Messiah*, but there have been many changes made in how it is performed. Handel himself changed the work according to the musical resources he had on hand: sometimes orchestra, sometimes organ alone; sometimes a male alto, sometimes a female one. The result is considerable confusion about just what Handel wanted. The work was reorchestrated in 1789 by Mozart to suit changing tastes, and that is the version we usually hear today. In the nineteenth century it became popular to have huge festival choruses, and there would sometimes be as many as five thousand voices performing the work that Handel wrote for a chorus of about twenty-four.

Today the *Messiah* is thought of as a Christmas work; at least, that is when most performances of it are presented. Actually, the work is divided into three sections, only the first of which deals with Christmas. Starting with the prophecies about Christ's birth, the first part is highlighted by the joyous chorus "For Unto Us a Child Is Born" and the angels' song to the shepherds. There is very little actual narrative, containing more descriptions of the emotions produced by the joyous tidings. The second part tells of Christ's Crucifixion and Resurrection, again without actually telling a story. The second part ends with the "Hallelujah Chorus" and is often referred to as the Easter section, the first part being called the Christmas section. The third part is a contemplation on the meaning of Christ's ministry and its promise of resurrection for all believers.

The text, mostly a compilation of biblical writings, was provided to Handel by his friend Charles Jennens, although there is some doubt whether he actually wrote it or merely took credit for what his secretary had written. Jennens did not appreciate what Handel had done. He wrote to a friend: "I shall show you a collection I gave Handel, called *Messiah*, which I value highly, and he has made a fine entertainment out of it, though not near so good as he might and ought to have done. I have with great difficulty made him correct some of the grossest faults in the composition." A more monstrous example of misplaced egotism would be difficult to find.

The *Messiah* is a living part of our Christmas tradition. In a major city, one usually has a choice of several complete performances. Radio and TV broadcast the presentations of famous orchestras as part of Christmas Eve programming.

The *Messiah* is one of the supreme achievements of human art. Its polyphonic writing, the weaving of melody against melody in the different voice and instrumental parts, has few equals in all the world of music; and the lyricism of its gentle airs is truly touching. But it goes beyond the bounds of mere ability and rises to inspiration. As Milton Cross puts it, "Never a religious man in the same sense as Bach, Handel became the God-intoxicated man while writing *Messiah*." Sheer joy and glory fill the whole work and make it especially appropriate to the Christmas season when the joy of Christ's birth fills all our hearts.

A curious footnote: Handel is buried in Westminster Abbey. Above his grave stands a statue of him holding a score of *Messiah* while angels wheel above his head. The word Messiah is misspelled.

The Nutcracker

Tchaikovsky's *The Nutcracker* is the best-loved and, in fact, the only major Christmas ballet in the standard repertory of today's companies. *The Nutcracker* is so popular that many ballet troupes finance all the rest of their productions with their profits from the many performances of *The Nutcracker* that they put on each Christmas. Thousands of children are brought to the Christmas holiday matinees, and yet this is a ballet for adults as much as for children. Like Christmas itself, *The Nutcracker* is a delight for all ages.

The original story, "The Nutcracker and the Mouse King," was written in 1816 by the famous writer of fantastic tales E.T.A. Hoffmann. (Hoffmann had many connections with music: he was himself a composer and took the middle name Amadeus as homage to his idol Wolfgang Amadeus Mozart; not only were his stories adapted as ballets and operas, he was himself made the leading character in Offenbach's opera *The Tales of Hoffmann*.) The story was translated from its original German into French by Alexandre Dumas (the elder), the author of *The Three Musketeers,* in 1845. In 1891 the great French choreographer Marius Petipa wrote a scenario with his assistant Lev Ivanov which was based on Dumas' translation. The commission for writing the music went to the great Russian composer Peter Ilich Tchaikovsky, with whom Petipa had previously collaborated on the *Sleeping Beauty* ballet.

In March of 1892 Tchaikovsky conducted an orchestral performance of a suite of music from the soon-to-be-produced ballet. The music was a grand success and boded well for the premiere of the ballet itself. This suite is still heard in its original form both on recordings and as a standard in light classical concerts.

The ballet was first performed on December 17, 1892, at St. Petersburg.

It was not a success! The main reason may have been the complaint, still sometimes heard, that the entire first act of the ballet is dominated by children, and that the real ballet is located almost entirely in the second act. Another problem was that audiences still weren't ready for such symphonic ballet scores as Tchaikovsky gave them. They were used to music that merely accompanied the dancing without attempting too much on its own. This had caused the same confusion and lack of success in Tchaikovsky's two previous ballets, *Swan Lake* and *Sleeping Beauty*. Yet it was Tchaikovsky's contributions to the field of ballet music that eventually raised the standard of such compositions and made it worthwhile for serious composers to venture into the field. The ballet scores of Tchaikovsky are among the most beautiful and familiar ever written.

The story of *The Nutcracker* takes place on Christmas Eve. Two children, Clara and Fritz, are given a number of magical presents by a magician named Drosselmeyer. One of them is a nutcracker shaped like a small man. The children quarrel over him before going to bed. Clara sneaks out of bed because she cannot sleep for thinking of her nutcracker. She finds a full-scale battle in progress between an army of toy soldiers, led by the nutcracker, and an army of mice led by the seven-headed King of the Mice. In an act of great bravery, Clara hurls her slipper at the Mouse King, stunning him and turning the tide of battle. The nutcracker is transformed into a handsome prince. In gratitude for her help, the nutcracker prince takes Clara on an enchanted journey to the Kingdom of the Sweets, which is presided over by the Sugarplum Fairy. There are dances by snowflakes and Arabian, Chinese, and Russian dancers. The finale is provided by the famous "Waltz of the Flowers."

One of the reasons for *The Nutcracker*'s popularity is the opportunity it offers for spectacular scenic effects. Sleds fly, snowflakes dance, hordes of mice throng the stage. For many New York children, it just wouldn't be

Christmas if they didn't go to the City Ballet and see the giant Christmas tree that magically grows out of the stage floor until it touches the ceiling of the high stage. *The Nutcracker,* both as music and as ballet, is filled with Christmas magic. Some of the major companies that present annual Christmas productions of this perennial favorite are the American Ballet Theatre, the New York City Ballet, the San Francisco Ballet, and Ballet West in Salt Lake City. The music of *The Nutcracker Suite* also provides the accompaniment for some of the most magical dancing in Walt Disney's *Fantasia.*

More Serious Music for Christmas

CHRISTMAS CONCERTO

An orchestral piece by the seventeenth-century Italian composer Arcangelo Corelli, officially titled *Concerto Grosso in G Minor.*

CHRISTMAS EVE

Nicolai Rimsky-Korsakov wrote this Russian opera in 1895 based on a Gogol fairy tale.

THE CHRISTMAS TREE

The virtuoso composer Franz Liszt arranged Christmas hymns and carols into a piano solo.

L'ENFANCE DU CHRIST

A French oratorio by Hector Berlioz, this 1854 work is not directly concerned with Christ's birth but with his childhood.

FANTASIA ON CHRISTMAS CAROLS

English composer Ralph Vaughan Williams created this work for baritone, chorus, and orchestra in 1912.

ST. NICHOLAS

This Christmas cantata by the English composer Benjamin Britten tells the story of St. Nicholas' life and first appeared on CBS television in 1959.

Christmas on the Page

Stories

Hans Christian Andersen

"THE FIR TREE"

—⁂—

Hans Christian Andersen, the great Danish writer of fairy tales, wrote a number of stories that we connect with winter, such as "The Little Match Girl." But only one actually takes place at Christmas, "The Fir Tree." For those of us who only remember reading this story long ago, a rereading comes as something of a shock, since it is not just a nice little children's story. The tale has a moral, and it pursues it relentlessly.

The fir tree begins as a very small tree surrounded by the delightful sights and sounds of the forest. But he is not satisfied. He dreams of seeing the world. He sees his larger comrades cut down and taken away at Christmas and he longs to go too, sure that they are going to a glorious new life. But then the time comes when he is big enough and he is cut down and taken away. He is set in a salon and heavy ornaments cause his limbs to droop. Candles scorch his branches. He is frightened by the children who dance and sing about him and finally swoop down on him to rob his braches of the goodies concealed there. When Christmas is over, he is thrown out in the yard. To see the sky and the trees once again is a joy to him, and he realizes he never knew when he really had it good. Then a servant comes and chops him up for firewood.

THE SECOND SHEPHERD'S PLAY

All of our modern Western theater, strange as it may seem, grew out of the liturgical church service of the Middle Ages. The question-and-answer format between priest and congregation was almost a form of drama itself, and at some point actual dialogue was added to bring the biblical stories more to life. The first instance of this was at Easter. It told how the women who came to find Jesus in the tomb were met instead by an angel who asked whom they sought and told them He was not there, but was risen. This simple three-line exchange was the beginning of modern drama.

This acting out of biblical stories became very popular. It got more and more elaborate until whole plays were being performed, first at the altar and then at the porch of the church. As the subject matter broadened and the natural rough humor of the times began to creep in, the plays were moved out of the church entirely, into the streets. There were great festival days on which whole cycles of plays were given, sometimes as many as forty-eight or more. These plays told everything from the creation of the world and the great flood down to the more modern miracles of favorite saints. The plays were performed by the different guilds of tradesmen in the town. Each guild had its own play; for instance, the shipbuilders' guild might do the story of Noah's Ark. Every year the same guild would do the same play. The plays were mounted on wagons so that they could be taken through the streets of the town. Thus, by sitting in one place, one could behold the whole history of the world in a single day.

Most of these plays are lost to us now, but several complete or near-complete cycles have survived, and one of them seems to be the work of a master. This is the Wakefield Cycle, from Yorkshire, England. It contains the Christmas masterpiece *The Second Shepherds' Play*. This work was written around 1385, which means that the language is extremely archaic.

There are, however, many good modern versions, and the work is well worth reading and performing. The blending of honest good humor and devotion is extraordinary. (It is the *"Second" Shepherds' Play* because there was another play about shepherds in the cycle.)

Three shepherds are tending their herds on a bitter cold night. They grumble and complain amusingly. Along comes Mak, a shepherd with a bad reputation. He complains that he has been given a bad deal, that no one ever trusts him. They trust him, but make him lie down between them as they go to sleep, just in case. Mak uses a spell to keep them asleep and steals a sheep, which he takes home to his wife, Gill. When the three shepherds come looking, the couple bundle up the sheep to look like a newborn baby. Gill groans as if she has just finished labor, and Mak sings a lullaby. The shepherds can't find their sheep anywhere about the hut, although they comment they never met with a more foul-smelling infant. Mak takes an oath that he doesn't have the sheep, saying, "If I have your sheep, may I eat my newborn son!" The shepherds are about to go away when they realize that they have been un-neighborly in not offering any presents for the child. They go back and ask to see him. Mak tries to stop them, but they are insistent. The size of the baby's nose makes them suspicious. Mak claims the nose was broken, that's all. The shepherds give Mak a good bouncing in a blanket and go off. Suddenly an angel rises up and announces the birth of Christ. The three shepherds hurry to Bethlehem and give present of cherries, a bird, and a ball to the newborn Babe. They go off singing happily in the cold night.

In a more sophisticated age, this juxtaposition of Mak's "son" with the Son of God would have been a blasphemous parody. But to the people of the Middle Ages it was perfectly natural for religion to spill over into everyday life. No one questioned how far it was to Bethlehem and no one saw anything wrong with laughing riotously at Mak's antics and a moment later standing in awe at the side of the cradle. Jesus was a part of their lives, and He could join in their pleasures. Simple happiness and simple devotion blend beautifully in this little masterwork from the Middle Ages.

Charles Dickens

After the period of prohibition imposed by the Puritans, Christmas returned to England with the Restoration. But it was not Christmas as it had once been. The splendor was gone out of it. The elaborate feastings and pageantry passed out of favor, and Christmas became a quiet celebration in individual homes. This was a good thing in that it helped eliminate the abuses of Christmas, but many fine old traditions also began to disappear.

The Industrial Revolution further hastened what looked like the imminent death of the old-style Christmas with its innocent feasting and games, plum pudding and mince pie, evergreens and mistletoe. The motto of the time was "Work!" and the poor were too oppressed to celebrate, while those who were well off did not want to waste the time and money. Christmas became a workday.

A number of writers wrote in praise of Christmas, but their writing had a flavor of nostalgia over the all-but-gone past. They spoke of what Christmas had once been, not what it now was or what it could become. This attitude has endured to the present day and is part of the bittersweet pleasure of all Christmas celebrations: no matter how delightful the present day, it can never hold a candle to those brisk Christmas mornings of memory.

One writer believed that Christmas could still be alive and well-and almost single-handedly made it so. Charles Dickens felt what Christmas could do for himself, and he set about doing the same for the rest of the world.

His first blow struck for the cause was a short sketch called "A Christmas Dinner," which described the conviviality of a family as it gathers around the Christmas table. The past is forgiven and forgotten as all join in the spirit of the season.

Dickens' next story on the subject will sound more familiar. It tells of an unpleasant, cranky type who is annoyed by other people's cheerfulness on Christmas Eve. He is taken by supernatural beings to view scenes of family happiness and goodness, which convince him of the error of his ways and cause him to reform when he awakens the next day. Sound familiar? You may be surprised to learn that this story was not Dickens' best-known work but was a short story called "The Goblins Who Stole a Sexton," contained in *The Pickwick Papers*. The story is an entertaining one, but it does not capture the imagination because the Christmas setting is almost incidental to the tale. It is merely a ghost story told around the fire at an old-time Christmas festivity. The description of the other Christmas games and frivolities is much more delightful and points more to what was to come in his later writings. Dickens wrote rhapsodically of the time of year which was so important to him:

> Christmas was close at hand, in all his bluff and hearty honesty; it was the season of hospitality, merriment, and open-heartedness; the old year was preparing, like an ancient philosopher, to call his friends around him and amidst the sound of feasting and revelry to pass gently and calmly away. . . .
>
> And numerous indeed are the hearts to which Christmas brings a brief season of happiness and enjoyment. How many families whose members have been dispersed and scattered far and wide, in the restless struggles of life, are then reunited, and meet once again in that happy state of companionship and mutual goodwill which is a source of such pure and unalloyed delight, and one so incompatible with the cares and sorrows of the world that the religious belief of the most civilized nations and the rude traditions of

the roughest savages alike number it among the first joys of a future condition of existence provided for the blest and happy! How many old recollections and how many dormant sympathies does Christmas time awaken!

We write these words now, many miles distant from the spot at which, year after year, we met on that day, a merry and joyous circle. Many of the hearts that throbbed so gaily then have ceased to beat; many of the looks that shone so brightly then have ceased to glow; the hands we grasped have grown cold; the eyes we sought have hid their lustre in the grave; and yet the old house, the room, the merry voices and smiling faces, the jest, the laugh, the most minute and trivial circumstances connected with those happy meetings, crowd upon our mind at each recurrence of the season, as if the last assemblage had been but yesterday! Happy, happy Christmas, that can win us back to the delusions of our childish days, that can recall to the old man the pleasures of his youth, that can transport the sailor and the traveller, thousands of miles away, back to his own fireside and his quiet home!

A Christmas Carol

Seven years passed before Dickens found his fullest expression of the Christmas spirit. The year 1843 was not a good one for him. He had had unparalleled popular success with his previous works, *Pickwick Papers, Nicholas Nickleby, Oliver Twist, The Old Curiosity Shop,* and *Barnaby Rudge.* But in 1843 he was in the midst of writing and publishing his new serial novel *Martin Chuzzlewit.* It was not well received, yet he had to keep turning out the monthly installments and trying desperately to regain the public's favor before his financial situation became impossible. He was also in a mental turmoil over the terrible plight of the poor. During October 1843 he went to Manchester to make several speeches appealing for aid to the working class. While he walked the streets with these images in his mind, an idea came to him for *A Christmas Carol.* He modeled it roughly on the "The Goblins Who Stole a Sexton" and decked it out with details from his own life, and he worked on it feverishly while still writing *Martin Chuzzlewit.* He finished it and took it to his publisher by the second week in November. Because he wanted it to be of the first quality, he worked on the design of the book himself, selecting the illustrator, the bindings, and the paper, having the illustrations hand-tinted, and keeping the price as low as possible so that his work could be afforded by the people he aimed it at. A few days before Christmas, the new little book appeared.

Financially, *A Christmas Carol* was not a success. Dickens had succeeded too well in keeping down the price of the book. Although it sold well, he made very little from it in its initial sales. He also had to suffer the indignity of seeing many cheaply made pirated versions of his work appear on both sides of the Atlantic. The copyright laws were not very strict then, and almost anyone could steal a writer's work. Dickens brought suit against one such pirate. This unethical publishing firm defended its version of Dickens' story by saying that it had made "very considerable improvements." Dickens won the suit, but the firm's bankruptcy left him with no settlement and court costs to pay.

It took Dickens a good while to realize just how completely he had succeeded even though he had not made much money. He wrote other Christmas books, one each year. In 1844 he wrote *The Chimes,* of which he said, "I believe I have written a tremendous book, and knocked the Carol out of the field." He was wrong. *A Christmas Carol* remains to this day, next to the Nativity itself, the best-known and best-loved Christmas story of all. Scrooge has passed into the language as a synonym for "miser," and the Ghosts of Christmas Past, Present, and Future have haunted us all.

Christmas has bloomed again as a time to think of one's fellow man and to strive to deserve the ultimate compliment that is paid to the reformed Scrooge:

> . . . and it was always said of him, that he knew how to keep Christmas well, if any man alive possessed the knowledge. May that be truly said of us, and all of us! And so, as Tiny Tim observed, God Bless Us, Every One!
>
> A Christmas Carol was the ultimate embodiment of what Dickens called "the Carol philosophy," that Christmas was "a good time: a kind, forgiving, charitable, pleasant time: the only time I know of, in the long calendar of the year, when men and women seem by one consent to open their shut-up hearts freely, and to think of other people below them as if they really were fellow-passengers to the grave, and not another race of creatures bound on their journeys."

There is a famous story, which may not be true but which should be, about a poor costermonger's girl in Drury Lane who was told of Dickens' funeral. "Dickens dead?" she asked tearfully. "Then will Father Christmas die too?"

MARLEY

The first spirit to visit Scrooge is the ghost of his dead business partner, Marley. Dickens selected the name of this ghostly and far-from-silent partner in an amusing fashion. At a St. Patrick's Day party the year in which he wrote and published *A Christmas Carol,* Dickens met a doctor who practiced medicine in Piccadilly. Knowing that Dickens peopled his stories with unusual names, this doctor suggested that his own family name was quite unusual: Marley. According to the story, Dickens merely replied,

"Your name will be a household word before the year is out." Thus the spirit of the forgotten Dr. Miles Marley is aroused every day by the clanking
chains of his namesake, the late Jacob Marley.

TINY TIM

In came little Bob, the father, with at least three feet of comforter
exclusive of the fringe, hanging down before him; and his thread-
bare clothes darned up and brushed, to look seasonable; and Tiny
Tim upon his shoulder. Alas for Tiny Tim, he bore a little crutch,
and had his limbs supported by an iron frame! . . .

"And how did little Tim behave?" asked Mrs. Cratchit. . . .

"As good as gold," said Bob, "and better. Somehow he gets thoughtful, sitting by himself so much, and thinks the strangest things you
ever heard. He told me, coming home, that he hoped the people saw
him in the church, because he was a cripple, and it might be pleasant to them to remember upon Christmas Day, who made lame
beggars walk and blind men see."

The Spirit of Christmas Yet to Come shows Scrooge that same
happy Cratchit household as it will be in the future. But there is
one difference, "a vacant seat in the poor chimney corner, and a
crutch without an owner, carefully preserved."

"But however and when ever we part from one another, I am sure
we shall none of us forget poor Tiny Tim-shall we-or this first parting that there was among us."

"Never, father!" cried they all.

"And I know," said Bob, "I know, my dears, that when we recollect how patient and how mild he was; although he was a little, little child; we shall not quarrel easily among ourselves, and forget poor Tiny Tim in doing it."

"No, never, father!" they all cried again.

"I am very happy," said little Bob, "I am very happy!"

Mrs. Cratchit kissed him, his daughters kissed him, the two young Cratchits kissed him, and Peter and himself shook hands. Spirit of Tiny Tim, thy childish essence was from God!

We all know that Tiny Tim did not die, that the converted Scrooge helped to save him. Tiny Tim is one of the most familiar names in popular English literature, and it is difficult to imagine a Christmas season without Tiny Tim in one of his many movie or TV incarnations waving his tiny crutch and crying, "God bless us, every one!" Yet the original manuscripts of A Christmas Carol show that Tiny Tim was to be called Little Fred. Most of us would agree that the name change was a wise one. It is difficult to hold back the tears at the thought of Tiny Tim; it is hard to imagine being anything but annoyed at someone named Little Fred.

The inspiration for the character of Tiny Tim probably came from a visit to Dickens' sister Fanny and her invalid son Harry Burnett in 1843, the year that the book was published. Unlike Tiny Tim, Harry Burnett did not find a second father and live happily ever after; he died while still a child.

"A merry Christmas, uncle! God save you!" cried a cheerful voice. It was the voice of Scrooge's nephew, who came upon him so quickly that this was the first intimation he had of his approach.

"Bah!" said Scrooge, "Humbug!"

He had so heated himself with rapid walking in the fog and frost, this nephew of Scrooge's, that he was all in a glow; his face was ruddy and handsome; his eyes sparkled, and his breath smoked again.

"Christmas a humbug, uncle!" said Scrooge's nephew. "You don't mean that, I am sure."

"I do," said Scrooge. "Merry Christmas! what right have you to be merry? what reason have you to be merry? You're poor enough."

"Come, then," returned the nephew gaily. "What right have you to be dismal? what reason have you to be morose? You're rich enough."

Scrooge having no better answer ready on the spur of the moment, said, "Bah!" again; and followed it up with "Humbug."

"Don't be cross, uncle," said the nephew.

"What else can I be," returned the uncle, "when I live in such a world of fools as this? Merry Christmas! Out upon merry Christmas! What's Christmas time to you but a time for paying bills without money; a time for finding yourself a year older, but not an hour richer; a time for balancing your books and having every item in 'em through a round dozen of months presented dead against you? If I could work my will," said Scrooge, indignantly, "every idiot who goes about with 'Merry Christmas,' on his lips, should be boiled with his own pudding, and buried with a stake of holly through his heart. He should!"

———⁂———

"At this festive season of the year, Mr. Scrooge," said the gentleman, taking up a pen, "it is more than usually desirable that we should make some slight provision for the poor and destitute, who suffer greatly at the present time. Many thousands are in want of common necessaries; hundreds of thousands are in want of common comforts, sir."

"Are there no prisons?" asked Scrooge.

"Plenty of prisons," said the gentleman, laying down the pen again.

"And the Union workhouses?" demanded Scrooge. "Are they still in operation?"

"They are. Still," returned the gentleman, "I wish I could say they were not."

"The Treadmill and the Poor Law are in full vigour, then?" said Scrooge.

"Both very busy, sir."

"Oh! I was afraid, from what you said at first, that something had occurred to stop them in their useful course," said Scrooge. "I'm very glad to hear it."

"Under the impression that they scarcely furnish Christian cheer of mind or body to the multitude," returned the gentleman, "a few of us are endeavouring to raise a fund to buy the Poor some meat and drink, and means of warmth. We choose this time, because it is a time, of all others, when Want is keenly felt, and Abundance rejoices. What shall I put you down for?"

"Nothing!" Scrooge replied.

"You wish to be anonymous?"

"I wish to be left alone," said Scrooge. "Since you ask me what I wish, gentlemen, that is my answer. I don't make merry myself at Christmas, and I can't afford to make idle people merry. I help to support the establishments I have mentioned: they cost enough: and those who are badly off must go there."

"Many can't go there; and many would rather die."

"If they would rather die," said Scrooge, "they had better do it, and decrease the surplus population."

———— ❧ ————

"A Merry Christmas to us all, my dears! God bless us!"

Which all the family re-echoed.

"God bless us every one!" said Tiny Tim, the last of all.

He sat very close to his father's side, upon his little stool. Bob held his withered little hand in his, as if he loved the child, and wished to keep him by his side, and dreaded that he might be taken from him.

"Spirit," said Scrooge, with an interest he had never felt before, "tell me if Tiny Tim will live."

"I see a vacant seat," replied the Ghost, "in the poor chimney corner, and a crutch without an owner, carefully preserved. If these shadows remain unaltered by the Future, the child will die."

"No, no," said Scrooge. "Oh, no, kind Spirit! say he will be spared."

"If these shadows remain unaltered by the Future, none other of my race," returned the Ghost, "will find him here. What then? If he be like to die, he had better do it, and decrease the surplus population."

Scrooge hung his head to hear his own words quoted by the Spirit, and was overcome with penitence and grief.

But he was early at the office next morning. Oh he was early there. If he could only be there first, and catch Bob Cratchit coming late! That was the thing he had set his heart upon.

And he did it; yes he did! The clock struck nine. No Bob. A quarter past. No Bob. He was full eighteen minutes and a half behind his time. Scrooge sat with his door wide open, that he might see him come into the Tank.

His hat was off, before he opened the door; his comforter too. He was on his stool in a jiffy; driving away with his pen, as if he were trying to overtake nine o'clock.

"Hallo!" growled Scrooge, in his accustomed voice as near as he could feign it. "What do you mean by coming here at this time of day."

"I am very sorry, sir," said Bob. "I am behind my time."

"You are?" repeated Scrooge. "Yes. I think you are. Step this way, if you please."

"It's only once a year, sir," pleaded Bob, appearing from the Tank. "It shall not be repeated. I was making rather merry yesterday, sir."

"Now, I'll tell you what, my friend," said Scrooge, "I am not going to stand this sort of thing any longer. And therefore," he continued, leaping from his stool, and giving Bob such a dig in the waistcoat that he staggered back into the Tank again: "and therefore I am about to raise your salary!"

Bob trembled, and got a little nearer to the ruler. He had a momentary idea of knocking Scrooge down with it; holding him; and calling to the people in the court for help and a strait-waistcoat.

"A merry Christmas, Bob!" said Scrooge, with an earnestness that could not be mistaken, as he clapped him on the back. "A merrier Christmas, Bob, my good fellow, than I have given you, for many a year! I'll raise your salary, and endeavour to assist your struggling family, and we will discuss your affairs this very afternoon, over a Christmas bowl of smoking bishop, Bob! Make up the fires, and buy another coal-scuttle before you dot another i, Bob Cratchit."

———&———

Scrooge was better than his word. He did it all, and infinitely more; and to Tiny Tim, who did NOT die, he was a second father. He became as good a friend, as good a master, and as good a man, as the good old city knew, or any other good old city, town or borough, in the good old world.

Maxim Gorky

"CHRISTMAS PHANTOMS"

～⚬≈⚬～

The great Russian writer Maxim Gorky wrote a very unusual Christmas story. It was a bitter response to the sentimental tragedies that are too often decked out in Christmas garb with no attention paid to the realities of the world around us. The story begins with the author relating the Christmas story that he wrote for the annual Christmas publications. It featured a blind beggar and his wife who wandered off into the snow and froze to death. But before they died, a vision of Jesus came to the beggar and so he died happily if poignantly. But that night, in a dream, the author's bedroom was crowded with all those pathetic figures he had used so lightly in so many stories over the years and a booming voice chastised him.

> "And all the others are also heroes of your Christmas stories-children, men and women whom you made to freeze to death in order to amuse the public. See how many there are and how pitiful they look, the offspring of your fancy! . . ."

I was staggered by this strange indictment. Everybody writes Christmas stories according to the same formula. You take a poor boy or a poor girl, or something of that sort, and let them freeze somewhere under a window, behind which there is usually a Christmas tree that throws its radiant splendor upon them. This has become the fashion and I was following the fashion.

> "You wish to arouse noble feelings in the hearts of men by your pictures of imagined misery, when real misery and suffering are nothing to them but a daily spectacle. . . . If the reality does not

move them. And if their feelings are not offended by its cruel, ruthless misery, and by the fathomless abyss of actual wretchedness, then how can you hope that the fictions of your imagination will make them better? . . ."

I awoke in the morning with a violent headache and in a very bad humor. The first thing I did was to read over my story of the blind beggar and his wife once more, and then I tore the manuscript into pieces.

Surely sentiment and sometimes sadness are a valid part of our Christmas literature. But this odd little tale serves as a timely warning to us not to weep over those things in a story which we would turn our heads away from in real life. The Christmas spirit must live in our day-to-day lives if it is to have any meaning at any time.

O. Henry (William Sidney Porter)

"THE GIFT OF THE MAGI"

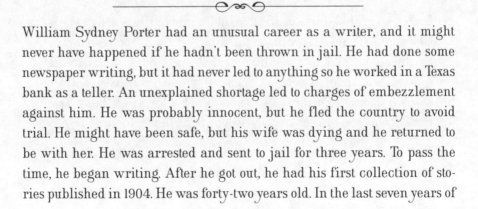

William Sydney Porter had an unusual career as a writer, and it might never have happened if he hadn't been thrown in jail. He had done some newspaper writing, but it had never led to anything so he worked in a Texas bank as a teller. An unexplained shortage led to charges of embezzlement against him. He was probably innocent, but he fled the country to avoid trial. He might have been safe, but his wife was dying and he returned to be with her. He was arrested and sent to jail for three years. To pass the time, he began writing. After he got out, he had his first collection of stories published in 1904. He was forty-two years old. In the last seven years of

his life he wrote hundreds of stories, enough to fill fourteen volumes. The pseudonym which he chose, and which has become far more familiar than his own name, was O. Henry. The greatest popular strength of his stories was also their greatest weakness: the surprise ending. Because of these often contrived plot devices, critics refused to take his work seriously, although his readers loved them.

One of his most successful stories was "The Gift of the Magi," first published in 1905. Here the surprise ending was not a gratuitous plot twist, but the revelation and embodiment of the theme of the story. The plot is a very familiar one. Jim and Della live in the city and have almost no money. Christmas is coming, and Della worries how she will be able to afford a present for Jim. Finally she decides to sell the thing she loves most, her beautiful long hair, to get money to buy a silver chain for Jim's watch, which is his proudest possession. When she gives it to him, he reveals that he has sold his watch to buy a beautiful set of combs for her to wear in her hair.

The style of the story is mildly chatty, with many author's asides and a light air of cynicism. But the final point is deeply felt and beautifully expressed. O. Henry closes by saying, "The magi, as you know, were wise men-wonderfully wise men-who brought gifts to the Babe in the manger. They invented the art of giving Christmas presents. Being wise, their gifts were no doubt wise ones, possibly bearing the privilege of exchange in case of duplication. And here I have lamely related to you the uneventful chronicle of two foolish children in a flat who most unwisely sacrificed for each other the greatest treasures of their house. But in a last word to the wise of these days let it be said that of all who give gifts these two were the wisest. Of all who give and receive gifts, such as they are wisest. Everywhere they are wisest. They are the magi."

Since its publication as a story, "The Gift of the Magi" has appeared in many forms. It has been done as a musical both off-Broadway and on television with Gordon MacRae and Sally Ann Howes. The American Ballet Theatre turned it into a ballet. And it appeared on film in 1952 starring Farley Granger and Jeanne Crain as one of five stories in O. Henry's Full House.

Washington Irving

When Charles Dickens wrote his Christmas pieces, there was another author whose writing on Christmas he probably had in mind. Two years before the composition of *A Christmas Carol,* Dickens wrote to this American author: "There is no living writer, and there are very few among the dead, whose approbation I should feel so proud to earn. And with everything you have written, upon my shelves, and in my thoughts, and in my heart of hearts, I may honestly and truly say so. . . . I should like to travel with you, astride the last of the coaches, down to Bracebridge Hall." The author he addressed was Washington Irving, and he was referring to that writer's famous story of the Christmas celebration at the mythical home of an English squire, Bracebridge Hall. This sketch was published in 1819 in *The Sketch Book of Geoffrey Crayon,* which also contained Irving's most famous story, that of the Headless Horseman in "The Legend of Sleepy Hollow." The story of Bracebridge Hall, with its celebration of all the antique customs, was a first reminder to the British people of the glorious traditions they were in great danger of allowing to fall into total ruin. It kept smoldering the coals that would be blown into glorious life a few years later by the literary bellows that was Charles Dickens. Let us go down by coach with Irving and Dickens to see how Old Christmas may be truly kept.

> The dinner was served up in the great hall, where the squire always held his Christmas banquet. A blazing crackling fire of logs had been heaped on to warm the spacious apartment, and the

flame went sparkling and wreathing up the wide-mouthed chimney. . . .

We were ushered into this banqueting scene with the sound of minstrelsy, the old harper being seated on a stool beside the fireplace, and twanging the roast beef of old England, with a vast deal more power than melody. Never did Christmas board display a more goodly and gracious assemblage of countenances; those who were not handsome were, at least, happy; and happiness is a rare improver of your hard-favoured visage. The parson said grace, which was not a short familiar one, such as is commonly addressed to the deity, in these unceremonious days; but a long, courtly, well-worded one, of the ancient school. There was now a pause, as if something was expected, when suddenly the Butler entered the hall, with some degree of bustle; he was attended by a servant on each side with a large wax light, and bore a silver dish, on which was an enormous pig's head, decorated with rosemary, with a lemon in its mouth, which was placed with great formality at the head of the table. The moment this pageant made its appearance, the harper struck up a flourish; at the conclusion of which the young Oxonian, on receiving a hint from the squire, gave, with an air of the most comic gravity, an old carol, the first verse of which was as follows:

> Caput apri defero
> Reddens Laudes Domino.
> The boar's head in hand bring I,
> With garlands gay and rosemary.
> I pray you all synge merily,
> Qui estis in convivio. . . .

When the cloth was removed, the butler brought in a huge silver vessel of rare and curious workmanship, which he placed before the squire. . . . The old gentleman's whole countenance beamed with a serene look of in-dwelling delight, as he stirred this mighty bowl. Having raised it to his lips, with a hearty wish of a merry Christmas to all present, he sent it brimming round the board, for every one to follow his example according to the primitive custom; pronouncing it "the ancient fountain of good feeling, where all hearts met together." . . .

After the dinner table was removed, the hall was given up to the younger members of the family, who, prompted to all kind of noisy mirth by the Oxonian and Master Simon, made its old walls ring with their merriment as they played at romping games. I delight in witnessing the gambols of children, and particularly at this happy holiday season, and could not help stealing out of the drawing room on hearing one of their peals of laughter. . . .

The door suddenly flew open, and a whimsical train came trooping into the room, that might almost have been mistaken for the breaking up of the court of Fairy. That indefatigable spirit, Master Simon, in the faithful discharge of his duties as lord of misrule, had conceived the idea of a Christmas mummery, or masqueing; and having called in to his assistance the Oxonian and the young officer, who were equally ripe for any thing that should occasion romping and merriment, they had carried it into instant effect. The old housekeeper had been consulted; the antique clothes presses and wardrobes rummaged and made to yield up the reliques of finery that had not seen the light for several generations; the younger part of the company had been privately convened from the parlor and hall, and the whole had been bedizzened out, into a burlesque imitation of an antique masque.

Master Simon led the van as "ancient Christmas," quaintly apparel'd short cloak and ruff, and a hat that might have served for a village steeple, from under which, his nose curved boldly forth, with a frost bitten bloom that seemed the very trophy of a December blast. He was accompanied by the blue-eyed romp, dished up as "Dame Mince Pie," in the venerable magnificence of a faded brocade, long stomacher, peaked hat, and high-heeled shoes. The young officer figured in genuine Kendal Green as Robin Hood; the fair Julia in a pretty rustic dress as Maid Marian. The rest of the train had been metamorphosed in various ways; the girls trussed up in the finery of their great grandmothers, and the striplings bewhiskered with burnt cork, and fantastically arrayed to support the characters of Roast Beef, Plum Porridge, and other worthies celebrated in ancient masqueings. The whole was under the control of the Oxonian, in the appropriate character of Misrule. . . .

It was inspiring to see wild-eyed frolic among the chills and glooms of winter, and old age throwing off his apathy, and catching once more the freshness of youthful enjoyment. I felt an interest in the scene, also, from the consideration that these fleeting customs were posting fast into oblivion; and that this was, perhaps, the only family in England in which the whole of them was still punctiliously observed. There was a quaintness, too, mingled with all this revelry, that gave it a peculiar zest; it was suited to the time and place; and as the old manor house almost reeled with mirth and wassail, it seemed echoing back the joviality of long-departed years.

Dylan Thomas

"A CHILD'S CHRISTMAS IN WALES"

⸺⸺⸺⸺⸺⸺⸺◦⸎⸎◦⸺⸺⸺⸺⸺⸺⸺

Dylan Thomas gave the twentieth century some of its greatest poetry, filled with the songlike rhythms of his native country, Wales. This reminiscence of Christmas is in prose, but it sings like poetry and its song transcends all national boundaries. It was originally a radio script that Thomas read over the Welsh region station of the British Broadcasting Corporation as part of a regular series of programs he had. It was later published separately and has been recorded on records and turned into a television drama.

The story is not a straightforward narrative, but rather poetic memories that blend together into a single great memory called Christmas. As Thomas puts it, "All the Christmases roll down the hill towards the Welsh-speaking sea, like a snowball growing whiter and bigger and rounder, . . . In goes my hand into that wool-white bell-tongues ball of holidays resting at the margin of the carol-singing sea, and out comes . . ." And the memories come pouring out. They are everyday and special, tinged with the glow of reminiscence. There is the fire Thomas remembers trying to put out with snowballs; he and his friends carol the haunted house, and when a thin little voice joins the harmony from inside they run for the comfort of home; there are feasts, and there are gifts. Thomas describes all the glories that lurk in and overflow his stocking of a Christmas morning, including "a celluloid duck that made, when you pressed it, a most unducklike noise, a mewing moo that an ambitious cat might make who wishes to be a cow; and a painting-book in which I could make the grass, the trees, the sea, and the animals any colour I pleased: and still the dazzling sky-blue sheep are grazing in the red field under a flight or rainbow-beaked and pea-green birds." This wonderful story is rather like that painting-book, full of the colorful memories of childhood which were probably never like that, but are nonetheless real.

Henry Van Dyke

"THE OTHER WISE MAN"

American clergyman, author, and educator Henry van Dyke is chiefly known today for his two Christmas stories, "The First Christmas Tree" and "The Other Wise Man." "The First Christmas Tree" was merely a retelling of the legend of St. Boniface and how he replaced the sacred German tree with the fir tree of Christmas. His other story was written in 1896 and is a more original parable of Christmas.

In far-off Persia, Artaban, a Wise Man, observes a new star in the heavens, a star he has been waiting for. He believes the star signifies the coming of the newborn King and Savior. Selling all his possessions, he buys three precious jewels: a sapphire, a ruby, and a pearl. He will give these to the newborn King. He hears of the other Wise Men and sets out to join them. On the first leg of his journey, he comes upon a sick traveler and cares for the man. Because of this, he arrives at the place where he expected to meet the other Magi too late. Going on to Bethlehem alone, he sees neither the other Wise Men nor the Christ Child. Grieved, Artaban begins a lifelong search for the King of Kings. His gifts-the sapphire, the ruby, and the pearl-are one by one used to help the poor and the sick. Artaban is an old man when he comes to Jerusalem on the fateful day of Christ's crucifixion. An earthquake strikes the city as Jesus dies, and Artaban is seriously injured. As his life slips away, a gentle voice comes to him ears: "Inasmuch as you have done it unto one of the least of these my brethren, you have done it unto me." He knows that he has met his Lord.

Poetry

Christmas has inspired some of our greatest poets. John Milton, T. S. Eliot, Robert Browning, and Sir Walter Scott all penned words in honor of the joyous season; so did Ogden Nash, for that matter. Christmas is one of those subjects that almost everyone has to write about eventually. This makes the realm of Christmas poetry a rather large one. Entire books have been devoted to the subject. Therefore, we will not attempt to cover the whole field, but will rather offer some samples of the delights to be found in this particularly evergreen branch of literature.

"A Christmas Carol"

CHARLES DICKENS

Besides *A Christmas Carol*, the novel, Charles Dickens actually wrote a carol for Christmas. It was published in the famous Christmas chapter of *The Pickwick Papers*, and later set to the tune of "Old King Carol" and published in a songbook.

I care not for Spring; on his fickle wing
Let the blossoms and buds be borne;
He woos them amain with his treacherous rain,
And he scatters them ere the morn.
An inconstant elf, he knows not himself,
Nor his own changing mind and hour,
He'll smile in your face, and, with wry grimace,
He'll wither your youngest flower.

Let the Summer sun to his bright home run,
He shall never be sought by me;
When he's dimmed by a cloud I can laugh aloud,
And I care not how sulky he be!
For his darling child is the madness wild
That sports in fierce fever's train;
And when love is too strong, it don't last long,
As many have found to their pain.

A mild harvest night, by the tranquil light
Of the modest and gentle moon,
Has a far sweeter sheen, for me, I ween,
Than the broad and unblushing noon.
But every leaf awakes my grief,
As it lieth beneath the tree;
So let Autumn air be never so fair,
It by no means agrees with me.

But my song I troll out, for CHRISTMAS stout,
The hearty, the true, and the bold;

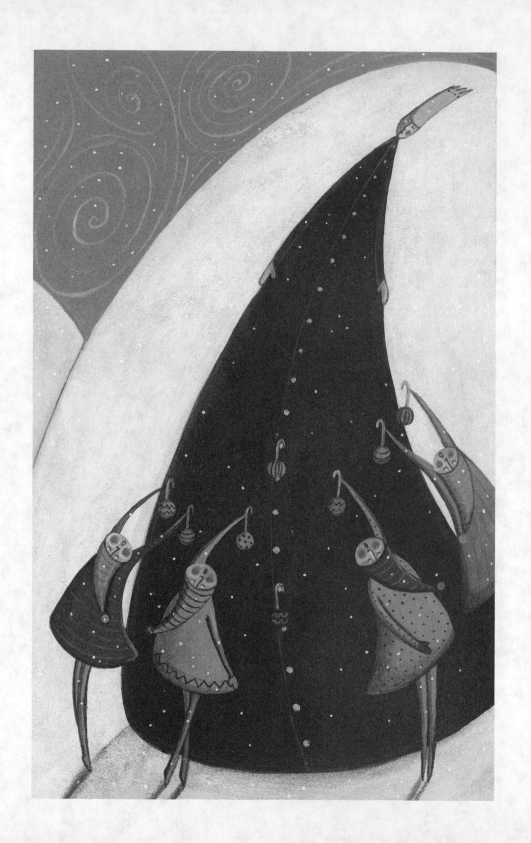

A bumper I drain, and with might and main
Give three cheers for this Christmas old!
We'll usher him in with a merry din
That shall gladden his joyous heart,
And we'll keep him up while, there's bite or sup,
And in fellowship good, we'll part.

In his fine honest pride, he scorns to hide
One jot of his hard-weather scars;
They're no disgrace, for there's much the same trace
On the cheeks of our harvest tars.
Then again I sing till the roof doth ring,
And it echoes from wall to wall-
To the stout old wight, fair welcome to-night,
As the King of the Seasons all!

As in most of his Christmas writings, Dickens is not concerned with the
specifically religious nature of the holiday but with the cheerfulness and
good feeling between people. Also, Christmas to him is not just a day but an
entire season, just like spring, summer, and autumn in the other stanzas.
His overflow of fellow-feeling could not be confined to a mere day.

"Christmas" (1836)

LEIGH HUNT

Christmas comes! He comes, he comes,
Ushered in with a rain of plums;
Hollies in the windows greet him;
Schools come driving post to meet him,
Gifts precede him bells proclaim him.
Every mouth delights to name him; . . .
And he has a million eyes
Of fire, and eat a million pies,
And is very merry and wise;
Very wise and very merry,
And loves a kiss beneath the berry. . . .

O plethora of beef and bliss!
Monkish feaster, sly of kiss!
Southern soul in body Dutch!
Glorious time of great Too-Much!
Too much heat, and too much noise,
Too much babblement of boys;
Too much eating, too much drinking,
Too much ev'rything but thinking;
Solely bent to laugh and stuff,
And trample upon base Enough;
Oh, right is thy instinctive praise
Of the wealth of Nature's ways.
Right the most unthrifty glee,
And pious thy mince-piety! . . .

"Christmas Night of '62"

In The Army of Northern Virginia, 1862

WILLIAM G. MCCABE

The wintry blast goes wailing by,
The snow is falling overhead;
I hear the lonely sentry's tread,
And distant watch-fires light the sky.

Dim forms go flitting through the gloom;
The soldiers cluster round the blaze
To talk of other Christmas days,
And softly speak of home and home.

My sabre swinging overhead,
Gleams in the watch-fire's fitful glow,
While fiercely drives the blinding snow,
And memory leads me to the dead.

My thoughts go wandering to and fro,
Vibrating 'twixt the Now and Then;
I see the low-browed home again,
The old hall wreathed with mistletoe.

And sweetly from the far-off years
Comes borne the laughter faint and low,
The voices of the Long Ago!
My eyes are wet with tender tears.

I feel again the mother kiss,
I see again the glad surprise
That lightened up the tranquil eyes
And brimmed them o'er with tears of bliss,

As, rushing from the old hall-door,
She fondly clasped her wayward boy-
Her face all radiant with the joy
She felt to see him home once more.

My sabre swinging on the bough
Gleams in the watch-fire's fitful glow,
While fiercely drives the blinding snow
Aslant upon my saddened brow.

Those cherished faces all are gone!
Asleep within the quiet graves
Where lies the snow in drifting waves,-
And I am sitting here alone.

There's not a comrade here to-night
But knows that loved ones far away
On bended knee this night will pray:
"God bring our darling from the fight."

But there are none to wish me back,
For me no yearning prayers arise.
The lips are mute and closed the eyes-
My home is in the bivouac.

"The Bells"

EDGAR ALLAN POE

In the first section of his poem "The Bells," Edgar Allan Poe describes the sound of the sleigh or sledge bells that are such an important part of our nostalgic Christmas sounds.

Hear the sledges with the bells,
Silver bells!
What a world of merriment their melody fortells!
How they tinkle, tinkle, tinkle,
In the icy air of night!
While the stars, that oversprinkle
All the heavens, seem to twinkle
With a crystalline delight;
Keeping time, time, time,
In a sort of Runic rhyme,
To the tintinnabulation that so musically wells
From the bells, bells, bells, bells,
Bells, bells, bells-
From the jingling and the tinkling of the bells.

"A Christmas Carol"

CHRISTINA ROSSETTI

Before the paling of the stars,
Before the winter morn,
Before the earliest cock-crow
Jesus Christ was born:
Born in a stable,
Cradled in a manger,
In the world His hands had made
Born a stranger.

Priest and King lay fast asleep
In Jerusalem,
Young and old lay fast asleep
In crowded Bethlehem:
Saint and angel, ox and ass,
Kept a watch together,
Before the Christmas daybreak
In the winter weather.

Jesus on His mother's breast
In the stable cold,
Spotless Lamb of God was He,
Shepherd of the fold:
Let us kneel with Mary maid,
With Joseph bent and hoary,
With Saint and angel, ox and ass,
To hail the King of Glory.

"Excerpt from Hamlet"

WILLIAM SHAKESPEARE

Some say that ever 'gainst that season comes
Wherein our Saviour's birth is celebrated,
The bird of dawning singeth all night long:
And then they say, no spirit dare stir abroad;
The nights are wholesome; then no planets strike,
No fairy takes, nor witch hath power to charm,
So hallow'd, and so gracious, is that time.

It is a curious fact that this passage from Hamlet is the only one devoted to the topic of Christmas in all of the writings of Shakespeare. The great poet who dealt so completely with all the emotions of humanity for some reason was uninterested in that most joyous season of the year. He uses the word "Christmas" only three times in all the mass of his works, each time to describe a time of year only, not to talk about the day itself.

"A Christmas Carol"

GEORGE WITHER

In this seventeenth-century poem Wither happily describes the boisterous joy of Christmas in that long-gone era.

So, now is come our joyfulst FEAST;
Let every man be jolly.
Each Roome, with Ivie leaves is drest;
And every Post, with Holly.

Though some Churles at our mirth repine,
Round your foreheads Garlands twine,
Drowne sorrow in a Cup of Wine.
And let us all be merry.

Now, all our Neighbours Chimneys smoke,
And CHRISTMAS blocks are burning;
Their Ovens, they with bakt-meats choke,
And all their spits are turning.
Without the doore, let sorrow lie:
And, if for cold, it hap to die,
We'll bury't in a CHRISTMAS Pie.
And evermore be merry.

Now, every LAD is wondrous trim,
And no man minds his Labour.
Our Lasses have provided them,
A Bag-pipe, and a Tabor.
Young men, and Mayds, and Girles & Boyes.
Give life, to one anothers Joyes:
And, you anon shall by their noyse,
Perceive that they are merry.

The Client now his suit forbeares,
The Prisoners heart is eased,
The Debtor drinks away his cares,
And, for the time is pleased.
Though other purses be more fat,
Why should we pine or grieve at that?
HANG SORROW, CARE WILL KILL A CAT.
And therefore let's be merry.

"A Visit from St. Nicholas"

CLEMENT CLARKE MOORE (ATTRIBUTED)

—————— ❧ ——————

According to legend, Clement Clarke Moore, an ordained minister and professor of literature, recited the now famous line, "'Twas the night before Christmas" at a party in his New York City home on December 22, 1822. A young lady who was one of Moore's guests copied the poem down for her own pleasure. The following Christmas, she sent the poem anonymously to the *Sentinel* newspaper in Troy, New York, which published it on December 23, 1983. In the years that followed, versions and excerpts of the poem appeared in newspapers, almanacs and periodicals throughout the country, but it wasn't until 1844 that Clement Clarke Moore accepted authorship of the poem, formally entitled "A Visit from St. Nicholas," and later even included it in a volume of his own poetry. Some historians believe that Henry Livingston, a Revolutionary War veteran residing in upstate New York, may have actually authored the poem as early as 1807, but today most Americans still associate it with the now-legendary Clement Clarke Moore.

'Twas the night before Christmas, when all through the house
Not a creature was stirring, not even a mouse;
The stockings were hung by the chimney with care,
In hopes that St. Nicholas soon would be there;
The children were nestled all snug in their beds,
While visions of sugar-plums danced in their heads;
And mamma in her kerchief, and I in my cap,
Had just settled our brains for a long winter's nap,
When out on the lawn there arose such a clatter,
I sprang from the bed to see what was the matter.
Away to the window I flew like a flash,
Tore open the shutters, and threw up the sash;
The moon, on the breast of the new-fallen snow,
Gave a lustre of midday to objects below;
When what to my wondering eyes should appear
But a miniature sleigh and eight tiny reindeer,
With a little old driver, so lively and quick,
I knew in a moment, it must be St. Nick.
More rapid than eagles his coursers they came,
And he whistled and shouted and called them by name:
"Now *Dasher!* now *Dancer!* now *Prancer!* now *Vixen!*
On, *Comet!* on, *Cupid!* on, *Donder* and *Blitzen!*
To the top of the porch! to the top of the wall!
Now dash away, dash away, dash away, all!"
As dry leaves that before the wild hurricane fly,

When they meet with an obstacle, mount to the sky,
So up to the house-top the coursers they flew,
With the sleigh full of toys and St. Nicholas too.
And then, in a twinkling, I heard on the roof
The prancing and pawing of each little hoof.
As I drew in my hand and was turning around,
Down the chimney St. Nicholas came with a bound.
He was dressed all in fur, from his head to his foot,
And his clothes were all tarnished with ashes and soot;
A bundle of toys he had flung on his back,
And he looked like a peddler just opening his pack.
His eyes: how they twinkled! his dimples: how merry!
His cheeks were like roses, his nose like a cherry;
His droll little mouth was drawn up like a bow,
And the beard of his chin was as white as the snow.
The stump of a pipe he held tight in his teeth,
And the smoke, it encircled his head like a wreath:
He had a broad face, and a little round belly,
That shook, when he laughed, like a bowl full of jelly:
He was chubby and plump, a right jolly old elf;
And I laughed, when I saw him, in spite of myself,
A wink of his eye and a twist of his head
Soon gave me to know I had nothing to dread.
He spoke not a word, but went straight to his work,
And filled all the stockings; then turned with a jerk,
And laying his finger aside of his nose,
And giving a nod, up the chimney he rose.
He sprang to his sleigh, to his team gave a whistle,
And away they all flew like the down of a thistle;
But I heard him exclaim, ere he drove out of sight,
"Happy Christmas to all, and to all a good-night!"

Letters

Robert E. Lee Writes to His Wife

December 25, 1861

I cannot let this day of grateful rejoicing pass without some communion with you. I am thankful for the many among the past that I have passed with you, and the remembrance of them fills me with pleasure. As to our old home, if not destroyed it will be difficult ever to be recognized.

. . . It is better to make up our minds to a general loss. They cannot take away the remembrances of the spot, and the memories of those that to us rendered it sacred. That will remain to us as long as life will last and that we can preserve. . . .

"Yes, Virginia . . ."

Dear Editor,

I am 8 years old. Some of my little friends say there is no Santa Claus. Papa says, "If you see it in The Sun, it's so." Please tell me the truth, is there a Santa Claus?

∾ Virginia O'Hanlon

The year was 1897 but the question is a timeless one. The *New York Sun* assigned Francis P. Church, a veteran newspaperman who had been with the Sun for twenty years, to answer this seemingly unanswerable question. His reply is one of the most famous newspaper editorials of all time:

Virginia, your little friends are wrong. They have been affected by the skepticism of a skeptical age. They do not believe except what they see. They think that nothing can be which is not comprehensible by their little minds. All minds, Virginia, whether they be men's or children's, are little. In this great universe of ours, man is a mere insect, an ant, in his intellect as compared with the boundless world about him, as measured by the intelligence capable of grasping the whole of truth and knowledge.

Yes, Virginia, there is a Santa Claus. He exists as certainly as love and generosity and devotion exist, and you know that they abound and give to your life its highest beauty and joy. Alas! how dreary would be the world if there were no Santa Claus! It would be as dreary as if there were no Virginias. There would be no childlike faith then, no poetry, no romance to make tolerable this existence. We should have no enjoyment, except in sense and sight. The eternal light with which childhood fills the world would be extinguished.

Not believe in Santa Claus! You might as well not believe in fairies. You might get your papa to hire men to watch in all the chimneys on Christmas eve to catch Santa Claus, but even if you did not see Santa Claus coming down, what would that prove? Nobody sees Santa Claus, but that is no sign that there is no Santa Claus. The most real things in the world are those that neither children nor men can see. Did you ever see fairies dancing on the lawn? Of course not, but that's no proof that they are not there. Nobody can conceive or imagine all the wonders there are unseen and unseeable in the world.

You tear apart the baby's rattle and see what makes the noise inside, but there is a veil covering the unseen world which not the strongest man, nor even the united strength of all the strongest men that ever lived could tear apart. Only faith, poetry, love, romance, can push aside that curtain and view and picture the supernal beauty and glory beyond. Is it all real? Ah, Virginia, in all this world there is nothing else real and abiding.

No Santa Claus! Thank God! he lives and lives forever. A thousand years from now, Virginia, nay 10 times 10,000 years from now, he will continue to make glad the heart of childhood.

Peace in the Trenches, 1914

W.R.M. Percy, London Rifle Brigade

We had a rather interesting time in the trenches on Christmas Eve and Christmas Day. We were in some places less than a hundred yards from the Germans, and we talked to them. It was agreed in our part of the firing line that there should be no firing and no thought of war on these days, so they sang and played to us several of their own tunes and some of ours, such as "Home Sweet Home" and "Tipperary"' etc., while we did the same for them.

The regiment on our left all got out of their trenches and every time a flare went up they simply stood there, cheered and waved their hats, and not a shot was fired on them. The singing and playing continued all night, and the next day (Christmas) out fellows paid a visit to the German trenches and they did likewise. Cigarettes, cigars, addresses etc. were exchanged, and everyone, friend or foe, were real good pals. One of the German officers took a photo of English and German soldiers arm in arm, with exchanged caps and helmuts.

On Christmas Eve the Germans burnt coloured lights and candles along the top of their trenches, and on Christmas Day a football match was played between them and us in front of the trench. They even allowed us to bury all out dead lying in front, and some of them, with hats in hand, brought in one of our dead officers from behind their trench so that we could bury him decently. They were really magnificent in the whole thing, and jolly good sorts. I have now a very different opinion of the German. Both sides have now started firing and are deadly enemies again. Strange it all seems, doesn't it?

Christmas on Film

The history of Christmas in the movies is somewhat difficult to trace because it is hard to determine exactly what is a Christmas movie. The simplest way to define it would be as a movie about the birth of Jesus, but if you define it that way, then there are very few Christmas movies. There were a few silent films as early as 1909 which dealt exclusively with the Nativity, but this was possible because movies were so much shorter then and did not have to have all the elements of good drama.

Other films set in Christ's time have included the nativity scene briefly as part of the story. Often this appears almost as a frozen picture with voice-over narration telling the story. Thus, movies such as *King of Kings, The Greatest Story Ever Told,* and *Ben Hur* deal briefly with the Nativity, but can hardly be considered Christmas movies.

Many other movies that are not really about Christmas use the holiday season as a setting or background. This is an old writer's device. If you want to write a story in which something sad happens, the best way to do it is to set it as the happiest time you can think of. The contrast between the sad occurrence and the cheerful background make it all the more poignant. Thus the viewer must be prepared in dramatic movies when everyone sits down to a happy Christmas dinner. It probably means that news of a death is about to arrive, romance is about to sour, or the boat is about to sink.

Perhaps the best and only definition possible of a Christmas movie is that it takes as its theme some aspect of the Christmas spirit, be it Santa Claus, gift-giving, or the joy of family reunion.

Three Godfathers (1936, 1948)

This western shows allegorically how the birth of Christ touches even the most hardened souls. The movie was made twice: once in 1936 with Chester Morris, Lewis Stone, and Walter Brennan; and again in 1948 with John Wayne, Pedro Armendariz and Harry Carey, Jr., with John Ford directing. The story tells of three bandits escaping from the law across the Arizona desert. They come upon a dying woman who is about to give birth. Their hearts are melted and they aid her in delivering her child. When she dies, they are left with the self-imposed rather joyful responsibility of caring for the infant. This symbolic Christ Child causes them to reform, even in the face of approaching death.

Beyond Tomorrow (1940)

This is a fantasy story of three rich, lonely men played by Charles Winninger, Harry Carey, and C. Aubrey Smith. They hit on the idea of dropping their wallets in the street and sharing Christmas with whoever is honest enough to return them. Only two are returned, by Richard Carslon and Jean Parker. The three men play Cupid, and all seems to be on the right track until a plane crash kills all three. Trouble sets in for the young couple, as the man has become a successful singer and is being wooed away by the traditional gorgeous vamp. The three men return as ghosts to try to finish up what they started before they receive their final call the "Great Beyond."

Christmas in July (1940)

This excellent movie has little to do with Christmas except its infectious spirit of the delight of gift-giving. Preston Sturges, the master of the screwball comedy, directed this often-hilarious film. Dick Powell plays a man who thinks he has won a slogan contest. He immediately begins playing Santa Claus to everyone in the neighborhood—all on credit. Christmas overspenders will appreciate his plight when he finds that he didn't win the contest.

Remember the Night (1940)

This touching film features Fred MacMurray as an assistant D.A. preparing to go home for the Christmas holidays. A shoplifter is to be held until after the recess for her day in court, but MacMurray is concerned about her having to spend Christmas in jail. When he finds she has no place to go, he invites her to his home in Indiana. Played by Barbara Stanwyck, the worldly-wise shoplifter goes to take advantage of him, but learns from the influence of a simple and modest Christmas and ends up loving him. When the case is brought up in court, he tries to lose it, but she pleads guilty to save him from jeopardizing his position. They promise to wed after she has paid her debt to society. Mitchell Leisen directed this film, scripted by Preston Sturges, well known as the writer and director of some of the greatest "screwball comedies." The 1997 remake, *On the 2nd Day of Christmas,* stars Mary Stuart Masterson and Mark Ruffalo.

Meet John Doe (1941)

This film is sometimes warm and amusing, sometimes hard-bitten and cynical. A bored newspaper reporter (Barbara Stanwyck) fills a slow news day by making up a letter from "John Doe," an average citizen so upset by modern conditions that he is going to jump from the roof of City Hall on Christmas Eve. Tremendous publicity results and she has to produce a real John Doe. She hires an out-of-work baseball player (Gary Cooper) to play the part. Easy-going and simple, he sees nothing wrong with the scheme. A national cult springs up of organizations devoted to helping all the "John Does" in the land and learning to be friends and good neighbors. It all looks wonderful, but then Cooper finds that he is being used to realize the political ambitions of an unscrupulous millionaire (Edward Arnold). When he tries to tell the people the truth, Arnold reveals him as a fake and all the John Doe clubs are disbanded in a fit of disillusionment. Cooper disappears for months. Then on Christmas Eve, he goes to the roof of City Hall. He is going to jump, not to prove a point, but because had has become the real John Doe and he owes it to all the people who believed in him. Arnold's men try to stop him from becoming a martyr, but it is Stanwyck who saves him. The tough reporter has seen the truth, that people can be good, that a bunch of average men can stand up to anyone if they'll just believe. She reminds him of the "first John Doe," whose birthday is celebrated on Christmas. He comes down with her to begin the fight again.

Holiday Inn (1942)

The story of this popular movie concerns a song-and-dance man who creates an inn that opens only on holidays. This gives the excuse for a dozen holiday songs by Irving Berlin. Love interest is provided by Bing Crosby and Fred Astaire good-naturedly competing for the heart of Marjorie Reynolds. This film would have no more to do with Christmas than any other month of the year if it weren't for Bing's crooning of "White Christmas," which won the Oscar for Best Song of 1942 and turned into the biggest-selling record of all time.

Christmas in Connecticut (1945)

This pleasant film is a welcome and frequent part of TV's holiday fare. Released in 1945, it stars Barbara Stanwyck as an unmarried writer who has sold a number of articles describing the joys of married life on a Connecticut farm from a first-person viewpoint. Her publisher, Sydney Greenstreet, decides it would be good for her to have a war hero, Dennis Morgan, as her family's Christmas guest. The fun concerns her attempts to produce a reasonable facsimile of a farm and a husband so she won't lose her job.

I'll Be Seeing You (1945)

This sentimental drama stars Ginger Rogers as a convict who is allowed to go home for Christmas. On the train she meets Joseph Cotton, a soldier returning home from World War II with severe emotional problems as he must adjust to civilian life. Their love affair helps to restore both of them to the joys of life. The supporting cast includes Shirley Temple, Spring Byington, and Chill Wills.

It's a Wonderful Life (1946)

This is perhaps the best-known Christmas film of all time. Jimmy Stewart plays a small-town banker whose biggest dream has always been to leave his small town and to see the world where he can amount to something. But he is always thwarted in his efforts to leave because he keeps sacrificing himself for the other people of the town. When it looks as though his company will fail and a lot of people will lose their savings, it is his honeymoon money that goes to save them; when the unscrupulous millionaire Lionel Barrymore tries to take the company over after the death of Stewart's father, it is Jimmy who cancels his travel plans to stay and preserve the company; when his uncle (Thomas Mitchell) foolishly loses a great sum of money, it is Jimmy who takes the blame and faces jail.

This is the situation on Christmas Eve. He has devoted his life to his family and his town, and now he faces ruin and disgrace. He stands at the edge of the bridge and looks down into the ice-clogged, swirling waters below him. He climbs the rail. But before he can jump, there is another splash. With the same selflessness that he has shown all his life, he leaps to rescue the other person from the dark waters. But this is not just an ordinary person he has saved but his own rather inept guardian angel, Clarence, played by Henry Travers. In a self-pitying moment, Jimmy wishes that he had never been born. Clarence, who is hoping to earn his wings on this case, grants his wish and takes him on a tour of his hometown to see what it would be like if he had never lived. It is a hopelessly different world. The corrupt millionaire runs the town as a vice jungle; a misguided girl he helped at a crucial moment is a dance hall girl; the pharmacist he saved from a fatal error when he was just a delivery boy is an ex-convict and a drunk. The whole town reeks of the cynicism and the self-disgust that he has always stood against without even knowing it. He begs for his life to be restored, willing to face personal shame and ruin if these people he has known and loved can be restored, too. His wish is granted and he waits happily to be taken to jail. But it is not to be. There are earthly miracles, too, and the townspeople pour out their love and their money to save him in a joyous affirmation that one man's life can make a big difference in the world.

And Clarence wins his wings.

Even if this film were set on the Fourth of July, it would be a Christmas film, perhaps the best of all. It is filled with unsickly sentiment and with principles that are unashamedly part of the American and the Christmas spirit. Frank Capra directed and co-authored this 1946 film. Donna Reed plays Jimmy Stewart's wife and equals him in some of the most amusing, touching, and honest love scenes imaginable. What do you call a tearjerker that inspires only tears of joy?

The Bishop's Wife (1947)

This comedy features Gary Grant as an angel named Dudley. He is sent to earth to aid David Nivin, the bishop, who is having troubles with his wife, Loretta Young, as well as financial troubles in raising money for a new cathedral. Dudley performs a number of delightful Christmas miracles to set all to rights. Also on hand is an excellent supporting cast, including Monty Woolley, James Gleason, Elsa Lanchester, and Gladys Cooper.

Christmas Eve (1947)

In this comedy-drama, Ann Harding plays an eccentric and wealthy widow who faces a dilemma on Christmas Eve. Her unscrupulous nephew is going to have her committed to an asylum in order to gain control of her financial affairs. She depends on her three adopted sons to show up and save her, even though they are scattered around the world. The three wards are played by George Raft, George Brent, and Randolph Scott. With that threesome on your side, could there be any doubt that good triumphs?

Miracle on 34th Street (1947)

This is probably the best-known and one of the best of all Christmas movies. It has had two interesting side effects: probably more people know which street Macy's Department Store is located on than the address of any other store in the world; and this film solidified for all time the idea that Kris Kringle is just another name for Santa Claus. (It is actually a corruption of Christkind, the Christ Child or angel who brings gifts to much of northern Europe at Christmastime.)

Edmund Gwenn plays Kris Kringle, a harmless old eccentric who lists eight reindeer as his next of kin and claims that he really is Santa, although he lives in an old folks' home on long Island. He is hired by Macy's to play Santa Claus, but doubts about his sanity lead to a courtroom trial. The final proof of his identity is provided by the Post Office, which decides to dump all the Santa Claus mail they have on him as an easy way of getting rid of it. He is therefore proclaimed authentic by an agency of the United States Government.

The story is also about the romance of John Payne, who sort of believes, and Maureen O'Hara, who has taught her daughter Natalie Wood that it is wrong to believe in fairy tales and Santa Claus. Without ever really finding definite proof, all come by the end to realize the importance of believing in things that can't be proved.

Twentieth Century-Fox didn't realize what it had on its hands when it released this film in 1947. It came out in the spring, of all times. It was a tremendous hit and won three Academy Awards, including Best Supporting Actor for Edmund Gwenn. The film was made into a book, appeared three times in TV adaptations, and was the basis for Meredith Wilson's Broadway musical *Here's Love.* According to National Telefilm Associates, this film appears on TV more often than any other.

Tenth Avenue Angel (1947)

This sentimental movie came out in 1947 (a good Christmas year for the streets of New York; besides this and *Miracle on 34th Street,* New York City was also the setting for the film *It Happened on Fifth Avenue*). The story is of a little dreamer growing up in New York's tenements. Margaret O'Brien is the little girl who has trouble distinguishing between reality and make-believe as she plays matchmaker for her aunt, Angela Lansbury, and an ex-convict, George Murphy. The climax comes when she sees a calf kneel in the deserted stockyards at midnight on Christmas Eve, proving her mother right in her assertion that the animals kneel at the moment of Christ's birth.

Holiday Affair (1949)

Janet Leigh stars in this pleasant comedy-drama as a young war widow with a child. She is working as a comparison shopper when she meets Robert Mitchum, a toy salesman, at Christmastime. They are great opposites-she needs someone who can accept responsibility and he just wants to run away and build boats-but of course they fall in love. Wendell Corey is on hand as the stuffy lawyer she finally throws over to go with her heart.

The Lemon Drop Kid (1951)

This Damon Runyan story has twice been made into a movie, the first time in 1934 with Lee Tracy and Helen Mack. The much better known and still-shown version was made in 1951 with Bob Hope and Marilyn Maxwell. The story concerns a typical Runyan character, played by Hope, who gets into trouble when he gives a big gangster's moll a wrong tip at a dog track. To atone, he has to come up with ten grand by Christmas morning. From that point, the lot becomes typically confused, but it basically concerns Hope dressing up as Santa in a wild scheme to get the necessary cash. Hope and Maxwell introduce the well-known song "Silver Bells" in this film, which is chockfull of topically amusing gags and antics by Hope and a supporting cast that includes Lloyd Nolan and William Frawley.

The Holly and the Ivy (1954)

This excellent English film takes a family Christmas reunion as its setting. A strong-willed vicar comes to realize that he has failed his children in the ways they most needed him. All is gradually set right against the background of the English Christmas scene. This somewhat slow story is kept strongly alive by the cast, headed by Ralph Richardson and featuring Celia Johnson, Margaret Leighton, and Denholm Elliott.

White Christmas (1954)

"If at first you do succeed, try again bigger" often seems to be Hollywood's motto. Occasionally it works out well, as in this remake of *Holiday Inn*. This version is more lavish and was the first film shot in Vista Vision, a process for improving the quality of the print. Wisely, Bing Crosby was back to sing the title song and also introduced the song "Count Your Blessings" as part of the revised score. He was most ably assisted by Danny Kaye, Rosemary Clooney, and Vera-Ellen.

All Mine to Give (1958)

This film stars Glynis Johns and Cameron Mitchell as the pioneer parents of six children in early Wisconsin. Much of the film traces their hardships in carving out a place for themselves. With the untimely death of the parents, the oldest boy is faced with the impossibility of caring for the younger children. On Christmas morning he sets out to find homes for them among the neighboring families. The Christmas setting heightens the poignancy of this touching story.

Mickey's Christmas Carol (1983)

This is an animated adaptation of Charles Dickens' classic 1843 tale of the miser Ebenezer Scrooge, here voiced by Alan Young. Donald Duck and other Walt Disney mainstays appear.

It Came Upon a Midnight Clear (1984)

In this tender Christmas tale, Mickey Rooney stars as Mike, a retired New York City policeman who promises to take his grandson from California to New York to show him a white Christmas, but dies before it can happen. After striking a deal with the Archangel of Heaven, Mike returns to Earth for one week to fulfill his promise.

Santa Claus (1985)

This Christmas tale, which traces the origins of St. Nicholas, was a hit with both young and old audiences when it premiered in 1985. Starring Dudley Moore as the hero elf Patch, this is a beautifully filmed, light-hearted Yule comedy.

National Lampoon's Christmas Vacation (1989)

Chevy Chase stars as the head of the Griswold family in this Lampoon comedy. Despite its slapstick nature, the film is nevertheless poignant and appealing in its holiday spirit. The film was the highest-grossing at the box office the week of its release. Cast members include Beverly D'Angelo, Randy Quaid, E.G. Marshall, Diane Ladd, John Randolph and William Hickey.

Home Alone (1990)

This Christmas film was the top box office film of 1990. A simple enough tale of a family on Christmas holiday who mistakenly leave one child behind. Home alone, the child (played by Macaulay Culkin) must hold down the fort and deal with house burglars who prove to be no match for the youngster. Not since *Miracle on 34th Street* has a Christmas film been so talked about. This perfect family Christmas film also includes cast members Joe Pesci, Daniel Stern, John Heard, and Catherine O' Hara, as well as the hit song by John Williams, "Somewhere in My Memory."

All I Want for Christmas (1991)

In this charming comedy set in New York City, two siblings use their wits to fulfill their one Christmas wish: to have their divorced parents back together again. The cast includes Leslie Nielsen and Lauren Bacall.

Yes Virginia, There is a Santa Claus (1991)

This endearing film has become a television favorite at Christmas time. Based on a factual occurrence, Charles Bronson stars as Francis Church, a journalist for the *New York Sun* in 1897 who answers a letter from a little girl named Virginia (played by Katherine Isabelle). (See page 291.)

Christmas in Connecticut (1992)

A television remake of the 1945 film which originally starred Barbara Stanwyck and Dennis Morgan, this new version imbues each scene with a pleasant Christmas spirit. Starring Tony Curtis, Dyan Cannon, and Kris Kristofferson, and directed by Arnold Schwarzenegger.

Home Alone 2: Lost in New York (1992)

The family is on vacation for Christmas once again, but due to a mistake at the airport, the young boy (again played by Macaulay Culkin) finds himself on a plane to New York City. Starring much of the same original cast, including the house burglars portrayed by Joe Pesci and Daniel Stern, this film yields touching and hilarious results.

The Muppet Christmas Carol (1992)

Miss Piggy and Kermit the Frog help carry off Charles Dickens' Christmas tale of long ago in Victorian England. A genuine Christmas treat for children, this film conveys the true joys of the holidays and is enlivened by its Muppet performances.

Mixed Nuts (1994)

Sunny California is the setting of this Christmas comedy about a crisis hotline during the holidays. Steve Martin and Madeline Kahn head a funny cast in this lighthearted film, complete with Santa Claus and a manger scene.

The Santa Clause (1994)

Tim Allen makes an impressive film debut as a dad who actually becomes Santa Claus, infusing the audience's hearts with warmth as he bestows gifts of hope and love at Christmas.

Jingle All the Way (1996)

Arnold Schwarzenegger stars in this Christmas comedy as a father who must race against the clock to find a popular gift for his son. This funny and touching film also stars Harvey Korman and James Belushi as Santa Claus.

The Preacher's Wife (1996)

This remake of the 1947 Cary Grant film *The Bishop's Wife* is the story of an angel who visits earth to help mend a troubled marriage. Denzel Washington stars as Dudley, an angel who answers the prayers of Reverend Henry Biggs, played by Courtney B. Vance. Whitney Houston stars as Reverend Biggs' wife, and lends her voice to much of the film's soundtrack.

How the Grinch Stole Christmas (2000)

Based on the children's bestseller by Dr. Seuss, this is a live-action retelling of the original 1966 made-for-television animated film, with Jim Carrey in the starring role. Anthony Hopkins narrates this tale of a dastardly malcontent's attempt to steal Christmas from the town of Whoville. Directed by Ron Howard, the film is complete with lively songs the memorable performances of supporting cast members Bill Irwin, Christine Baranski and Jeffrey Tambor. Makeup artists Rick Baker and Gail Ryan won Oscars for their artistic talents.

The Santa Clause 2 (2002)

Tim Allen stars as Santa Claus in this feature film. At the behest of his elves, he re-reads his Santa Claus contract, which obliges the Christmas gift-giver to search for a wife. Critics loved this film, which was rich with high comedy and joyous Christmas music.

Elf (2003)

This is a lively comedy about a man raised as one of Santa's elves in the North Pole, who travels to New York City to find his father and discover his true identity. Saturday Night Live alum Will Ferrell stars as the six-foot tall high-spirited elf Buddy, while James Caan plays his selfish and irritable father who is in need of some holiday spirit. Also starring Bob Newhart, Mary Steenburgen, and Zooey Deschanel.

Actors Playing Santa

Edmund Gwenn won the Best Supporting Actor Oscar for playing Kris Kringle in *Miracle on 34th Street* in 1947, and has since become the model for that role. But a great number of other actors-including some rather unlikely choices-have donned the red suit and beard for even just a few minutes in the course of a movie:

ACTOR	MOVIE AND YEAR
Frank Morgan	Dangerous Nan McGrew (1930)
Jimmy Durante	The Christmas Party (1931)
Robert Livingston	Three Godfathers (1936)
Tex Ritter	Down the Wyoming Trail (1939)
Cary Grant	My Favorite Wife (1940)
Edward G. Robinson	Larceny, Inc. (1942)
Monty Woolley	Life begins at 8:30 (1942)
Robert Cummings	The Bride Wore Boots (1946)
Errol Flynn	Never Say Goodbye (1946)
Bob Hope	The Lemon Drop Kid (1951)
Mickey Rooney	The Year Without a Santa Claus (1974)
Mickey Rooney (again)	Rudolph and Frosty's Christmas in July (1979)
John Malkovich	Rabbit Ears: Santabear's High Flying Adventure (1987)
Lloyd Bridges	In the Nick of Time (1991)

Richard Attenborough....................Miracle on 34th Street (1994)
Edward Asner.................................The Story of Santa Claus (1996)
John Goodman................................Rudolph the Red-Nosed Reindeer: The
                                                                Movie (1998)
Leslie Nielsen...................................Santa Who? (2000)
James Earl Jones............................Recess Christmas: Miracle on Third
                                                                Street (2001)
Kelsey Grammer.............................Mr. St. Nick (2002)
Joe Piscopo.......................................Dear Santa (2002)
Edward Asner (again)...................Elf (2003)

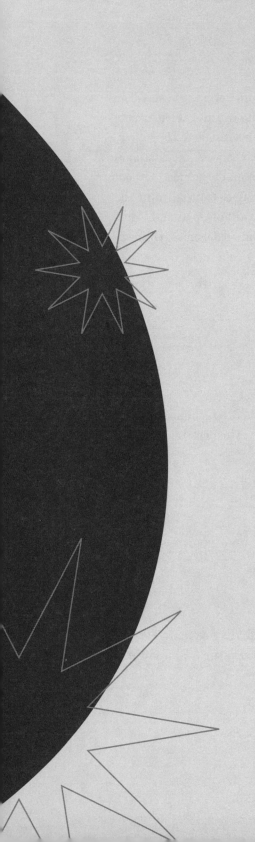

Christmas on the Table

The food of Christmas has always been one of its glories. The Christmas meal is a festive and decorative one, and what it may lack in subtlety, it more than makes up for in substance. The following recipes offer a mere introduction to the full range of international Christmas foods, as entire books have been written on the subject without exhausting the possibilities. These traditional recipes from all over the world represent some of the wonderful diversity available to us at this joyous time of year. The recipes are arranged into four categories: Dinners, Breads, Desserts, and Drinks.

Dinners

❖ Spiced Pork ❖

Pork is a common Christmas meat in the United Kingdom. It is best served hot and with mashed potatoes and gravy. The pork in this spice-rubbed recipe takes about 24 hours to prepare.

1 6-lb. boneless pork shoulder, tied
¼ cup packed light brown sugar
¼ cup kosher salt
2 tbsp. dried juniper berries
1 tbsp. whole black peppercorns
1 tbsp. whole allspice

Finely grind the juniper berries, peppercorns, and allspice in an electric coffee/spice grinder, then stir together with the brown sugar and salt in a small bowl. Rub the spice mix all over the pork and chill for 1 day in a sealed plastic bag.

Transfer the pork to a large pot and cover with cold water by 1 inch. Bring to a boil, then reduce heat and simmer, covered, adding more water as needed to keep the pork submerged, about 3–3 ½ hours.

Transfer the pork to a cutting board and let stand 25 minutes before slicing.

⁙ Turkey ⁙

Turkey is the main course in more Christmas dinners than any other type of meat or fowl. The high proportion of meat to unusable bone and fat makes it an ideal bird for a feast. Turkeys were domesticated in Mexico long before Spanish explorers found them and introduced them into their homeland. From there they spread throughout Europe and gradually replaced most of the native Christmas feast foods.

BASIC PREPARATION FOR COOKING

Remove paper of giblets from body (save giblets for gravy or use in stuffing). Also remove any loose fat from body cavity. Wipe bird with a damp cloth but do not wash (most birds coming to market today are beautifully cleaned and dressed: washing them merely destroys some of their flavor). Singe off any hairs and remove pinfeathers. Sprinkle neck and body cavity with salt.

HERBED BREAD STUFFING

There are many possible stuffings for turkey. This is a good basic one. It makes about 2 quarts, enough to stuff a 10-12 pound bird.

  10 cups 1-inch cubes of crusty country-style bread
  3 medium onions, chopped
  3 celery ribs, thinly sliced crosswise
  1 tsp. dried thyme
  ½ tsp. dried sage
  ½ tsp. dried rosemary
  1 stick unsalted butter
  1 ½ cups chicken broth
  ½ cup water

Preheat oven to 325° F.

Toast bread in a large shallow baking pan in middle of oven until just dry, 25-30 minutes.

Cook onions, celery and herbs in butter in a large heavy skillet over moderately low heat, stirring occasionally, until celery is softened, about 10 minutes.

Stir together bread, vegetables, broth, water, and salt and pepper to taste. Then cool completely, uncovered. Proceed to stuff the turkey.

NOTE: Do not stuff a bird until *just* before roasting; and *do not* let a stuffed bird stand at room temperature because of the danger of food poisoning.

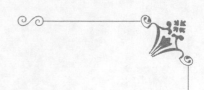

TO TRUSS A BIRD

After stuffing bird, skewer or sew openings shut, then truss by folding the wings back and underneath body and tying drumsticks close to body so bird will have a more compact shape and roast more evenly.

BREAST-UP METHOD FOR A WHOLE BIRD

This is the preferred way today; it produces an exquisitely brown bird. Preheat oven to 325° F. Prepare turkey as above and place breast side up on a rack in a shallow roasting pan. Insert meat thermometer in thigh or stuffing, not touching bone, and roast uncovered, according to times given below. Baste, if you like, with melted butter or margarine every ½-¾ hour. If bird browns too fast, tent breast loosely with foil.

Roasting times with oven temperature of 325°F

4-8 pounds	2 ½-3 ½ hours
8-12 pounds	3 ½-4 ½ hours
12-16 pounds	4 ½-5 ½ hours
16-20 pounds	5 ½-6 ½ hours
20-24 pounds	6 ½-7 hours

Internal temperature when done will be 180-85° F.

BREAST-DOWN METHOD FOR A WHOLE BIRD

Though this method produces juicier breast meat, it has disadvantages: The breast skin is apt to stick to the rack and tear as the turkey is being

turned, and the act of turning a hot, hefty turkey is both difficult and dangerous. Preheat oven to 325˚ F. Prepare turkey for roasting as directed and place breast side down in a V rack in a shallow roasting pan. Roast uncovered until half done according to the above roasting chart, turn breast side up, insert thermometer in thickest part of inside thigh, not touching bone, and continue roasting, uncovered, until done. Baste, if you like, during cooking with drippings or melted butter.

FAST FOIL METHOD FOR A WHOLE BIRD

This is the method to use for birds, especially big ones, that must be cooked in a "hurry." Turkeys cooked this way will have more of steamed than roasted flavor. Preheat oven to 450˚ F. Prepare turkey for roasting as directed and place in the center of large sheet of heavy foil: brush well with softened butter, margarine, or shortening. Bring foil up on both sides of breast and make a simple overlapping fold at the top, smooth down around turkey, then crumple ends of foil up to hold in juices. Place turkey breast side up in a shallow roasting pan and roast as follows:

Ready-to-Cook Weight	Total Roasting Time
6-8 pounds	1 ½-2 hours
8-12 pounds	2-2 ½ hours
12-16 pounds	2 ½-3 hours
16-20 pounds	3-3 ½ hours
20-24 pounds	3 ½-4 hours

About 30-40 minutes before turkey is done, open tent of foil and fold back and away from bird so it will brown nicely.

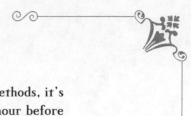

NOTE: When roasting turkey by any of the three preceding methods, it's a good idea to cut string holding drumsticks to tail about 1 hour before bird is done so that inner legs and thighs will brown.

⁘ Classic Gravy ⁘

This recipe utilizes the juices left over in the pan after cooking the turkey.

3 cups chicken broth (or less, depending on
how much pan juice there is)
3 tbsp. butter
3 tbsp. all-purpose flour
1 tsp. chopped fresh thyme (or ½ tsp. dried)
1 small bay leaf
2 tbsp. apple brandy (optional)

Strain the pan juices from the turkey into a large measuring cup, and skim any solids and visible fat from top of the juice. Add enough chicken broth to the pan juices to measure 3 cups total. Transfer the liquid to a heavy medium saucepan and bring to a boil.

Mix together the butter and flour in a small bowl to form a smooth paste. Whisk the paste into the broth mixture. Add chopped fresh thyme and the bay leaf.

Boil the mixture until it reduces down to a sauce consistency, whisking occasionally, about 10 minutes. Mix in apple brandy, if desired, and season to taste with salt and pepper.

❧ Cranberry Sauce ❧

When paired with roast turkey, this fruity sauce can be a refreshing alternative to gravy.

1 12-oz. package of cranberries (can be fresh or frozen)
1 cup water
⅞ cup sugar
¼ cup apricot or pineapple preserves

Place the cranberries in a large bowl of cool water. Fresh cranberries should float in water, so any cranberries that sink should be removed. Also remove any stems left on the berries, and discard any berries that are discolored or very hard. Drain the water off and set the berries aside.

In a medium saucepan, mix the sugar and water over medium heat, stirring until the sugar is dissolved. Bring to a boil and add the cranberries. The cranberries will expand and begin to pop. Carefully stir the mixture until all the cranberries have popped.

Add the preserves and continue to stir until a consistent texture is achieved. Remove from heat and allow to cool. If a smoother sauce consistency is desired, mix it in a food processor, or use a wire strainer to remove the skin and seeds. Pour into a serving bowl and refrigerate until ready to serve.

❧ Goose ❧

Before the European advent of the turkey, the goose was one of the favorite Christmas meals. Goose is still a prime contender in some countries such as Denmark, where it is traditionally stuffed with apples and prunes.

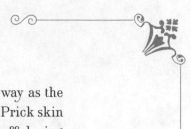

Preheat oven to 325° F. Prepare bird for roasting in the same way as the turkey. Also rub insides well with half a lemon before stuffing. Prick skin well all over with a sharp fork so fat underneath will drain off during cooking. Rub skin well with salt (this helps to crispen skin).

Place bird breast side up on a rack in a shallow roasting pan and roast uncovered, draining off drippings as they accumulate and pricking as needed.

NOTE: For a particularly crisp skin, raise oven temperature to 450° F during last ½ hour of roasting. Also, drain all drippings from pan and spoon ¼-½ cup ice water over bird.

Roasting times with oven temperature of 325°:

4-6 pounds	2 ¾-3 hours
6-8 pounds	3-3 ½ hours
8-12 pounds	3 ½-4 ½ hours
12-14 pounds	4 ½-5 hours

GOOSE STUFFING

8 oz. prunes
8 oz. bread crumbs
1 lb. cooking apples, cored, peeled and chopped

Wash the prunes and soak them overnight in cold water. Use the same water the next day to simmer them until moderately soft. Drain and pit the prunes. Chop them finely and mix with the bread crumbs. Add the apples and a little of the prune juice if necessary to bind the mixture.

⚜ Baked Country Ham ⚜

Country ham is a traditional part of Christmas dinner in the Southern states. This recipe is for one with an orange juice and brown sugar glaze.

    1 12- 14-lb. country ham
    2 tsp. whole cloves
    8 cups apple cider or apple juice
    Orange Juice and Brown Sugar Glaze (recipe below)

Place the ham in a sink and cover with cold water. Soak overnight, changing the water once. Next day, scrub ham in warm water with a stiff brush and rinse well. Cut the skin from the ham and trim off fat. Insert cloves into the ham.

Preheat oven to 325° F.

Place the ham, fat side up, in a large roasting pan. Insert a meat thermometer into the thickest portion of the ham, making sure it doesn't touch fat or bone. Pour the apple cider or apple juice over the ham.

Bake the ham, covered, for 4-4 ½ hours, or until the meat thermometer registers 160° F. Drain off pan juices, glaze, and serve.

ORANGE JUICE AND BROWN SUGAR GLAZE

    1 ¼ cups packed light brown sugar
    3 tbsp. orange juice
    ½ tsp. ground cloves

Mix sugar, orange juice and cloves together in medium bowl to form thick paste. Set aside until ready to glaze the warm ham.

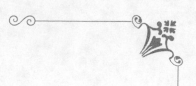

✤ Vegetarian Lasagna ✤

While Christmas feasts are often associated with an assortment of juicy meats, fowl, and fish, vegetarian dishes are becoming a more prevalent feature on the contemporary Christmas table.

9 lasagna noodles
20 oz. chopped spinach, fresh or frozen
    (if frozen, thawed and squeezed dry)
2 cups sliced mushrooms
1 cup grated carrots
½ cup finely chopped onion
1 ½ cups sliced zucchini, optional
2 8 oz. cans tomato sauce
1 6 oz. can tomato paste
2 eggs
2 cups ricotta cheese
2 ½ cups shredded mozzarella cheese
2 tbsp. dried parsley
1 ½ tsp. oregano
1 tsp. basil
1 tsp. coarsely ground black pepper, preferably fresh
½ tsp. garlic powder
Parmesan cheese

Cook lasagna noodles until just done. Drain and run cold water over them to cool, then lay the noodles out on paper towels.

In a saucepan cook the onions, carrots and zucchini until just tender. Add the mushrooms and cook until tender as well. Then add the tomato sauce, paste, spices and garlic powder. Once all the ingredients are mixed well, set aside.

In a mixing bowl, whip together the ricotta cheese, parsley and eggs. Add a dash of black pepper.

Grease a deep 9x13-inch dish or foil lasagna pan. Lay 3 noodles along the bottom, then layer with half of the ricotta cheese mixture, followed by half of the spinach, approximately one-third of the mozzarella cheese, and then one-third of the tomato sauce mixture. Repeat the layers. Top with the remaining 3 lasagna noodles, the final third of the tomato sauce, and the last bit of mozzarella cheese. Liberally grate some Parmesan cheese over the top.

Bake in an oven at 375° F for 45 minutes. Let stand 15 minutes before cutting and serving.

⁂ Cold Ginger Chicken ⁂

Hawaii

Because of Hawaii's multi-ethnic population, any holiday feast is resplendent with a blend of Hawaiian, Asian and European cuisines. This dish is a popular choice for luaus and other large gatherings.

  1 whole chicken
  ¼ cup ginger, minced
  ¼ cup green onion, minced
  salt to taste
  ½ cup cooking oil (peanut or vegetable)

Clean chicken and carefully immerse in a pot of boiling water. Lower heat to a simmer, and poach chicken for 45 minutes to 1 hour. Cool, and cut into serving pieces.

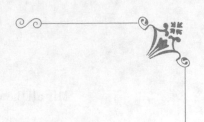

Heat cooking oil until it is near-smoking

NOTE: Be very cautious when handling oil at such extreme temperatures.

Combine the ginger, onion and salt in a heatproof container, and carefully pour the hot oil into the mixture. Allow to cool.

Place chicken pieces in a serving dish and spread the ginger sauce over it.

⁎ Ensalada de Navidad ⁎

Mexican Christmas Salad

This fruity salad is a refreshing accompaniment to the traditional Mexican Christmas feast of roast turkey, tamales, *atole* (a thick beverage made from corn or rice) and *ponche* (a warm fruit punch with tequila).

2 small cooked beets, peeled and diced
1 large cooked carrot, diced
1 orange, peeled and chopped
1 apple, peeled and diced
¼ fresh pineapple, peeled, cored and diced
1 large banana, diced
½ cup unsalted almonds or peanuts
seeds of ½ pomegranate
1 tbsp. lime or lemon juice
3 tbsp. salad oil
½ tsp. sugar
dash of salt

Mix all the vegetables and fruits together in a salad bowl.

Combine the lime or lemon juice, salad oil, sugar, and salt in a jar and shake until it is well blended and the sugar has dissolved. Pour the dressing over the salad and toss well.

Garnish with the nuts and pomegranate seeds. Let stand in the refrigerator until ready to serve. Serve chilled.

⚜ Tamal Navideño ⚜

Costa Rican Christmas Tamales

These little Costa Rican rolls are filled with an assortment of ingredients. The principle ingredient in the tamal dough is masa, which is white field corn that has been dried, treated with a lime-water solution, and then ground to a flourlike consistency.

TO MAKE THE TAMAL DOUGH

5 lb. masa
1 cup concentrated pork broth
1 cup concentrated chicken broth
4 chicken bouillon cubes
1 tbsp. Worcestershire sauce
6 strips bacon, cooked and crumbled
½ tsp. black pepper
2 cups mashed potatoes

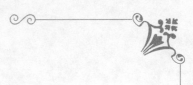

Combine all ingredients in a large pot and mix well. Bring to a boil on low heat, stirring constantly to prevent sticking. Remove the mixture from heat as soon as it starts to boil.

TO MAKE THE TAMALES

Take 2 pieces of banana leaf, one on top of the other, and place 3 tbsp. of tamal dough in the center. Into the dough press:

1 small piece cooked pork
1 small piece cooked chicken
4-5 green peas
1 green olive
4-5 raisins
1 small piece cooked carrot
4-5 capers
1 strip bell pepper
4-5 chickpeas
1 tsp. cooked rice, flavored with paprika powder

Wrap up the sides of the leaves, forming a brick shape. Stack the tamales together, seams facing inward, and tie with a string or twine. Place the tied tamales in hot water and boil for half an hour. Serve hot.

⁂ Tourtiére ⁂

This savory pie dish is traditionally served at Christmas and New Year's in the French-influenced provinces of Canada. Customarily, it is a double-crust pie with a spiced mixture of ground pork, beef, and potato; however the ground meat can be replaced with a vegetarian meat substitute.

Pastry for a 9-inch double-crust pie
½ lb. ground pork
½ lb. ground beef
1 large baking potato, boiled and mashed
2 tbsp. vegetable oil
1 large onion, diced
2 garlic cloves, minced
1 bay leaf
1 tsp. dried thyme
½ tsp. salt
½ tsp. coarse black pepper
¼ tsp. cloves
¼ tsp. ginger
¼ tsp. dry mustard

Preheat oven to 425° F, and line a 9-inch pie plate with the pastry. Roll out the remaining pastry to a flat round for the top of the pie, and set aside.

Brown the beef and pork in a large skillet and drain the fat. In another skillet, heat the oil and sauté the onion and garlic until tender. When the onion and garlic are cooked, remove from heat and add the meat, potato and spices. Combine well and allow the mixture to cool slightly.

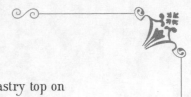

Spread the mixture in the prepared pie shell and place the pastry top on the pie. Seal the edges with a little water, turning the crust under and fluting decoratively. Bake for about 20 minutes or until browned.

Let stand 5 minutes before cutting into wedges.

⚜ Aardappel Kroketjes ⚜

Belgian Potato Croquettes

This vegetarian dish is a versatile accompaniment to almost any entrée.

    3 russet potatoes
    ½ cup water
    3 tbsp. unsalted butter, cut into pieces
    1 tsp. salt
    pinch of nutmeg
    ½ cup all-purpose flour
    2 eggs
    vegetable oil for frying

Preheat oven to 425° F. Place whole potatoes on a baking sheet and bake until soft, about one hour. Let the potatoes cool slightly, then peel and mash them. Measure out 2 cups of mashed potatoes and set aside.

Combine water, butter, salt, and nutmeg in a medium saucepan. Bring to a boil and stir in the flour. Reduce the heat to medium and beat the mixture with a wooden spoon until the paste pulls away from the sides of the pan and forms a ball, about 3 minutes. Remove from the heat and add the eggs, one at a time, beating well after each one. Beat the mixture until smooth and shiny.

Add the 2 cups of mashed potatoes and mix well.

Heat oil on high in a deep frying pan. Scoop potato mixture with a large tbsp. and drop into the oil, flattening each croquette with the back of the spoon. Cook until crisp and golden on one side, then turn over and repeat. Transfer to paper towels, dry and serve.

⊰ Graavilohi ⊱

Freshly-Salted Salmon

A customary Christmas dinner in any of the Scandinavian countries will include a wide selection of fresh and pickled fish. While most fish can be bought pre-prepared, this Finnish recipe for salted salmon is simple enough that many people still prefer to make their own. In America, it is most often referred to as gravlax, and often served with a light mustard vinaigrette and boiled potatoes.

  2 lbs. fresh filleted salmon
  1 ½-2 tbsp. coarse-ground salt
  1 tsp. sugar (optional)
  1 tsp. freshly ground white pepper
  plenty of fresh dill

Cut the fillet into 2 pieces. Combine the sugar and salt and rub the fillet pieces with the mixture. Sprinkle with the pepper and some sprigs of dill.

Press the two fillets together, with the skin sides outwards. Take a plate or shallow dish and sprinkle some more salt on the bottom, then place the fillets on it. Sprinkle some more salt on the top.

Cover with plastic wrap and place a weight on top to ensure that the fillets are pressed together tightly—a cutting board often works well. Refrigerate the fish for 1-2 days, turning it every so often.

Before serving, cut the fish away from the skin into thin slices or strips. Arrange on a plate with slices of lemon and more sprigs of fresh dill.

❖ Svenska julköttbullar ❖

Swedish Meatballs

Meatballs are only a small part of the smorgasbord of Swedish delicacies featured on the traditional Christmas buffet. Other dishes include beet salad, pickled fish, braised cabbage, sausage and pâtés.

18 oz. ground meat (half pork, half beef)
4 tbs. fine, dried breadcrumbs
½ cup water
½ cup cream
1 onion, finely chopped
1 egg
1 ½ tsp. salt
dash white pepper
pinch sugar
butter for frying

Combine the breadcrumbs, water and cream in a large bowl, and allow the breadcrumbs to expand.

Sauté the onion in a skillet until soft, but not colored. Allow to cool.

Stir the ground meat, onion, egg, salt, and spices into the breadcrumb mixture and blend well. Shape into small meatballs.

Fry the balls in a frying pan with the butter. Shake the occasionally to ensure that the meatballs are browned on all sides. Rinse and wipe out the pan between each addition of new, unfried balls.

⁘ Kuba ⁘

Czech Barley Pudding

This Czech barley casserole dish is traditionally served on Christmas Eve.

2 cups dried mushrooms
1 cup barley
7 cups water
½ cup butter
¾ cup onion, finely chopped
2 tsp. salt
2 cloves garlic, finely minced
¼ tsp. pepper

Cook the onion with the butter in a large pot until translucent. Make sure

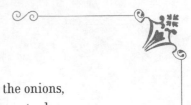

the mushrooms are washed and free from grit before adding to the onions, along with the barley, water, and salt. Cook, uncovered, until the water has evaporated, stirring frequently (the mixture will be very thick). Add the remaining ingredients.

Place the mixture in a greased casserole or baking dish, and bake at 350°F for 30-35 minutes.

⁓ Fufu ⁓

African Vegetable Balls

In Western and Central African cooking, fufu is a typical accompaniment to almost any stew or dish served with sauce. The starchy balls are most commonly prepared with yams, but can also be made with plantains, maize, semolina, and even rice.

   2-4 lbs. large white or yellow yams
   (or equal parts yams and plantain bananas)
   1 tsp. butter

Place yams in a large pot and cover with water. Bring to a boil and cook until the yams are soft, about half an hour. Remove pot from heat and cool yams under running water. Drain and peel. Add butter and mash together until the yams reach a smooth consistency.

Shape the fufu into balls and serve immediately with meat stew or any dish with a sauce or gravy. To eat, tear off a small handful of fufu and use it to scoop up meat and/or sauce.

Breads

⁂ Panettone ⁂

Italian Christmas Bread

Makes a tall 9-inch loaf.

1 ½ cakes fresh baker's yeast
¼ cup granulated sugar
6 tbsp. warm milk
6 egg yolks, lightly beaten
zest of one lemon, finely grated
1 tsp. vanilla extract
pinch of salt
2 ½ cups flour
6 tbsp. butter, cut into small pieces
4 tbsp. sultana raisins
6 tbsp. minced candied citron
or mixed candied fruits
4 tbsp. currants

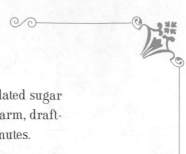

In a large mixing bowl, sprinkle yeast and 1 tbsp. of the granulated sugar over the warm milk and let sit 3 minutes; mix and let sit in a warm, draft-free place until the mixture has doubled in volume, about 5 minutes.

Add egg yolks, lemon zest, vanilla, salt, and the remaining sugar. Gradually knead in 2 cups of the flour by hand, until a smooth consistency is attained (the dough should easily form into a ball). Add the butter and beat until the dough becomes smoother and more elastic. Then add ½ to 1 cup more flour until the dough is firm and soft, but not sticky.

Place the dough on a floured surface and knead until the dough is smooth and shiny, about 10 minutes. Place dough in a buttered bowl, dust lightly with flour, cover with a kitchen towel, and allow to rest in a warm, draft-free place until it has doubled in volume, about 45 minutes.

With the dough still in the bowl, punch it down firmly and flatten it out as much as possible. Add the candied citron/mixed fruits, raisins and currants, and knead until well distributed but without working the dough more than necessary.

Preheat oven to 400° F. Line a large bread pan with brown paper that has been well-buttered on both sides; place the dough in the pan and trace a cross on the top. Cover with more buttered paper and let rise again for 15 minutes. Remove the paper from the top and brush with softened butter. On the middle rack of the oven, bake for 10 minutes; then reduce heat to 350°F and continue baking for another 30-40 minutes, occasionally brushing with melted butter. The surface should be golden and crispy.

⊹ Stollen with Almonds ⊹

Classic German Christmas Bread

This sweet German bread can be served with an icing glaze dribbled over the top or simply on its own.

FOR THE SPONGE

1 ⅓ cups plus 1 ½ tsp. lukewarm milk
1 ½ tsp. lukewarm water
1 ½ tsp. sugar
1 fresh yeast cake
2 ⅔ cups all-purpose flour

Stir 1 ½ tsp. lukewarm milk, 1 ½ tsp. lukewarm water and 1 ½ tsp. sugar in a large bowl. Add yeast and sir until smooth. Let stand until foamy, about 10 minutes. Add flour and remaining 1 ⅓ cups lukewarm milk and mix well. Cover and let sponge rise in warm, draft-free area until doubled in volume, about 1 hour and 15 minutes.

FOR THE DOUGH

3 ½ cups plus 3 tbsp. all-purpose flour
1 ⅓ cups raisins
⅔ cup blanched, slivered almonds
⅔ cup chopped, candied fruit
1 cup unsalted butter, room temperature

1 cup sugar
2 eggs
1 tbsp. ground cardamom
1 tsp. vanilla extract
½ tsp. salt

Mix 3 tbsp. flour with the raisins, almonds and candied fruit in a medium bowl. In a large bowl, beat the unsalted butter and sugar with an electric mixer until light and fluffy. Beat in eggs, cardamom, vanilla, and salt. Beat in the sponge mixture. Stir in the fruit and nuts. Slowly mix in enough of the remaining flour (about ½ cup at a time) to form a slightly sticky dough. Turn the dough out onto a lightly floured surface and knead until smooth and elastic, adding more flour if very sticky, about 10 minutes.

Lightly oil a large bowl. Add dough, turning to coat the entire surface. Cover bowl with plastic wrap and allow dough to rise in a warm, draft-free area until doubled in volume, about 2 ½ hours.

After dough has risen, punch down and divide in half. Pat each half into a 10x16-inch oval and fold in half lengthwise. Place the two pieces on a large, greased cookie sheet. Cover and let rise in a warm, draft-free area until the dough doubles in volume again, about 2 hours.

Position rack to the lowest third of the oven and preheat to 350° F. Bake until loaves are golden and sound hollow when tapped on bottom, about 1 hour. Transfer to a rack and cool slightly. Serve warm or at room temperature

NOTE: Stollen can be prepared up to 1 day ahead.

⁂ Christopsomo ⁂

Greece

This traditional sweet bread is baked for the Christmas holiday in various parts of Greece. A truly authentic recipe calls for masticha flavoring. It is a flavoring made from the sap of a mastichodendro bush, which grows only on island of Chios, and is a difficult product to find outside of Greece. Vanilla extract makes a suitable substitute.

1 ½ packages active dry yeast
¼ cup lukewarm water
¾ cup plus ½ tsp. sugar
3 ½-4 cups plus 1 tbsp. all-purpose flour
½ tsp. salt
3 eggs
¾ cups milk, scalded and cooled
½ tsp. masticha flavoring or vanilla extract
1 stick unsalted butter, melted
½ cup blanched, slivered almonds
¼ cup white raisins
½ tsp. grated lemon peel

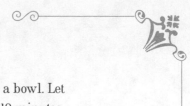

Combine yeast, water, ½ tsp. sugar, 1 tbsp. flour, and ¼ tsp. salt in a bowl. Let stand in a warm place until mixture bubbles and foams, about 10 minutes.

In a large bowl, beat the remaining sugar together with the remaining salt, 2 eggs, cooled milk, and the yeast mixture. Add 1 ½ cups of the remaining flour, along with the vanilla extract. Next add melted butter, almonds, raisins, and lemon peel. Continue to add the rest of the flour, kneading well until dough is stiff but elastic.

Place the dough in a greased bowl and cover first with plastic wrap, and then with a damp towel. Let the dough rise in a warm place until it doubles in volume. Punch down and turn over in bowl. Cover and let rise for 30 minutes more.

Preheat oven to 350° F. On a flat surface, shape the dough into three ropes and braid together. Place the braid on a lightly-greased cookie sheet and let rise for 40 minutes.

Beat the remaining egg and brush the braid with it. Bake for 30 minutes or until golden brown.

❖ Makowiec ❖

Poland

This traditional roll containing a gooey poppy-seed filling is especially popular during the holiday season.

FOR THE DOUGH

4 tsp. active dry yeast
1 tbsp. sugar
1 pinch salt
1 cup warm milk
3 cups flour
1 egg
1 egg yolk
4 tsp. vanilla extract
4 tbsp. butter, melted

Mix together yeast, sugar, and salt in a large bowl. Pour in milk and stir until dry ingredients dissolve. Whisk in 1 cup of flour, cover, and let rise in a warm place until doubled, about 15 minutes.

Stir in egg, egg yolk, and vanilla extract. Knead remaining 2 cups flour and the butter into mixture, a little at a time. Continue to knead until smooth and elastic, about 15 minutes. Place dough in a large bowl, cover, and let rise until doubled, about 1 hour.

FOR THE FILLING

1 cup poppy seeds, rinsed
½ cup sugar
4 tbsp. butter
¼ cup raisins
¾ cup almonds, ground
¼ tsp. vanilla extract
4 tbsp. honey
1 egg white
1 egg white, lightly beaten

Simmer poppy seeds in a medium saucepan with water until soft, about 40 minutes. Drain and purée in a food processor, about 4 minutes. Return purée to same saucepan; add sugar, butter, raisins, almonds, vanilla extract, and honey. Cook, stirring over medium-low heat for 15 minutes. Set aside to cool.

MAKING THE ROLL

Preheat oven to 350° F and roll out dough to a 16x12" rectangle.

Whisk unbeaten egg white in a bowl until stiff peaks are formed, then fold into the poppy seed filling. Spread over the dough, leave a 1-inch border for the edges. Fold dough lengthwise in thirds to form a long log, and pinch ends to seal.

Place roll on a nonstick baking sheet. Brush with beaten egg white and bake for about 50 minutes, or until it sounds hollow when tapped. Cool before serving.

Desserts

⁂ Bûche de Noël ⁂

This classic French Christmas cake is shaped and decorated to resemble a Yule log (*bûche*" means "log" in French). Light and airy meringues resembling mushrooms are the traditional garnish.

FOR THE CAKE

1 ¼ cups cake flour
1 tsp. baking powder
½ tsp. salt
7 large eggs, separated
1 cup sugar
1 tsp. vanilla extract
3 tbsp. confectioner's sugar
½ tsp. ground cinnamon

Preheat the oven to 375° F, and line a 17x11-inch jelly roll pan with parchment paper. Brush with melted butter and dust with flour.

Sift the flour, baking powder, and salt together onto a sheet of parchment paper. Beat the egg yolks and ¾ cup of the sugar with a whisk attachment in an electric mixture until the mixture is thick and lemon colored. Add the dry ingredients at a low speed, mixing until just incorporated. Add the vanilla, mix quickly and thoroughly, and set aside (the batter should be quite thick).

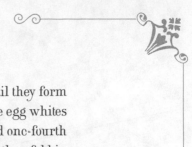

In a separate bowl, whisk the egg whites with a pinch of salt until they form soft peaks. Add the remaining ¼ cup of sugar and whisk until the egg whites are glossy and form peaks that stand up, but are not too stiff. Fold one-fourth of the egg whites into the cake batter until they are incorporated, then fold in the remaining egg whites, working quickly. Be sure not to overmix.

Spread the batter in the prepared pan and bake until the cake is golden and a slight indention is made in the top of the cake when pressed, about 8-10 minutes.

While the cake is baking, sift the confectioner's sugar over a clean kitchen towel. Remove the cake from the oven, and immediately invert it onto the sugar-dusted towel. Peel the parchment paper from the cake, and starting from one long side, gently roll the cake up in the towel. Allow it to cool for 30 minutes.

FOR THE FILLING AND FROSTING

21 oz. bittersweet chocolate
1 ½ cups crème fraîche or heavy, non ultra-pasteurized cream
½ cup chestnut purée

Melt the chocolate and the cream together in a medium-sized saucepan over medium heat. Shake the pan occasionally, and when the chocolate has completely melted, whisk the mixture so it is completely combined. Let it cool to room temperature, so it will be thick enough to spread. To make the frosting, transfer ¾ cup of the chocolate mixture to a small bowl and whisk in the chestnut purée. Season with vanilla if desired.

When the cake has cooled, unroll it and trim off the edges so it is perfectly even, reserving the trimmings. Spread the filling evenly over the cake, leaving ⅛-inch from the edges, and roll the cake back up. Roll the trimmings into 2 spirals, and affix them to the sides of the cake with any leftover filling.

Using the frosting, generously frost the cake, including the spiral ends. Let the cake rest for about 15 minutes, then decorate it in the traditional manner. First, using the tines of a fork, create the texture of a log by gently dragging the fork along the length of the cake. Then continue with other decorative pieces. Allow the cake to sit for at least 8 hours before serving.

⸎ Chocolate Haupia Pie ⸎

Hawaii

Haupia is a traditional coconut pudding that is a staple dessert at every Hawaiian luau. It can be served on its own, but also makes a creamy addition to other dessert recipes for more special occasions.

1 9-inch pie crust (can be homemade or store-bought)
1 can coconut milk
1 cup sugar
1 cup milk
½ cup cornstarch
1 cup water
7 oz. semi-sweet chocolate
1 ½ cups heavy whipping cream
¼ cup confectioner's sugar
chocolate shavings, for garnish

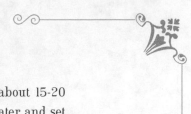

Preheat oven to 350° F. Bake pie crust until golden brown, about 15-20 minutes. In a medium bowl, whisk together cornstarch and water and set aside. In a medium saucepan, whisk coconut milk, milk and sugar. Bring mixture to a boil, stirring often. Reduce heat to a simmer, and whisk in cornstarch mixture until thickened. Set aside.

Melt semi-sweet chocolate and combine in a bowl with half of the coconut mixture (haupia). Pour into the pie shell. Layer the rest of the coconut mixture on top. Cool the pie in refrigerator for at least 1 hour.

Whip heavy cream with sugar until stiff peaks form. Garnish the pie with whipped cream and chocolate shavings. Chill for at least another hour before serving.

❖ Christmas Crescents ❖

These nutty half-moon-shaped cookies are a tasty alternative to the traditional chocolate-chip cookie—Santa will be grateful for the change!

    1 cup butter, softened
    5 tbsp. sugar
    2 tsp. vanilla extract
    2 tbsp. water
    ½ tsp. salt
    2 cups flour
    2 cups chopped pecans

Preheat oven to 325° F.

Cream butter with the sugar, water, and vanilla extract. Combine thoroughly. Mix in flour and salt. Add chopped pecans.

Take approximately one tablespoon of dough and roll into a walnut-sized ball. Using the palms of your hands, roll the dough into a tube shape and then curl it into the shape of a crescent.

Place on a cookie sheet and bake for 25 minutes. While still warm, roll the crescent cookies in powdered sugar.

❧ Date Pudding ❧

Although plum pudding is the dessert most commonly associated with the traditional British Christmas feasts evoked by writers such as Charles Dickens, date pudding is a more popular dish for today's tastes and much easier to prepare.

FOR THE BATTER

1 cup brown sugar
1 tbsp. butter
1 tsp. baking powder
½ tsp. salt
1 tsp. cinnamon
1 cup milk
1 cup chopped dates
½ cup walnuts
2 cups flour

Cream together brown sugar and butter; add milk. Blend in baking powder, salt, cinnamon and flour until smooth. Add dates and walnuts. Set aside batter.

FOR THE BOTTOM LAYER

2 cups water
½ cup granulated sugar
2 tbsp. butter

Preheat oven to 350° F.

Combine water, granulated sugar and butter in a saucepan and bring to a boil. Remove from heat. Pour the mixture into a 9x12-inch pan, and then pour the batter on top of it.

Bake in oven for 30 minutes, or until lightly brown. Serve hot with ice cream or whipped topping.

⚜ Eskimo Doughnuts ⚜

Alaska

These savory deep-fried snacks are a popular treat to hand out to carolers.

5 lbs. flour
palm full of yeast
palm full of salt
raisins

Mix the ingredients together and add warm water to form a soft dough. Put in a dry, warm place, and allow to rise until the dough has a pot belly. With greased or floured hands, pull doughnut-sized pieces off the dough and make a hole in the middle with a finger. Work the dough in your palms to make a doughnut shape. Fry in hot oil until golden brown and place on paper towels or cloth to absorb excess oil. Serve warm or at room temperature.

⨝ Glorious Golden Fruitcake ⨝

This is a traditional season favorite which can be served with an optional pineapple glaze.

    4 cups sifted flour
    1 ½ teaspoon baking powder
    ½ teaspoon salt
    2 cups butter or regular margarine
    2 ½ cups sugar
    6 eggs
    ¼ cup milk
    4 cups chopped walnuts
    ½ cup chopped candied pineapple
    1 cup golden raisins
    ½ cup chopped red candied cherries
    ½ cup chopped green candied cherries
    1 tablespoon grated lemon rind
    Pineapple Glaze (recipe below)
    pecan halves

Sift together flour, baking powder and salt. Reserve ¼ cup of the mixture and set aside.

Cream together butter and sugar until light and fluffy. Add eggs, one at a time, beating well after each addition. Add sifted dry ingredients alternately with milk, beating well after each addition.

Combine walnuts, pineapple, raisins, candied cherries, lemon rind and the reserved ¼ cup flour; toss gently to coat. Stir into batter. Spread batter in greased and waxed paper-lined 10-inch tube pan.

Bake in oven at 275° F for 2 hours 45 minutes. Cool in pan on rack 30 minutes. Remove from pan and allow to cool on rack longer.

Wrap fruitcake tightly in foil. Store in refrigerator up to 4 weeks. (Fruitcake keeps better if stored unfrosted.) Can be served alone or drizzled with pineapple glaze and pecan halves sprinkled on top.

PINEAPPLE GLAZE

Combine 1 cup sifted confectioners' sugar and 2 tablespoons pineapple juice; mix until smooth.

❧ Moravian Ginger Cookies ❧

These dark ginger-molasses cookies store beautifully, so you can make them well ahead of the Christmas rush. The Moravian women of Old Salem, North Carolina, roll them paper thin and cut in fancy shapes, but the same recipe can be used to make Gingerbread Men. Makes 4 ½ dozen.

    4 cups sifted flour
    1 teaspoon ginger
    1 teaspoon cinnamon
    1 teaspoon mace
    ½ teaspoon cloves
    ¼ cup butter or margarine
    ½ cup lard
    ½ cup firmly packed dark brown sugar
    1 cup molasses
    1 ½ teaspoons baking soda
    1 teaspoon very hot water

In a large bowl, sift flour together with ginger, cinnamon, mace, and cloves.

In a separate bowl, cream butter, lard, and sugar until light and fluffy; add molasses and beat well. In a heatproof container, dissolve the baking soda in water. Mix one-quarter of the dry ingredients into creamed mixture, then stir in soda-water. Work in remaining dry ingredients a little at a time. Wrap dough and chill 4-6 hours.

Preheat oven to 350° F. Roll dough, a little at a time, as thin as possible. Cut with Christmas cutters. Place cookies 1 ½-inches apart on lightly greased baking sheets, and bake about 8 minutes until lightly browned. Cool 1-2

minutes on sheets, then transfer to wire racks. When completely cool, store in an airtight container.

TO DECORATE

Make a simple icing by mixing 1 cup sifted confectioners sugar with 2-3 teaspoons heavy cream. Trace outlines of cookies with icing by putting through a pastry tube fitted with a fine tip.

⁙ Nanaimo Bars ⁙

Canada

Nanaimo bars are immensely popular layered bar cookies, which originated in Nanaimo, British Columbia. These bars consist of three layers, each of which require little preparation and cooking time, but make for an absolutely decadent treat.

FOR THE BOTTOM LAYER

½ cup unsalted butter
¼ cup sugar
5 tbsp. cocoa
1 egg, beaten
1 ¾ graham cracker crumbs
½ cup finely chopped almonds
1 cup shredded coconut

Melt the butter, sugar and cocoa using a double boiler. Add egg and stir to thicken. Remove from heat and mix in the crumbs, almonds and coconut. Press the mixture firmly into an ungreased 8x8-inch pan.

FOR THE SECOND LAYER

½ cup unsalted butter
3 tbsp. cream
2 tbsp. vanilla custard powder
2 cups confectioners sugar

Cream together all the ingredients, and beat until light. Spread over the bottom layer.

FOR THE THIRD LAYER

4 oz. semi-sweet chocolate
2 tbsp. unsalted butter

Melt the chocolate and butter over low heat. Remove and allow to cool slightly (make sure the mixture doesn't harden). Drizzle over the second layer, and place the pan in the refrigerator to chill.

⊰ Pfeffernüsse ⊱

German Peppernuts

The secret of good "peppernuts" is to ripen the dough 2-3 days before baking. Makes 3 ½ dozen.

    3 cups sifted flour
    1 tsp. cinnamon
    ⅛ tsp. cloves
    ¼ tsp. white pepper
    3 eggs
    1 cup sugar
    ⅓ cup very finely chopped blanched almonds
    ⅓ cup very finely chopped mixed candied orange peel and citron
    Vanilla sugar or confectioners' sugar (optional)

Sift flour with cinnamon, cloves, and white pepper and set aside. In a large mixing bowl, beat eggs until frothy, slowly add sugar, and continue beating until thick and lemon colored. Slowly mix in flour, then almonds and fruit peel. Wrap dough in foil and refrigerate 2-3 days.

When ready to bake, preheat oven to 350° F. Roll out about one-third of the dough at a time, ¼-½–inch thick and cut with a 1 ¾-inch round cutter. Place cookies 1-inch apart on greased baking sheets and bake 15-18 minutes until light brown. Cool on wire racks. If desired, dredge in vanilla sugar or dust with confectioners sugar before serving.

❧ Ris al'amande ❧

Danish Rice Pudding

Every Scandinavian country has a similar recipe for a traditional Christmas rice pudding. It is customary to place one whole almond in the pudding. The diner who finds it will have good luck throughout the coming New Year.

- 1 cup short grain rice
- 2 cups milk
- 1 tsp. vanilla extract
- ⅔ cup chopped almonds
- 2-3 tbsp. sugar
- 1-2 tbsp. Madeira or sherry (optional)
- 1 ½ cups whipping cream

Smear the bottom of a medium saucepan with some butter, then add the milk and heat to almost boiling. Gradually add the rice while stirring. Turn the heat down, cover, and allow to simmer for about 50 minutes.

Once the mixture has been removed from heat and allowed to cool, add the vanilla, almonds, sugar, and wine.

Whip the cream and gently fold it into the pudding. Serve pudding on its own or with a dollop of warm or cool cherry sauce.

⁙ Speculaas ⁙

Netherlands

These ginger cookies are a traditional St. Nicholas Day treat in the Netherlands.

 4 cups sifted flour
 1 cup butter
 1 ½ cups brown sugar
 1 tsp. salt
 4 tsp. baking powder
 1 tsp. cinnamon
 1 pinch cloves
 1 pinch nutmeg
 1 pinch ginger
 1 pinch black pepper
 milk
 blanched almonds or candied fruit peel (optional)

Preheat oven to 325° F. Mix all ingredients together, and add enough milk to make a stiff paste that can be rolled out. Roll dough into sheets and press blanched almonds or candied peels on top, if desired.

Cut dough into small rectangles (or any other shape if desired), and transfer to a greased cookie sheet. Bake until light golden brown.

❊ Sugarplums ❊

These dry-candied fruit treats are made by rolling fondant around small pieces of fruit such as candied cherries, small pitted dates, cubes of preserved ginger and pieces of dried apricots.

FOR THE FONDANT

2 cups sugar
1 ½ cups hot water
⅛ tsp. cream of tarter or ¼ tsp. lemon juice

Heat and stir all ingredients in a large, heavy saucepan over moderate heat until sugar dissolves; cover and boil 3 minutes. Uncover, insert candy thermometer that has been heated under hot tap water, and cook *without stirring* to 238° F or until a drop of fondant forms a soft ball in cold water.

NOTE: Wipe crystals from sides of pan with a damp pastry brush as they collect—fondant will be less apt to turn grainy.

Remove fondant from heat and let stand 1-2 minutes until bubbles subside; pour-*without scraping pan*-onto a marble slab or large, heavy platter rubbed lightly with a damp cloth; cool undisturbed until barely warm.

NOTE: If you have an extra candy thermometer, insert as soon as fondant is poured.

When fondant has cooled to 110° F, scrape from edges with a broad spatula in toward center again and again until it thickens and whitens; pick up and knead until velvety. Wrap fondant in cloth wrung out in cold water and set aside at least ½ hour before using.

NOTE: Covered with damp cloth and stored in an airtight jar, fondant will keep 3-4 days.

TO FLAVOR FONDANT

Knead in about ½ tsp. extract (vanilla, almond, rum, spearmint, rose or orange water) or a few drops oil of peppermint or wintergreen. Add these by the drop, tasting as you go so you don't overflavor.

TO COLOR FONDANT

Dip a toothpick in desired food color, then pierce fondant in several places. Knead to distribute color; if too pale, repeat-but keep colors pastel. Once fondant is prepared, it can be rolled around any small fruits of choice.

❧ Twelfth Night or King's Cake ❧

New Orleans

This brioche-style cake is eaten on the twelfth day of Christmas, also known as Epiphany (January 6), to celebrate the arrival of the Three Kings. The cake is often circular in shape and usually decorated with colored sugars in green, gold, and purple. The cake traditionally contains a hidden bean, pea, or a tiny figurine symbolizing the baby Jesus; whoever finds it shall receive good luck. In New Orleans, King's Cake is prepared in bakeries for the entire period between Epiphany and Ash Wednesday and is a popular treat during Mardi Gras celebrations.

FOR THE CAKE

½ cup lukewarm water

2 packages active dry yeast

½ cup plus 1 tsp. sugar

3 ½-4 ½ cups flour, unsifted

1 tsp. nutmeg

2 tsp. salt

1 tsp. lemon zest

½ cup warm milk

5 egg yolks

1 stick butter, softened and cut into slices,

plus 2 tbsp. more softened butter

1 tsp cinnamon

1 egg slightly beaten with 1 tbsp. milk

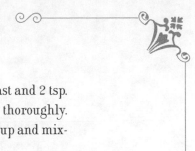

Pour the warm water in a small shallow bowl and sprinkle yeast and 2 tsp. sugar into it. Allow the mixture to sit for 3 minutes, then mix thoroughly. Set bowl in a warm place for 10 minutes, or until yeast bubbles up and mixture almost doubles in volume.

Combine 3 ½ cups of flour, remaining sugar, nutmeg and salt, and sift into a large mixing bowl. Stir in lemon zest. Separate center of mixture to form a hole, and pour in yeast mixture and milk. Add egg yolks and slowly combine the dry ingredients into the yeast-milk mixture using a wooden spoon. When the mixture is smooth, beat in the butter slices, a few pieces at a time, and continue to beat for 2 minutes or until the dough can be formed into a medium-soft ball.

Place ball of dough on a lightly floured surface and knead like bread. While kneading, sprinkle enough of the remaining cup of flour over the dough (1 tbsp. at a time) until it is no longer sticky. Knead 10 minutes more until shiny and elastic.

Using a pastry brush, evenly coat the inside of a large bowl with 1 tbsp. of the softened butter. Place the dough ball in bowl and rotate until entire surface is buttered. Cover bowl with a kitchen towel and allow the dough to rise in a warm, draft-free area until it is doubled in volume, about 1 ½ hours.

Remove dough from bowl and place on a lightly floured surface. With a fist, punch down forcefully. Sprinkle cinnamon over the top, then pat and form dough into a cylinder. Grease a large baking sheet with the remaining tablespoon of butter and lay the dough on it, curling it to form an oval. Pinch the ends together to complete the oval. Cover dough with towel and set aside until the oval of dough doubles in volume again, about 45 minutes.

Preheat oven to 375° F. Brush top and sides of the dough with the egg and milk mixture, and bake on the middle rack of the oven for 25-35 minutes until golden brown. Place cake on a wire rack to cool. If desired, the plastic baby or bean can be hidden in the cake at this time.

FOR THE ICING

3 cups confectioners sugar
¼ cup lemon juice
3-6 tbsp. water

Combine sugar, lemon juice and 3 tbsp. water until smooth. If icing is too stiff, add more water until spreadable. Spread icing over top of cake. Immediately sprinkle with green, purple and yellow colored sugars.

✥ Zimtsterne ✥

Austrian Cinnamon Stars

As Christmas approaches, markets throughout Austria fill with little cakes called kekse. There are countless varieties, flavored with cinnamon, vanilla, or jam, in the shape of stars, Christmas trees or crescents. Zimtsterne is a light, star-shaped cinnamon cookie flavored with kirsch, a dry, clear brandy distilled from black morello cherries.

    5 egg whites
    4 cups confectioners sugar
    18 oz. almonds, finely ground
    2 tsp. cinnamon
    1 tbsp. kirsch
    granulated sugar for rolling out the dough

Beat the egg whites to stiff peaks. Slowly sift in the confectioners sugar, continuing to beat. Set aside one cup of this mixture to decorate with later.

Add the almonds, cinnamon and kirsch. Knead the dough quickly and allow to rest in the refrigerator for an hour, covered.

Sprinkle a flat surface with the granulated sugar and roll out the dough to a ⅜-inch thickness. With a cookie cutter, cut and remove star shapes. Cover the stars with the reserved sugar and egg white mixture, and let rest overnight at room temperature.

Bake at 325° F for 7-8 minutes. The stars should be soft, and their tops should remain white.

Drinks

⁙ Angel Punch ⁙

1 cup sugar syrup
1 pint lemon juice
1 qt. strong green tea
2 qts. white grape juice
1 block ice
2 qts. chilled club soda

Combine all ingredients except ice and soda; and refrigerate for an hour or two. Pour over ice in a punch bowl and add the soda. Serve in punch glasses.

⁙ Eggnog ⁙

This nonalcoholic version of a traditional favorite makes 6 servings.

4 eggs, separated
½ cup sugar
2 cups cold milk
1 cup cold light cream
1 ½ tsps vanilla
⅛ tsp. salt
¼ tsp. nutmeg

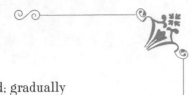

Beat egg yolks and ¼ cup sugar until thick and cream colored; gradually add milk, cream, vanilla, salt, and ⅛ tsp. nutmeg and beat until frothy. Beat egg whites with remaining sugar until soft peaks form and fold over.

Cover and chill until serving time. Mix well, pour into punch bowl, and sprinkle with remaining nutmeg.

⁒ Classic Hot Chocolate ⁒

¾ cup heavy cream
3 ¼ cups milk
1 ½ tsp. vanilla
6 oz. bittersweet chocolate, chopped fine
miniature marshmallows for garnish

In a saucepan, combine the cream, milk, vanilla, and a pinch of salt, and bring the mixture just to a boil over moderate heat.

In a small heatproof bowl, combine the chocolate with about ⅔ cup of the hot milk mixture and whisk the mixture until the chocolate is melted and the mixture is smooth.

Whisk the chocolate mixture into the remaining milk mixture and simmer the hot chocolate, whisking, for 2 minutes. (For a frothy result, blend the hot chocolate in batches in a blender.)

Serve topped with the marshmallows.

❧ Spiced Christmas Coffee with Whipped Cream ❧

Brandy can be a flavorful addition to the whipped cream, however the recipe is delightful on its own.

¾ cup chilled whipping cream
1 ½ tbsp. powdered sugar
1 tbsp. brandy (optional) 1 cup freshly ground coffee
5 tsp. ground cardamom
1 tbsp. sugar
2 tsp. ground cinnamon
1 tsp. ground nutmeg
7 cups water

Using an electric mixer, beat whipping cream in a large bowl to soft peaks. Add powdered sugar and optional brandy; beat to stiffer peaks. Cover and keep refrigerated (can be prepared up to 4 hours ahead).

Using a coffee maker, place ground coffee, cardamom, sugar, cinnamon and nutmeg in a coffee filter, and mix gently with a spoon. Add water to the coffee maker and brew according to manufacturer's instructions.

Divide coffee among cups and garnish each serving with a dollop of whipped cream. Serve immediately.

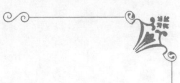

❧ Hot Chocolate with Hazelnut and Coffee Liqueurs ❧

6 tbsp. sugar

6 tbsp. unsweetened cocoa powder

dash of salt

½ cup water

3 ½ cups whole milk

16 tbsp. coffee liqueur

16 tbsp. hazelnut liqueur

grated semisweet chocolate

¾ cup chilled whipping cream

Beat cream in medium bowl until peaks form. Cover and refrigerate (can be made up to 4 hours ahead).

Whisk sugar, cocoa powder, and salt in medium saucepan to blend. Gradually add the water, whisking until the mixture is smooth. Bring the mixture to a simmer over medium-low heat, whisking constantly. Simmer for 1 minute. Gradually whisk in milk and return to simmer. Divide hot chocolate among mugs and stir 2 tablespoons of each liqueur into each mug. Top with a dollop of whipped cream and sprinkle with grated chocolate.

❧ Wassail ❧

2 cinnamon sticks, plus additional sticks for garnish

10 whole allspice

8 whole cloves

1 qt. cranberry juice cocktail

1 qt. apple cider

2 tbsp. sugar

1 Granny Smith apple

1 cup apple liqueur

Make a "spice bag" by wrapping the 2 cinnamon sticks, allspice, and cloves in a cheesecloth and tie it with string. Simmer cranberry juice, cider, sugar and the spice bag in an uncovered 5-quart pot, skimming froth occasionally, for 10 minutes.

Halve apple and cut into ¼-inch slices. Add slices and apple liqueur to the cider mixture and simmer for 2 more minutes. Serve hot and garnish with cinnamon sticks.

⚜ Hot Buttered Rum ⚜

1 cup firmly packed dark brown sugar
2 sticks unsalted butter, cut into pieces
2 tsp. cinnamon, plus additional for garnish
2 tsp. freshly grated nutmeg, or to taste
½ tsp. ground cloves, or to taste
4 cups water
1 ⅓ cups dark rum

In a saucepan, combine all the ingredients except the rum and bring the mixture to a boil, whisking constantly. Simmer the mixture for 5 minutes and stir in the rum. Ladle the buttered rum into mugs and serve with some of the additional cinnamon sprinkled on top.

⁑ Finnish Christmas Glögg ⁑

1 bottle of red wine
2-3 tbsp. Madeira (optional)
½ cup raw sugar, or to taste
⅓ cup raisins
1-2 sticks cinnamon
5-6 whole cloves
grated orange peel
¼ cup blanched, slivered almonds
¼ cup vodka (optional)

In a large kettle, combine all the ingredients except the vodka. Heat slowly, until the mixture is steaming hot, but not boiling, stirring every once in a while. Before serving, add vodka if desired.

⁑ Warm Beaujolais Kir ⁑

1 bottle of Beaujolais
¾ cup crème de cassis, or to taste
a couple of strips of lemon or orange zest,
removed with a vegetable peeler
lemon or orange slices for garnish

Stir together the ingredients in a saucepan and simmer, covered, for 5 minutes. Discard the zest and divide the mixture among wineglasses. Garnish each drink with a lemon or orange peel.

Christmas Decorations

THAT OLDER CHRISTMAS WAS ONE WE SEEMED TO HOLD IN OUR HANDS. AFTER ALL, OUR HANDS SEEMED TO CREATE SO MUCH MORE OF IT THEN THAN NOW.

〜 **Paul Engle**, "A Handmade Christmas"

Have we lost the meaning of a homemade Christmas? Is it a chore each year to break out the boxes of decorations and store-bought ornaments that look exactly like everyone else's? Most of us wouldn't let a stranger cook our Christmas dinner, so why do we put up decorations that are strange or generic to us, that show no reflection of ourselves?

There is a wealth of possibilities for homemade decorations. String popcorn, cherries, or cranberries on the tree. (Taking down decorations isn't such a chore if you can eat them, too.) Decorate your tablecloths for Christmas dinner by sewing on bells or other appropriate symbols. Make a crepe-paper "stained-glass window" for the lights to shine through, or cut out a silhouette and stick it to your windows to share Christmas with passersby.

Ingenuity is the keyword in homemade Christmas decorations. The simplest objects that you find lying around can be combined with a touch of imagination into delightful ensembles. Natural objects that you find in your yard or in the woods can make lovely additions to your Christmas festivities.

The following ideas are just to get you thinking.

Advent Calendar

An Advent calendar to mark the days from the first of December to Christmas Eve is easy to make if you have a supply of old Christmas cards at hand. Use the designs and trimmings on cards to finish the shutters of the calendar's windows and trim the edges of the house.

Start with a 9x12-inch sheet of dark-blue construction paper. Draw a line through the center, lengthwise, on the wrong side of the paper to serve as a guide.

Measure down 4 inches on each side and draw a line from that point to the center of the top. This will form the roof. Draw in the chimney about midway down one side of the peak—the chimney is 1¼ inches wide—and cut out the house. It will be 9 inches wide and 12 inches tall at the center of the roof's peak.

On the right side of the paper, mark off the windows, starting 3 inches down from the top of the roof. All windows are ¾ inch wide and ¾ inch tall, except the three in the third row. These are 1 inch tall and ¾ inch wide, just for variation. The top row of windows has three windows; the second, five; the third, three; the fourth, five; the fifth, three; and the sixth has two windows on either side of the door.

Leave ½ inch between all windows, and about ¼ inch between the rows, and center your rows on the house, leaving the same amount of space on each side.

The door is 1½ inches wide and 1½ inches tall.

With an X-Acto knife and a ruler edge, cut across the top and bottom of all windows and the door, and then down through the center of each. Bend back the shutters. *Don't* cut down each side of our windows, or you will lose your shutters.

Paste on strips of gold or colored designs from old Christmas cards, trimming each row of shutters with the same color. Use stick glue—it will not mar the paper.

Trim the edges of the roof and the walls of the house with strips of gold, and top the chimney with gold.

Cover the door with gold pieces; give the door and the windows on each side of it a triangular lintel of gold, and paste two golden steps below the door.

On the back of the calendar paste a lining of red shelf paper, placing it so the red side of the paper will show through the little windows. Use stick glue and fasten the red paper securely.

In each window paste a tiny picture cut from a Christmas card-a toy, an animal, a candle, or whatever you can find. Paste the cutout onto the red shelf paper. Paste a Christmas tree in the doorway.

Starting on December 1, open one window each day, until the door is opened on the twenty-fourth, revealing the Christmas tree.

When all the windows are open, stand the calendar in front of a lamp. The light will shine through the red paper, giving the little house a Christmas glow.

Natural Decorations

The great outdoors offers many materials for making decorations. Most of them can be found lying around on the ground, often in your own backyard.

Make wreaths and festoons with wire or rope, grapevine rings, or even bent wire hangers. Any kind of greenery or foliage can be used to create the base. Traditional wreaths have bases made from pine or balsam, but you can also use leaves from magnolia, juniper, and tallow trees. To dress the wreath up a bit, add pinecones, holly, acorns and clusters of berries. Finish by attaching a decorative bow made from the ribbon of your choice.

Kissing balls—a favorite Christmas decoration hung from doorways or hallway light fixtures—can be made with cones, pods, all of the greens available in your area, and dried berries. Using a large Styrofoam ball as the base, attach florist's wire to the materials and then insert the ends of the wire into the Styrofoam until the ball is completely covered. Accents of gingham or plaid ribbons can add an old-fashioned touch of color.

Besides being used as garnish for Christmas wreaths, pinecones make a variety of decorative pieces, and best of all, they're readily available if you live near a forested area. After collecting and bringing the pinecones home, be sure to remove all the dirt and bugs they may have on them. This can be done by placing them on a foil-covered baking sheet in the oven at 200° F for ten minutes. Not only does the heat from the oven melt the sap, which adds a natural glaze to the pinecones, it also causes closed pinecones to open up and releases a wonderful seasonal smell throughout the house. Pine cones and their sap very flammable, so place them on a baking sheet and watch them carefully. Scatter the cones throughout the table for a holiday dinner, or place them in a dish, bowl, or basket in the center. Accentuate the pinecones by spray painting them in festive colors such as white, gold, or silver, or you can even use glitter. Use ribbon to make a bow around the basket or add some pine branches to enhance the natural beauty of the cones—anything goes! Pinecones also make excellent Christmas tree ornaments. Glue or tie ribbon to the stem and simply hang on the tree as they are, or garnish them with glitter, paint, and even small leaves.

Nuts can be painted, or, in a tradition that goes back a very long time, they can be wrapped in gold or silver foil or in colored paper to be used as Christmas tree ornaments. Nuts can be wired into grape-like clusters or made into small trees. (Pierce them with a drill or a red-hot pin and insert wire.)

Cookie Ornaments

This delicious kind of homemade decoration is easy to make, and a fun project to involve the kids in.

Most Suitable Cookies

Large decorated rolled cookies; shapes such as stars and candy canes can be cut out of the centers of circular cookies.

To Attach Hangars to Unbaked Cookies

Fasten large loops of thin ribbon or thread to backs of unbaked cookies with tiny dabs of dough. Bake as directed, then decorate.

To Attach Hangars to Baked Cookies
(good only for those that are not shattery-crisp)

While cookies are still warm and pliable, quickly draw coarse thread through top, using a sturdy needle. Don't insert too close to edge or cookies may break. Allow 6-8 inches of thread for each cookie. Decorate as desired.

Christmas Macaroni Garland

This is another kid-friendly project-not only will it give the children something to do, but it will also help them feel like they're really making a contribution to the household decorations.

~[MATERIALS]~

macaroni noodles (or any kind of noodles with holes)
fishing line or string
red and green food coloring
vinegar
2 small bowls
small bells (optional)

In each of the bowls, mix a small amount of vinegar with several drops of the food coloring, green in one bowl and red in the other (Note: the more drops of food coloring used, the deeper the color.)

Immerse some noodles in each of the bowls. Once colored, spread the pasta on a cookie sheet to dry. After the macaroni has dried, it can be threaded onto fishing line or string to make the garland. Optional: Alternate the macaroni with bells or other ornaments that are easy to thread string through.

Pomanders

Pomanders make delightful Christmas gifts or fragrant tree decorations and can freshen closets and drawers for years to come. Any kind of fruit may be used, but apples and oranges are the easiest to start with.

For 6-8 apples or oranges you will need:

½ lb. whole long-stemmed cloves
¼ cup ground cinnamon
¼ cup ground cloves
2 tbsp. ground nutmeg
2 tbsp. allspice
¼ cup powdered orris root

Holding the fruit firmly, insert the whole cloves at ⅛ to ¼-inch intervals.

After cloves are pushed into the fruit, make a spice mixture by combining all the other ingredients. Roll the pomander in the mixture, coating it completely to keep out air.

Let the pomanders sit in the excess spice mixture in an open bowl in a warm, dry place for about a week. They can even be placed in an area where the fragrant smell of the curing pomanders penetrates the entire house. At the end of a week, the pomanders should be sufficiently hardened. Dust off the spices and hang with a ribbon, or wrap up as a gift.

Spice and fruit pomanders will be fragrant for several years. When their aroma fades, wash your pomanders in warm water, roll them in a fresh spice bath, and add a drop or two of clove or cinnamon oil. Let them remain in the spices for a few days, then tie with fresh ribbons.

Holiday Scents

To infuse your home with a spicy holiday aroma, all you need to do is simmer the following ingredients in a pot of water. Most can already be found in your kitchen cupboard:

3 cinnamon sticks
1 orange peel, in pieces
6 tbsp. star anise
4 tbsp. whole cloves
2 tbsp. crushed nutmeg
6 tbsp. juniper berries
2 tbsp. allspice
20 drops of the following essential oils
(optional): orange, clove or cinnamon

Allow the mixture to simmer throughout the day; add more water as needed.

Stained "Glass" Windows

Transform one or more of your windows at Christmastime and create the illusion of having a beautiful, costly, stained glass window. These effects are easily attained by anyone with a little patience. If you have a window that is already distinctive, such as a semi-circular one over your door, this is the best type to choose for decorating, as decorating only one window in the living room will leave an unfinished appearance.

The most beautiful effect can be attained by the use of crepe paper and black cardboard; the cardboard simulates the lead and the crepe paper the glass. Trace a design on the cardboard, then cut it into a stencil of ½-inch wide "lead" outlining the design. Trace each open section on the desired color crepe paper and cut a trifle larger to allow space for pasting.

Apply the paste to the cardboard rather than the crepe paper. You may produce gradations in the tints of the "glass" by stretching the paper before you put it on. Sometimes we may use several layers of crepe paper to modify the color, such as yellow over green to produce yellow-green.

Tree Trimmings

The following homemade ornaments are easy to make, yet they lend a truly unique and enriching character to your holiday decorations.

Foil Flakes

Cut a strip of metallic paper 22 inches long and 2½ inches wide. Fold the paper into ½-inch pleats. Cut angular designs along both sides of the folded foil. This will form the cutout pattern of the snowflake when unfolded. Start with just a few cuts and add more as you see how they look. Run a threaded needle through each fold ½ inch from the bottom. Tie the ends of the thread together loosely. Open the snowflake like a fan until the ends come together. Join them with glue or staples, and your snowflake is ready to hand on the tree.

Stained-Glass Oranges

Citrus fruits make beautiful ornaments resembling tiny stained-glass windows. Simply place thin fruit slices on a cookie sheet and dry in a warm area or in an oven on low. Sprinkle with sugar to add a sparkly effect, or leave as is to show their natural beauty.

Picture Frame Ornaments

These personalized ornaments are something you definitely won't see on anyone else's tree. Mini picture frames can be converted to ornaments by simply attaching ribbon hangers to the backs with a glue gun. Remove the glass from the frames while decorating, then insert photo and replace.

Ribbon Ball Ornaments

These gorgeous ornaments are nothing more than ribbons of various colors wrapped around a Styrofoam base. Hang these balls on your tree or pile them in a bowl for a lovely centerpiece. Using a 3-inch Styrofoam ball, wrap ribbon of one color around the ball, dividing it in half, and pin in place with a straight pin. Wrap another ribbon around the ball in the opposite direction, dividing it into quarters. Continue with other colors-as many as desired-until the ball is entirely covered.

Some More Suggestions

Christmas is the greatest blending of the secular and the religious in all the year. It is best to realize that it is both and not try to exclude one or the other. Anything indulged in to excess is bad for us, but the pleasures of Christmas can be joyous and even worshipful when entered into in the right spirit.

Everyone knows that Christmas is a special time for children; why can't it be that special for adults? Are we so afraid of being childish that we cannot let ourselves be childlike? Try to see everything afresh, taste everything for the first time. Read the Bible story as if you never heard it before; notice the smell of the pine and admire the brightness of the lights. Really hope for snow this year.

There is very little pleasure in giving gifts to the person who has everything and wants nothing. Do everyone a favor and really want something this year. Drop hints. Get excited. Try to decipher everyone else's hints. Care if you got the right thing. Try to find out the right size without asking outright. Be secretive. Hide everyone's presents. Try to find where they hid yours. No matter how unsuitable your gifts turn out to be, wear or use them once. That ugly pink and orange tie will remind you of Christmas no matter when you wear it.

Don't trim the tree with whatever the dime store has on special. Do your ornaments have memories for you? How can they if they're all the same? Have a tree-trimming party and invite everyone to come for a donation of one ornament. You'll have a tree filled with both variety and the memories of good friends.

Don't let the store gift-wrap anything. Do it yourself, even if it's lumpy and uneven-especially if it's lumpy and uneven. Try Julklapping. Wrap it as outlandishly as possible. If the gift is the size of a postage stamp, put it in an old carton and fill the carton with three rolls of tissue paper. Write a verse on the card. The more homemade, the better.

Christmas Trivia

Christmas Superstitions

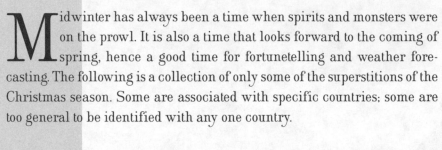

Midwinter has always been a time when spirits and monsters were on the prowl. It is also a time that looks forward to the coming of spring, hence a good time for fortunetelling and weather forecasting. The following is a collection of only some of the superstitions of the Christmas season. Some are associated with specific countries; some are too general to be identified with any one country.

- At midnight on Christmas Eve, all water turns to wine; cattle kneel facing toward the East; horses kneel and blow as if to warm the manger; animals can speak, though it's bad luck to hear them; bees hum the Hundredth Psalm.

- In Ireland, it is believed that the gates of heaven open at midnight on Christmas Eve. Those who die at that time go straight through without having to wait in Purgatory.

- A child born on Christmas Day or Christmas Eve is considered very lucky in some countries, but in Greece he or she is feared to be a Killikantzaroi; in Poland he or she may turn out to be a werewolf.

- The weather on each of the twelve days of Christmas signifies what the weather will be on the appropriate month of the coming year.

- The branch of a cherry tree placed in water at the beginning of Advent will bring luck if it flowers by Christmas.

- In Devonshire, England, a girl raps at the hen house door on Christmas Eve. If a rooster crows, she will marry within the year.

- You burn your old shoes during the Christmas season in Greece to prevent misfortunes in the coming year.

◦[It's bad luck to let any fire go out in your house during the Christmas season.

◦[It's bad luck to let your evergreen decorations fall or to throw them away. You should burn them.

◦[If the husband brings the Christmas holly into the house first, he will rule the household for the coming year; if the wife is first, she will hold sway.

◦[If you eat a raw egg before eating anything else on Christmas morning, you will be able to carry heavy weights.

◦[From cockcrow to daybreak of Christmas morning, the trolls roam the Swedish countryside. Stay indoors.

◦[During the recitation of Christ's genealogy at Christmas Eve Midnight Mass, buried treasure reveals itself.

◦[If you don't eat any plum pudding, you will lose a friend before next Christmas.

◦[If you refuse mince pie at Christmas dinner, you will have bad luck for a year.

◦[A loaf of bread left on the table after Christmas Eve dinner will ensure no lack of bread for the rest of the year.

◦[Eating an apple at midnight on Christmas Eve gives good health for a year.

◦[You will have as many happy months in the coming year as the number of houses you eat minced pie in during Christmas.

There is some truth behind some of these superstitions. For instance, if you eat everything during Christmas that you're supposed to eat for good luck, the rest of the year has got to be an improvement once you get over your stomachache.

Famous People Born on Christmas

[Isaac Newton (1642)........................Mathematician, scientist

[Clara Barton (1821).........................Nurse/Founder of American Red Cross

[Aristide Maillol (1861)....................Sculptor

[Evangeline Cory Booth (1865).....Salvation Army General
                                                        USA/Canada/England

[Helena Rubinstein (1870)..............Cosmetics merchant

[Giuseppe de Luca (1876)................Opera singer

[Conrad Hilton (1887)......................Hotel mogul

[Rebecca West (1892).......................English author/critic/feminist

[Robert Ripley (1893)......................Cartoonist, "Believe It or Not"

[Humphrey Bogart (1899)..............Actor

[Raphael Soyer (1899)....................Painter

[Clark Clifford (1906).....................Government official

[Cab Calloway (1907)......................Band leader/entertainer

[Lord Gray (1906)............................Entertainment entrepreneur

[Quentin Crisp (1908).....................Actor

[Mike Mazurki (1911).......................Actor

Tony Martin (1913).........................Singer

Oscar Lewis (1914).........................Sociologist

Anwar Sadat (1918)......................President of Egypt (1970-81)

Rod Serling (1924)........................Writer, "The Twilight Zone"

Nellie Fox (1927)............................Pro baseball player

Carlos Castaneda (1931)..............Anthropologist

Little Richard (1935)....................Singer

Ismail Merchant (1936)...............Film director

O'Kelly Isley (1937)......................Singer, "The Isley Brothers"

Gary Sandy (1945)........................Actor

Alice Cooper (1945).....................Singer

Jimmy Buffett (1946)...................Singer

Larry Csonka (1946)....................Hall of Fame pro football player

Barbara Mandrell (1948)............Singer

Sissy Spacek (1949).....................Actress

Annie Lennox (1954)....................Singer

Rickey Henderson (1960)............Pro baseball player

Dido (1971)....................................Singer

The Twelve Days' Accounting

If you add up all the presents in the old carol "The Twelve Days of Christmas," you find that the twelfth day's shipment brings the menagerie to the following total:

[12] drummers drumming

[22] pipers piping

[30] lords a-leaping

[36] ladies dancing

[40] maids a-milking (presumably they brought cows with them)

[42] swans a-swimming

[42] geese a-laying

[40] gold rings

[36] calling birds

[30] French hens

[22] turtle doves

[12] partridges in a dozen pear trees

There have been some feeble attempts to figure the net worth of this Christmas package, but it all breaks down when you try to fix a price scale for such unusual gifts as leaping lords. Fortunately, this medieval sender didn't have to face today's postal rates.

A Warning to Hunters

This article appeared in the Milwaukee Journal on December 26, 1950:

It seems that a successful deer hunter, with his quarry on the fender stopped en route home to regale his cronies with the story of his triumph. The telling took longer than he planned, and certain low comedy characters utilized the pause to sow seeds of his undoing. They sent for red paint and while the hunter recounted the glories of his hunt inside, they painted the nose of his slain buck a ruby red.

At this point, by no accident, the youngsters were homeward bound from school. And the enemies of our hero, not satisfied with leaving the red-nosed buck out there in naked view, stopped some of the moppets and horrified them with a whispered alarm. "Look! Rudolph!"

By the time our hero emerged, fifty youngsters were dug in for battle equipped with snowballs, rocks and righteous wrath. Well he escaped with his life, and on Christmas Eve, it turned out that Rudolph was all right after all. So now the tale can be told.

Santa Claus Investigated

I t might have been a movie like *Miracle on 34th Street,* except it didn't have a happy ending.

In 1914 in New York City, John D. Gluck formed an organization called the Santa Claus Association, whose stated purpose was "to preserve children's faith in Santa Claus." It obtained from the Post Office letters addressed to Santa Claus and would investigate them to see if the cases were needy. If they were, it would try to help answer the requests for toys and presents and even sometimes meet rent payments. Obviously, this was financed by the contributions of Christmas-spirited citizens.

It sounds too good to last, and it was. In 1928 federal postal authorities refused to turn over any more mail and instituted an investigation into the organization. There were rumors of fraud and other irregularities, but nothing was ever proved. Still, the organization was criticized and disbanded. The organization's founder said, "All I ask is that these people don't sock it to us at this time of the year and spoil the faith of little children."

Things Named for Christmas

P eople have always named things after other things that they love. Christmas and the symbols of Christmas have appeared in many other names. Consider the following:

Place Names

⊶[Bethlehem is located in Connecticut, Georgia, Indiana, Kentucky, Maryland, New Hampshire, New York, and Pennsylvania.

⊶[Holly is in Colorado, Michigan, and West Virginia.

⊶[Mount Holly is in New Jersey and Vermont.

⊶[Noel is in Missouri and Virginia.

⊶[Santa Claus is in Idaho and Indiana.

⊶[Christmas itself is in Florida and Michigan.

⊶[Christmas Cove is in Maine.

⊶[Mistletoe is in Kentucky.

There are two Christmas Islands: one in the Indian Ocean, administered by Australia; the other in the Gilbert Islands and claimed by the United States. Ironically, this second island with its peaceful name was the scene of nuclear test explosions in 1957, 1958, and 1962.

Christmas Ridge is an underwater mountain chain in the Pacific Ocean.

Plant Names

The Christmas bell is an Australian flower that is widely used in Christmas decorations down under. It blooms in the warm Decembers of the Southern Hemisphere. It has bright green leaves and a red flower, fringed in yellow, shaped like a bell.

The Christmasberry is also called California holly. It grows on the West Coast of North America. It is an evergreen tree or shrub with white flowers and, later, bright red berries.

The Christmas bush is another Australian decorative plant. It has many tiny flowers growing in soft clusters.

The Christmas cactus is also known, less pleasantly, as the crab cactus. It blooms in mid-December in its native Brazil and Central America. It has pink ornate flowers and light green, oval-shaped leaves.

The Christmas fern is a North American woodland fern, a dark evergreen.

The Christmas Rose, or black hellebore, is an Eurasian perennial. It has white or greenish blossoms that look much like wild roses. The leaves are evergreen.

Odd Christmas Trees

The pyramid-shaped assembly of pipes, valves, clamps, and so on, that stands over an oil well and controls the output of oil is called a Christmas tree.

The control panel of a submarine, with its flashing red and green lights, is also called a Christmas tree.

In CB radio jargon, a Christmas tree is a truck or any other vehicle with lots of bright lights (and a Christmas card is a traffic ticket).

To World War II aviators, a Christmas tree was the shower of bright metallic foil that they dropped over enemy targets to jam radar and communications systems. The name probably derived from the similarity to a well-tinseled tree.

At a drag strip, a Christmas tree is the set of flashing red, green, and yellow lights that signal the start of the race.

A Disease

Christmas Disease is a bleeding disease very much like hemophilia and similarly caused by a genetically determined deficiency of one of the several factors present in blood plasma that bring about normal clotting. Also like hemophilia, it is transmitted by carrier mothers (who themselves do not show symptoms) to their sons, half of whom are thus affected. The name is not taken directly from the season of Christmas but rather from the first known victim of the disease, a young lad named Stephen Christmas.

An Appropriate Name

A book now out of print called *A Christmas Dictionary* was published in 1959, and was by the appropriately named author Holly Bell.

Traditional Christmas Gift-givers

- Austria.................St. Nicholas or Christkind
- Belgium................St. Nicholas
- Brazil...................Papa Noël
- Chile.....................Viejo Pascuero
- China....................Lam Khoong-Khoong or Dun Che Lao Ren
- Costa Rica............Christ Child or Santa Claus
- England...............Father Christmas
- France..................Père Noël or le Petit Noël
- Guatemala............Christ Child

Holland...............St. Nicholas

Italy...................Befana

Japan.................Hoteiosho

Mexico.................Three Kings

Norway...............Julesvenn

Poland.................Star Man

Puerto Rico.........Both Santa Claus and the Wise Men

Russia.................Babouschka

Spain...................Wise Men

Sweden...............Jultomten

Switzerland.......Christkind, St. Nicholas, or Father Christmas and Lucy

Syria....................Smallest Camel of the Wise Men's caravan

U.S.A...................Santa Claus

The Knighting of the Sirloin of Beef
by Charles the Second

This anonymous poem suggests how a Christmas joke might have given us the name of one of our favorite foods.

The Second Charles of England
Rode forth one Christmas tide,
To hunt a gallant stag of ten,
Of Chingford woods the pride.

The winds blew keen, the snow fell fast,
And made for earth a pall,
As tired steeds and wearied men
Returned to Friday Hall.

The blazing logs, piled on the dogs,
Were pleasant to behold!
And grateful was the steaming feast
To hungry men and cold.

With right good-will all took their fill,
And soon each found relief:
Whilst Charles his royal trencher piled
From one huge loin of beef.

Quoth Charles, "Odd's fish! A noble dish!
Ay, noble made by me!
By kingly right, I dub thee knight-
Sir Loin henceforward be!"

And never was a royal jest
Received with such acclaim;
And never knight than good Sir Loin
More worthy of the name.

"Merry Christmas" Around the World

Argentina .... Felices Pascuas

Armenia .... Schenorhavor Dzenount

Belgium (Flemish) ...... Vrolijke Kerstmis

Brazil (Portuguese) ..... Boas Festas

Bulgaria .... Chestita Koleda

Chile .... Feliz Navidad

China .... Kung Hsi Hsin Nien or Bing Chu Shen Tan

Columbia .... Feliz Navidad y Próspero Año Nuevo

Croatia .... Sretan Bozic

Czech Republic .... Vesele Vanoce

Denmark .... Glaedelig JulEsperanto/Gajan Kristnaskon

Estonia .... Roomsaid Joulu Puhi

Finland .... Hauskaa Joulua

France .... Joyeux Noël

Germany .... Fröhliche Weinachten

Greece .... Kala Christouogena

Hawaii .... Mele Kalikimaka

Holland .... Zalig Kerstfeest

Hungary .... Boldog Karacsony

India (Bengali) .... Shuvo Naba Barsha

Iraq .... Idah Saidan Wa Sanah Jadidah

A Christmas Tree

I have been looking on this evening, at a merry company of children assembled round that pretty German toy, the Christmas-Tree. The tree was planted in the middle of a great round table, and towered high above their heads. It was brilliantly lighted by a multitude of little tapers; and everywhere sparkled and glittered with bright objects. There were rosy-cheeked dolls, hiding behind the green leaves; there were real watches (with movable hands, at least, and an endless capacity of being wound up) dangling from innumerable twigs; there were French polished tables, chairs, bedsteads, wardrobes, eight-day clocks, and various other articles of domestic furniture (wonderfully made, in tin, at Wolverhampton), perched among the boughs, as if in preparation for some fair house-keeping; there were jolly, broad-faced little men, much more agreeable in appearance than many real men—and no wonder, for their heads took off, and showed them to be full of sugar-plums; there were fiddles and drums; there were tambourines, books, work-boxes, paint-boxes, sweetmeat-boxes, peep-show-boxes, all kinds of boxes; there were trinkets for the elder girls, far brighter than any grown-up gold and jewels; there were baskets and pincushions in all devices; there were guns, swords, and banners; there were witches standing in enchanted rings of paste-board, to tell fortunes; there were teetotums, humming-tops, needle-cases, pen-wipers, smelling-bottles, conversation-cards, bouquet-holders; real fruit, made artificially dazzling with gold leaf; imitation apples, pears and walnuts, crammed with surprises; in short as a pretty child, before me, delightedly whispered to another pretty child, her bosom friend, "There was everything and more."

∽ **Charles Dickens**

Solution to a Christmas Dilemma

Robert Louis Stevenson, author of *Treasure Island* and *Dr. Jekyll and Mr. Hyde,* as well as many other stories, found a whimsical solution for the problem of having a birthday that falls on Christmas. Here he is writing to the young daughter of an American Land Commissioner in Samoa.

∽ **Vailima, June 19, 1891**

I, Robert Louis Stevenson, Advocate of the Scots Bar, author of *The Master of Ballantrae* and *Moral Emblems,* stuck civil engineer, sole owner and patentee of the Palace and Plantation known as Vailima in the island of Upolu, Samoa, a British subject, being in sound mind, and pretty well, I thank you, in body:

In consideration that Miss Annie H. Ide, daughter of H. C. Ide, the town of Saint Johnsbury, in the country of Caledonia, in the state of Vermont, United States of America, was born, out of all reason, upon Christmas Day, and is therefore out of all justice denied the consolation and profit of a proper birthday;

And considering that I, he said Robert Louis Stevenson, have attained an age when O, we never mention it, and that I have now no further use for a birthday of any description:

And in consideration that I have met H. C. Ide, the father of the said Annie H. Ide, and found him about as white a land commissioner as I require:

Have transferred, and do hereby transfer, to the said Annie H. Ide, *all and whole* my rights and privileges in the thirteenth day of November, formerly my birthday, now, hereby, and henceforth, the birthday of the said Annie H. Ide, to have, hold, exercise, and enjoy the same in the customary manner, by the sporting of fine raiment, eating of rich meats, and receipt of gifts, compliments, and copies of verse, according to the manner of our ancestors:

And I direct the said Annie H. Ide to add to the said name of Annie H. Ide the name Louisa—at least in private; and I charge her to use my said birthday with moderation and humanity, *et tamquam bona filia familiae,* the said birthday not being so young as it once was, and having carried me in a very satisfactory manner since I can remember:

And in case the said Annie H. Ide shall neglect or contravene either of the above conditions, I hereby revoke the donation and transfer my rights in the said birthday to the President of the United States of America for the time being:

In witness whereof I have hereto set my hand and seal this nineteenth day of June in the year of grace eighteen hundred and ninety-one.

> ∽ SEAL, Robert Louis Stevenson
> WITNESS, Lloyd Osbourne
> WITNESS, Harold Watts

Christmas Grades

The distinguished Professor of English William Lyon Phelps gave an unusually difficult examination to his students just before the Christmas holidays. One befuddled student turned in a blank page with his season's greeting:

God knows the answer to these questions.
Merry Christmas!

In the spirit of the season, Professor Phelps responded:

God gets an "A." You get an "F."
Happy New Year!

A Christmas Wish

It is my heart-warm and world-embracing Christmas hope and aspiration that all of us, the high, the low, the rich, the poor, the admired, the despised, the loved, the hated, the civilized, the savage (every man had brother of us all through-out the whole earth), may eventually be gathered together in a heaven of everlasting rest and peace and bliss, except the inventor of the telephone.

∽ **Mark Twain**

Our Family's Christmas

❧ HOW WE DECORATE THE HOUSE ❧

_____

_____

_____

_____

_____

_____

_____

❧ HOW WE DECORATE THE TREE ❧

_____

_____

_____

_____

_____

_____

_____

HOW WE CELEBRATE CHRISTMAS EVE

_____
_____
_____
_____
_____
_____
_____

HOW WE CELEBRATE CHRISTMAS DAY

_____
_____
_____
_____
_____
_____
_____

OUR FAVORITE CHRISTMAS DISHES

_____
_____
_____
_____
_____
_____
_____

OUR FAVORITE CHRISTMAS DESSERTS

OUR GIFT-GIVING TRADITIONS

OUR FAVORITE CHRISTMAS SONGS

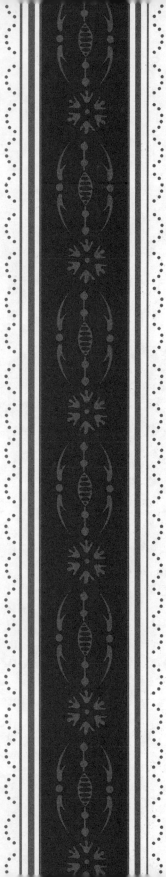

OUR FAVORITE CHRISTMAS MOVIES

OUR FAVORITE CHRISTMAS STORIES AND POEMS

OUR FAMILY'S OTHER CHRISTMAS TRADITIONS

Christmas is a time for top-heavy joy. Humanity's hope has been reborn in the bleakness of midwinter. Bells are ringing, people are singing out loud in the street. There is no such thing as a quiet Christmas. The whole world trembles with the thrill of Christ's coming.

Join in the song.

THE BAD MOTHER'S HANDBOOK

Kate Long

WINDSOR
PARAGON

First published 2004
by
Picador
This Large Print edition published 2005
by
BBC Audiobooks Ltd by arrangement with
Pan Macmillan Ltd

ISBN 1 4056 1165 0   (Windsor Hardcover)
ISBN 1 4056 2152 4   (Paragon Softcover)

British Library Cataloguing in Publication Data available

Printed and bound in Great Britain by
Antony Rowe Ltd., Chippenham, Wiltshire

For Lily

Acknowledgements

For their encouragement and guidance:
David Rees, Kath Pilsbury, Ursula Doyle, Leslie
Wilson, Katherine Frank and Simon Long.

For helping to get the ball rolling:
Judith Magill, Adrian Johnson, Lynn Patrick
and Peter Straus.

For invaluable practical support:
the Headmaster and staff of Abbey Gate College.

For inspirational background material,
and a whole lot of Oldham Tinkers LPs:
Mum and Dad.

I'll tell thee a tale
About a snail
That jumped in t' fire
And burnt its tail

I'll tell thee another
About its brother
Did t' same
Silly owd bugger.

In the battle between handbag strap and door handle, far better to knacker your handbag than let the door handle feel it's won.

CHAPTER ONE

NAN DREAMS:

When I was twelve I fell and broke my elbow. It was election day 1929 and we were mucking about on top of the wall by the polling station. It was about six feet up and you were all right as long as you sat astride the coping stones, only I'd turned side-saddle so as to spot the people who'd voted Conservative, my dad said you could see it in their faces. Jimmy nudged me and we started singing:

> *'Vote! Vote! Vote for Alec Sharrock*
> *He is sure to win the day*
> *And we'll get a salmon tin*
> *And we'll put the Tory in*
> *And he'll never see his mother any more.'*

I swung my legs to make the words come out better and the next thing I knew I was sprawled on the ground with my arm underneath me. Jimmy tried to make a sling out of the yellow muslin banners we'd been waving but I screamed and he started to cry in panic. It hurt so much I was afraid to get up in case I left my arm on the floor.

The following day, when we heard Labour'd got in, Dad got so drunk he couldn't open the back gate.

'I'll go and let him in,' Jimmy volunteered.

'Tha'll not!' said Mother. 'Leave him where he is.'

So I lay on the sofa with my arm all strapped up and watched him struggle. Finally he fell over and my mother drew the curtains on him.

It was funny, we'd never known him touch a drop before.

His vices lay in other directions.

JANUARY 1997

The day after it happened everything seemed normal. Even from behind my bedroom door I could hear Mum going on at Nan. She tries not to get cross but it's the only emotion my mother does these days.

'Come on, Nan, it's time for your bath.'

'I can't. My arm hurts.'

'No, it doesn't. You've been dreaming again. Come *on*.'

Ours is a house of lost things; keys, hearing aids, identities. There was a row about sausages this morning. My mum had cooked two sausages for Nan's dinner and left them on a plate to cool. Then the window cleaner came to the door, and when she got back they'd gone.

'What have you done with them?' she asked Nan (patient voice).

'I han't touched 'em.'

'Yes, you have, you must have.'

'It were t' dog.'

'We haven't got a dog, Nan. Where are they? I just want to know, you're not in trouble. Have you eaten them?'

'Aye, I might have done. Yesterday. I had 'em for my tea.'

'How can you have had them yesterday when I've only just cooked them? God Almighty, it's

2

every little thing.' My mother ran her hand wearily over her face and sighed. It's something she does a lot.

'By the Crin! There's no need to shout. You're a nowty woman. You're like my daughter Karen, she gets her hair off at nothing.'

'I am your daughter Karen.'

'Hmph.'

It was me who found the sausages next day, wrapped in two plastic bags inside the bread bin.

Not that Nan has the monopoly on confusion.

I know my name is Charlotte and that I'm seventeen, but on a bad day that's as far as it goes. 'Be yourself' people, older people, are always telling me: yeah, right. That's *so* easy. Sometimes I do those quizzes in *Most!* and *Scene Nineteen*. Are you a Cool Cat or a Desperate Dog and What's Your Seduction-Style, how to tell your personality type by your favourite colour, your favourite doodle, the hour of your birth. Do I

a) believe this crap?
b) treat it with the contempt it deserves?

Depends on my mood, really.

Sometimes my nan thinks I am her own childhood reincarnated. 'Bless her,' she says, rooting for a Mintoe, 'her father beat her till she were sick on t' floor and then he beat her again. He ran off and her mother had to tek in washin'. Poor lamb. Have a toffee.'

This drives my mum up the wall, round the bend and back again. She doesn't like to see good sympathy going to waste, particularly in my direction, because she thinks I Live the Life of Riley.

3

'You have chances I never had,' she tells me. 'Education's everything. How much homework have you got tonight?' She bought me a personal organizer for Christmas but I lost it—I haven't had the balls to tell her yet. 'You must make something of your life. Don't make the mistake I made.'

Since I am part of the Mistake ('I was a mother by the age of sixteen, divorced at twenty-one') this leaves me in an unusual position: I am also her redeemer, the reassurance that her life has not in fact been wasted. My future successes will be hers and people will say to me, 'Your mother was a clever woman. She gave up a lot for you.'

Or so she hopes.

Actually I'm in a bit of a mess.

When Nan walked in on me and Paul Bentham having sex yesterday afternoon she didn't say a word. She's surprisingly mobile, despite the bag. The colostomy was done donkey's years ago, pre-me, to get rid of galloping cancer.

'THE QUEEN MOTHER HAS ONE, YOU KNOW,' the consultant had shouted.

'Ooh. Swanky,' replied Nan, impressed. 'Well, Ivy Seddon reckons Cliff Richard has one an' he dances about all ovver.'

I thought she might let it slip that evening while we were watching *Coronation Street*. Suddenly she said: 'She were too young, she didn't know what she were doing. I towd her, tha maun fret, I'll tek care of it.' My mum, coming in with a cup of tea for her, banged the saucer down so that the tea spilt on the cloth, and gave me a look.

Christ, Nan, please don't say anything or I'm done for. ('A thirty-three-year-old woman was today formally accused of bludgeoning to death her

4

teenage daughter with what police believe may
have been a personal organizer. Neighbours
reported hearing raised voices late into the
night . . .')

It still hurts a bit. I didn't know it would hurt like
that. I knew there'd be blood because I read
somewhere about them hanging the bed sheets out
of the window in olden days so that all and sundry
could see the bride had been virgo intacta. I used
an old T-shirt and rinsed it out afterwards; if she
asks, I'll tell my mother it was a nosebleed.

I'm not a slag. It's just that there's not a lot to do
round here. You can walk through Bank Top in
fifteen minutes, a small dull village hunching along
the ridge of a hill and sprawling down the sides in
two big estates. From the highest point it affords
panoramic views of industrial Lancashire; factories,
warehouses and rows and rows of red-brick
terraces, and on the horizon the faint grey-green
line of millstone-grit moorland. To the south
there's the television mast where a German plane
is supposed to have come down fifty years ago; to
the north there's Blackpool Tower, just visible on
the skyline. I used to spend hours squinting to see
the illuminations, but they're too far away.

There are three types of housing in Bank Top.
Victorian two-up two-downs line the main street,
while on the fringes of the village it's all modern
boxes with garages and uniform front lawns. None
of the people in these Prestige Developments talk
to each other but you can hear everything your
neighbour's doing through the cardboard walls,
apparently. Beneath these shiny new houses the
foundations shift and grumble over defunct mine
shafts—the last pit closed forty years ago—making

5

Bank Top a sink village in every sense.

Then there's the council estate, thirties semis, where dogs roam free and shit on the pavement with impunity. This is where we live. We bought our house in the boom of '84 (also Divorce Year) and my mother celebrated by having a Georgian front door fitted and mock leaded lights on the windows. The front box room, which is mine and minute, looks out over the Working Men's Club car park; some rum things go on *there* of a Saturday night, I can tell you.

In the centre of the village is the church and the community centre and a rubbish row of shops, a newsagent, a launderette, a Spar. Two pubs, more or less opposite each other, battle it out but one is for old people and families off the new estates with quiz nites and chicken tikka pizza, and the other's rough as rats. I don't go in either. For kicks I get the bus to Wigan from a bus shelter smelling of pee. Fuck off, it says over the lintel, so I generally do.

I don't belong in this village at all. Actually, I don't know where I do belong. Another planet, maybe.

*   *   *

So there I was, on my back, entirely naked and rigid as a corpse, when Nan totters into my bedroom and says to Paul, 'A horse has just gone past the landing window.'

'Which way did it go?' asks Paul.

'*Which way did it go?*' I said later. 'What are you, mad as her?'

'I was only trying to make conversation.' He

6

shrugged his bony shoulders under the sheets. 'What's up with her? Is she mental, like?'

'No more than a lot of people,' I said, a bit sharply. I get defensive about her, even though she is a bloody nuisance. 'Some days she's more with it than me. She's just old. You might be like that when you're old.'

'I'd shoot myself first.'

'No, you wouldn't. That's what everyone says, but they wouldn't.'

Part of the problem in this house is hormones. There are too many undiluted women for one small ex-council house. Huge clouds of supercharged oestrogen drift about and react sending showers of sparks into the atmosphere; the air prickles with it. Nan hasn't got any left, of course, although she hung onto hers longer than most (had my mum at forty-six! Didn't realize people even had sex at that age), but I've got more than I know what to do with. Certainly more than my mother knows what to do with. She suspects I have tart DNA (passed on from her, presumably). If she finds out I've been having sex she will kill me. Really.

This would be my worst nightmare:

Bloody bloody bloody hell. Bloody Nan for making a mess on the bed. Again. Not her fault but I DON'T CARE, nobody cares about me. COME OFF, you bloody fitted sheet, bastard son of a sheet HELL. Trailing this armload off to the washing basket and HELL I've dropped a pair of tights HELL I've dropped a pair of knickers trying to pick up the tights, whole bloody lot's gone now all over the floor. Navy sock in with the whites, that was a close shave. Charlotte WILL NOT put her dirty clothes in the right baskets, what kind of a slut have I produced, you'd think she'd have more consideration. Dying for a cup of tea, cotton with pre-wash, heavily soiled, everything's heavily soiled in this house. Not Nan's fault, that bloody tape doesn't stick to her skin if she gets Nivea under it, what's this, what's this? What's just fallen out of the dirty pillowcase onto the floor?

Oh, Jesus, it's a condom. Charlotte's been having SEX.

*   *   *

I've known Paul Bentham since primary school. Funny to think of all the small events that lead up to a big one. Once, when I was about ten, we were down on the rec, watching the lads play five-a-side. Paul went for an extra big kick, got it wrong and smacked me really hard in the face with the football. The girls all marched off to tell on him and he thought he was in big trouble. Even his ears went red. But I didn't cry, even though I thought my nose had changed shape. I think he appreciated that.

Then there was the Valentine's Day before we moved schools. I knew he'd made a card for me, his friends had all been teasing me about it, and I waited; morning playtime, dinnertime, afternoon playtime. It wasn't till four o'clock he thrust it into my hand, and even then he'd changed the words on it:

8

Roses are red ~~Roses are red~~ ~~Vilots are blue~~ ~~If you go with me~~ ~~I'll go with you~~

Vilots are blue
Roses are red
If I went with you
I'd be off my head

I wasn't that fussed, though. I knew it was Martin Hedges who'd made him do it.

I was more upset when he didn't dance with me at the leavers' disco. We knew we were off to different schools, him to the comp and me to the grammar, so I thought he might be up for a kiss, but he never came near me, just raced around hitting his mates with balloons and stuffing streamers down their backs. I told my mum about it afterwards (we got on in those days). She said, 'Well, what can you expect, he's a little boy.' It made me wonder when he'd be grown up.

Luckily it's impossible to avoid anyone on a place as small as Bank Top. We'd meet at the bus stop, blank each other out and sit as far apart as possible on the red leatherette seats, so I knew there was a chance he was interested. When he was with his friends he'd spread himself out over the back of the 214 to Wigan and talk loudly and swear a lot, writing on the windows and converting the sign EMERGENCY EXIT to VIRGIN EXIT by scratching off bits of the lettering. Then the boys would say to each other, 'That's *your* door, that is. That's the door *you* should use.' Such a stigma.

Now neither of us would be able to use it.

I thought it would make me feel different, not being a virgin, but mainly it's made me feel scared.

'Have you done this before?' he asked as he unzipped his jeans.

We knew what was going to happen. It was my

9

New Year's resolution and I'd told him. I don't think he could believe his luck.

'No. Have you?'

'Does it matter?'

I didn't trust myself to answer so I took my skirt off. Like we were changing for PE; hand your valuables over. I was sure we should be undressing each other, or at least kissing, but that seemed too intimate. I started to shiver with nerves and the cold. 'Can you stick the heater on? You're nearest.'

CLICK went the thermostat and we got into bed.

Then time seemed to hang for a moment and I was back at last August's carnival, sitting on our front wall watching the streamered floats go past and waving at toddlers dressed as bees, when he came sauntering over with his bucket of coins. He was wearing a pirate costume and he'd drawn a black curly moustache over his soft top lip, but the skin only looked more smooth and bright, almost girlish. 'It wrecks, this eyepatch,' he said, peeling it off and rubbing at the red mark on his cheek. 'I'm sure I'm doing myself damage. And these boots are killing me, an' all.'

So he sat down and we chatted shyly, then we walked to the field together to hear the judging and watch the endless teams of high-stepping knee-socked majorettes waving giant pompoms about. The megaphone squawked the names of princesses and queens. 'Why is there always a fat one in every troupe?' he'd said, and the brass band played 'Oh When the Saints' while the air glittered around us. Little children ran about screaming, teenage girls lay on the grass and exposed their midriffs to the sun. Before he went home he said, 'You'll have to come round some time and we'll listen to some CDs or summat.' The sun flashed on his dagger. 'Yeah,' I said. 'All right.'

CLICK.

He was fumbling between my legs and pushing a finger inside me then, Christ, two, stabbing and rotating clumsily. (Wasn't that what the boys boasted about, the girls at school said, how many *fingers* they'd managed?) No. I'd changed my mind. This was a bad idea. Stop. I looked for his gaze to tell him to slow down, to abandon the whole thing and go downstairs and watch *The Simpsons*. But the fierce desire in his eyes paralysed me. I'd heard of people's eyes burning, but I'd never seen it in real life. It was like all his maleness concentrated there, shocking.

Suddenly he paused and half turned away. My heart lurched, then I realized he was rolling on a condom. His vertebrae were clear through his skin and I followed their curve down to the shadow at the base of his spine. Were all men so angular?

CLICK.

Then he turned back to me, grasped his cock like he meant business and forced his way in. Ow ow OW it stung so much it was all I could do not to cry out. A football in the face was nothing compared to this. I held myself rigid and clung on to his back, wondering why something so universally billed as brilliant could be so awful. Why didn't they warn us at school? I'm sure if some teacher had said, 'Oh and by the way, it feels like someone sandpapering your cervix,' they needn't have bothered with all the Aids warnings and morality stuff. I'd certainly have thought twice. He came quickly with a series of great shudders and

11

then collapsed into me, hiding his face against my neck.

It was at this point that Nan walked in, so all credit to him really that he managed anything coherent at all.

Afterwards it was embarrassing. Even though I ran over and locked the door I still felt the horror of Nan's blank stare and half-smile. Neither of us knew what to say and there was blood and we were still naked. Down the landing we could hear Nan singing:

'You know last night, well you know the night before
Three little tom-cats come knockin' at the door
One had a fiddle, another had a drum
And the third had a pancake stuck to its bum.'

'Don't put that in the bin!' I shouted as he scooped up the condom and neatly tied a knot in it. 'Hell's bells, if my mother finds that in with the tissues . . .'

'So what am I supposed to do with it? Do you not want to keep it forever?'

He dangled it from his finger then made as if to throw it at me. I screamed and flinched. He lunged and we rolled about on the bed, then somehow it became a pillow fight. I bet that never happens in my mother's Aga Sagas. His ribs moved under his pale skin and his blue eyes shone, and I thought, He's still just a boy really. He was panting and smiling, and I knew then I'd done the right thing.

At last we rolled into the bedhead. He banged his chin and I knocked a picture off the wall which fell down the back.

'Aw, shit, sorry. I'll get it.'

12

He dived under the bed, all sharp shoulder bone, and brought out the photograph; two hand-tinted ginger kittens in a basket above the legend *Happy Hours!*.

> *Hoping always for a meeting*
> *With a friend I love so true*
> *Dear I send this simple greeting*
> *May the world deal well with you*

'The frame's a bit jiggered.'

He handed it over. The thin black wood was split at the corner and the glass was cracked.

'I can get a new one. Best not let my mother see, though.' I opened the bedside cupboard and slid the picture in under some magazines. 'I know it's naff but it's got sentimental value. It's one of Nan's birthday cards from when she was little, she used to have it in her room and I always wanted it. I nabbed it when her mind began to go. Sort of a way of preserving a piece of my childhood, do you know what I mean? Against all the change . . . She's never noticed.'

'Very nice. Do you want to come round on Saturday? Everyone's out so, only I've got to get back to let Daniel in now. Sooner he gets his own key the better.'

He was pulling on his sweater as he spoke.

'Can you not stay just a bit longer?'

'Sorry. Little brothers and all that. Have you seen my sock?'

I scrambled to put something on, we found the sock and then he went home. I lay on the bed wishing he'd kissed me goodbye instead of ruffling my hair. Should've asked. Or maybe that's not cool. What are the rules, anyway? Perhaps some men

13

just aren't all that demonstrative; it doesn't necessarily mean anything, it's the way they are.

So there it is, the great seduction. I suppose I've made the whole thing sound pretty gross. Some of it was. But the point is, the point is, I'm a woman now, an adult. Perhaps people will be able to tell just by looking at me (God, I hope not! The girls at school used to say you walked funny afterwards). But the point is I have a life that is not my mother's and it is the beginning of some big changes round here.

I know things are going to be different from now on.

*　　　*　　　*

I'D MET Billy when he ran across the street to help me carry a basket of washing. It was blowing about, a great white sheet on the top, and I knew if it hit the ground and got dirty my mother would chow. It happened once before when I was little and Jimmy had hold of one handle and I had the other. We were staggering down the street to Dr Liptrot's with his week's wash when a big gust of wind took two or three shirts right off and they fell in t' road. We were two-double laughing as we picked 'em up, but when we got home and showed my mother she laid her head on the table and wept.

Billy had been courting a girl he'd met in the TB sanatorium, a bonny woman but it made no difference. We had ten for the wedding tea, then caught the train to Blackpool. At Chorley some lads got in and saw all t' confetti in my hair so they started singing, 'We have been married today, We are on our honeymoon all the way.' When we got

14

to the bed and breakfast I gave a fish to the landlady so she could cook it for our supper. The next evening she said, 'Mrs Hesketh, are you ready for your fish now?' And I never took her on because I wasn't used to the name.

When I got back to the mill I had such a colour all the girls said I must be pregnant.

*   *   *

WHERE'S CHARLOTTE? Gone to Wigan for the afternoon, no doubt to spend money she hasn't got on crap she doesn't need. Nan? Asleep in the chair, legs apart, mouth slightly open. God, if I ever get like that. And why are there never any pens in this house? You put them down and they walk. Useful Drawer; what a flamin' mess, I don't know why we keep half this rubbish. Sandpaper, candles, napkin rings—like we're ever going to use *those*—Stain Devil's leaked all over the clothes brush now. Had a big row with the hoover and a table leg today; broke one of the attachments, so that'll be something else to sort out. Bingo! Black biro, bit fluffy round the nib, still, be all right. Here goes nothing.

Love 'n' stuff

Finding You a Partner for Life's Adventure

Outline Questionnaire

Please try to answer as honestly as possible

Name Karen Cooper

Status *Very low actually.* Divorced.

Address 21, Brown Moss Road, Bank Top, Nr Wigan, Lancs WI24 5LS. *Moving in with my mother was supposed to be a fresh start.*

Age 33. *Feel about 60 sometimes.*

Children One. *17-year-old madam.*

Occupation ~~Teacher.~~ Part time classroom assistant. *At my old primary school! My life's just gone round in a big loop.*

Educational Qualifications 10 'O' levels. *Yes, 10. I could have had a degree if I'd wanted. What the hell does it matter anyway? I've been to the University of Life (though I had originally set my sights on Leeds).*

Salary (approx) Crap. *Funded this caper out of Nan's present (I just withdraw it from her savings account, Merry Xmas Happy Birthday etc, even buy my own damn card).*

Do you consider yourself to be
❑ working class ☑ middle class
❑ upper class ❑ not sure

Political Persuasion *If push came to shove I suppose I'd say Conservative. I mean, they're going to*

16

be in forever, aren't they? Anyway, if it wasn't for Maggie Thatcher we couldn't have bought this house (although I can't say I rate John Major much). Truth is, nothing ever changes for people like us, whoever's swanning about in Number 10.

Religion None. *Mum'll put in a good word for us all when she gets to heaven.*

Height 5'9". *That's going to put a lot of men off for a start.*

Weight/dress size 12/14. *Depends how bloody Nan's being. Some days I can eat a whole packet of gypsy creams at one sitting.*

Hair colour Brown. *Currently. I'm always looking for the perfect hairstyle, the one that'll solve my life for me. Growing out a perm in the meantime.*

Eyes *Sort of grey. Charlotte's got her dad's blue eyes. Nan's are brown. None of us bloody match in this house.*

Special Interests *Reading, drinking, watching tv. Doesn't sound too clever, does it? But believe me, when the alternatives are changing your mother's colostomy bag or arguing with your daughter, there's no contest. Always meant to take up something worthy, but there you go. Actually I do read quite a lot. Joanna Trollope, Rosamunde Pilcher, that kind of thing. It helps.*

Personality

Do you consider yourself to be any of the following? (It may be useful to ask a friend or relative.) *You must be kidding. Charlotte would wet herself laughing if she saw this.*

❑ extrovert ❑ generous ❑ organised

❑ shy ❑ patient ❑ creative

❑ optimistic ❑ thoughtful ❑ spontaneous

❑ loyal ❑ down-to-earth ❑ understanding

To be honest, none of these seems quite right.

Please feel free to add your own ideas below:
Knackered, bitter, unfulfilled, self-sabotaging. Hence this questionnaire.

What kind of relationship are you hoping might develop out of our introductions?
Christ. Just forget it.

MY LAST DATE was a classic. We'd met in the Working Men's. It's a bit common, but I go there occasionally because it's cheap and local, and if Nan gets up to anything really mad Charlotte can nip across the road and let me know. Sometimes I need to get out of the house in a hurry.

Anyway I was sitting at the bar cradling a Bacardi Breezer and feeling bleak when he came over. Greyish—well, grey, but not balding; normal shape; about my height. He was wearing a check shirt with the sleeves rolled up, and jeans, which gave no clues. I clocked hairy forearms, no wedding ring, clean fingernails as he proffered his money to the bar man.

'Can I get you a drink while I'm here?'

18

That gave me licence to have a better look at his face. He just seemed ordinary, pleasant, not weird or anything.

'Thanks. I've not seen you in here.' It was true; it's always the same faces in the Working Men's.

'No. I used to live up Bolton way, I'm revisiting old haunts. What about you? Is this your regular?'

'Not really.' God, what a thought. 'I just drop in from time to time. When it all gets too much.' I laughed loudly but really I felt like banging my forehead against the bar. Stupid thing to say.

He only smiled, which made his face crinkle up. I wondered how old he was, not that it mattered. I get like that sometimes; desperate.

See, I know you shouldn't look for a man to solve your life for you, but it's easier said than done when you're out in the throng on your own. Sometimes it would be so nice for somebody else to take the flak for once, never mind have some decent sex. A hundred million sex acts a day worldwide, there are supposed to be; you'd think one of them might waft its way over in my direction. Nobody in our house understands that I have Needs as well, it's like Montel Williams says. He was on Channel 4 yesterday afternoon, a show called 'I Hate My Mom's New Boy-friend'. 'Doesn't Mom have a right to some happiness too?' he kept asking these sulky teenagers. The audience were all clapping. I nearly called Charlotte down but she was revising for her modules.

Six Breezers later and for all his grey hair I was out in the car park kissing him long and full, putting off the moment when I had to go home and change Nan and face Charlotte's scowls. Even light rain and sweeping headlights weren't putting me

19

off my stroke. It was so nice to be held, even for a few minutes. Then a car nearly reversed into us, which broke the mood slightly. I disentangled.

'I'd invite you back but my daughter's around . . . It's a bit difficult . . .'

'Can I see you again?'

Jackpot.

He fished in his back pocket and gave me His Card, very swish, and said there was no pressure but to give him a call. 'Soon.' I liked that, it seemed gentlemanly; also it meant I didn't have to sit around waiting for him to ring me. I should have known it was all looking too good.

The next day at school I was telling Sylv, the secretary.

'He wasn't sex on a stick but he was all right. I'd see him again.'

'*What* was his name?' she asked with a funny look on her face.

I gave her the card.

She studied it and pursed her lips. 'You do know this is Vicky's ex, don't you?' She handed it back smugly. I don't like Sylv any more, I never really liked her. She draws her eyebrows on and wears skirts that are too tight.

'Vicky? Deputy Head Vicky? Vicky Roberts?'

'Yep.'

'The one she divorced just before I started here?'

'The one who couldn't *get it up* unless he wore *special rubber knickers*.' Sylv dropped her voice and mouthed exaggeratedly.

'Jesus.'

'Wanted her to wear *some kind of mask*, too. That's when she asked him to leave.' Sylv smacked her lips with satisfaction. She'd be dining out on this for months, I could tell. I am never going to tell her anything personal again. I wanted to sink to my knees and beg her not to pass it on but I knew it would be a waste of time; Rubber Man would be all round the staff room by lunchtime. For once I was glad I was on playground duty. So instead I said:

'Well, he was too old, anyway.'

'So you won't be seeing him again, then?' she called after me as I swept out of the office.

It's just as well Sylv didn't catch me photocopying my practice run at 'Love 'n' Stuff' in school. I reckon perhaps I'm ready to do the questionnaire properly now.

NEVER LET IT be said that when things are looking their grimmest, they can't get worse.

I was sound asleep when I heard the crash. I struggled with the bedsheets, tangled from some overheated dream, threw on a dressing gown in case it was an intruder, although I knew it wasn't, and hurried downstairs.

It was completely dark in the lounge but there were muffled sounds coming from the kitchen. I opened the door and blinked in the light.

'What are you doing, Nan?'

Actually I could see what she was doing. She was pulling out drawers and emptying Tupperware boxes onto the floor. Six tins of salmon were stacked at her feet.

'Are you looking for something to eat?'

'I've lost my key.'

'Which key?'

'To t' back door. Bloody hell fire.' She wrestled with a plastic lid and flung it across the tiles. Then

21

she sat down wearily.

'You don't need a back door key. What would you want to go outside for? It's the middle of the night. And it's freezing.'

'I need to check the bins.'

'No, no you don't. You did them this morning. Don't you remember? Charlotte helped you.'

What it is, she worries if we put envelopes with our name and address into the wheeliebin, in case someone roots through and takes them. 'Then what, Nan? What would they do with the envelopes?' 'Ooh, all sorts,' says Nan mysteriously. 'There's some wicked people about.' It clearly worries her, so we let her rip them up into tiny pieces. It's one of our routines which has become normal. This nocturnal activity was something new, though.

'Come on, Nan, come to bed, you'll catch your death. I'll clear up in the morning.'

'The bins!'

'We did them. Tiny pieces. And the bin men come tomorrow.' And I'm bloody cold and Christ it's twenty past *three* in the morning and I've got to go to work in five hours and nobody cares that my life is a complete fuck-up.

'I'll just put this salmon back.'

'LEAVE IT! Just COME to BED and LEAVE this mess. Please.' I used to cry before the divorce but I don't seem able to any more. I get angry instead. She didn't move, so I lunged over and pulled her up roughly. She's only small and pretty light. We staggered together and I fell into the edge of the unit and banged my arm.

'Hell.'

Nan looked up with watery eyes.

22

'You'll want some knit-bone for that.'

'Shut up.' I was trying not to swear at her.

'Or Dr Cassell's Miracle Cure-All Tablets. They cured Uncle Jack and he had malaria. Caught it in Mesopotamia during the Great War. He always had to have the doors shut and a big fire. When he emigrated he sent us a lamb. My mother took it to t' butchers to be jointed up but she never got back what she should have done.'

'WILL YOU COME TO BED!'

She turned and stared at me, trying to focus. Then she put her face close to mine.

'I don't have to do what you tell me,' she said quietly. 'You're not my daughter. Your mother was called Jessie. Didn't you know? You're not mine.'

*   *   *

'**Did you have** an orgasm? I want to give you an orgasm, Charlotte.' Behind him David Beckham grinned confidently; no sexual hang-ups for him. We were lying under a Manchester United duvet and it was four weeks since we'd first done it. Outside children were screaming and an Alsatian barked from behind wire netting in next door's garden. His house is no quieter than ours. I glanced up at the window (Man U curtains).

'Is it snowing yet? It's cold enough. Snow's about the only thing that makes our estate look any better.'

'Did you hear what I said?'

'Sorry. Yeah. Well, no. It doesn't matter. It was nice.'

'Nice? Is that it?' Paul rolled away onto his back and gazed at the ceiling, hands behind his head. He

23

had little tufts of hair under his arms that I loved to stroke. 'I want it to be fantastic for you, fireworks going off, that kind of stuff. I don't feel you're always . . .'

'What?' I leant up on an elbow and watched his face struggle.

'Sort of, I dunno, *with* me. Oh, I can't explain. It's not like it is on the telly, is it?'

'Nothing is. This is Life.' I lay back down and put my face close to his. 'It's loads better than it was, though.' This was true. It wasn't painful any more, for a start, especially now I'd sorted out the cystitis. And when we did it at his house it felt more relaxed; no leaping up and legging it afterwards, no fear of interruptions. Paul's mum left two years ago, and his dad was so laid back about his son's sex life I got the impression we could be having it off on the living-room carpet and he'd only complain if we got in the way of the TV screen.

'Yeah, well. Practice makes perfect, eh?' He reached over and ran his hand over my breasts. 'These are great.' He circled a nipple with his finger and watched it firm to a peak. 'Brilliant.' Then he moved sideways and put both palms flat over my chest. He sighed happily. 'You'll get me goin' again.'

It was thrilling, this power I never knew I had. I pushed the duvet back and watched his cock grow and twitch against his pale thigh; it wasn't scary any more. I felt like the goddess of sex. I wriggled against him and he groaned.

'Touch it.'

I still didn't know the proper technique but it didn't seem to matter. Whatever I did he rolled his eyes back as if he was having a fit, and panted.

There was all this loose skin below the tight, shiny stalk. I fiddled experimentally and he began to swear quietly.

'Like that, yeah. Fuck. Fucking hell.'

When my hair fell forward and brushed his stomach he drew his breath in sharply.

'Wait a minute.'

He groped around on the bedside table and snatched up a condom, which he dropped with shock when I dipped my head and kissed his navel.

'I'll get it.' I leant over and retrieved the little foil packet from off the floor.

'Put it on for me. Go on. It'd be so sexy.'

I must have looked doubtful.

'I'll show you how.'

I thought, you have to learn these things if you're a woman, it'll be another string to my bow.

He tore off the packet end and squeezed out the slimy ring. I watched closely, the way I used to in science lessons when Bunsen burners were being demonstrated. Then he handed it to me. I tried not to flinch.

'Keep it this way up. Pull that pointy thing in the middle, just a bit, gently. Gently! It's my last one. Now, put it on the top like this—' he guided my hands to his groin—'and, that's it, roll it down— Jesus—'

And then he was on me, in me again, jerking his hips and burying his face against my shoulder.

'I'm going to make you come,' he whispered savagely. It sounded like a threat.

I moved my hips under his and he slowed his pace, adding a sort of grind to the thrust.

'What does that feel like?'

'Ni— fantastic,' I breathed. But I was panicking.

I didn't know how to rise to the occasion. Perhaps I had come and didn't realize it. No, because the girls at school said you definitely knew when you'd had an orgasm. It was like a sneeze, Julia had said. A *sneeze*?

Meanwhile Paul ground on. 'Ooh, that's so good.'

'Mmm.'

Should I fake it? I tried panting heavily and moaning a bit, but I didn't have the confidence to pull it off. He would guess, and then it would be awful. But what to say?

He humped away and I stroked his back absently, gazing round the room at his collection of football programmes pinned to the walls, his red and white scarf draped over the lintel, the rosette stuck to his computer. The rhythm of his pelvis became a playground skipping song: *Keep* the kettle *boil*ing, *keep* the kettle *boil*ing—

Suddenly he stopped. 'Have you come yet?'

There was a brief pause then I smiled dazzlingly.

'No, but it was great. Have you?'

He looked hurt. 'Yeah. Ages ago. At the beginning. I was only keeping going for you. Do you think you might be close?'

'I don't know,' I said truthfully.

'Do you want to try a bit longer?'

I shook my head and tried not to shudder.

'Look, Paul, it really doesn't matter. It'll, it'll sort itself out. I probably just need to relax more. Don't worry about it. I'm not.' I smiled again, reassuring. 'It's great. You're great.'

'OK, then.' He grinned. 'God, I'm knackered.' He pulled away, then, 'Shit.'

'What's the matter?' He was looking down in a

horrified sort of way. 'Have you hurt yourself? Have *I* hurt you?'

'The condom. It's . . .' he gestured at his limp and naked cock. 'It's still . . . Can you . . . ? Look, I think it's still inside you. Bloody hell. Do you want to, er, have a feel?'

I was seeing stars of panic but I did what he said. I leant flat on the bed, drew my knees up and put my fingers gingerly inside myself. 'Don't watch!' It felt raw and strange in there. I kept trying to take deep breaths and not clench up. 'I can't . . . Oh, God! Paul!'

'Let me have a try. I'm at a better angle.' He giggled nervously.

As he turned back to me I closed my eyes. It was like being at the doctors. Once there'd been a girl at school, in the first year, who'd got a tampon stuck up her and a teacher had had to fish it out: I remember the horror of simply being told. I wanted, now, at this very moment, to die with fear and shame. I opened my eyes a fraction as he probed and concentrated, and saw his tongue poking out slightly between his lips.

'Sorted!' He pulled out the slimy thing and held it up for inspection. Then he nodded. 'Phew! We're OK, it's not bursted or anything. I'll stick it in t' bin.' He threw it across the room. I hoped he wouldn't shout *Goal!* like he normally did, but he didn't. He just said, 'Christ, I can do without that!'

You can, I thought, rolling miserably up in the duvet. That was, would be, without doubt, the worst moment of my entire adult life.

'Cheer up. It weren't nothin'.' He ruffled my hair. 'I'll go and get us a Wagon Wheel in a minute. I'll stick t' kettle on too. Do you want to play Tomb

27

Raider when you've got dressed? I nicked it off Dan this morning.'

He was throwing on clothes as he spoke. So it must be all right, then. But why don't they tell you sex can be so bloody *embarrassing*? I have to admit, it isn't like I thought it would be. Perhaps I don't love Paul enough, or perhaps it's me. Either way, I need some answers and I think I know where to get them.

*   *   *

THE QUESTION IS, is Nan telling the truth? And if she is, what then? I have to, *have to* find out.

CHAPTER TWO

BY GOD, Bill were a clever man. I don't know what he saw in me. Sometimes, when he was a lad, they sent him home early from school because he'd done all his work. Teacher used to say, 'Hesketh! Come out with your sums, an' if they're not finished, you're in trouble.' An' he'd go up to t' front and it'd all be done, all correct, and he'd be sent home at half-past three instead of four. He should have stayed on, he had a 'ead for learning, but he had to leave at thirteen for the wage, same as me.

So he went down the mines, like his father had, and hated it. He never got any proper rest. In the evenings he used to go to Bob Moss's grocer's shop and pack orders, then tek 'em round in a wheelbarrow. Then he started with TB and that was it, off to the Co-Op Convalescent Home at Blackpool, where he met his fiancée. Her name was Alice Fitton, she lived up Chorley way, and she was a bonny woman. She was broken-hearted when he finished with her to start courting me. I should have felt sorry but I didn't. I had what I wanted. I'd seen the way my mother suffered and I knew the value of a good man.

After we married he got a job at Cooks's paper mill, and took up with Bank Top Brass Band, playing tenor horn. He used to say they were one of the finest second-class amateur bands in the league. They practised every other day in a barn over the smithy, and paid a penny a week into funds. Once they played at the Winter Gardens at Southport in front of an audience of four thousand, and won a cup, it were t' first time ever. The conductor, Mr Platt, was overwhelmed. By the time they got back home it was past midnight but he insisted they play Souza's 'Semper Fidelis' as they walked through the main street. 'I don't think as we'd better. We'll wake everyone up,' Bill had said. 'Well, then,' Mr Platt told him, 'we'll tek our shoes and socks off.'

His chest stopped him playing in the finish; there was the TB, and he'd been smoking since he were thirteen. It kept him out o' t' war too, more or less; he stayed at home and was an ambulanceman for th' Home Guard. We were never short of crepe bandage in this house. But it were his lungs that killed him in th' end. He was only sixty-three. We'd been married forty-two years. And it was a happy marriage, oh it was. Except for the one thing.

*   *   *

29

Where do you go to get the answers when you're seventeen? Well, you start by pushing your way through the Enchanted Forest of people around you who *think* they know the answers: parents, teachers, solve-your-life-in-twenty-minutes-magazine-article writers. Mum thinks ballsing up her own life makes her an expert on mine (now where's the logic in *that*?), but what she fails to see is that I am about as much like her as she is like Nan, i.e. not at all. To look at us both you'd think I'd been found under a hedge. Bit of a relief if I had been, in some ways. It would certainly explain a lot.

Dad, of course, is conspicuous by his absence. Oh, I *know* where he lives, and it's not so far away, but if I turned up on the doorstep and started asking for Advice about my personal life, he'd have kittens. It's not his field. Anyway, I think I scare him.

Teachers, they mean well, most of them, but they just see everything in terms of exam results, as if your 'A'-level grade print-out will have magically at the bottom a projected CV to tell you exactly where you're going next. 'A A B B, Accountancy at Bristol, followed by a meteoric career with Touche Ross, marriage at twenty-six, a nice house in Surrey and two healthy children by the time you're thirty (suggested names Annabel and Max).'

I suppose a normal girl would ask her friends, but I only have acquaintances, people I hang around with but never Talk to. Is it geography or psychology? John Donne wrote, 'No man is an island', but he didn't live in Bank Top. Lucky bastard.

30

Part of the problem is that the village is at the back of beyond and there's no one else from my form lives there. All the other kids from my class at primary school swarmed off to the Comp, sneering over their shoulders at me as they went: I see them around but they don't want anything much to do with me now I'm officially A Snob. Most of the people who go to the Grammar live on the other side of Bolton (in, it's got to be said, much bigger houses). I can't drive—no money for lessons and though Dad's promised faithfully to teach me I know this will *never* happen—and the buses stop running at 10.30. Mum can't be ferrying me about because she doesn't like to leave Nan unattended for fear of mad accidents. So here I am. It's never worried me till now.

Don't get me wrong, I'm not Billy No-mates, I know where to sit in the Common Room, I go out (and return early). I just don't seem to have that need for intimacy that some girls do. Strolling around the field at lunch-time, sharing confidences, not my thing. But maybe I'd be like that wherever I lived. I was always on the outside at St Mary's; the one helping Mrs Ainscough in the library at dinner break rather than playing Scott and Charlene by the bins. 'You spend too much time in your own head,' my mother once told me during a blazing row over nothing at all, and I hate to say it, but I think she was right.

So where was I going? Here, to this ordinary-looking modern semi on the outskirts of Bolton, a mere bus ride away from our house. Behind this front door with its glass panels of tulips, a figure moved.

'Hang on a sec. I'm trying not to let the cat out.'

31

The door opened a fraction and a woman's plump face appeared, squashed against the crack. 'Can you—oh damn.' A grey shape squeezed past our feet in an oily movement and was gone. 'Never mind. Come in.'

I stepped into a white hallway full of swathed muslin and stippled walls, church candles and statuettes, *Changing Rooms* gone mad.

'Hiya, I'm Jackie. Is it Charlotte? Great. Come through. Mind the crystals.'

I dodged the swinging mobiles as she led me along to a room at the back. This was all black and red and stank of patchouli. On the walls were pictures of Jackie when she had been younger (and slimmer) together with framed testimonials and a poster of a unicorn rearing up under a rainbow. The table was covered with a scarlet chenille cloth. Jackie lit an incense burner in the corner.

'Now. Take a seat and we'll start with a palm reading.'

We sat with the corner of the dining table between us and she took my hand. The contact made me shiver and it was all I could do not to pull away.

'Relax,' she murmured, touching the soft pads of skin carefully. It felt really freaky. What the hell am I doing here, I thought. Jackie's blonde head was bent and I could see her dark roots. Her nails were immaculately manicured and her fat fingers full of rings.

'I bet you're wondering what you're doing here,' she said without looking up.

Shit shit shit. 'No, not at all.' I could feel myself blushing. 'You were recommended. A girl at school, you told her not to panic when suitcases appeared in the hall, and then her dad left home, but he came back again two weeks later. She was dead impressed. She's been telling everyone.'

'Right.' She shifted her bottom on the chair and leaned back, scrutinizing my face. 'Only a lot of people feel self-conscious consulting a psychic.'

'Yeah, well, I'll be honest . . . I don't know what to think. Does it matter? Am I going to interfere with the vibrations if I don't, er, completely believe . . . ?'

'No.' Very assured. 'What is it you want to know, Charlotte?'

'I, um, oh God, now you're asking. I think I need to know what to do with my life. I want somebody to tell me how to get out of Bank Top, 'cause it's a dump, and where I'd be happy. Is there, like, somewhere I should be headed? Point me in the right direction. Show me how to change things.' She was really listening, which unnerved me, I wasn't used to it. 'Because I thought I had, but everything's just the same . . . Does any of this make sense?'

Her lids and lashes were heavy with make-up as she frowned, leaned forward again and studied my hand. Then she began to talk quickly and confidently, her gaze still fixed on my palm.

'You're an independent person. You are surrounded by conflict. You have moments of confusion and at times you feel nobody understands you.'

Welcome to the World of the Average Teenager, I thought.

'There are a lot of choices coming up for you. You don't know which path to take. Difficult times are ahead but things will resolve themselves by the end of the year.'

Presumably I'd have sorted out my university application by then.

'You need to take particular care of your health over the next twelve months.'

'My mother's always on at me to eat fruit,' I joked. No reaction.

'Your love life will be complicated. Basically you have too soft a heart, but you try to hide it. You will find true love in the end, though.'

Yeah, well, I wouldn't have expected to hear anything else. She wasn't going to say, 'You'll shack up with a one-legged dwarf from Adlington and he'll beat you nightly.' My lips were forming a cynical smile when she pulled in her breath and whispered, 'There's somebody from the Other Side looking after you. He's here now.'

A faint sad cry, like a child, made me freeze.

'Oh, God.' I half turned round, appalled. 'A dead person?' But there was only my reflection in the patio doors and the grey cat mewing to be let in.

'A little boy.'

She waited for my response. I shrugged.

'About eight or nine I'd say, dressed in old-fashioned clothes, a cloth cap and short trousers. Big thick boots, like clogs. He won't tell me his name, he's too shy. But he's holding out forget-me-nots to you.' Jackie's face had gone blank-looking and she was focusing on a spot by my shoulder. It was beginning to spook me.

'I don't know any dead children. God, this is so weird.'

'He's very cold, very cold. He says you're lucky, you're a lucky person. He says you should make the most of your opportunities in life.'

The tension made me laugh. 'He's been talking to my mum. It's a conspiracy.'

Jackie glared at me and let go of my hand. 'He's gone now.' She made it sound as if it was my fault.

'Good.'

'But he's never far away.'

'Christ, don't say things like that, I'll never sleep at night.'

'He's a friend.'

'Right.'

She got up and pulled the curtains across roughly. I could tell she was annoyed with me and I smirked nervously in the gloom. Then she lit candles and brought over a Tarot pack.

'Do you want me to carry on with this?' She had a penetrating stare; I felt like I was back in the first year at school.

'Yeah, absolutely. Sorry.' Might as well get my money's worth.

'Pick a card, then,' she said.

'Dirty little bugger,' said Paul when I told him. 'Here, this'll shift him.' He aimed a trainer at the empty space by the end of my bed. 'Shoo. Go spy on someone else, kinky devil. Go back to your cloud and play with your harp or your pitchfork or whatever.'

'Do you think there could be anything in it?' I was sitting up with the duvet wrapped round me. I hadn't felt properly warm since I'd come home. 'Well, it's the middle of bloody winter, in't it?' had been Paul's response when I told him.

'Ghosts in cloth caps? Sounds like one of the Tetley Tea folk. Get a grip, Charlie.'

I giggled in spite of myself. 'I didn't believe her up till then. But she went sort of creepy after that. You'd have been rattled. You *would*. Stop laughing.'

'And how much did you pay this old hag?'

'Sod off. I only told you because I thought you'd be interested.'

'I am. Take off your bra.'

I unhooked resignedly. 'I know it was all just a load of rubbish . . .'

'So stop worrying.' He was kissing my neck and shoulders and his body heat was wonderful.

'Anyway, you're in the clear.'

'Mmm?'

'She told me a dark-haired boy would hurt me "more than I'd ever been hurt before". It was in the cards. So you're all right.'

'How do you mean? Because I'm blond?' He took his mouth away from my skin reluctantly.

'Yeah.'

'Smashing. Do you want to stop talking now?' he said.

There wasn't the usual mad scramble afterwards because Mum had taken Nan for a hospital appointment and the Metro had died so they'd gone by bus. The journey to hell and back, I'd have thought.

'Did you get that picture sorted?' Paul asked, his eyes roving round the room. We were getting better at the post-coital business. 'The one you broke that time.'

'The one you broke, you mean? While we were scaling the heights of passion? No. Although I did get as far as buying a new frame. I couldn't get the

36

old one off so I gave up.'

'Bloody feeble girly. Do you want me to have a go? Give it here.'

I fished about in the bedside cabinet under the magazines and brought it out.

'Couldn't get it off? What is it, super-glued or summat?'

'Just you have a look.'

He turned the frame over in his hands and examined the back. 'Jesus. I see what you mean.'

Wires criss-crossed the thick cardboard; they had been stapled into the frame at irregular intervals. Blobs of ancient brown glue bulged from the corners. 'I took off another layer of card and Sellotape to get to that. I thought I'd damage the picture if I went any further. Does it need a screwdriver or something to lever the staples out? We have got one but I don't know where.'

'Nah, a penknife should do it. Pass us my jeans.'

He set to work, absorbed. I watched him and thought about my little ghost.

Finally the sections eased apart. 'There you go. Just needed the masculine touch.' I took the pieces in my hands and laid them on the covers. 'If you bung us the new frame I'll put that on for you an' all.'

'Hang on a minute.' I was taking off the layers of card. 'There's something in here. My God, look at that, it's a letter.' I unfolded two sheets of thin yellowing paper. 'It looks like . . . Shit, listen to this.' And I started to read.

Dear Miss Robinson,

Re Sharon Pilkington.

Thank you for your letter informing me that the Adoption Committee have accepted this little girl for a direct placing adoption. I am as certain as it is possible to be in these cases that the mother is quite definite about the adoption. She will not change her mind.

Yours sincerely,

P Davis

'Sharon Pilkington? Who's she when she's at home? Somebody's cut the top off so you can't see the address or date.' I turned the paper over but it was blank. 'Let's have a see what's on the other.'

Notes for the Information of the Case Committee

Name of child: Sharon Anne Pilkington
Weight at birth: 7lbs 2oz
Date of birth: 13.4.63
Present weight: 9lbs (at 3 weeks)
Child of: Miss Jessie Pilkington
Occupation of Mother: mill worker   Aged: 16 years
The Natural Father is: Aged:
Whose occupation is:
Recommended by: Mrs P Davis
The Child is at present: with mother at Mother and Baby Home, Hope Lodge, 46 Walls Road, London N4

General Remarks

Jessie Pilkington is unable to keep and support her baby, she is only 16 and has several young sisters and brothers at home. She feels that it would be unfair on her parents and particularly her mother to bring up another young child. She is unwilling, or unable, to supply the identity of the father, so there is no possibility of support from that quarter. Therefore Jessie feels it is in the child's best interests to be adopted and have the chance of being brought up in a happy family atmosphere.

She has asked that the baby be placed with an acquaintance of hers, a Mrs Nancy Hesketh, who is unable to have children of her own. Jessie feels sure that she has made the right decision to give her baby up and will not go back on it.

Particulars of Mother

Character: good character and reputation
Appearance: good complexion, 5ft 7ins, grey eyes
Health: a strong and healthy family

Particulars of baby

Mrs Davis has seen this baby and she says she is a nice little baby with light brown hair and grey eyes. Her skin is very slightly dry in parts. She has a tendency to colic but a lovely smile.

Additional notes

No history of mental illness, nervousness, alcoholism, bad temper, brutality, delinquency, history of crime in the mother's family.

'So what do you reckon to all that, then?' Paul was busy fanning out all the blades on his penknife and admiring them. 'Charlie? Y' all right?'

I didn't know what to say for a minute so I read the pages again. 'Oh, Paul . . . I don't believe this . . .' I went back up to the date of birth at the top and my throat went tight. 'Paul, stop a minute. I think this is my mum.'

'Who?'

'This Sharon Pilkington. Because, because Nancy Hesketh is Nan, and it's the right birthday, let me just count on . . . 63, 73, 83, 93, 97, yeah. And, oh God, it all makes sense, Nan was really old when she supposedly had my mum and everyone said it was a miracle because she'd tried for years. That's the word Nan used to use herself, a miracle.' I'd put the letter down on the bed and was holding my head between my hands. 'I can't take it in. She doesn't know, surely? My mum, I mean. Oh, Jesus, Paul, this is just amazing. It means Nan's not my nan. It's this Jessie woman. Whoever she is. Wherever she is.'

Paul shrugged. 'Well,' he said closing up his penknife with a click. 'There's summat your psychic didn't mention.'

*   *   *

'THERE'S BLOOD in your shoe.' I spotted the smear on Nan's tights as she knelt to pick up half a Rich Tea she'd spotted under the table. Her joints really are amazing for the age, the doctor at the hospital couldn't believe it. Wouldn't believe me either when I told him how mad she gets, because Sod's law, she was on top form and completely coherent, chatting away as if she'd known him all her life. Even flirted with him. 'I feel champion today. Are you courtin'?' she asked him. 'You're a bonny lad. Have you a car?' He thought it was sweet; I thought it was monstrous. I wanted to hit her over the head with a bedpan, only that would probably have got me admitted instead. Maybe that wouldn't have been such a bad idea.

I spotted the blood in the morning as I was opening the post. Sylv reckoned—I know I said I'd never tell her anything again but she's got this *way*—Sylv reckoned I could just write off for a copy of my birth certificate and that would tell me who my mother was. So I'd been running to pick up the letters from off the mat ever since.

'Have you hurt yourself?'

'No. Where?' She turned her head this way and that, trying to see down her own body.

'Your leg, your ankle. Sit down a minute. Leave the biscuit. Sit, Mother.'

She sank down and pulled at her tights. 'Where? I can't see owt.'

Then I saw her heel was filled with blood.

'Oh, God, lift your foot up.' I squatted down and gently eased off the shoe.

'That's not my blood,' she said immediately.

'Well, who the hell's is it?' I didn't mean to shout so loudly.

'Eeh, you're nowt. I know what's up wi' you. What you want is another baby.'

'Jesus, Mum. You are so wrong. What would I want with a baby when I've got you, eh?'

In the end it was only a scab she'd knocked on

her ankle and nothing like as bad as it first looked. But pulling her shoe on again I thought, Why am I doing this for you? Who are you, anyway? And when I went back to the post, there it was; my birth certificate. And she was right. I'm not her daughter. I'm Sharon Anne Pilkington, from London, from limbo.

1	2	3	4	5
When and where born	Name, if any	Sex	Name and surname of father	Name, surname and maiden surname of mother
Thirteenth March 1963 Hope Lodge Mother and Baby Home 46 Walls Road East Finchley	Sharon Anne	Girl	——	Jessie Pilkington 56 Prentis Road Wigan

So my mother—real mother, birth mother, whatever you call it—is from round here. What I was doing popping out in London, God only knows. She must have run away. I can understand that. Only it's funny I ended up back in the north. Perhaps it was policy then. Maybe they thought babies with northern genes needed weaning on cow heel and parkin. Or maybe they didn't want me polluting southern stock.

I'd like to say I still can't believe it, except that's not true. It kind of confirms a feeling I've always had, that I never fitted in. When I was little and Dad was still alive, on winter evenings we used to

42

draw the curtains and all sit round watching rubbish: *Wheeltappers and Shunters*, or *Bullseye* (super-smashing-great!). Mum's favourite was *The Golden Shot*. I'd have a bottle of pop and a big bag of toffees to pass round, and there'd be this crackly telephone voice droning on: *left, left, stop, right a bit, down, stop, up a bit, up a bit, fire!* Silence, groans or the rattle of coins and cheers. Once Dad dropped his coconut mushrooms in the excitement and there were white flakes in the rug for weeks.

Happy times, sort of, but even then I used to feel I didn't really belong. Somewhere out there was a Beatrix Potter sort of a childhood that wasn't like mine, dandelion and burdock and Jim Bowen. I can remember thinking, Is this all there is? So perhaps I should have stayed in London. With my *mother*.

I imagine her looking like Julie Christie, swinging her bag and wearing a short belted mac and black eyeliner. I bet she sat in cafes and looked soulful when she was pregnant, with the rain lashing down outside and people hurrying past. Everyone's always in a hurry in London. Or maybe that's just an image from some film I've seen. It seems like a real memory, now I know the truth. Can you do that, tune into other people's memories?

The next step, apparently is to contact the Adoption Register. It's a list of people who want to trace each other, so if Jessie Pilkington wants to find me, she can.

I'm sure she'll want to. I can hardly wait.

*　　　*　　　*

People were moving as if they were under water,

43

ponderously. The air was thick and warm, you could tell it had just been in someone else's lungs. The beat of the music pummelled your chest, and then the strobe started up making everything look jerkily surreal. I closed my eyes but the light cut straight through the lids.

Fifty-five minutes to go till closing.

I was in Krystal's Nite Club in Wigan, and it was one of those times where you think, I should have stayed in.

Gilly Banks' birthday and at least half the lower sixth were there, maybe all of us; I hadn't exchanged two words with her since the beginning of term and *I'd* got an invite, so she wasn't being particularly discriminating with her guest list. '+ friend' it had said on the gold-coloured card, but I was on my own because I'd had a row with mine.

'Do you think we ought to try summat different?' Paul had said after the last session. When his hair's all ruffled from sex he looks almost too pretty, like something out of a Boy Band. That day, though, it was irritating, not cute.

'What, you mean like actually going out somewhere? Or talking to each other? That would be a novelty.' I'd been in a temper all week, what with the burden of the Nan revelation and the next History module coming up, and feeling sort of generally not myself. He'd also managed to locate the only Valentine card in the universe which didn't have the word Love on it.

'All right, there's no need to take my head off. We'll go to t' pictures if you're that bothered, bloody hell. I just meant we could try some new positions, I've been reading up on it.' He pulled out a magazine from under his bed and began to flick

44

through. 'There's this one where you get on top but face my feet.'

'Sounds charming, what a view.'

'No, come on, don't be like that. It's supposed to mean you can, er, Control your own Pleasure. Or summat. I can't remember exactly. Oh, forget it.' He flung the magazine across the room and began feigning interest in a ragged fingernail. 'I just thought . . .'

'What?'

'Nothing.'

'It's this orgasm thing again, isn't it?' I reached for my knickers so I could argue with more dignity. 'Why do you keep going on about it? What's the big deal? It's not an issue. But I'm beginning to feel like there's something wrong with me.'

He opened his mouth and the words dropped out. 'Well, you could nip down the doctors and get yourself checked over. Check there's nothing . . . *amiss.*'

('YOU OK?' shouted Gilly over the racket. 'HAVING A GOOD TIME?' She was breezing past on her way to the bar, birthday girl, in combats and a little vest, bra strap showing. She's one of those people who doesn't give a toss. I bet she has loads of orgasms.

'OH, YES. EXCELLENT. NICE ONE.' I raised my glass through the smoke and smiled at her and Paul's voice said again in my ear, 'Get yourself checked over.' Bastard.)

'Bastard!' I'd shouted at him, before pulling on the rest of my clothes in a frenzy. 'I can't believe what you just said! What the hell are you suggesting? That I'm *abnormal*?'

He lay there chewing his nail and watched me

45

struggle with my trousers. I'd got my toe caught in the hem and was pushing at the stitching, making it rip, wanting it to rip.

'You want to watch it, you'll tear 'em.'

'Jesus!' Some threads gave and my foot shot out. I staggered against the bed end.

'All I meant was, it's not been, oh, you know. Like you hear it's going to be.' He looked embarrassed, but resolute, like he was going to say his piece whatever. He held out his hand to me in a gesture that might have been meant to reassure. 'Did you not think the same though, really?'

'And could it not be,' I put my burning face close to his, 'and could it not perhaps be that it's *you* who's getting it wrong? That it's *your* amazing technique that's failing to deliver?' I nodded at his flaccid cock which lay across his thigh innocently. 'That your mighty equipment is not quite *up to the job*?'

He pulled the sheets across himself and flushed.

'No,' he snapped. ' 'T i'nt, actually.'

'Really?'

'No. An' I'll tell you why.'

'Go on.' I sensed what was coming.

'Because. Because Jeanette Piper never had any trouble, that's why.'

So I finished dressing and let myself out. Past next door's sad Alsatian, past the bench with no slats left, and the tyre-marked verges, past the shattered bus shelter and home to my room where I cried for half an hour.

It's true, he never actually said he was a virgin. But then again, he didn't say he wasn't. I should've kept asking, only, what do you do if you don't hear the answer you want? 'Stop, it's all off, put your underpants back on; I only sleep with the undefiled!' I don't think so. And it's not something he could have done anything about, you can't rewind time. Once It's gone, It's gone. I should bloody know.

No, it wasn't the fact that he was one step ahead, though to be honest it's not nice knowing he's dipped his wick elsewhere (thank God I don't even know this Jeanette Piper, I think she lives in Standish. He did say she was a bit of a dog before I slammed out, but that was probably only to make me feel better). No, it's what he said before. About me. My defective body. What if it turned out to be true?

'OVER THERE, BY THE BAR. I THINK YOU'VE GOT AN ADMIRER!' twinkled Gilly as she squeezed past, a pint glass in each hand.

I squinted across the room but it was all heads and bodies and there was a great fat man in front of me. I stepped backwards into a bit of a gap and immediately trod on someone's toe.

'Sorry. SORRY.'

It was Daniel Gale, recently arrived in our sixth form from somewhere down south and already dismissed as a boring swot. He swept a hand through his wild hair and grinned weirdly. What was someone like him doing here, for God's sake? He should have been at home chasing Internet porn.

'ACTUALLY,' he leaned closer, 'IT'S A PROSTHETIC.'

'A WHAT?' I was still trying to see over to the bar.

'GALVANIZED STEEL AND PLATINUM BONDED. BIONIC. I HAD IT FITTED AFTER

A TERRIBLE FREAK ACCIDENT. YOU COULD DROP A MINI COOPER ON HERE AND I WOULDN'T FEEL A THING. IT'S FULLY MAGNETIZED TOO. IF YOU DROPPED ME IN THE SEA MY TOES WOULD POINT NORTH.'

'YOU WHAT?'

His shirt lit up dramatically as the ultraviolet came on: it made his head look disembodied and wobbly. I don't know what my face was doing but I don't think it was registering anything very positive. His glasses flashed reproachfully at me and he opened his mouth, then shut it again. 'JOKE,' he finished sadly and drifted away, shoulders hunched.

It was then I spotted him; a tall bloke leaning against a pillar, watching me. Black jacket slung over his shoulder like a catalogue model, dark curly hair, thin nose, might have been all right but it was difficult to tell from a distance. He waved. I looked away. I looked back. He started to come over, smiling. Bollocks, I thought. Then, well why the hell not? Teach that bastard Paul, wouldn't it?

It wasn't till he got really close that I could see the leather pants.

Now the only stuff I know about leather pants, not owning a pair myself, is what I heard some stand-up cockney comedian say once, that they turned your privates into a fiery furnace. As he got closer I could see he was quite nice-looking, but the thought of the turkey-neck testicle skin and the accordian-wrinkled penis cooking gently in there persisted and my brow furrowed.

'PENNY FOR THEM,' he said as he reached me.

I could hardly say I was thinking about his

48

genitals.

'YOU LOOK LIKE YOU'RE IN ANOTHER WORLD. YOU DO. WITH YOUR BIG EYES. LIKE YOU'RE WAITING TO BE RESCUED. LIKE A PRINCESS.' He put his hand on my arm. I didn't move. 'SO WHERE *DO* YOU COME FROM?'

I couldn't think of an appropriate reply to this— there was no way I was going to utter the words 'Bank Top'—so I reached up and glued my lips to his. Out of the corner of my eye I could see Daniel Gale watching us, so I shifted round and put my back to him.

This guy knew how to kiss, that was for sure. No bits of escaping spit, no feats of ridiculous jaw-stretching or clashing front teeth, just a nice lazy action. I let myself go with it and after a while we found ourselves a corner and settled in for what was left of the night. The leather pants felt odd under my hands but also safe in a reinforced sort of way. You couldn't feel anything *personal* through them, just the lumps and bumps of folds where they creased. We had the last dance together, well we stood on the dance floor and snogged while slowly pivoting, then the lights came on and we were suddenly blinking at each other and looking sheepish. It was then I realized how much older he was.

Outside in the quiet cold air his pants squeaked.

'Can I see you again?' he murmured over the creaking. My ears were still ringing slightly and it took a moment to register what he'd said.

'How old are you?' I found myself asking. Around us crowds of people moved into knots and couples, shouting or embracing, slapping passing cars on the roof. Someone was throwing up in a shop doorway amid cheers.

He held up his palms to me, head on one side. I was sure I could see crow's feet in the lamplight. 'Hey. What's up? Does it matter?'

Does it matter? That's what Paul said when I asked him if he'd done it before. And yeah, it bloody well did, as it turned out. So not a great question, Rawhide.

'I'll take *your* number. I'll give you a call.'

He shrugged. Then, with difficulty, he extracted a pen from his back pocket and wrote it on my hand, held onto my fingers afterwards. He was staring into my eyes.

'I'm twenty-eight, if you must know. God.' He shook his head. 'Still don't see what the deal is. Why, how old are you?'

'Like I said, I'll give you a call.' I loosed my hand from his grip. 'See you.' And I joined Julia and Gilly on the taxi rank, feeling as if, somehow, I'd got one back. On somebody.

See the doctor. I should bloody cocoa.

*   *   *

IT WERE summat an' nowt, only a dance at the Mechanics', but I got in a row over it. It were a regular thing when I was about sixteen. I'd throw my lace-up shoes and best frock out of the window, then tell my mother I was off to Maggie Fairbrother's. Her mother used go out drinkin' so we could do as we liked. So then we'd walk it into Harrop and go dancin'. The last time though it were t' Carnival Dance and when I got back home I had confetti all in my hair and cuffs. I kept brushin' it out but it sort of clung. My mother spotted some of it on the floor, and I got a good hiding and sent to bed. She was allus angry, and tired to death, bent over her dolly tub or her scrubbing board or her mangle. And shamed. You see she could never hold a man, never had a home of her own. I think she were terrified I might end up the same.

*　　　*　　　*

I HAD A TRIP into Wigan to find out what I already knew.

There was a time, late sixties I suppose it'd be, when approaching the town was like driving through a war zone. Nan and I would get the bus in and I'd stare out of the windows at rows and rows of shattered terraces, brick shells, piles of rubble. Sometimes there'd be a square of waste ground with just a line of doorsteps along the edge of the pavement, or ragged garden flowers sprouting through the masonry or a tiny patch of floor tiling in the mud. On the horizon there would always be those huge swinging metal balls on cranes. It made me shudder to think what they could do. That was the progressive period when they were busy putting people into tower blocks (I don't know what they called the period when they moved everybody back out again).

The journey through all those ruins always unsettled me. We'd have reached the Market Hall by the time I felt right again. Nan would visit each stand, chatting and joking with the stallholder over every purchase, and I'd turn on my heel and gaze upwards at the steel rafters where pigeons fluttered, and escaped balloons dawdled tantalizingly. You could smell the sarsparilla from the health-food booth, and ginger and hot Vimto. If I was good I had a hair ribbon off the trimmings stall, and I got to choose the colour.

So now I drove through the outskirts of a reinvented Wigan with grassed-over areas and new, prestige estates with names like 'Swansmede' and 'Pheasant Rise'. Imaginative chaps, these developers. I got through Scholes and onto the one-way system, over the River Douglas, past the Rugby League ground, under Chapel Lane railway bridge. Huge hoardings promised faithfully to change my life if I bought a new car, cereal, shampoo: if only. Then I was out the other side, glancing over at the *A–Z* spread out on the passenger seat. Finally I was turning into Prentis Road.

Streets like this used to be cobbled, but the council tarmacked them over years ago. At the beginning of the road two short blocks of terraces nudged the pavement. I know these back-to-back houses, there's enough of them in Bank Top. The flat red fronts, the white doorsteps that nudge the pavement and, at the back of each house, a flagged yard walled round six foot high and a door opening onto a cinder track. The original outside privies would all have been demolished in the sixties, and little narrow kitchens built on to free up what had been the parlour. Then in the seventies everyone had to go Smokeless, so the coal sheds went. While they were at it, most people had the two downstairs rooms knocked through and folding screens put in (so much more versatile!). Anything so long as it didn't look Victorian. (You want to get them

52

picture rails tekken off an' all.)

This was where my Real Mother grew up.

I parked the car and walked slowly along the pavement, this stupid song going through my head, the one we used to chant on school trips when I was in the juniors.

We're goin' where the sun shines brightly
(BLACKPOOL!)
We're goin' where the sea-hee is blue (RIVER
DOUG-ER-LAS!)
We've seen it in the movies
Now let's see if it's true (IS IT BUGGERY!).

Christ, I thought, I'm turning into Nan. But that should have been impossible. At least I wasn't singing out loud.

I started counting door numbers although I could see, ages before I got to the end, that I was going to run out. 28 was the last in the row, then there was a grassy space with a sign saying 'Hollins Industrial Park'. Past this was the first building, a sort of hangar, Naylor's Body Work Repairs. A row of courtesy cars was parked outside and one of those revolving signs turned sluggishly: *OPEN/ SUNDAYS*. A young lad in overalls came out, saw me staring and shouted over.

'Y' lookin' for summat? Boss is out the back.'

'It's OK,' I called.

He shrugged, climbed into one of the cars and started revving the engine with the door open. I walked a bit further, to where I reckoned 56 would have been, and silently blessed my mother. I knew she wouldn't be here. I'd known it all along. She was in London, with a Life.

Talking of which.

53

I'm supposed to be holding out for Mr Right, but what do you do in the meantime? I was prepared to settle for Mr Do For Now If You're Not That Fussed, while I was waiting. 'Love 'n' Stuff' had sent me Davy, looked a bit like that actor who played Jesus of Nazareth in the '70s, only not so holy. Same age as me but a completely different attitude to life. Dressed young, smoked roll-ups. Tall and lean. I'd seen him twice, once for a quick drink at the Wagon and Horses (he had an appointment with somebody), and once for an Italian meal in Bolton (we went Dutch, but that was OK, it is the nineties). Right from the word go he let it be known that he had a full and active social diary. Well, I thought, I bet you don't have a mother with a high-maintenance colostomy and a daughter ready to hurtle off the rails at any moment. I just smiled and said, 'Good on you. Hope you can fit me in somewhere,' which sounded naff and desperate (again).

At Luciano's he told me he was divorced, which I think even now was probably the truth, and that he'd been in a few different dating agencies but 'Love 'n' Stuff' was the best so far (he gave me a little wink when he said this line). Then he did some tricks with a bread-stick which I thought were screamingly funny, although in retrospect I'd had quite a lot to drink by then. He also said he was a rep and so the only way he could be contacted with any regularity was through his mobile. Yeah, well, I know it's the oldest trick in the book, but when you want to believe someone, you do.

I wouldn't have brought him back to the house but he claimed to be Mr I Might Be Able To Fix Your Metro too. Also it was Saturday afternoon,

54

Nan's nap time, and I knew Charlotte had gone into town as usual, so the coast should have been clear. Hah. When is my coast ever bloody clear?

He'd not been under the car two minutes when Nan appeared at the front door. I motioned her to go back inside but she only waved back, put her hand to the jamb and lowered herself down the step. Then she waddled down the path holding some bit of paper aloft.

'I've won a Range Rover,' she said, pushing a letter in my face. 'Charlotte can have it, she can have it for school.'

I thought there hadn't been any post that morning, but Nan had been up before me.

'Let's have a look.' I whipped it off her and scanned the contents. 'Load of rubbish. No, you haven't, Mum. It's junk mail. And it's for me anyway.'

'It never is.' Nan looked cross.

'Look, what does that say?' I pointed at the address window. 'See?'

She peered forward and huffed at me. Then she spotted Davy, who had wriggled himself back out from under the chassis while we'd been talking. 'Who's this?'

'Davy, Mum.'

'Jamie? Eeh, you favour a German.' She reached down and touched his leg. 'Is he foreign?'

'No. Come on back inside and I'll make you some tea.'

She gave him a glazed smile before retreating. 'You want to watch them swanky pants,' was her parting shot. 'Don't get muck on 'em.'

We went back up the path, me holding her elbow to stop her escaping, and I got her ensconced in her chair and put the telly on. *Love Boat*, ideal. Then I came out again.

The Ribble bus went past and stopped at the corner. Charlotte got off, face like thunder.

When she got close enough she held up a carrier bag and snapped, 'They wouldn't take it back! Can you believe it! Just because I'd washed it! I tell you what, I'm never shopping there again, bunch of rip-off merchants.'

She stepped angrily over Davy's legs, then paused as she realized they were coming out from under my car.

'Bloody hell,' she said staring down. 'Mum? Mum, who is this?'

'It's Davy. A, er, friend of mine.'

She shot me a withering look.

Davy shuffled out, grin at the ready, wiping his hands on the oily rag. Then his face fell. There was a pause.

'Jesus, Mum; we've met, actually,' said Charlotte in icy tones. 'Last week, at Krystal's. I'm sure you remember, all those *teenage girls*. God, how disgusting. Twenty-eight, my arse! You're really wrinkly in the daylight, Mr Leather Pants. Don't you ever wear anything else? They must be beginning to *stink* by now.'

The penny was beginning to drop.

'You old, sick bastard,' she said, and turned on her heel. I gaped after her. *Charlotte?*

'Small world,' said Davy.

'I'll give you small world,' I snarled. My leg twitched with the effort of not kicking him. 'You want reporting. Get your hands off my car and leave my daughter alone, or I might do something vicious with that socket set.'

'You'll laugh about this one day,' I heard him saying as I walked away.

When I got inside Charlotte had stropped off upstairs, but Nan was still watching *Love Boat*. A soft-focused couple were embracing to a backdrop of blue sea, and from the bridge a little boy was watching them, a big smile on his face. The captain put his hand on the boy's shoulder and a tear twinkled in his eye. 'I guess your mom's found what she was looking for, Jimmy,' he said as the music swelled and the credits rolled.

'I forgot to tell you, I've won a Range Rover,' said Nan, pulling out an envelope from under the cushion.

'Jesus Christ,' I said, snatching it off her. But this time it wasn't junk mail. It was from Social Services Adoption Department.

CHAPTER THREE

I didn't know what to do.

If I contacted him first, would that make me look like a total Sad Act? Would it be reported to his mates that I was turning into some mad stalker, unable to accept the bleeding obvious, that her boyfriend had blown her out? Because he had, hadn't he? Or was it me who gave him the boot? Or was it neither?

Or what if I'd got it all wrong and he was sitting alone in his room, broken-hearted, too dispirited to pick up the phone? After the initial fog of anger had cleared I'd got to thinking we'd make it up, maybe sulk for a few days but then fall into each other's arms, and out of the ether he'd pull some magic words which would wipe my head clean forever of Jeanette Piper and her writhing limbs and panting cries.

But that had been two weeks ago. Oh WHY hadn't he been in touch? Even to finish it. You know, if you've shared bodily fluids with someone then they ought at least to tell you where you stand. Surely it's manners. It wasn't just my pride, there was my hymen too. Or perhaps best to forget about that.

Bloody Paul bloody Bentham, bloody men.

So in the end I went round to his house.

I practised all the stuff I was going to say before I went, and on the way as well, trying to get the inflections exactly right, the face, the body language. *I just want to get things cleared up*, I told my bedroom mirror, folding and unfolding my arms to assess the different effects.

Clothes had been a problem too. I didn't want to wear anything which implied I'd made an effort, only for him to give me the elbow, that would make me look really pathetic. On the other hand, I didn't want to look like something the cat dragged in, in case he had wanted to get back together but changed his mind when he saw the state I was in. God knows, I didn't want him to think I'd been *pining* for him. In the end I'd settled for washing my hair and worn my second-best jeans.

I think it's best for both of us, I told my friend the Alsatian, and it wagged its tail slowly and grinned. Then I marched up and rang Paul's doorbell, shaking. *Paul Bentham is no good, chop him up for firewood*, my head kept chanting, which wasn't exactly helpful. There was a funny metallic taste in my mouth.

Chimes echoed in the distance but no one stirred. I waited a long time, then turned to go, half relieved, only to hear the door open behind me.

'Sorry, love, I was on the toilet.' Mr Bentham, naked to the waist, bare-footed, embarrassed and embarrassing. I tried not to look at his pink rubbery nipples, and the line of wiry hair which came up from inside his trousers and touched his paunch. His face was shiny and he had too much forehead. You could tell he'd been pretty once, like Paul, but everything had begun to blur and slide. It made me think of my dad, about the same age, mid-thirties, but sharp-featured, built like a whippet, all his own hair—extra, actually, if you count the recent moustache. I hate it when old people let themselves go.

Mr Bentham stared at me for a moment. 'He's norrin. Went off to Bolton, I think. He'll be back about tea time. Shall I tell him you called?'

'Yeah.' My heart sank. I was going to have to go through all this palaver again. 'No. Actually, can I just scribble him a note? I won't be a minute.' I smiled nicely.

'Aye, awreet, love. Come in.' I followed him down the hall to the back kitchen. 'Want a cup of tea? There's one brewed.'

I glanced round the mess and took in the dish of gritty butter, the weeping Brown Sauce bottle, top askew, the open bag of sliced bread stuck on the table. I knew without looking what state the sink would be in. Even if it was clear of dirty pots there'd be Christ knows what clogging and breeding in the plughole. My mum has her faults, God, but at least our house is fairly clean. Three

59

men living on their own: possibly even worse than three women.

'No, ta, you're all right.'

Mr Bentham followed my gaze. 'I work shifts,' he said simply. 'Oh, you'll need some paper.'

We doubled back and stopped at the telephone table, which stood under a rectangle of lighter-coloured wallpaper, a little hook still protruding at the top. 'Used to be their wedding photo,' Paul had pointed out on my very first visit. 'You'd have thought he'd have stuck something over it,' I'd said to Paul, who'd shrugged.

'Anyway, give me a shout when you've done. Like I said, he's gone off to t' shops. After some video or summat, I don't know.' He shook his head. 'He dun't talk to me you know, I don't have a clue what he's up to from one day to t' next. But that's lads for you.' He scratched his neck and dropped his gaze to the floor.

'Thanks.' I brandished the pen and pad. 'I won't be long.'

Mr Bentham wandered off into the lounge and *Grand-stand* came on.

> Dear Paul,
>   I ~~came~~ popped round to say can I have my CDs back sometime? If you want we could ~~get together~~ meet up for a drink and a ~~talk~~ chat (but only if you've got time). I've got loads on at the minute and I bet you have too!! Give me a ring.
>   Love ~~Charlie~~ Charlotte

This masterpiece of literature took me nearly ten minutes to draft; I kept thinking, at any point Mr Bentham's going to re-emerge to check I'm not up to anything dodgy, like rifling through his wallet. And what if Paul came back early and caught me off guard? An RNIB envelope came though the letter box and I jumped about a mile. 'Get a grip,' I remembered Paul saying, which irritated me so much I lost my thread even more. But finally it was finished.

'Shall I leave it in the hall?' I shouted towards the lounge.

Mr Bentham ambled out. 'No, give it here, we put them on a board in the kitchen. See?'

'Oh, yeah. Right.'

I thought that was a bit civilized, but then I registered the gingham frame round the cork and I realized it was just another bit of Mrs B that she'd left behind. He impaled the note with a map pin, underneath a take-away menu and next to, oh God, next to a note for Paul, written in childish handwriting, must be Darren's, saying 'Phone Chrissy about Sat eve!'

Of course, Chrissy could be a bloke. Or a friend. No need to panic yet.

*   *   *

I WANTED TO get back so I could read the letter again, just in case I'd missed something, because I still hadn't decided what to do. But shopping with Nan takes forever because we have to stop and chat to all and sundry. Forty-five minutes it took us to walk back up from the butcher's; we could have done it in ten, and all the while the blood seeping out of the cold chops and pooling in the corner of the plastic bag. Little Jim by the Post Office, with his flat cap and muffler, wanted to know how

61

Reenie Mather's operation had gone ('She were the colour of this envelope when th' ambulance men carried her out, she were, honest'). Then he detailed his own ailments for us (why should he think I want to know about his prostate? Nan was all ears, though).

Next it was Skippy, our local tramp, so called because he spends a lot of time ferreting about on the Corporation tip. He was turning on his heel outside the library, blagging change and spitting on the pavement.

'Awreet?' Nan asks, cheerful as anything. I can never tell what Skippy says, so I left them to it and went in to see if the new Mary Wesley was in (it wasn't). When I came out Skippy was on his hands and knees making a sort of yipping noise and Nan was two-double, Christ knows what was going on there. I didn't stop to ask, just dragged Nan away. 'Eeh, he's a rum 'un,' she said, wiping her eyes with a hanky. 'Filthy old deviant, more like,' I muttered, but she was blowing her nose and didn't hear.

Then, when we were on the home stretch, up pops Mr Rowland, the newish vicar. Don't know what it is about vicars, they always make me feel guilty, then annoyed with myself for feeling guilty. I mean, I know I don't go to church but on the other hand, I'm not especially sinful either. Not on the world scale of evil, anyway.

'Lovely to see you,' he calls across the road like he means it. Nan beams, and he bounds over and starts to describe at length how the vicarage is shaping up and how Mrs Rowland's knee has been poorly because she fell off a stepladder trying to get to a cobweb and it's started an old hockey injury off again. Nan tuts and shakes her head sympathetically while I lean on the wall and look over his shoulder. Hanging baskets are going up in the High Street; they'll last all of two minutes.

He finally remembers some appointment and dashes off (where does he get his energy from? God, presumably). Nan watches him go fondly. 'Now *he's* a good man. Not like that Mr Shankland, playing guitars and tambourines, what have you. I'm not surprised he didn't last long. Clapping in church! He went off somewhere foreign i' th' end, didn't he?'

'Surrey, Mum. Mr Shankland went to form a Charis-matic group in Farnham. You told *me* that.'

'Nay, I never did. Are you sure? Well, who was it went to Japan?'

'I've no idea.' I bundled her up the step and shut the door. I felt like I'd run the London Marathon. 'I'll get the kettle on. Give us your coat.'

I pulled the letter out of the table drawer and took it into the kitchen to scan it again while the water boiled.

> In the past it was thought best for all concerned that an adopted child's break with his birth family should be total. Parents who placed a child for adoption were generally told that a child would not have access to his birth record. The current legislation reflects increased understanding of the wishes and needs of adopted people. It recognises that although adoption makes a child a full member of a new family, information about his or her origins may still be important to an adopted person.
>
> People adopted before 12 November 1975

63

are required to see a counsellor before they can be given access to their records because in the years before 1975, some parents and adopters may have been led to believe that the children being adopted would never be able to find out their original names or the names of their parents. These arrangements were made in good faith and it is important that adopted people who want to find out more about their origins should understand what it may mean for them and others.

This means that *if you were adopted before 12 November 1975*, you will have to see an experienced social worker called a counsellor before you can obtain further information from your original birth record.

There was something in the phrasing that had made me pause. *What* might it mean for me? And who else was it going to affect if I began my search properly? The Adoption Contact Register had drawn a blank. All they'd said was that 'my details had been entered in Section 1', so that must mean there was nothing in Section 2 which matched up. But Jessie Pilkington probably didn't know the Register existed: why should she? She'd been told nobody could trace anybody, when she handed me over That was That. However you looked at it, I was going to be a bolt from the blue. Best not to over-analyse the situation, really. I mean, if you went through life examining the minute consequences of everything you were about to do, you'd end up so bloody paranoid you'd do nothing. We might as well all live under the table.

I shut the letter inside a Trex cookbook and

shoved it to the back of the cupboard.

'Phyllis Heaton's had a hysterectomy, did I tell you?' Nan was playing with a piece of toast left over from breakfast; God knows where she'd stowed it.

'No, Mum. No, she hasn't. She's gone ex-directory. You misheard.'

'And she can't accept it.' Nan carried on as if I hadn't spoken. 'If you ask her, she denies it. Eeh, it's a shame for some folk. We don't know as what we'll come to, any on us.' She gnawed at the toast like a terrier.

It was then I noticed the amaryllis.

'God, Mum, what's happened to my flower?'

Instead of two brilliant red trumpets, a naked green spike rose two feet into the air, and stopped. The pot had been pushed back to the left of the windowsill, behind the curtain, so I knew who'd done it. I leaned across the table and slid it back out.

'Mum? Mum, look at me. Mum, what happened to the flowers on the end? Where have they gone?'

Nan laughed uncomfortably. 'I were closing t' curtains and I must have caught it. It came away in my hand. It'll be all right.'

'How can it be all right when you've knocked its head off? Honestly! I can't keep anything nice in this house, if it's not you it's Charlotte with her magazines and clothes all over the floor, I ask her and ask her to tidy them up but she takes no notice, neither of you do. What's the point of me reading *Homes and bloody Gardens* when you're busy mutilating my plants and hiding bits of food around the place?'

Nan glanced guiltily at the sofa.

65

'Oh, hell, you've not got butter on the cushions, have you?' I flipped them up angrily, one after the other. But it wasn't toast, it was the amaryllis, tattered and flaccid like a burst balloon, and sporting a little Sellotape collar round the base. I held it up, speechless.

'It'll be all right,' said Nan. 'We'll just stick it back on. It'll be all right.' But she didn't sound convinced.

'No, Mum. It won't be all right.' The flower heads came apart and I squashed them up hard in my palms, feeling the cool petals bruise and smear. When I opened my hands it was like the stigmata. Nan stared. I looked over to where the letter was hidden, waiting. 'There are some things you can't mend.'

*   *   *

There is *no privacy* in this house. My mum, probably just to spite me, has the phone wall-mounted in the hall, which is just about big enough for two medium-sized people to stand chest to chest. Since there is no room even for a chair, let alone those swanky telephone seats she drools over in the catalogues, I have to sit on the stairs to have a conversation. It's bloody freezing, too, I don't know why we bother having a fridge. We could just keep the milk on the doormat. The letter box doesn't fit properly and she's never got round to fixing it (waiting for a man to sort it for her, dream on, Ma), so it blows open at the slightest breeze. You can, of course, hear everything that's going on in the next room and vice versa. So all in all, it's pretty crap. I'm *definitely* having a mobile for my

66

birthday.

I could have sneaked out to the public phone box, but knowing my luck my money would jam or run out, or there'd be some pervo outside listening in. I needed this call to go well, I had to be on top of it. I didn't want to lay my heart on the line in a stinky glass box.

As I dialled the number I could hear Mum picking on Nan again, something to do with some stupid flower. Like it matters. I pulled Nan's scarf down from the hook above and wound it round my neck. It smelt of Coty L'Aimant.

Ringing. Ringing. Click.

Paul: Hello?

Me: Hello.

Paul: Hello?

Me: It's me, Charlotte. I was—

Paul: Oh yeah, right, Charlotte—

Me: Yeah . . .

Paul: I was going to give you a ring.

Me: Did you get what you were after?

Paul: You what?

Me: Your video. Your dad said you'd gone into Bolton.

Paul: Oh yeah, oh, I see what you mean. Yeah, *England's Pride*, top twenty goals of the decade. Narrated by David Beckham. I've not watched it yet.

Me: Sounds fantastic. Look, when you do, can I be the first to borrow it?

Paul: Ha bloody ha. It's better than a video on, I dunno, make-up or summat, girly stuff.

Me: Sod off. Look, did you want to meet up for a drink some time? Only . . .

Paul: Oh, yeah, right, that would be great. Em,

yeah. I'll give you a ring . . . we'll get summat sorted. Maybe next week. If it's not too busy. All right?

Me: Yeah. All right. Well . . .

Paul: I'll call you.

Me: Paul?

Paul: What?

Me: Who's Chrissy?

Pause, click, dialling tone.

The door to the lounge opened and Nan wandered out. There were crumbs all down her front.

'Phyllis Heaton's had a hysterectomy,' she said sadly, and sat down on the step next to me.

I unwound the scarf and draped it round us both. I wanted to cry.

'There's some things as can't be mended,' she whispered.

*   *   *

'WELL, YOU WOULDN'T catch me even thinking about it,' said Sylv, swinging her knees to and fro on her swivel chair like she does; she'll come a cropper one of these days and unswivel herself completely. I was sitting in the office to cut out my thirty daffodil shapes because Year 6 were watching a science programme on TV and the classroom was too dark to see what I was doing, not that it was exactly taxing stuff. Sylv, however, had been delighted to see me. 'I *mean*, what if they want your bone marrow?'

'You what?'

Sylv looked at me as if I was stupid. 'Don't you watch the news? When these long-lost relatives

68

meet up there's always someone wanting your bone marrow, or your kidneys or what have you, and then if you don't give it to them *you're* the villain. It's not on. I was reading about a case in *Woman's Own* last week. This woman didn't even know she had a twin brother until he turned up on the doorstep wanting her organs. It's a hell of a risk. No, Karen, I wouldn't touch it in your shoes.'

Thanks, Sylv, I thought, these heart-to-hearts we have are invaluable. You've helped me make up my mind. I'm going to find my birth mother if it kills me.

Just then the Head came into the office with a letter for typing. Sylv quivered like a pointer.

'What do you think, Mr Fairbrother?' She ignored my desperate expression and plunged on. 'Do you think Karen should try to find her natural parents?'

Give him his due, Mr F didn't bat an eyelid. I suppose he's used to it, he sees Sylv all the time whereas the rest of us only consort with her at break times.

'I really couldn't give an opinion,' he said and put the letter down on the desk. 'Can you get this out to Gavin Crossley's parents by the end of the day? We'll have to have them in, it's no good. Daryl Makinson's had to have stitches.' Then he turned to me. 'A difficult decision for you. Not one I should like to be faced with.' He gave me a nice smile and left us to it.

'Such a shame,' said Sylv as soon as the door was shut. She means because he's past forty, possibly fifty, and still single, and used to live with his parents till they both died and now he lives on his own in that big house up Castleton Road, he must

69

rattle around in it, why he doesn't buy a little bungalow, and maybe he's homosexual but doesn't realize it, not that it matters in this day and age. And he's losing his hair, poor chap. I've heard Sylv's musings on the subject more times than I can count. But he's actually a pleasant man and really quite OK as a boss, especially when you think the staff are all women: you'd think we'd drive him mad. He's great when I need to take time off for Nan, and he buys us all Christmas presents; just bits and pieces, but it's the thought. This year it was cacti. Sylv got a squat, spiky number. Mine was tall and sort of hairy, as if a gang of spiders had run amok over it. I don't like them as plants, I tend to think they're a bit common. You never see cacti on 'Inspector Morse'. So I put Mr F's effort on the back kitchen windowsill, behind the terracotta garlic jar, but I didn't throw it out, that would have been ungrateful.

The bell was about to go for break so Sylv tottered off to the ladies' to re-do her lipstick and rearrange her underskirt, and I gathered up my daffodils and set off for the classroom. As I got to the corner some of them began to escape and flutter to the floor. Any minute now and they'd be stampeded by a bunch of ten-year-olds, so I put the rest of the pile on the Nature Table and got down on my hands and knees and began swishing up the little paper shapes with my hands.

'Let me help.' Mr F, with his clipboard and stock cupboard invoices under one arm, was stooping to pick at a lone petal which had welded itself to the grey vinyl floor tiles. 'Tricky customers, aren't they? Look, I'm sorry about earlier.'

I must have looked blank.

'In the office. Sylv.' He lowered his voice. 'Sometimes her enthusiasm to, ahm, *help* gets the better of her.'

'It's not your fault, you've nothing to apologize for.'

'Well. Rest assured, it won't go any further.' He handed me my daffodil. 'And if you'd like someone to talk it through with sometime, someone objective . . . I can see it must be a difficult situation, with your mother being as she is . . . Anyway, I'm usually in the Feathers of a Sunday lunchtime, the Fourgates Ramblers meet there. It's quite a nice atmosphere, I don't know if you've ever been in. No jukebox, which is a rarity these days.'

Before I had time to do anything other than smile vaguely we heard the click of heels behind us. Sylv's face, newly drawn on, was eager with news. 'You might like to know we're running short of paper towel in the ladies',' she said as she drew level. Mr F gave a small salute and walked off towards his room. 'He's very much on the short side for a headmaster, isn't he?'

*   *   *

My dad always says, 'As one door shuts, another one slams in your face.' Mind you, he's not nearly as bitter as my mum, because according to her, he didn't have anything like as much to lose. He was an apprentice with British Aerospace when she got caught, and he just carried on, finished his training and got a full-time job there. He's still on the machines, despite waves of redundancies and his appallingly casual attitude. 'He thinks it's beneath him,' my mum often says, and we know who to blame for that idea. A blue-collar worker? Nah. She wanted to land a professional, a doctor or a lawyer, that sort of league.

Anyway, he's wrong. About the doors. I was asked out by someone else the very next week.

I was in the senior library, because I often am. I love it in there. It smells of furniture polish, and the wicker-bottom chairs creak under you as you lean back against the radiator to chew your pen and think. On sunny days the light makes beams of sparkly dust that drifts like random thoughts. The calm is intoxicating. It's about as unlike our house as you can get.

The one thing my mum can't get at me for is, I do work. I'm after four As, mainly to get me away from her. Don't know if I'll get the grades, but it won't be for want of trying. There was another module coming up and an essay to get out of the way (what I want to know is, why can't teachers communicate with each other so you don't get about twenty deadlines at once?).

So I had my Keats out and my Brodie's Notes and my Oxford pad and I was just getting into my spider diagram when someone put an illegal cup of hot chocolate down on the desk next to me.

'Absolutely NO food and drink to be consumed in the library,' said Daniel Gale brightly. 'It's OK, the librarian's outside arguing with Mr Stevens over the budget. She'll be there for the duration. Cheers.' He produced a KitKat and snapped it in half. 'There you go. Eat up.'

Out of the corner of my eye I saw two Year 11 girls half turn to gawp.

'What's that for?'

72

He ran his hand through his wiry hair like he does and pushed his glasses against the bridge of his nose. 'You looked in need.'

'Of what, exactly?'

'Chocolate.'

'I think you ought to know I never accept sweets from strangers.' I bit into the KitKat and felt better. 'Thanks.'

'My big sister always swore by chocolate. Contains iron and antioxidants, boosts your immune system, relaxes your arterial walls making strokes less likely. Really. It ought to live in the medicine cabinet. And, most importantly, it lifts your mood through the mystic power of everyone's favourite chemical neurotransmitter, ta-daah, serotonin.'

The Year 11s were hunching their shoulders suspiciously and nudging each other. Girls that age are *so* immature.

'Right. Do I look like a miserable bugger, then?'

He had the grace to look uncomfortable. 'I overheard Julia telling Anya that you'd split with your boyfriend. Although, and I know I'm almost certainly going to regret saying this, he was somewhat lacking in sartorial discretion.' Daniel sat down opposite me and leaned forward across the desk. 'He dressed like a tosser.'

I was genuinely confused. He didn't even know Paul.

'Spooky leather trousers. Give you crotch-rot. Apparently. Not that I've ever worn them.'

'Oh, I get you. He—it wasn't—' I stopped. If I started to explain he'd think I was a right tart. Bloody hell. Why did I attract these weirdos? What bloody business was it of his anyway? 'It's not really

73

your place to comment,' I snapped and stuffed the rest of the KitKat into my mouth.

For a moment he seemed crushed. 'No, fair enough. Scrub that bit. Foot in bloody mouth again. The Aztecs used cocoa beans as a simple form of currency, you know.' He snatched up the hot chocolate and took a deep swig. Then he put the plastic cup back down on my spider diagram and grinned hopefully. I scowled back. He took the scrap of silver foil and scrunched it deftly into a four-pointed star shape, which he stuck on the end of his finger and waved around. The star dropped off and skittered away, leaving a red dent in his skin. Finally he picked up my retractable biro and began clicking it on and off rapidly.

'Right, well, having fucked up big time I might as well go the whole hog.' He fixed his gaze on me. 'Would you—*go out* with me?'

And it seemed to me he shouted those words and they went echoing round the ceiling, because the hum of chat suddenly dropped, like it always does exactly when you don't want it to.

I was completely amazed. It wasn't only that he looked a bit odd and talked posh bollocks, but it had been popularly assumed since he arrived at the school that he wasn't interested in girls. Electrical gadgets, maybe; human relationships, no. He'd been here a term and a half and never asked anyone out, never got off with anyone at a party, never even seemed to notice the opposite sex in any way. Julia had reckoned he might be one of these God-botherers. There was an intensity about him that made you feel fidgety. He certainly wasn't like anyone else in the year.

'Shit, shit, shit. I've done it wrong, haven't I? I

74

ought to have said, "I've got two tickets for a gig," or "Do you fancy coming for a drink sometime." ' He threw down the biro and scrumpled up the KitKat paper in anguish. 'And then you'd say, "No, sorry, I'm bathing the dog that night," and I'd crawl off and die quietly in a corner somewhere. Much as I'm going to do now.' He flushed and rose to his feet, scraping the chair loudly on the parquet so that the Year 11s put their pens down and turned right round to watch the show. 'Don't know what I was thinking of. Sorry. Catch you later,' he muttered. Then he slunk off, banging the double swing doors behind him.

I slumped forward and bowed my head till my brow touched the wooden desk. Absolutely fucking marvellous. Just what I needed at the moment, to be responsible for someone else's misery.

That lunchtime I watched him in the common room. He was sitting, as usual, with The Two Nerds (subjects: Maths, Further Maths, Maths With Knobs On, Complete Bastard Maths). One's tall, the other's short but they both have bad haircuts, crap clothes and look about forty. Daniel looked almost elegant beside them, with his good suit and expensive shoes (I don't think they're short of a bob or two in his house).

The Nerds were playing chess and Daniel was making a show of reading an Asterix book. There was this *aura* of unhappiness around him. I edged my chair closer to Julia and laughed loudly at something Anya said. The realization made the hairs on my neck prickle: he reminded me of myself.

*   *   *

75

I DIDN'T MIND school, on the whole. Now our Jimmy hated it. As soon as it were time to go, he'd want the toilet. He'd stay in, and when the factory whistle went at nine he'd come out. Of course it were no good then, 'cause you got the stick across your hand if you were five minutes late. He were worst on Monday mornings when his class had to go through the books of the Old Testament. **Gen**-esis, **Ex**-odus, **Levit**-icus, **Num**-bers. He had a block, he said; he could do them at home. First and Second **Sam**-uels, **First** and **Second** Kings. You could hear him chanting it through the toilet wall. But the minute he got his bum on t' long wooden form with th' others, it went straight out of his head. So he'd get t' stick again.

One day there were a bit of excitement. The big lads in the top class—some of them were fourteen, and tall—turned on the headmaster, Mr Avis. He were a vicious man, he had it coming. He used to cane pupils for nowt, humiliate them, just to show who was boss. Nobody ever learned anything in his class, you were too frightened. Six of 'em carried him to the window, opened it up, pushed him out and held him over the sill by his ankles. It was his good luck that there were some workmen in the hall below who heard his shouts and came running. The pupils pulled him back in sharpish and sat down meek as you like at their desks, so by the time the workmen arrived the only evidence that summat had been going on was Mr Avis's red face and his broken suspender. He was far too embarrassed to admit the truth in front of them, it would have finished him in the village, and we weren't going t' say owt, so he picked up his cane, laid it across his desk and said he was going home because he felt unwell. He resigned t' same day. I think he went to teach at Lytham in the finish.

Startin' work wasn't much of an improvement. You still got the stick—well, you did at our place anyroad, and across your legs too. At thirteen I started in the cotton mill; it was that, or the bleachworks or pickin' coal at Pit Brow. You hadn't a right lot of choice in the matter. I had to clean under four looms before they started up, and you got sixpence extra for that, what they called your 'spender'. But it meant gettin' there early, and y' ad to walk it in all weathers. You got put wi' a woman as 'd learn you how to piece ends, that were called tentin', but if you were slow she'd rap your legs. They got paid by how much cloth they wove, you see, an' they didn't want to waste time on sortin' out such as me. And every mornin' the boss'd be waitin' outside, ready to knock money off if you were late, which was worse than any stick.

They say 'The Good Old Days', but they weren't nice times, not really.

*   *   *

I think worries are like Russian dolls; almost anything can be eclipsed by something worse. You think a terrible emergency is, say, a monster spot or a bad grade, but that would be nothing if your house burnt down, which would still not be as bad as if you found out you had incurable cancer. (I suppose the only calamity that could top that would be full-on nuclear war.) So it's a matter of scale.

I wondered, as I searched desperately for my completed Keats essay that Thursday night, why on earth I'd ever been concerned about a loon like Daniel Gale. I'd left the essay on my desk, in a blue Slimpick wallet, ready to hand in next day, which would leave the weekend free to do some last-minute revising for the exam. But it had vanished. I looked in all the pockets of my school bag, my course books, my Oxford pad; I got down on my hands and knees and peered under the bed, moved magazines, shoes, clothes; school bag course books Oxford pad under the bed again, then downstairs: house magazines, table drawer, letter rack, under the sofa, under the chairs, in the sideboard, kitchen surfaces, kitchen cupboards, bread crock, bin inside, bin outside (quickly, because it was dark and smelly), airing cupboard, bathroom cabinet, top of the cistern. There aren't that many places in a house the size of ours. Then I really started to panic.

'Mum. Mum! *Mum!*' I bounded back up the stairs and burst into her bedroom.

'God, Charlotte. Is there no privacy in this house?' she snapped, shutting the wardrobe mirror quickly. I vaguely took in the fact that she was wearing a black miniskirt and a shiny white blouse, like a waitress, and she'd been blow-drying her hair in a sad attempt at a Rachel. 'Do you think you might knock before you come barging into my room?' Crossly she pulled on her old grey sweater over the blouse; it was nearly as long as the skirt. She saw me staring. 'I'm only thirty-three. Look at Madonna.'

'Thirty-four tomorrow. What's Madonna got to do with it? Look, Mum, I'm desperate. Have you moved a blue folder from off my desk?'

She clocked the state I was in. 'Give me a

minute,' she said reaching for her leggings.

We both knew it was Nan. 'Let me talk to her, you're too hyper.' She went into Nan's room and I heard low voices. Please God, let her remember where she's put it, I prayed as I hung outside the door biting my thumbnail. But Mum's face was glum as she came out.

'Oh, God, Mum! I spent *hours* on that essay! I haven't even got my notes any more! Can't you have another go at her?'

We could hear Nan singing, so I knew it was hopeless.

> *'Oh the moon shines bright on Charlie Chaplin*
> *His boots are crackin'*
> *For want of blackin'*
> *And his owd fustian coat is wantin' mendin'*
> *Before they send 'im*
> *To the Dardanelles.'*

'I know where we'll find it.' Mum's expression was suddenly bright and I noticed then she'd got lip gloss on.

'Go on.'

'The Tin.'

She slipped back into Nan's room and I heard the wardrobe door go, a scuffle as Mum shifted footwear aside, then the lid of the large biscuit tin Nan keeps full of Spam and canned baked beans in case of war. I twisted impatiently and peeped round the jamb. Nan was flat out on the bed, staring at the ceiling.

At last Mum stood up. 'Sorry, nothing. We'll try downstairs again.'

'Jesus! Why do I have to live in this bloody hole!' I exploded at her. 'You can't put *anything* down without someone interfering with it. I'm completely *sick* of this house! When I get my "A" levels, which I probably won't do at this rate, you'll not see me for dust. God Almighty! What am I going to tell them at school? My nan ate my homework?' I was close to tears. 'I *can't* do all that work again. I'm so tired, and what about my revision? I haven't *time* to do both, I'm just going to fail. I don't know why I *bother*.'

'You're hyperventilating. Calm down. We'll have another look and I'll write you a note.' She squeezed past me and began to go downstairs.

'A *note*?' I shouted over the banisters at the top of her head. 'Do you know how old I am? It's not like I need to be excused games! A *note* won't do any good.'

She turned her face up to me. 'Do you want me to help you or not?'

'Christ!' I turned on my heel and threw myself into my bedroom, slamming the door. Papers fluttered off the desk, but not the right ones. I sank onto the bed in a welter of self-pity. No one else had to put up with this continual family sabotage. Why hadn't I been born into a different life?

Except, I nearly was, wasn't I?

I'd been trying not to think about it, because the implications were too big and too scary. Only you can't *not* think of something, it's impossible. By making a conscious effort to blot it out, you give it life. Try *not* thinking of a blue elephant. See?

Later on, it must have been about 2 a.m., I crept in to see Nan. She looked awful without her teeth, her head lolling, little snores coming from the back of her throat. Close to you could see the pink scalp through her thin hair. One day she'll be dead, I thought, she'll be lying like this but there'll be no breathing and her skin will be cold. I took her small hand, loving and hating her at the same time. I'm here, in this house, in this life, because of you, I told her. She didn't stir.

Just before I went to sleep I remembered Mum's birthday present. *The Stately Semi: How To Achieve The Neo-Classical Look In The Suburban Home*. She's forever decorating, trying to paint out the council house, rag-roll away her roots. I supposed I ought to wrap it, so I tiptoed downstairs for some Sellotape and there, as I clicked on the light, sitting on the table were some narrow-ruled sheets covered with my handwriting. My heart leapt. But it wasn't the essay, it was only my notes. There was orange spaghetti bolognaise sauce on the top page which my mum had tried to wipe off. She must have trawled through the wheeliebin after I'd gone to bed. I wrapped the present quickly and left it for the morning.

*　　　*　　　*

WHAT IS IT about kids? I'd lie down in front of a tram for Charlotte without a second thought, but most of the time I want to beat her about the head with a blunt instrument. Do all mothers feel this way?

*　　　*　　　*

WHEN THEY laid her in my arms I thought I was going to die with happiness. I used to wheel her up the street in that big pram and old Mrs Moss used to be leaning on her gate, and she'd say

81

every time, 'Whose babby's that? Wheer's tha getten' it?' And I'd say, 'She's mine.' Mrs Moss would suck her teeth. 'She never is.' I'd look down at the little fingers poking out over the top of the crocheted blanket. 'Oh, yes she is. She's mine. She's mine.'

*   *   *

'**Not enough** sex. That's what causes aggression in middle age.' Daniel Gale was twittering at me as I blew my nose into his enormous handkerchief. 'It's true. Those ones who write in to *Points of View* to complain about the pronunciation of "controversy", or constantly moan on to the council about their neighbour's Leyland hedges, those maniacs shouting their mouths off in restaurants and reducing the waitresses to tears, those are the types you know just don't get laid enough. You've got to feel sorry for them, really. I mean, Mrs Stokes must weigh about fifteen stone, and she's got that moustache. We know there's a Mr Stokes, but I don't suppose he's panting to exercise his conjugal rights of an evening. That's why she was such an A1 bitch. Nothing to do with you at all.' He hovered at my chair, not touching it, not sitting down. We were in the library; he'd followed after seeing me storm out of cow-bag Stokesy's office.

'But I've never been late with a piece of work for her, *ever*.' I was still crying with temper. 'She said, "Oh, I'm sorry, Charlotte, you're the fifth person today with an excuse. I can't make an exception for you. Monday, 9 a.m." So *I* get penalized because of someone else's laziness.' I put my head down on

82

my arms. 'And I'm *so* tired. I want to sleep all the time.' I'd been too angry to be embarrassed with him at first so he got it all, blow by blow, from Nan downwards. Now I'd finished, though, I wanted him to go away. 'Here.' I lifted my head up and gave him back his handkerchief. I knew my mascara must have run, so it was imperative I get to a mirror as soon as possible.

'You can keep it, if you like.'

'No, really.'

'You've got a bit of . . .' He gestured to his own cheek. 'Do you want me to . . . ?' He was wrapping the hanky round his finger, the way mums do with mucky toddlers.

'No! Sorry, no, it's OK. I need to wash my face anyway.'

'Right.'

'I'm fine now. Nothing a hatpin and a voodoo doll won't cure.' I smiled feebly.

'Right.'

He hesitated.

'See you.'

'Yeah.'

'And thanks,' I called after him faintly. He didn't acknowledge me.

But on Monday, after I'd handed in my essay and before the exam started, he found me again.

'You been here all weekend? Sorry, stupid joke. I won't hold you up.' He nodded at my open textbook. 'I just wondered if this was any use.' He plonked a plastic bag down on the table. I peered in, and nearly swallowed my biro in shock.

'My God, Daniel, it's a laptop! You can't give me this!'

His hands went fluttery and he swept his hair

back several times. 'No, no, it's simply a glorified typewriter. We've had it for ages. My dad was literally throwing it out, well, he was going to put it in the loft, anyway. He doesn't bother with it now he's got the PC. It's yours to borrow—indefinitely—if you think it'll help.'

'How do you mean?'

'You can save your essays on disk as you type them. That way it wouldn't matter if you lost a copy, you'd always have a backup. It's an absolute doddle to use. The instruction booklet's in there, and I've formatted a couple of disks for you so it's all ready to go. Just be careful not to pull the lead out while you're in the middle of something, that deletes it all. Best to save your text as you go along.' He was gabbling now. 'Oh, there's this as well.' He fished out a small cardboard box and flashed it at me before dropping it back into the bag. 'Iron tablets. You're probably a bit anaemic, that's why you're so tired. My sister used to take them, before she ran off to join the circus, well, read medicine at Birmingham. Not these actual tablets, obviously. I'm not trying to palm you off with drugs that are past their sell-by date.' He gave a high-pitched laugh. 'Anyway, give them a try—or not—as you like.'

He let go of the back of the chair he'd been gripping, and stalked off towards the doors.

Well, bugger me, I thought. You've got to give the lad credit for trying.

I picked up the bag and ran after him, squeak squeak across the parquet. Everyone looked.

I bundled him outside and held up the typewriter.

'I understand. You can't accept it. Say no more.'

He sighed and made to take the handles of the bag off me.

'No, no, it's fab. I'm really grateful. Tell your dad thanks. And—if you want, if you're not doing anything on Saturday afternoon, I usually go to Tiggy's for a coffee about three. Do you know where I mean? So . . .'

'I'll see you there.' He grinned manically and all but ran off down the corridor.

Straight away I wished I hadn't done it. He was bound to get the wrong idea.

In the event it didn't matter. Not at all. That Saturday, at about three, Daniel, the essay, the exam were a million years ago. I was in my bedroom, amongst the posters and the pictures of impossibly beautiful women, staring at my naked body in the full-length mirror. Downstairs Mum was lecturing Nan at top volume, and through the chink of curtain I could see the light of a keen, bright spring afternoon.

I was trying to see if my breasts had got any bigger. I had to contort a bit because of the old Take That stickers which refused to peel off the glass properly. Robbie Williams leered at me unhelpfully but Gary Barlow looked sympathetic, even though the top of his head was missing. I turned side-on to check out my stomach. I grabbed some flesh and pinched. Impossible to tell. Then I let out my breath. That did look pregnant. I sucked in my muscles again quickly.

I heard Mum pounding up the stairs; thank God I'd locked the door. She was shouting down to Nan to stay where she was or she'd get it all over her clothes. There was the sound of drawers slamming, then footsteps on the stairs again. I blanked it out and continued gazing.

I wasn't sure where the idea had come from. I hadn't felt sick in the mornings, but my bra had definitely got tighter. If only I had X-ray vision. What would I see? A little fishy tadpole thing, wriggling its limbs and nodding its outsize head? Probably the length of a baked bean, if I was right about the dates. Oh, please let me not be right. Would it have *implanted* itself in me yet? Burrowed in? God.

It was paranoia. I looked exactly the same. There was no baby. I started to put my clothes back on and checked my knickers once more for blood. Virgin white, alas. Still, I'd been late before, that meant nothing. My jeans still fitted, so it was probably all right.

Suddenly there was a clattering noise from the hall. I pulled my fleece on, unlocked the door and ran across the landing to see. Mum was bending down to pick up the pile of CDs that had been posted hastily through the letter box. I saw her open the front door in puzzlement, and beyond her, Paul's retreating figure hurrying across the road.

Without a second thought I dashed down the stairs, whipped a pistol out the pocket of Nan's Welsh wool coat which was hanging in the hall, and fired. In the distance Paul crumpled into a denim heap.

'Nice shot,' said Mum admiringly.

No, not really. What actually happened was that together we craned to watch him disappear round the corner then I turned and ran back into my room, banging the door shut.

CHAPTER FOUR

I stayed put for two hours and would ideally have spent the rest of my life there only the need to pee drove me downstairs.

The table was laid and tea was in progress, the TV blaring. Next to the pepper mill sat a neat tower of CDs.

'They catch seagulls off the rubbish tip and pass them off as chicken,' Nan was saying.

'Charles Darwin!' shouted my mother, oblivious to everything except *University Challenge*. '*The Magic Flute*!'

I hurried through and gained the bathroom. Nan had taken all the guest soaps out of their little pot and lined them up along the cistern, as she always does. Usually I put them back, it avoids another row, but this time the lavender perfume pushed right up my nostrils and made me feel queasy. I leaned forward and laid my forehead on the rim of the cold sink. There was still no blood.

At last I got myself together and went to face the inquisition.

'You tell me,' Nan was poking a drumstick round her plate and shivering theatrically. 'You tell me what chicken has four legs. It's never right, that. Four legs.'

'They came out of a bag of chicken pieces off the market.' Mum was busy eyeing up Jeremy Paxman. 'There were three wings as well.'

'Good God.'

'Yours is in the fridge, Charlotte, under some

87

clingfilm.' Mum tore herself away from the screen. 'Oh! What's happened to your head?'

In the mirror over the fire I could see the red furrow left by the edge of the sink. Christ.

'Nothing!' I said venomously and plonked myself down in the armchair.

And waited.

Bleak House. A. A. Milne. The Dissolution of the Monasteries.

'Was that the boy you were seeing before Christmas?' she hazarded finally.

Hah, Mother! You know *nothing*! You have no idea how long it's been going on! You miss what's *right under your nose*. You'd have a *blue fit* if you even knew the half of it. I *never* tell you anything because you'd always construct the worst (and all right, in this case you'd be right, but that's *not the point*). It's none of your business, I'm an adult. Get yourself a life then you can stop interfering with mine!

I said, 'Yeah.'

'I take it . . . it's finished?'

I wanted to wrestle her to the ground and bang her skull repeatedly on her precious white marble hearth.

'What do *you* think?' I hunched my knees up under my fleece and pulled in my arms so that the sleeves hung empty. I waited for her to say, 'Take your feet off the chair,' but she didn't. I hated her so much I could hardly breathe.

'They eat frogs' legs in France,' said Nan jabbing a fork in the direction of the TV. 'The dirty buggers.'

'He's not French, Nan, I've told you before. He does *Newsnight*.'

'Of course he is. Look at his nose.'

How long would I have to live in this madhouse, I wondered, before my head caved in.

*   *   *

I WAS IN the bedroom trying on clothes again when the telephone rang.

I'd just been thinking, maybe I don't look so bad for my age, actually, you see a lot worse on reality TV. I haven't got those road-map veins you see some women with, and my teeth are all my own. You've got to be realistic. Anyway, I reckon we could all look like Jennifer Aniston if we had a few million in the bank and a personal trainer. I wasn't fat, not *fat* fat. Size 14 isn't fat. I pulled my stomach in and turned sideways on to the mirror. Now that didn't look bad at all. If I could stand in this pose for the rest of my life people might think I was quite slim. I did a film-star smile at myself and arched my eyebrows. Then I tilted my head and tried a wistful gaze; nice. If I ever released an album, this would be the covershot.

I fluffed my hair up—currently mid-length, lightened, Brauned to within an inch of its life— and slicked some shimmery lipstick on my pout. You see, I told myself, if you had the *time* you could look half-decent. But it's so hard with Charlotte and Mum. Sometimes it's like a conspiracy, I only have to get the can of shaving foam out of the cupboard and there's some domestic crisis, so back it goes on the shelf, and I get hairier. Thank God for opaque tights.

Charlotte would have had a blue fit if she knew how much I'd just spent on the catalogues; thank

God you get to pay by instalment. *So What If I'll Never See Thirty Again, I've Got Legs*, favourite outfit of the new batch, lay on the bed slinkily; I'd have to get the razor on my shins for that. You should have seen Charlotte's face when she saw me in it. Bit of a shock for her, seeing her mum look like a proper woman for a change. Serves her right for barging in.

She's a sly devil, though! Some daughters talk to their mothers, I've seen it on *Trisha*, but Charlotte's like a clam. I never know what's going on in her mind. Then again, if I'm being absolutely honest, I don't want to. It's not worth the row to ask, anyway. She'll snap your head off if you ask her what she wants on her toast, never mind how her love life's going.

You walk on eggshells in this house.

And this boy, nice-looking but cocky with it; I can't say I particularly liked him. I think he was called Paul, she used to go to St Mary's with him, years ago. I'd only met him twice and even then she whisked him away before I could say much to him. What would you say, though? Paws off my daughter till she's finished her education? She wouldn't thank me for that.

I wish I could have told her 'It doesn't matter, you're better off without him,' but that would have sounded pretty hollow coming from me. We might be about to enter a third millennium but a woman's still a non-person without a man in tow. At least that's been my experience.

Anyway the phone rang while I was still wearing *Semi-Casual Sunday Luncheon In A Pub With Mr Fairbrother*. No chance of Charlotte stirring her stumps at the moment, she's far too traumatized, and Nan can't hear through the receiver properly so she won't touch it: probably just as well. The ringing continued as I wrestled with the top button. 'Buggeration!' I yelled at my reflection. Album cover girl had vanished. My face was hard and cross and my hair had gone all staticky.

'Telephone!' Nan shrieked up the stairs.

I gave in, shoved my slippers on and nipped down to the hall. It was a woman from Bolton Social Services.

'We just need you to give us a couple more details. I think you missed a page out on the form. Have you got your National Insurance number at all?'

I ferreted it out of the Useful Drawer in front of Nan's glassy stare, then returned to the phone.

'I thought you were ringing to tell me you'd found my birth mother,' I said, knowing it was stupid. They'd only had the forms a week.

The woman gave a short laugh. 'We have to process the information first. Then you get assigned a social worker, and have an interview. It's the procedure.'

'Will it take long?'

'You should hear back from us in two to three months' time. Give us a call if you haven't heard anything by then.'

'Two to three *months*?'

'It's the procedure.'

'No sooner?'

'We're very overstretched at the moment.'

Aren't we all, love, I felt like saying.

Nan opened the door as I was hanging up. She was focusing again and gave me the once-over. 'Ooh, swanky. Turn round. You're a bonny woman when you want to be. I never see you in a dress.' She stroked the sleeve thoughtfully. 'You want a nice pair of courts with that. Did you know you've a button loose?'

'You're one to talk,' I said. 'If anyone's got a button loose, it's you. Now look, I'm off upstairs to reinvent myself. Stick the telly on and *don't* touch the kettle till I come down again.'

*   *   *

A miracle! A *bloody* miracle! Well, two actually, although one's quite small-scale. And Fate can go stuff itself. Start the clocks again, open the champagne, exhale.

We were in the hall for the last assembly of term. We'd had the sermon, some gubbins about how all the people in hell have to eat with six-foot-long chopsticks, where do they get this bilge from? Then it was the hockey and football results, then some Year 7 kids got a road safety award then, finally, it was the dismissal prayer. The Head put his fingertips together in that way that always makes me want to give him a good kicking, bowed his oily head and began.

'Lord, thou knowest how busy I must be this day . . .'

I prayed: Oh, God, please make me not be pregnant, please please, I'll make such an effort with Mum and Nan and I'll revise really hard and never have sex again until I'm at least twenty-five, and then only with the pill, a condom and a cap as well, please, God. Amen.

Someone was digging me in the ribs.

'Get a move on, cloth ears,' Julia hissed, and I

looked up and saw the line of upper sixth nearly out of the door and a big gap where I should have been following. I lurched forward and scuttled after them, aware that all the Year 11s behind were watching and sniggering. 'What's up?' asked Julia when we got outside.

'Nothing. Just . . . I've got to go somewhere.'

'Not coming into town with Anya and the twins?'

'Gotta go straight home, sorry. Thanks.'

I knew the bus was waiting, but first I had to go check the state of my knickers.

The cubicle was narrow and the lock put up a fight. I closed my eyes, pushed my underwear down quickly and stared. Blood. BLOOD. Thank Christ. My knees buckled and I sat down on the toilet rim, still staring. Not much blood, but that didn't matter. It was OK, everything was going to be OK. Outside girls came and went, cisterns flushed, then it all went quiet. I'd missed the bus but I didn't care. Catch another one. I could fly home, if it came to that.

Oh, the other little miracle, hardly worth mentioning really but one less thing to worry about. I'd been dreading seeing Daniel Gale and having to invent some lie about why I stood him up. Then, when he wasn't in on the Monday I began to wonder if he'd chucked himself off a motorway bridge or something, that'd be just my luck. Any minute now, I thought, the head of sixth is going to walk into the classroom with a stony face and ask us if we knew of any reason why he might have been feeling depressed. Then he was in registration on Tuesday, a tad paler than usual perhaps, but definitely not dead. He kept trying to catch my eye, and I kept staring at the floor. I tried for a quick getaway out of the common room but he beat me to the door and put his hand on my shoulder, all breathless and earnest. Here we go, I thought, clenching my teeth.

'I am *so* sorry,' he began, making my mouth drop open.

'What?'

'About Saturday. God! I hope you didn't wait for long. I know you must be really angry with me, I mean it's the most awful manners, you must think I'm unbelievably rude—'

'No! No, not at all—'

We were hustled through the door in the general scrum. Someone pushed between us with a large art folder then the bell went above our heads. We grimaced at each other until the din stopped.

'Look, I'll be quick.' He pushed his hair out of his eyes and blinked. 'I did try to contact you. I went through the directory but there were stacks of Coopers and my mum was on the phone most of the night anyway. The thing is, we heard on Friday night that my grandfather in Guildford had died. Mum wanted to go down straight away but Dad persuaded her to wait till Saturday morning—'

'Oh, God, I'm really sorry.'

'Yeah, well. Thanks. These things happen. He was a nice guy but pretty old. Mum's all over the place, though, and so is my grandmother. So you can imagine, it was all a bit hectic over the weekend, travelling down there and back. But I really am sorry about leaving you in the lurch like that.'

I tried not to seem joyful. 'Forget it. Honestly. It must have been awful for you.' I laid a hand on his arm and he looked down at it in surprise. I took it off again hastily.

'The thing is, I was really looking forward to it.'

'No bother. Some other time.'

'We're down there again this weekend. It's the funeral on Friday.'

'We'll catch up at some point. I'm in town most Saturdays.'

The corridor had gone worryingly quiet.

'So, what, the Saturday after?'

'Whatever, yeah. Look, we'd better get a move on, it's nearly twenty-five past. Last day or not, Stokesy's a complete git if you're late for any of her lessons, she keeps records, you know, and then makes sarky comments on your report.'

'And I should be in physics, which is right over the other side, which means it'll be half-past by the time I make an entrance. Hardly worth going, in fact.' He furrowed his brow. 'Do you fancy bunking off, just for this session?'

'You *what*?' Daniel was even more law-abiding than me.

'I don't mean leave the building or anything rash like that. We could just go back into the common room and have a coffee. Quite a minor crime. *I'll* be OK, I can say I was overcome with sudden grief, and I'll put on an innocent expression and swear to Mrs Stokes that I compelled you to stay and counsel me. You'd get away with it because you're normally so good. And they think I'm so weird they wouldn't like to pursue it for fear of sending me into a mad fit.'

I began a laugh, then looked away in embarrassment.

'Sorry. I shouldn't be so flippant about the grandfather situation. I'm not, honestly. He was a

95

great guy and I'll miss him. Only it's so bloody serious at home, awful actually. Scary seeing your parents show their feelings.'

I thought of our house, where Feelings flowed like hot and icy water, constantly. I realized my mouth was open again, and shut it.

'So, what do you say?' He cocked his head and looked at me over his glasses.

'You're full of surprises, aren't you?'

'I like to think so.' He turned to go back through the door. 'Coming?'

'Nope. You might be a genius but I have to work my tail off to get a half-decent grade. She's going over past papers today and I need to be there. That's the trouble with me; I'm just so bloody conscientious.' I smiled and he smiled back. 'Enjoy the coffee, though. And I will use you as an alibi, if that's still OK.'

'I'll be ready to prostrate myself with misery at break time.'

And he did. And then I bled. Happy Easter.

*　　　*　　　*

IT DIDN'T GET OFF to a particularly auspicious start, that Sunday. I'd downed a couple of gins for luck, and put the new dress on. Then I stood in front of the wardrobe mirror, trying to decide on earrings, studs or danglies. Downstairs Nan was belting out 'Tell Me the Old, Old Story', presumably they'd had it at church that morning. From behind her bedroom door Charlotte was moaning like a cat in pain, which meant she must have her headphones on. And me? *Well, tonight, Matthew, I'm going to be . . .* I breathed on the glass and waited till the mist cleared: *Celine Dion!* (Sound of cheering, clapping, murmurs of amazement etc.) Pouting at my reflection I took a deep breath. I had to admit, the new highlights did look good.

'Baby think twice, for the sake—'

The smoke alarm began to go off in the kitchen.

'Fucking hell,' I said to Celine in the mirror, and legged it down the stairs. Nan met me at the bottom.

'Karen! The toaster's set afire. What do I do?'

I shouldered her aside and barged into the kitchen. Black smoke was rolling from the toaster slot. Nan appeared at my shoulder, wringing her hands.

'I were just mekkin' a bit o' dinner—'

'I was *going* to do it, if you'd just waited for two minutes!' I yelled and she shrank back into the lounge.

I wrenched the plug out of its socket and flung a dishcloth over the toaster. The smoke stopped. I opened the back door, put on oven gloves and carried the thing to the step, then stood looking at it. Thirty seconds later Charlotte came in, sniffing.

'What's that awful smell?' she said, then she spotted the trail of crumbs across the tiled floor, the dishcloth bundle. 'Oh, right, yeah. I bet Nan's been putting the cheese spread on again before the bread goes in, I caught her trying that one last week. She scrapes it on about an inch thick and it welds itself to the element.' She put on a sorrowful face. 'Poor old Nan. She doesn't understand, it's not her fault. Do you know she's crying on the sofa?'

I ignored her; it was that or stab her to death

97

with a fork. I didn't know why she was being so bloody reasonable all of a sudden but I could do without it. The doorbell rang.

'That'll be Ivy. I'll go. By the way, you've got odd earrings in, Mum.'

'AND IVY IS?' Mr Fairbrother took a sip of his pint. He'd moved his chair a little off from the rest of the Fourgates Ramblers and we were sitting at the end of a long table in the lounge bar of the Feathers. Thank God he'd seemed pleased to see me: thank God he'd been there at all.

'One of Nan's friends from her Mothers' Union days. Ivy Seddon and Maud Eckersley take her up to church every Sunday, then Ivy comes and sits with her in the afternoon. They take her to the Over Seventies' Club on a Wednesday across at the Working Men's, and Maud visits on a Tuesday morning and stays for her dinner. And if one's ill, the other comes, they never let me down. Then I have a woman from Crossroads Carers on a Monday and a cleaner for three hours on Thursday, which I pay for out of the Allowance. I mean, I could leave her with Charlotte, and I do, sometimes, but I try not to. And anyway, Charlotte's at school most of the time, so I couldn't even do part-time work without some help. It's funny how these things creep up on you. Ten years ago, even five, Nan was fine, just a bit forgetful, then . . .'

Mr F looked sympathetic. 'Your mother's lucky to have that support network. That's the marvellous thing, though, about community. Our parents grew up in a time when everybody knew everybody else in this village. Times may have been hard, but they all helped each other out. There's too much isolation these days.'

I nodded, thinking of myself. Where was my little network of support, my social life? At fifteen there was a big group of us, out every weekend. More energy than we knew what to do with, on the phone all hours; it used to drive Nan mad. We all had plans, we were going to set the world on fire. Then Dee, my best friend, moved to Cheltenham, and then I got pregnant, and there was just this *gulf* between me and the other girls, even though they tried to be nice about it.

Some of it was not understanding. They got fed up of me moaning about always being tired, and they didn't see at all why I couldn't leave the baby and just go off places at the drop of a hat. And I couldn't confide about the horror of veins all over my boobs, peeing when I sneezed, the big jagged purple lines on my tummy.

Some of it was, too, they were scared it might happen to them, that they might 'catch' my pregnancy. I always remember one of them, Donna Marsden, coming to see me in hospital. She'd got a little rabbit suit for Charlotte and she'd come all prepared to coo. But she barely looked at the baby. What she couldn't keep her eyes off the whole visit was my saggy stomach, bursting out from under one of Nan's old nighties. She was clearly appalled. Finally she slinked off down the ward in her size-8 jeans and I sat in the metal-framed bed and cried my eyes out.

The bottom line was, I was going to be married with a baby while they were all buggering off to college to screw around and do things with their lives. And by the time some of them came back to

Bank Top to settle down and do the family stuff, I was divorced, and they didn't much rate that either.

Mr F was still speaking, fortunately, and didn't notice the tears of self-pity pricking my eyes.

'Sorry?'

'And, of course, your mother's lucky to have you. Too many people walk away from their responsibilities these days.' He smiled at me approvingly and I thought his face looked nice, fatherly. He was wearing an Aran sweater, canvas trousers and hiking boots. It was odd to see him out of a suit. 'By the way, I take it you've had lunch?'

I glanced down the long table and took in the dirty plates and screwed up paper napkins. Bloody hell, him and his rambling mates had already eaten.

'Oh, yes. I had something before I came out,' I lied, praying my stomach wouldn't rumble.

'Then I'll get you another, what was it, vodka and orange?'

'Lovely.' I'd have to scoff some peanuts in the loo soon or I'd be drunk as a lord. Pace yourself, I thought. On the other hand, the quicker I drank this round, the sooner I'd get something to eat.

'SO HOW LONG'S your mum been a widow?' Mr F's brow furrowed as he handed me my glass and sat down again.

'God, let me . . . nearly twenty years it'll be. January 1978, my dad died.'

'I'm sorry.'

'Yeah, it was pretty grim in the end. Lung cancer. It seemed to go on forever, him being ill, but then I didn't really know all the details. I was only fourteen, and Nan kept a lot of it to herself.'

'She sounds like a strong woman.'

'Oh, she is. They built them tough in those days. Once, when she was a little girl, she broke her elbow and she never cried. Her brother did, though, had the screaming hab-dabs, apparently, and they all thought it was him that was hurt because he was in such a state he couldn't get the words out to explain.'

Mr F smiled. 'But you're strong in your own way.'

'Not really.' If only he knew the truth. But it was flat-tering all the same. *This* date I wasn't going to spend the whole time dissecting my own inadequacies, I'd done enough of that in the past. His niceness, and seeing him in these unfamiliar surroundings looking like a real person rather than a boss, made me ridiculously nervous. I swigged at the vodka like it was going out of fashion and grinned inanely.

'Yet to cope with losing your father at that age. It must have been traumatic.'

The grin fell off my face. 'Yeah. It was, actually. We were really, really close, he'd have done anything for me . . . At least he didn't live to see . . . But then he'd have loved Charlotte, he really would. I think it's what pulled Nan through in the end, having a baby around. She was, I have to admit it, brilliant with Charlotte. I used to walk out of those screaming rows with Steve, go round to Nan's and dump the baby in her arms. I don't know how I'd have coped otherwise.'

'And yet you still want to look for your biological mother?'

I paused, and Mr F looked concerned.

'I'm sorry, do tell me if I'm stepping out of

line—'

'No, not at all. It's nice to have the chance to talk it over with someone. I was just thinking . . .' I drained my vodka and stood up. 'Ahm, while I'm up I'll get some more drinks in, you're on . . . ?' I glanced at his pint. Mr F had drunk about two inches. He tried not to look surprised.

'No, not for me, thanks.'

'Well, I'll just—'

I got two packets of dry roasted and headed off to the ladies'. Actually, peanuts take longer to eat than you think. I leant against the sink and munched madly like a demented hamster, then the door opened and I nipped into a cubicle. Several years later I finished the first packet, tore open the second, and poured them into my mouth. Next door the other person pulled the chain, and the shock sent a peanut nib down the wrong way. I started a choking fit, scattering bits of mashed-up nut and spit everywhere. Finally I got my breath back, but by then I'd totally gone off the whole peanut thing. I threw the plastic packets in the loo and flushed. They floated back up. I waited till the cistern filled, the theme tune to *Countdown* running through my head, then flushed again. When the bubbles cleared the packets had vanished but two stubborn peanuts still lurked in the bottom of the pan. Bugger it, that'd have to do.

I opened the door cautiously and saw my reflection in the mirror. My cheeks were bright red and my eyeliner had run. I moved over to the sink and started to repair the damage, trying not to catch the eye of the other woman who was making a right meal of washing her hands. Sod off, I told her silently. But she went on standing there, and, I thought, taking sneaky glances at me every so often. Then, just as I reckoned she was finished, she sidled over and murmured, 'You can get out of it, you know.'

'You what?' I hadn't a clue what she was on about.

'I used to be like you.' Since she was about ten years younger than me and a heck of a sight more glamorous, I wondered what she meant. She lowered her voice to a whisper. *'I used to have an eating disorder.'* She laid a comforting hand on my shoulder. 'You can break out of it, with help.'

Light dawned. She thinks I've been making myself sick.

'It's nothing to be ashamed of. Princess Diana . . .'

'Thanks, but you've got me wrong—'

She smiled and began rooting in her handbag. 'I always carry these. When you're ready, just give them a ring. Admitting you've got a problem is the first step.' She squeezed my elbow and placed a little card in my hand, then went out. *The Bulimia Helpline*, I read. *Together We Can Change Tomorrow.*

What about changing yesterday? Now that really would be worth ringing up about.

I got myself a spritzer and rejoined Mr F. Across the room the lady from the toilets gave me the thumbs up.

'You were saying?'

'About my mum? Yeah, well . . . It's difficult to explain, you probably won't have the foggiest what I'm warbling on about.'

He looked worried again. 'No, please . . .'

'Well, it's like—no, you'll think I'm mental.'

'Go on.'

'Well . . . well do you ever think you might be living the Wrong Life?'

He leant forward, as if getting his forehead closer to mine might help him understand.

'I mean, who we are, where we live, the jobs we do—everything, really—it's all just down to chance, isn't it? The lottery of where we were born, and who to. It's like, the same person could be born into two completely different homes, well not *really*, but imagine it.' I started shunting bar mats purposefully round the table. 'And in one home he might get loads of encouragement, go to a posh school, end up all confident and successful in some top job, while in another he might have awful scummy parents who don't care about him, and he might get in with a bad crowd and go to a rotten school and end up in prison or something . . . Am I making sense?'

'The Prince and the Pauper?'

'Yeah, that's it, sort of.' I leaned a pair of bar mats into a wigwam. 'And I don't mean I've been living like a pauper, God knows Nan did her best, but I've always felt like I belonged elsewhere. I mean, I'm nothing like her. She's never been that interested in my education, for one thing. As long as I behaved myself at school, that was enough for her. The comp was OK and I'd probably have done really well if, if—' I had a sudden flash of memory, Steve in school uniform leaning against the iron gates, arms folded: that was the afternoon before the First Time. I shook my head and the image cleared. 'But she'd never have even thought of the grammar, and I didn't because of my friends . . . And she's got, it's not her fault, it's the way she was brought up, oh, God, I sound like such a snob, but she's got terrible taste. In everything. Calendars with kittens in baskets, plastic flowers in miniature wheelbarrows. I knew what kitsch was before I ever realized there was a word for it. And I try and keep the house nice, you know, improve it, but no one else cares. I've got this vision of my real mother in a lovely drawing room somewhere, fresh flowers, long white curtains. Like the cover of a Mary Wesley novel. Because I think she'll be like me, she'll understand me. And then, then . . .' The wigwam slid apart and collapsed.

'What?'

'Then I can go on looking after Nan without hating her.'

I heard myself say it and I couldn't believe it.

'Oh God, I didn't mean that. I did not mean it, just pretend I never said it—'

But Mr F was putting his hand over mine.

'It's all right,' he said gently. 'You forget, I've been a carer too. I know what it's like. It's perfectly natural to feel as if you're at the end of your tether sometimes. When you love someone, that's when the other emotions are at their strongest. It's the most difficult job in the world. I know. But you do a marvellous job, keeping that house running, and your clever daughter . . .'

I started to fill up. This kindness was outfacing. 'I must nip to the loo again,' I said huskily, and went off to splash cold water on my face.

When I got back there was another vodka on the table for me.

'I got us some peanuts too,' said Mr F. 'Dry roasted all right?'

'Mmm. Then again,' I plonked myself down and

105

carried straight on, unstoppable, 'it might be a real can of worms. I mean, she might hate me, my real mother, I mean. Or Nan. Nan might hate me for finding this other woman. Not to mention Charlotte. She's unstable enough at the moment. But who do you live your life for, in the end? You've got to take some risks, or you might as well be dead. Don't I owe it to myself? Don't I owe it to my birth mum? What if she sobs herself to sleep on my birthdays, or kisses my picture every bedtime? There's more than one sort of duty.'

By now I was talking quite fast. I made a conscious effort to stop, took a deep breath and asked; 'So was it very hard, caring for both your parents?'

Mr F began to talk in a low, sad voice and I let my eyes unfocus. I felt very tired and slightly sick. After a while I realized he'd stopped speaking.

'Sorry?'

'Are you all right?'

My eyes smarted from the effort to keep them open. 'Mm, yeah. Fine. Look, it's been really nice, it really has, to talk, but I'll probably have to make a move soon.' The idea of getting up and walking anywhere seemed impossible. I could have put my head down on the table top and gone straight to sleep. I let out an enormous yawn. 'Sorry.'

'Do you want me to walk you home? If you're not—if you're a bit tired.'

'I'll be fine, really.' I reached round the back of my chair, then remembered I'd left my jacket in the hall; it had been a perfect spring day when I set out.

'Haven't you got a coat?'

'No. Well, it's gone so mild. You'd never think it

was only April.'

The pub door swung open and a middle-aged couple came in, shaking snow out of their hair.

'Don't worry. I always carry a spare cagoule,' said Mr F, rummaging in his rucksack. He drew out a little package of bright blue material and began to unfold it. 'You'll need your hood up by the looks of things.'

I struggled into the shiny sleeves and he zipped me up. The other ramblers looked across and nodded at us.

'Do you think it's possible to love somebody and hate them at the same time?' I asked, as he pulled the toggles tight.

'Oh, yes. Very much so. Now, out into the frozen wastes.' He squeezed my hand briefly, then steered me to the exit.

'*This is getting serious*,' sang Celine, quite out of the blue. Mr F looked puzzled, but politely held the swing door ajar and ushered me through.

'I have to say—' I began, but then with the icy air a wave of nausea swept over me and I had to stop and press my hand against the wall.

'Do you feel faint? Best to put your head—'

I didn't hear the end of the sentence because I found I was throwing up peanutty vodka against a half-barrel of pansies. Mr F's arms were round me as I bent and heaved, and when I could right myself he offered me a hanky and turned away while I sorted myself out. 'It must be something I've eaten,' I mumbled.

He took my arm and we walked home mutely through the blizzard, my small circle of exposed face getting redder and redder and my wet fringe sticking to my forehead. My feet, in their unsuitable courts, were agony. At my gate he said briskly: 'So, I'll see you tomorrow,' and I thought, Not if I go upstairs now and slash my wrists, except I'm too bloody cold to hold the knife steady and my veins have all shrunk to nothing anyway. I just smiled weakly. He gave his half-salute and strode off into the swirling white like Captain Oates.

Ivy Seddon opened the front door as I trudged up the path. 'They're smashing, them pack-a-macs, aren't they?' she shouted. 'We saw you coming, be quick and get by t' fire. And can you check her bag, I think it's come away again. I'll mek a brew.'

*   *   *

SHE'D ONLY been at the mill two weeks but I'd had her down as a hard-faced madam, sixteen or not. Then that Monday morning she went off for a break and didn't come back, and I found her crying out by the bins, nearly hysterical.

'T 'int fair!' she sobbed. 'He only has to hang his trousers ovver th' end o' t' bed and I catch on. Me mum'll kill him. She'd no idea it was still goin' on. An' she'll want me to see that foreign doctor in Salford again. I can't go through wi' it. I thought I were goin' t' die last time. They pull all your insides out, you're bleedin' for weeks and weeks after. I'll run away first. No one's layin' a finger on me, not this time!'

And I put my arm round her. 'You'll be awreet. Me an' Bill'll look after you,' I said.

*   *   *

Mum had said to take the washing in if it started to

rain and I wouldn't normally have bothered, but my best jeans were out on the line. So when Ivy shouted up that it was snowing I crawled out from under the duvet and thumped downstairs. I'd forgotten about the toaster on the doorstep and, in my haste to get at the jeans, accidentally booted it, sending it skidding across the flags. Crumbs and what looked like bits of singed paper sprayed out of the slot. I ran across the lawn, tugged at the clothes in turn till they pinged off the washing line, pegs left swinging on the blue nylon rope or catapulted onto the lawn, I didn't care, then laid the bundle over my arm and scooted back to the house. It was bitterly cold. On the way I scooped up the toaster, American-football style, and carried it under the other arm. I slammed the back door behind me and dumped everything in a heap on the floor.

'Nan says you're getting a Range Rover,' Ivy called from the lounge.

'Yeah, right,' I shouted back. Total bloody nut-house. I started to examine the toaster.

Dear Mrs *charred bit*
    Imagine what you could do with a loan for £10,000! A new *charred bit* perhaps, *charred bit charred bit* or maybe the holiday you've been promising yourself.

I extracted the rest of the letter and flipped open the pedal bin where it could go with all the other loan offers we'd had that week. Even Nan gets them. God knows what she'd spend £10,000 on. Pontefract cakes, maybe, except she's not allowed them because they play havoc with what's left of her bowels. Then I turned the toaster upside down and gave it a good shake. More flakes came out, devil's confetti, but there was something still wedged inside. I brought it over to the window and picked a table knife up off the draining board. I could definitely see folded paper when I tilted the slot towards the light. I fished around, got the blade underneath and eased the thing out.

'What's so funny?' asked Ivy from the doorway. She moved over to the pile of clothes and automatically began to pick them up one by one, smooth them out and stack them neatly on top of the fridge. 'Something's tickled you.'

'It'd take too long to explain,' I said, unfolding the ruined Keats essay and watching as it disintegrated in my hands. My shoulders shook uncontrollably and tears of laughter started to run down my face.

'Eeh, I like to hear her laugh,' called Nan. 'She's a bonny laugh but we never hear it these days.'

'Well, she's certainly laughing now,' commented Ivy as I lay down on the tiles, helpless, and put the essay over my face.

*   *   *

SHE WENT down to London first, the story was she was going to try for an actress, and I handed my notice in two weeks later. We'd found her a place at a Mother and Baby Home run by a charity, although they wouldn't tek her till she were six months. So we stayed down t' road wi' Bill's sister Annie in Finchley; she'd been widowed two years before, and she was glad o' t' company. She had a funny daughter, Theresa, face like a line of wet washin'. Now she must have been about sixteen too but very backward, and she kept asking why Jessie

110

was so fat. I heard Annie telling her afterwards it was because Jessie had been a Bad Girl, and to watch herself or she'd end up t' same way. Except I don't think any man ever went near her, she were so sour.

Hope Lodge, they called the home. I'd heard about it through the Mothers' Union: never dreamt I'd ever have anything to do wi' it. It weren't a nice place, though. Big Victorian brick house, slippery floors, long dark corridors. I can smell the disinfectant now. They had their own rooms, the girls, but that made it worse apparently. You could hear 'em cryin' at night, Jessie said, behind the doors. She'd not been there above a fortnight when she announced, 'I'm not stoppin' here, Nance. Let me come back to Annie's wi' you. It's awful. We're not allowed to use t' front door, did you know? And they make you go to church on Sundays but you have to stand at t' back so none o' t' congregation can see you.' I talked her round. I said, 'You have to stay where there's nurses and doctors. They have to keep a special eye on such as you, with you being so young. You'll get t' best care here, love. I'll come every day, look after you.' I were terrified she'd change her mind, if you want to know. Or disappear, or do herself a mischief. I knew she hadn't thought it through.

When she went into labour, five weeks early, it was at night and I didn't know. It was quick, too, just over four hours. The nurses said she was mustard. 'I've never known such a foul-mouthed creature,' one of them told me, 'and we hear some things within these four walls, I can tell you.' She said they were cruel, wouldn't give her anything for the pain. 'It was unbelievable. I'm NEVER goin'

111

through that again, I'll tell you that for nowt. An' the doctor, he came in near th' end and never spoke a word, not one word. I hope he rots in hell, I hope they all do.'

I couldn't think of anything except that baby. 'Do you still want me to take her?' I asked. My heart was in my mouth. 'Oh, yes,' she says straight away, 'you can have her. I don't want her.' And I went hot and cold all over.

Bill came down to bring me home, stayed a week, and when I got back everyone was agog. He'd put it about that I'd been nursing a sick relative. So then I told them that had been a white lie because, although I was thrilled to be expecting finally, I was worried it might go wrong, what with my age. I don't know if they believed me or not. It didn't matter. No one ever really asked, whatever they thought in private. A nine-day wonder, that's all it was. And that first Sunday they said prayers at church for me and t' little one, and I didn't feel a bit guilty. 'It's our secret,' I told the Lord. 'I won't say owt if you don't.'

*   *   *

We have no radiators in our house, of course, nothing so useful, so I had my jeans laid out on the bed with a hair-dryer nozzle up one leg. Downstairs the front door banged and I heard Ivy's voice, then Mum's (sounding strangely muffled). I transferred the nozzle to the other leg and thought about meeting up with Daniel, that it wasn't going to be the ordeal I'd first thought: I could almost say I liked him. Not *that* way, of course, he was too fucking weird. Funny, though. He seemed to

112

understand me more than anyone else at school. Maybe I was the weirdo.

I switched off the hairdryer, and in the sudden silence heard Mum's bedroom door click shut. Ivy shouted up, 'I'll bring you some Milk of Magnesia in a sec, love, you get your head down for half an hour. I'll just hang your mac out on the maiden.' Another crisis, then.

When I felt at the ankle cuffs the denim was more or less dry, so I pulled down my trackie bottoms, eased the elastic over my feet, and stepped into my jeans.

I stopped. Looked at myself in the full-length mirror. Something wasn't right. Even as they got to my knees I knew they weren't going to do up over my rounded belly.

Fate had got me after all.

CHAPTER FIVE

THIIIINGS CAN ONLY get better. It must be true, it was on TV. But you tell me what political party could sort out my problems. If I thought it would really make a difference I'd be down that polling booth at 7 a.m., but nobody really cares about people like us, stuck at home with only the insane for company.

We save this country a fortune and where does it all go? Bloody subsidies for bloody London opera houses and the like. I'd vote Monster Raving Loony if I could actually be bothered, but I haven't got the energy. It's all right them offering a lift to the polling station, but I bet none of them would be prepared to change Nan's bag while I was out exercising my democratic right.

Politicians, they want to try living in the real world.

* * *

'You'll have to do a test,' said Daniel, his face blurry through my tears. We were sitting in Tiggy's Italian coffee bar at a Formica-topped table covered with wet ring-marks. I hadn't meant to say anything, but it was all my head was full of, there wasn't room for anything else. Besides, somehow I thought he'd know what to do. He seemed that sort.

'I *can't.*'

'Yes, you can. Look, it's probably a false alarm. I mean, you don't *look* pregnant, if it's any consolation. How far are you meant to be along?'

'About three and a half months, if I'm right.' I began to draw miserable lines in the sugar with the end of my spoon. 'God, I just can't be. Not me. Anyone else, but not *me.*'

'It might simply be too many Easter eggs. Or a hormonal imbalance; have you been sprouting hairs on your chin?'

'Oh, for God's sake, Daniel, it's not something to joke about!'

He drooped his head. 'Sorry.'

'Do you *promise* not to tell anyone about this? I couldn't bear the thought of the other girls . . .'

'As if I would.' He seemed really hurt. 'I don't do that sort of thing. Besides, who have I got to tell? Look, if it's not too personal a question, have your periods stopped?'

'*Daniel!* Honestly!'

'Well, it's a bit crucial, Charlotte. I mean, I'm only a mere male but even I can see there might be a connection.'

'Well, yes and no. Oh, I can't start going into details, it's too gross. And especially not with you. You don't talk about things like that, it's not polite.'

He shrugged. 'We talk about everything biological in our house. It's with my dad being a GP. No bodily function is taboo. They used to take us to a naturist beach in Greece every year, until I started getting what my mother called "stirrings".'

'That's because you're Middle Class, probably. In our house everything's taboo, there are no safe subjects, so mostly we don't talk. Well, Nan does, but she doesn't count because none of it makes any sense.' The knowledge of why I was here settled on my shoulders again and I slumped forward. 'Oh, Daniel, what am I going to do?'

'Wait here,' he said, rising to his feet. 'Don't move a muscle.' And he dived out of the shop.

I waited and watched through the window. Shoppers crowded past, carefree. Every other figure was loaded with personal irony: the willowy pair of teenage girls with flat stomachs, laughing at some private joke; the smart brisk career woman whose life was clearly going places; the—oh, horror—hugely pregnant mum holding a toddler on reins and peering into the cafe, her hand shading her weary brow. I stared back. Surely it must hurt when your body got to that size? What happened to your skin? Might it not split, like a dropped tomato? How did her trousers not fall down? How could she see what she was doing when she went to the toilet?

115

'Give the woman a break,' said Daniel, sitting down again and sliding a Boots bag across at me. I realized I was gaping with horror, and looked away quickly.

'Is that what I think it is?'

'Uh-huh. Now, nip to the toilets, sort yourself out and then come with me.'

'Where?'

'Do as you're told. Come on.' He pulled me up and shepherded me to the back of the cafe.

Once in the cubicle I undid the cellophane, then opened the box. A white plastic felt-tip thing slid out. I had a good look at it, pulled the cap off, then fished out the instruction leaflet and unpleated it. So, you just peed on the end of the stick; two minutes later it was all over bar the shouting.

When I came out Daniel was waiting. 'Well?'

'I haven't looked yet.'

'Good.'

He grabbed my hand and pulled me out onto the street.

'Where are we going?' I shouted as he yanked me through the crowds.

'Just come on!'

We ran and ran, up Standishgate, down Market Street and Parson's Walk, into Mesnes Park Terrace and through to the park.

'Quick!' We dashed through the iron gates and dived for the grass. I sort of fell, then rolled over and lay back, gasping. 'It's not too wet, is it?' he asked, patting around with his palm.

'Yeah, it's bloody soaking but I don't care.' I was still panting like mad. 'What's going on?'

He squatted beside me. 'Unwrap the test. Go on.' He nodded encouragingly.

I sat up, drew the bag out of my jacket pocket and held up the box. My fingernail slid under the cardboard flap. 'I know what I'm looking for, I read the blurb. If the second window's empty, I'm in the clear . . . Oh, God, Daniel, oh, God. Oh, no.'

He leaned over to peer at the two blue lines. The air felt still around us. It was one of those moments when the universe pivots and you know nothing's ever going to be the same again.

Daniel looked shattered. 'Oh, Charlotte, I'm sorry. I was so sure it was going to be OK. I was so sure.'

Don't touch me! I thought, but he didn't. He set his jaw and gazed out to the tree tops. I could tell he didn't have a clue what to say and I wished to God I could snap my fingers and make him vanish.

I don't know how long we sat there on the damp grass. I wasn't thinking proper thoughts, just giving in to a squeezing sensation round my ribcage and a feeling like my heart was going to explode. I just kept staring at the sun going in, out, flirting with the clouds, but there was no heat. I was chilled right through.

'Your teeth are chattering,' said Daniel, wrenching his focus back to me. 'Maybe we should go.'

I hate you, I thought. If it wasn't for you, I wouldn't have known. It's your fault, you speccy weirdo bastard. I was waiting for the sky to cave in, or one of those giant pointing fingers to come pushing out of the heavens. *It could be YOU—and it IS!* How could things be going on as normal around me, the woman walking the Airedale, the kid wobbling around on a bike, when my life was over? It wasn't fucking FAIR.

But then I thought, it could still be wrong, the test. It only said 98% accurate. That meant two in every hundred *weren't*. So, say they sold, I don't know, five hundred a week nationwide, somewhere in Britain ten women would be shitting themselves for nothing. And one of them might be me. After all, I had had a period, so that proved it. It was probably OK after all. I'd sneak one of my mum's water tablets when I got home, see if I could shift some of this pot belly. Because, at the end of the day, I was me, Me, and there was no way *I* could be pregnant. Encouraged, I began to hunt in my pocket for the instruction leaflet.

'I think,' said Daniel cautiously, 'your next step is probably to get checked out at the doctor's. You might need to act quite quickly, depending . . .' He trailed off.

I think I went a bit mental.

'What the FUCK is it to do with YOU?' I gave him a shove and he nearly toppled. His glasses fell off and landed in the wet grass, and that made me hate him even more. 'It's MY body! MY problem! You have NO idea about ANYTHING. Just, just,' my arms were waving pointlessly, 'get out of my HEAD!' As Daniel tried to wipe his spattered lenses on his sleeve I struggled up, clutching the white plastic stick with its parallel lines of doom. 'And you can FUCK OFF too!' I told it, ramming it into the soil like a tent peg and stamping it down. I turned and stalked off, towards the wobbly kid.

'I don't know why you're so cross with *me*,' I heard Daniel call, then mutter, 'I'm not the one who got you pregnant.'

I broke into a run.

118

THE TRAINS IN my head came back again last night. Details change, but the dream's recurring in its basic plot: I'm trying to go somewhere (although the exact destination's always pretty vague) but the train I'm on never gets there. There's always some crisis; I'm on the wrong train, or it won't leave the station, or it turns into a wheelbarrow. Sometimes it never comes at all. I wake with a terrible sense of panic, and loss.

Not hard to interpret that particular sequence of symbols, any cod-psychologist could work it out. I wonder, though, if I ever got my life together, would the trains actually Get There, or would the dreams simply stop?

Sometimes in the morning, before I get up, I lie for a few seconds and my heart's strung out with nostalgia for something I can't even identify.

I got to school at 9.10 that Monday, even though I'm not technically paid till half-past: I wanted a clear field. It was eerily quiet. Everyone was in assembly (except for Sylv who's let off the daily spiritual injection to man the phones). I tiptoed past the main office, turned the corner and trotted quickly down the long corridor. That morning's hymn floated out to greet me.

> *'The trivial round, the common task*
> *Should furnish all we ought to ask'*

sang the children flatly, northernly. And yes, when I peeped through the double doors Mr Fairbrother was standing at the front, hymn book aloft, a trumpet and a traffic cone at his feet (he likes his visual aids, does Mr F. 'I hear and I forget, I see

119

and I remember,' he's always quoting at us). So I had about five minutes. I hurried back up to the reception area, peered round the corner, All Clear, and scuttled across to Mr F's office.

Once inside I dumped the carrier bag containing the cagoule on his chair where he couldn't miss it. I'd wondered about a note with it, but what do you say? 'Sorry I puked on your shoes'? My eyes travelled round the room for a moment. Shelves of box files and books, union memos and selected children's artwork displayed on a pinboard; on the floor by the far wall a giant ammonite, an inflatable hammer, a monkey puppet, a hamster cage, a devil mask (as I said, he does like his props); in the corner a box of confiscated footballs, cap guns, poking devices, etc. On his desk was his parents' wedding photo and a selection of horrible ornaments bought for him by various kids over the years. It was the room of a kind man. Oh how, how, how I had messed up.

Time to go. I listened at the door, then opened it slowly.

'Everything all right?' Sylv's voice made me jump about a mile in the air. She was standing across the corridor, lipsticked coffee cup in hand, waiting for me. 'He's in assembly. But you know that.'

I could have told her. I could have beckoned her into the office, closed the door and taken her through the whole sad story, she'd have loved that. Sworn her to secrecy (a slim chance but a chance nevertheless). But I couldn't do it. I said, 'I was just checking Lost Property,' and she stared at me so hard her eyebrows nearly disappeared into her hairline. 'Oh, piss off, you poisonous old witch,' I

120

nearly said. Nearly.

The morning seemed to last forever. By ten I was sitting in the quiet corner with the remedial group helping them fill in worksheets on Area. We'd all drawn round our hands and agreed that mine was the biggest, and I was trying to count away the recollections of Sunday with square centimetres.

'How old are you, Miss?' asked Dale. They do that, remedials, constantly try to distract you with personal chat.

'That's rude,' said Lisa promptly. 'You shouldn't ask a lady that.'

'I think she's about twenty-five,' persisted Dale. He had a long face with a large jaw, and chewed his pencils compulsively.

'No,' I smiled. 'I'm afraid I'm a bit older than that.'

'Fifty?' offered Lisa. 'You've a look of my gran, and she's just had her fiftieth birthday.'

'When's your birthday, Miss?' asked Dale, spitting splinters of mashed-up wood across the table.

'Mine's next week,' said fat Philip, waking up. 'I'm gettin' a Furby.'

'You big poof,' said Dale. 'You big girl.'

The groups moved round and I helped put up some backing paper for a display on Transport. Mr F's disappointed face and Sylv's peevish one were printed on every sheet of sugar paper. Each time I pulled the trigger on the staple gun it felt like I was driving staples into my own temples. Finally I asked Pauline if I could go and get a paracetamol.

'Then go and sit in the staff room,' she said.

121

'There's only ten minutes to break, I'll clear up here.' I must have looked really poorly.

Sylv's the guardian of the paracetamol unfortunately but, hooray, she wasn't in the office so I unlocked the cabinet and helped myself, swigging them down with a mug of cold water. From there I went straight to the staff room where I heard through the half-open door: '. . . *saw them embracing in the car park of the Feathers, apparently*'. So I did a smart U-turn and walked back along the corridor, and met Mr F coming in the opposite direction.

'Thanks for the, ahm, bag, ah . . .' he said as he drew near.

'Oh, no bother. Thanks.' I couldn't look him in the eye. Keep walking, I told him silently. He did, and I pushed out through the swing doors into the playground and breathed again. My whole body felt hot and I knew my cheeks were burning. Maybe it was the menopause, come early. That'd be just about my luck.

The bell went and children began to trickle out. I walked across the rec over the patches of slush and perched with the edge of my bottom on the low wall by the gates, wishing I had a coffee. 'Hey, Miss?' Dale appeared at my elbow. There were tiny flecks of red paint all over his lips off the crayon he'd been eating. 'Look! I did you a card. For your birthday. You can save it, like, and bring it out when it's time.' He handed me a folded piece of centimetre-squared paper with two pencil figures drawn on the front. One was lying down in what appeared to be a pool of blood. 'It's OK, he's a baddie,' explained Dale, pointing. 'The other's Gravekeeper, he saves the world.' He spread his arms out like wings, then let them flop to his sides.

'Nice trick if you can do it,' I said, opening the card up. *To a grat teasher*, it said. *Meny happy retuns*. You're not supposed to touch the pupils, the times being what they are, but I leant forward and gave him a hug. On these slender shafts of sunlight sanity seems to turn, at times. 'You've made my day,' I told him warmly. He stepped back slightly. 'No, really. You've redeemed the moment, you've given me the impetus to lurch forward into the next inevitable crisis. You've provided a tiny spark of light in a tunnel of gloom. Dale, you are a superhero within your own galaxy.'

'Steady on, Miss,' he said.

*   *   *

I waited a week and did another test, also positive, so that was that. Then I sorted all my clothes out and ended up with a capsule wardrobe of fleeces and baggy jumpers and tube skirts and leggings. Standing naked before the mirror now there was no doubt. My whole body had started to change. It wasn't mine any more. It belonged to the thing inside.

At school I avoided Daniel, avoided everyone, really. Spent a lot of time in the library, books open, looking out the window. Well, how could I join in the common-room chit-chat about clothes, and boys, and weight, and fall-outs? In the smart corner it was all Tony Blair and his New Vision, but I couldn't engage with any of it. The very word *Labour* turned my insides to water. None of it seemed real; it was as if there was a big glass wall between me and the others. I'd realized in the

123

park, nothing was going to be the same ever again, but it was taking time for the extent of it to sink in. I mean, I couldn't see further than the pregnancy. There was the immediate problem of trying not to look fat, and (more hazily) steeling myself up for the hoo-ha when everyone found out, not least my mother, who was definitely going to have some kind of breakdown. On the very far horizon was the prospect of giving birth, which I'd heard was quite painful, and I wasn't very good with pain. But after that? I knew there was going to be a baby at the end of it, but I couldn't get my head round it. Not *me*, not a *baby*.

Unless I decided there wasn't. But, as Daniel, damn him, had pointed out, I was going to have to get my skates on if I wanted to go down that route. I didn't even know what they did. Hoovered you out, a girl had once told me. It didn't sound too awful in that respect, but even I could see there was probably more to it than a quick trip to the Outpatients'.

I think it was the toes that were bothering me. We'd had a video on pregnancy, in Year 10. It showed the foetus wiggling about, sucking its thumb and kicking its skinny legs with their little splayed toes, then the narrator had said, *See if you can guess how old this baby is.* The teacher had paused the tape and we'd had a go, most of us thought about five months. Then she switched the video back on and the answer had been fourteen weeks. *See how the heart, with its four chambers, is already beating*, the narrator had continued. *In fact, a heart beat can be detected at just six weeks of development.* The miracle of creation. It was a sod.

So what a mature and sensible person would

have been doing at this stage of the game was weighing things up, the fucked-up life versus the other, differently fucked-up life, and seeing which she thought she could honestly cope with. What a mature person would do was tell their mother, see a doctor, get a counsellor. Face up to it all, and pronto.

But I was frozen. Because it still couldn't be true; it couldn't be me who was going through this. I was going to slide the pregnancy under the lining paper of the chest of drawers in the spare room of my mind. Something would turn up, surely.

*   *   *

HE CAME STRIDING across the tarmac, kids buzzing round him like flies.

'Here,' he said. 'No sugar.' I took the steaming mug off him and studied the ground while he scanned the sky above my head. 'Don't worry about Sunday, anyway. These things happen. I was once very ill after a rogue sausage roll from a garage.' He nodded at my bare forearms; my coat was still in the staff room. 'Don't catch cold, will you?'

He walked away, and was immediately accosted by a very small Year 1 boy, tugging at his trouser leg and pointing over to the football pitch. Mr F bent down to hear the tale and it was like a scene from *Goodbye Mr Chips*, except that Mr F looks more like Syd Little than Robert Donat.

I'd give them breaktime to get it out of their system, then I was going back inside.

*   *   *

I was having a conversation with Daniel in my bedroom. He wasn't actually there, I'd just conjured him up for the purposes of rational debate.

'I know you *want* to see Paul again. But all I'm asking is, have you thought through the reasons behind it?' Daniel sat scrunched up in the beanbag chair, his knees to his chin. I was at the desk, doodling boxes and clouds on the flyleaf of *Sense and Sensibility*.

'He's got a right to know,' I said sulkily. I wanted to see Paul so much it was like toothache; I couldn't keep still, couldn't get comfortable. Today was Sunday, which always makes things worse. There's something about Sundays which makes you rattle around inside yourself, even in these exciting days of car boot sales and extended trading hours. Mum had gone to Do-It-All to get some polystyrene coving and Nan was downstairs playing dominoes with Ivy. I'd paced up and down my room so much I had a stitch in my groin; I thought I was going to go mad with indecision. Hence Daniel.

'He will know, sooner or later. You can't keep it a secret much longer. Unless you . . .'

'Yes, all right,' I said testily. 'I know the score.'

'What do you honestly expect his reaction to be?'

I wasn't ready to answer this question, even from myself. We tried again.

'In an ideal world,' Daniel pushed his imaginary glasses further up the bridge of his imaginary nose, 'what would you expect his reaction to be?'

That was better. 'Well, he'd be totally supportive, for a start. He'd say, "Whatever you

126

want to do, Charlie, I'll stand by you." '

'And what *do* you want to do?'

'I want . . . I want not to be pregnant in the first place.' I heard my voice rise to a wail.

Daniel sighed heavily. 'Come on, Charlotte, grow up now. Are you saying you want an abortion?'

'I—' Suddenly, out of the corner of my eye, I saw the door handle turn and my heart jumped in horror. The door swung open and Nan shuffled in. 'Ivy's doin' some toasted teacakes, d' you want one?'

'Oh, Nan, thank God it's only you. I thought it was Mum.'

Nan smiled blankly. 'Toasted teacakes,' she said.

'Oh, no, you're OK. I'll wait till later. I'm not hungry.'

'Eeh, I don't know. Not hungry. I could eyt a buttered frog.' She chuckled at her own joke and retreated, pulling the door to after her. I waited till I heard it click, then turned my attention to Daniel again.

'Well, are you going to . . . ?'

'It depends what *he* wants. If he came with me while they did it, if he was really nice and we got back together and he let me talk about it afterwards, and he never mentioned Jeanette Piper or Chrissy . . .'

'If pigs went flying past the window.'

'Oh, ha-fucking-ha.' I vanished him, then sat in a temper drawing cartoon bombs and lightning bolts.

Julia and Anya materialized on the bed, unbidden.

'Isn't it the absolute worst thing you can think of, though,' Anya was saying.

'Oh, yeah. Well, cancer would be pretty bad, and losing both your parents in a car crash.'

'Or being permanently disfigured, with, like, acid or something. You know, having a glass eye or whatever.'

'Or being a quadriplegic.'

'Yeah.'

'But being pregnant's pretty horrendous. I mean, your whole life messed up. Can you imagine what your mum would say?'

They both pulled manic faces and Julia put her hands round her throat and made strangling noises. 'I'd just die. Wouldn't you?'

'Oh, God, yeah. Awful. Completely fucking awful.'

'What I don't understand, though,' Julia wound a strand of glossy hair round and round her finger, 'what I don't get is, how she let it happen. I mean, she's supposed to be so clever. She got an A in that last History module, the one she was supposed to have ballsed up.'

'Yeah, I know. And I tell you what, I didn't even really know she had a boyfriend. Actually, she can be a right miserable cow, she never tells you anything. To be honest, I still had her down as a virgin.'

'They say it's the quiet ones,' sniggered Julia. Anya began to giggle, then Julia started too. 'Oh, shit, we are awful. 'S not funny. Poor Charlotte.'

'Yeah, poor old Charlotte.'

Three identical culs-de-sac run off Barrow Road; Paul's house is down the second. Not much had changed since I last went, except the bus shelter now had no roof at all, and the form was completely slatless, just two thick concrete stands five feet apart rising out of the tyre-marked grass. I remembered when I was a little girl, three old men in caps and mufflers used to always be sitting there, smoking away, gossiping. They were sort of like custodians of the highway, Neighbourhood Watch. Nan knew who they all were, used to say howdo and get a nod. Then after a few years there were two, then only one old man, sitting on his own, clouded in blue smoke. One day there was no one at all, and after that the bench started to get taken apart. I think maybe Bank Top didn't used to be so crap, something went wrong with the people.

The Alsatian had gone too. The yard was bare except for a chewed rubber ball and a length of chain.

Mr Bentham let me in; I could tell he was surprised.

'Paul! Paul!' he shouted up the stairs. 'You've gorra visitor!'

Paul's face peered over the banister and he mouthed 'kin 'ell when he saw me. But when he didn't move I climbed up after him.

By the time we got inside his room I was out of breath and sweating.

'What d'you want?' he asked gracelessly.

I saw with a pang that he was still as handsome, that the Man U duvet looked sex-rumpled, that someone had bought him a white teddy with heart-shaped paws which he'd stuck on top of his computer.

'Can I sit down?'

He just shrugged, so I stayed where I was, shoulder to shoulder with David Beckham. The moment twisted slowly on its long thread. I

129

couldn't make my mouth work, though my brain was racing, until:

'Nice bear,' I said, like a pillock.

'Oh. Yeah.' He snickered awkwardly, looking all round the room, everywhere except at me. 'Shit, y' know, seems really weird—' He allowed himself a glance in my direction. *All those times I was here,* I was thinking, *and the last few weeks, we never knew, I had cells dividing inside me. 2, 4, 8, 16, an exponential time bomb. Cells all drifting to their allotted place like synchronized swimmers. Shape-shifting: amoeba to blackberry, to shrimp, alien, baby. There's a baby under this fleece. Hallo, Dad.*

'Hey, are you all right? You look a bit—funny.'

I took heart from what might have been concern in his voice and stepped forward. 'Paul, I—no, I'm not all right. I, I'm—' My hand dipped automatically to my stomach and his eyes followed it, then widened. Then his brows came down and his whole face went hard.

'Paul?'

'Oh, no. Oh, no, not that one. I do *not* want to hear this! I do not fucking want to hear this!' He turned right away and put his hands on the back of his neck, blocking me out. Any minute now, I thought, he's going to put his fingers in his ears and start humming.

'Paul, you've got to know—'

'Fuck OFF!' he shouted over me. 'Don't try and put this one on me. This is your fault. Christ! You stupid, stupid bitch!' He thumped the wall, then leant on it, shoulders hunched, still with his back to me. He looked like a three-year-old whose mum has refused to let him go on the Tigger ride outside Tesco's.

There was silence while I fought the urge to run down the stairs, through the door and across the Continent; run for ever, run the pregnancy away.

'I'm sorry, Paul, it's true.'

'Aw, Jesus.' He groaned and finally turned back round to face me. 'You've gotta be wrong. It weren't like we didn't use owt. Loads of girls have scares, it dun't mean a thing. You've just got yourself in a state.'

'I did a test.'

He put his hand over his mouth and swore behind it.

'It is yours.'

He took his hand away from his chin and stared at me. 'No, Charlotte. That's where you're wrong. It's yours. It's all yours. I don't want fuck all to do wi' it.'

At least you know where you stand. At least you know where you stand.

I don't remember walking back home but here I was under the duvet in my bedroom, so I suppose I must have done. Maybe I'd been asleep, because I was very hot and my mouth was dry. Maybe it had been a dream.—Maybe it had *all* been a dream!— But no, my hand strayed down over my bump, and Paul's parting shot still rang in my ears. I'd put my Walkman on but it'd made no difference, Paul was louder. That exact intonation would be etched into my brain all my life, long after his features had become vague. I'd probably die with that last sentence replaying itself.

I snuggled down further into the bed. When I was very little and Mum and I still got on, she used to let me make a Nest at bedtime out of the duvet.

131

Then she'd peer in and pretend she couldn't see me and that she was going. I'd shoot out from underneath, all flushed and ruffled, and shriek, 'Story!' and she'd pretend to be incredibly surprised. She used to read to me every night, long after I could read myself. If only I could be little again. You don't appreciate it at the time.

I must have drifted off again because the tape was on side two and Nan was shaking me gently.

'A shut mouth keeps flies out,' she was saying when I lifted up the earphones.

'You what?'

Nan settled on the bed and leant over to stroke my hair. Normally I'd have had to fight the urge to squirm away; not that I don't love her, I just get really touchy about my personal space sometimes. But this time I lay there quietly, glad of the sympathy. After a while she said; 'You're havin' a baby, then.'

I nearly jumped out of my skin.

'*Nan!*'

'Don't you worry, it'll be awreet. We'll see you through.' She fished under the duvet for my hand and took it in her gnarled fingers. The flesh moved loosely over the bones, as if it was ready to come away. I shuddered and closed my eyes, tears brimming out from between the lashes.

'Oh, Nan.'

'Charlotte, love.' She gripped my hand tighter.

'*Please* don't tell Mum. Not yet. I can't face her.'

She half-smiled. 'I know all sorts as I've never towd.' (Of course you do, I thought.) 'Tha maun fret, I'll not say owt till you're ready.'

Beside my ear the Walkman played:

132

You walk out of trouble
Into trouble
Out of trouble
Into trouble
And this is your life
This is your life

'Oh, Nan, why is everything such a mess? Why me?'

'Eeh, lamb,' she said. 'You'll be awreet, you'll see. God's good.'

'How *can* I be?'

But she just shook her head and carried on stroking my hair. I closed my eyes, let the earphones fall back.

*   *   *

MY MOTHER was eighteen when she had me, Jimmy was born two years later. But she couldn't hold my father. Harold Fenton was a restless soul, his own mother couldn't make moss nor sand of him. I think he loved us, though. He wouldn't marry my mother, but he gave us his surname for a middle name, so's everyone would know who we were. Nancy Fenton Marsh. I hated it, still hate it today. Fillin' in forms and such; whose business is it anyway? Because in them days, the sin fell on the childer as well as the mother. But there was a lot of it about.

She were allus short of money, that's why she had to tek in washin', an' it were a right palaver in them days; two dolly tubs, a coal boiler, scrubbing board, mangle, it took for ever. She never had a home of her own either. The summer before I was

133

born she'd sit out every evenin' in her parents' back yard wearing her nightie and her dad's overcoat, there were nowt else as'd fit. She said it was a terrible labour: when they held me up and said, 'Polly, it's a girl,' she told them she didn't care if it was a brass monkey so long as it was out.

Once, when I was about six and Jimmy four, we were waitin' at a bus stop to go to Wigan an' a smartish woman came and stood alongside us. There was a bus comin' and my mother just bundled us on. I said, 'Mam, this in't our bus, where are we goin'?' 'Never you mind,' she said. It turned out this woman was my father's latest fancy piece. We went all the way to Worsley before my mother came to herself. He had a lot of women, she told me before she died, but she said he was her man and that was that. 'At least he never drank,' she used to say.

She'd be thinkin' of her father, Peter Marsh. Her mother, Florrie, had a grim time of it even though she had a husband. They'd married because she was expectin' and then after, she had three children die in their first year. The doctor told her not to risk any more or she'd damage her own health—all she could think about was that at last she could sleep in the front bedroom with Polly, away from him. He were mean, you see; she allus struggled to get money out of him because he spent it all on drink. She used send Polly to the colliery gates to try to get some of his wages off him before he went in t' pub (he never came straight home when there was brass to spend) but then that would get him in a rage. I think she were relieved when he went to join the Loyal North Lancashires in 1917, except when he got there, there were so few on 'em left he had to join up with the East Surreys. He sent some beautiful silk postcards though, 'Greetings from France', all embroidered with flags and flowers, and his slow big pencil writing on the back. Then he was hit by a shell, or at least he jumped into a hole to avoid one, and got buried by a wave of mud. They'd just been wondering how to break it to him about the baby, me, when they got the telegram. He was only forty-two.

My father tried to join up as well at seventeen, but it'd finished by the time he got there, typically. I don't suppose he were too bothered. My mother's big fear was that she'd be made a widow too, but never being married she wouldn't have qualified anyway. She lost him young, though; two days after his thirty-first birthday he was knocked down in Manchester, outside the Corn Exchange. And I did miss him, even though he'd been in and out of our house like a cat. We both cried over him. He was my dad. And you need your dad when you're growing up. Well, I think you do, anyroad. Family's everythin' when it comes down to it.

*   *   *

I woke with a jolt. The tape had finished and my earphones were hissing. I unhooked myself and struggled out of the duvet.

'I can't have this baby, Nan. I've decided.'

From the end of the bed Nan snored gently. I folded the covers over her and tiptoed out of the room.

135

CHAPTER SIX

I WENT ON a blind date with Pauline's brother's friend from tai kwon-do class. 'He's got a smashin' personality,' Pauline had said. Ugly as sin, then, I thought. But it was worse than that. When I walked into the Working Men's and saw him propped against the bar it was like that old music hall joke, Don't stand up, oh I see you already have. He came about level with my nose. That wouldn't necessarily have been a problem, only he looked like Ken Dodd and talked like Roy Chubby Brown. I sat through fifty minutes of filth, then he said, 'I've got good manners, me. Tits before fanny,' and laughed uproariously. 'Wanker,' I hissed, picking up my bag. 'Ah, get away, you love it really, you ladies,' he grinned. 'Have you ever actually *had* sex with anyone?' I asked nastily. That shut him up.

'His twin brother's on a kidney machine, you have to make allowances,' said Pauline the next day.

I gave her a hard stare. 'Why? Why should I? No one does for me.'

She just turned away and started counting Tesco's computer vouchers. Cow.

*   *   *

'My God, you're here!'

Daniel was sitting in the window of Tiggy's, looking anxious.

'Did you think I wouldn't be?' he asked.

'Well, under the circumstances . . . I'd have

stood me up, without a doubt.' I slumped down beside him. My bulge nearly came up to the edge of the table. 'I don't know what to say. I've been such a bitch.'

'No, no, well yes, actually.'

We laughed nervously.

'Sorry.'

'Hormones under the bridge. This thing's too important to fall out over.' Fingers through hair, worried frown. 'So, you really have decided, then?'

'Oh, yeah.' I kept my voice low. 'It's not practical. I could no more look after a baby than fly to the moon. Think about it. Mum's life would be in tatters, I'd have to throw in my university place and stay, God, stay at home for *years*, it doesn't bear thinking about. And I know I'd make a terrible mother, I'm just not the sort. I've been really stupid, I should just have got on with sorting things out. I mean, the father . . .'

My voice began to quaver and my eyes pricked.

'Say no more.'

An enormously fat chef carrying a tray of dirty cups squeezed past our table, his apron straining over his stomach. 'Keep your hair on, we're short-staffed,' he barked at an old biddy in the corner. Everyone turned to see. The biddy stuck two fingers up at his back, then swept all the sachets of salt and pepper into her handbag.

'Now *he* looks pregnant. You're a positive sylph compared to him. Look, I'll get you a milkshake while you cast your eye over these.' Daniel began pulling some folded sheets of paper out of the pocket of his jeans.

While he was at the counter I looked through the pages he'd printed off the Internet. *An abortion is legal until the 24th week of pregnancy*, I read. *There is an initial consultation with a doctor, but the woman can also see a counsellor if she wishes.* Hmm. Now there was an idea. I didn't want my head screwed up any more than it was already. On the other hand, they might try to persuade me to change my mind, and now I'd made the decision there was no way I was going back on it. Toes or not.

'Banana,' said Daniel putting the tall glass down on the table. 'They're all out of chocolate. Drink up, anyway, you need your calcium or your teeth will fall out. And you don't want to be toothless on top of everything else, do you?'

I tried to smile.

In order to qualify for a same-day procedure, the woman must be under 19 weeks pregnant. If she is more than 19 weeks, she must stay overnight at the hospital or health care centre.

Same-day procedure!

It is generally accepted that there is very little risk associated with abortion.

Toes.

'How far are you on?' asked Daniel gently.

I thought back and counted. 'I'm fairly sure. Eighteen weeks, I think. So I might be just in time. I could go to the clinic in the morning and be back by teatime, tell my mum I'd been to Manchester shopping.'

Buy some extra-large pads, pretend I had flu and rest up for a day or so. Maybe it wouldn't be so bad after all.

Daniel looked uncomfortable. 'Yeah, you might just about be OK. Only, they have this funny way of calculating.'

'What do you mean?' My heart began to thump.

'It's something I've heard my dad mention. They don't calculate from the actual date of, er, conception.' He dropped his gaze. 'They take it from the start of your last period. So—'

'You *what*?'

'So, well, that means you're not actually pregnant for the first two weeks or so of your pregnancy. As it were.'

'You've got to be wrong about that. That's ridiculous, it doesn't even make sense. I've never heard that one before.'

'Forget it. I'm probably wrong.'

As soon as he said it I knew he was probably right. 'So what you're saying is, that would make me nearer twenty.' I put my hands over my face and dragged them down over the skin. What a fucking mess.

Fat chef came out from behind the counter again and began shouting at two boys for breathing on the window and drawing pictures of willies. 'If yours looks like that you need to see a doctor,' he bellowed. 'I'll be phoning your headmaster. Which school d'you go to, when you're not playin' truant?'

'Best go before he sits on us!' one of them shouted, and they slid out of their seats and barged past us, colliding with the table and sending the sauce bottle spinning on its axis. We watched it lurch and fall. Tomato ketchup blobbed out slowly, mesmerizingly.

Stupid I may be, but I'm not daft. I knew that nineteen-week cut-off point must be there for a good reason, that a later operation was going to be a lot more traumatic than an early procedure. I'd been really ill having a wisdom tooth out once, vomiting everywhere and swollen up like a hamster. My insides still scrunched up when I thought about it.

Did they use a general anaesthetic? It would be best if they just put you under so you didn't know what was going on, but what if they didn't? What if it really, really hurt and you *saw what came out* and it lived in your head for ever and ever?

'Do you know what they do, exactly?' I made myself ask.

'No. The website didn't go into details. Just what's on those pages.'

I couldn't tell if he was lying or not. We looked at each other for a long time but he held his gaze steady. Panic rose suddenly up my throat like nausea, catching me off-guard. *Not me! This can't be happening to me! I can't cope, there has to be another way!*

I struggled to get a grip. My mum has these breathing exercises, they use them on anger-management courses; she does them if we have a big row. She doesn't know I use them too. In through the nose, count five, out through the mouth. I had—breathe—to stop the scary thoughts—breathe—and face up to—breathe—the practicalities—breathe. There was no other way. Breathe. It was going to be all right if I kept my head.

'What you could do,' Daniel was saying, 'is tell your mum you're staying over at a friend's, a girlfriend's obviously . . .'

'Which is something I never do.'

'Work with me, Charlotte. You could tell her it was a special occasion, an eighteenth or something . . .'

'I'd have to bunk off school, they'd want a note.'

'It's half-term the week after next.'

'What if she rung up my friend's house to check?'

'Take your mobile.'

'I haven't got one!'

'Take mine, for God's sake!' Daniel sounded exasperated. 'You could tell her your friend lent it you so you'd always be contactable, even if you got in from clubbing very late. And give her a false number for the home telephone, then when you get back say, if she's tried it, that you must have made a mistake.'

Once again I looked at him with respect. 'God, you're a good liar.'

'Sign of intelligence.' He cocked his head, eyebrows raised. 'So, are we sorted?'

I closed my eyes and took another long deep breath. 'You are so . . . God, I don't know what to say.'

'It's no big deal. Just providing information.' He drained his cappuccino and leaned back.

'Well, yeah, then, I think I am, er, *sorted*. Bloody funny word for it, though.' I scanned the papers again while I waited for my insides to settle down. It looked as though everything might work out OK. Outside the two rude boys had returned and were busy writing FAT BASTAЯD on the steamed-up glass.

Then something on the papers caught my eye.

For details of our tariff please click on our homepage.

'Hey, Daniel, is this a private clinic?'

He nodded.

'Well, I can't afford it, how much is it going to

141

be?'

'About five or six hundred pounds.'

The milkshake straw pinged out from under my fingers. 'You're joking.'

'It's no big deal—'

'Pardon me, it bloody is!'

'If you'd *listen* for a minute. I was going to say, my grandfather left me a few thou, it's sitting in a savings account doing nothing.'

'Oh, God! No way. I am *not* taking your money for this. No way. That's final.'

He put his hand out to me across the table but I didn't touch him. 'Charlotte, what choice do you have? You can pay me back when you get your student loan, whatever, if it'll make you feel better.'

'NHS?'

'If you want to start from scratch and find out all about that route, it's up to you. But to be honest, you're leaving it all a bit late.'

I wanted someone just to sort it out for me, take it all out of my hands. I felt utterly weary.

'Can you book me in, then?'

'I'll telephone as soon as I get home.'

Like he said, what choice did I have?

*   *   *

THIS IS THE WAY my world collapsed.

I'd gone on a mug-hunt. Opened the kitchen cupboard and there was only Nan's china cup with roses, and an egg-cup with Blackpool Tower on it. Ridiculous, as we have about twenty mugs in this house.

I knew where they'd all be so I steamed upstairs and rapped on Charlotte's door. No answer. I didn't seem to have seen her properly for weeks, she kept disappearing off to her room with sandwiches and endless bloody yoghurts. She reckoned to be revising but I'd thought she might be brooding over that boy, so I'd left well alone.

I stood and listened: nothing. I hadn't heard her go out but she obviously wasn't in her bedroom. (Can I just say I don't normally go barging in; for one thing, I'm always frightened of what I might find—justifiably, as it's turned out. Oh WHY did I have to be RIGHT?)

I opened the door slowly, sniffing the fuggy teenage air, and looked round. Mugs, yes, several, dirty, dotted about; her fleece on the floor in a heap; Charlotte, *Charlotte* on the bed, half-sitting up against the headboard with her Walkman on and a book on her lap.

Her lap.

Through the thin T-shirt I saw, for the first time, the outline of her belly rising in an unmistakable swell. The paperback was perched on top and it looked like she was using one of those beanbag trays for the elderly. Her head whipped up and she stared. And the look in her eyes was mine, eighteen years ago.

*   *   *

Out of the corner of my eye something moved and my whole body jolted with shock. I was *sure* I'd locked the door, but there she was, like Nosferatu only with permed hair, pointing a sharp fingernail at my belly. OhGodohgodohgod, worstnightmarescenario, major panic for about five seconds, then, weirdly, something else. Something

143

else taking over.

The guitar solo on my Walkman faded out and a voice in my head spoke over it, *Don't panic. This is the worst it gets. What can she do to you, other than shout? And you're well used to that, it's water off a duck's back, isn't it? And, listen, you're her equal now, in this situation. You're one woman talking to another. She can't accuse you of anything she hasn't done herself. Keep calm and say what comes into your mind.*

*   *   *

EIGHTEEN YEARS AGO, sitting at the table in tears and Nan kneeling at my side trying to hold my hand, except I kept pulling it away. Nan saying over and over again, 'Tha'll be awreet, we'll sort it out.' Me saying, shouting, 'How CAN it be, for God's sake?' She was frightened—I think I bullied her a bit after Dad died—but very sure. Very sure.

*   *   *

Then I was ready, and from then on it wasn't like me speaking at all.

*   *   *

'YOU STUPID—'

Charlotte wrenched her earphones off. Her face was twisted with some emotion, but it didn't look like shame.

'Oh, Christ, don't start—'

'What do you mean, *don't start*? I cannot *believe* what I'm seeing—' I pointed in fury at her

144

stomach—'that my own daughter could have been so bloody bloody stupid—and, and *loose*!'

She put the book down deliberately on the duvet and shuffled herself more upright.

'What, like you, you mean? Exactly like you, Mum, or had you forgotten?'

She was too cool by half. I wanted to strangle her with my bare hands.

'Oh, no. How could I *possibly* forget? That's the point. All that sacrifice and now this slap in the face.' I clenched my fists so hard my nails dug into the palms. 'You should have taken notice of me, of my mistake! I thought, Jesus wept, if there was one thing I'd taught you, it was not to throw your life away—'

'Like you did.'

'Exactly!'

Her eyes were flashing anger back at me, as if *I'd* done something wrong.

'So, in fact, you wish I'd never been born? Isn't that what you've been burning to tell me for the past seventeen years?'

All that sacrifice.

'Well, you said it.'

'Well, then. That makes two of us, doesn't it?'

The words flew out and collided in midair. There was a moment of deafening silence.

Then Charlotte threw her book against the wall and it dropped down on top of her pot of pens, scattering them across the desk. At the same moment Nan walked in, wide-eyed with fear. She pushed past me and tottered over to the bed.

'Eeh, love,' she said, putting her hand on Charlotte's shoulder.

Rage boiled up inside me at the gesture. Just

who should be getting the sympathy here?

'Get OFF her!' I shouted, and they both flinched but stayed where they were. 'YOU,' I barked at Nan, 'it's YOUR fault, all this. We wouldn't be in this mess if it wasn't for you. Get out and leave us to it.'

They moved closer together and Nan lowered herself down on the edge of the bed. She put her arm round Charlotte's bulk.

'Talk sense, Karen,' Nan muttered.

I thought I was going to hit her.

'Talk sense? Talk sense? That's the pot calling the bloody kettle, isn't it? There's no one comes out with as much rubbish as you, and it's me who has to put up with it on a daily basis, it's a wonder I'm not off my head.'

'Are you sure you're not? Anyway it's not Nan's fault, Mum. Whatever else, it's nothing to do with her.' Charlotte's face looked small under her fringe, but very fierce.

'Oh, isn't it? *Isn't it?* Well, I'll tell you something you don't know, lady.'

'Karen,' said Nan faintly.

I didn't even look at her.

'For a start, it was Nan who made me keep you. Just hang on, she told me. Have the baby, and then if you're still not suited, put it up for adoption, there's plenty of women who'd jump at the chance. Of course when I'd had you she knew I'd never be able to give you up. She said she'd look after you—'

'She *did*!'

'Only some of the time. And that's not the point. She *changed my mind*, ruined my life. I had such plans . . .'

'Oh,' said Charlotte tartly, 'put another record

146

on. Come on, Mum, we all know it was *you* who fucked up. You can't blame it on anyone else. Not even Dad.'

'A lot you know. You're not even eighteen. You wait till you get to my age and the best years of your life are behind you and you know there's no redeeming them, see how you feel then about *decisions that got made for you*.' It was true what they said about a red mist coming down in front of your eyes. There was a buzzing sound too, and my heart was leaping with extra surges of boiling-hot blood. I stepped forward shakily and pointed down at Nan. 'She isn't even my real mother.'

Nan turned her face into Charlotte's shoulder and I waited for the thunderclap. She just stared back, cool as you like.

'Did you hear what I said? I'm adopted. *Nan isn't my mother.*'

'Well,' said Charlotte, 'same difference. She brought you up, didn't she? What's that make her, then?' She was breathing fast and clinging on to Nan, who had her eyes shut. 'At least she wanted you, which is more than I can say for *my* mother. From where I'm standing it looks like you got a pretty good deal. Now, would you get out of my room, please; I'm supposed to be watching my blood pressure.'

*   *   *

To my amazement Mum turned on her heel and swept out. I'd thought she was going to hit me at one point, or have a heart attack. Her cheeks had gone really pink and her eyes all stary. My own heart was pounding in my chest and my throat was

147

dry.

After a minute Nan and I untangled ourselves. She fished a hanky from her sleeve, wiped her eyes and blew her nose. Then she began rooting in her cardigan pockets.

'Have a Mintoe,' she said, offering one up in a shaking hand. 'She dun't mean it. She loves you. That's why she could never give you up.' She wrestled with the cellophane wrapper.

'I don't care,' I said, and at that moment it was true. My insides were churning but my head was clear. I gripped the Mintoe in triumph. 'Oh, Nan. I can't believe I said all those things to her face, they've wanted saying for so long. It feels brilliant. How did I manage it? It was like I was possessed.'

Nan turned to me and smacked her minty lips. Her bottom dentures jumped forward suddenly and she popped them back in with her index finger. 'Pardon,' she said. We both began to giggle with nerves.

Then the door flung open and Mum was there again.

'How *dare* you laugh at a time like this!' she shouted. She held up a photo frame in front of her face. It was the one she keeps on her dressing table; me on a stretch of mud at Morecambe in a white sun-hat and knickers, hair blowing across my face. 'Look! You were five when this was taken and just *look* at you! Picture of innocence! And it turns out in the end you haven't the sense you were born with. All those times I've warned you!'

Nan and I sat and watched as she tossed the photo onto the desk where it sent more pens clattering off and knocked over my clay elephant I'd made in Year 7.

'Bloody hell, Mum. You've broken its trunk off.'

'You're having an abortion.'

I could have said, 'Yeah actually, I am, in two days' time. You can come along and cheer if you like.' But at that very moment two things happened. Nan drew in her breath and put her hand over my bump; and I felt the baby move.

It wasn't the first time, I realized now; there'd been flutterings before, like when a nerve twitches, only deep inside. But I hadn't clocked what they were, until this moment.

'You're having an abortion,' Mum said again.

If it had been a request; if she'd sat down and held me like Nan was doing; if we hadn't said those awful things to each other five minutes ago. But Fate gets decided on littler things than that every day.

'You're wrong, Mum.' Flutter flutter. 'I'm keeping this baby.'

Nan's arms tightened around me.

'Don't talk soft. You're not fit.' Mum leaned forward and spat the words at me. And if I hadn't decided by then, that would have swung me.

'Well, I'm a damn sight *fitter* than you. At least I won't make this baby feel guilty all its life,' flutter flutter, 'at least I won't try and make it Responsible for my own shortcomings. If you didn't want me, eighteen years ago, that's fine. But I'm not going to do to this baby what you did to me. Poor bugger. It deserves a better chance than I had.'

Can foetuses clap? I was sure I could feel a round of applause down in the left side of my pelvis. Washed in adrenaline, the thing was going berserk.

Mum's face had gone that nasty colour again

149

and her legs were trembling.

'You'll change your mind. Or I'll never speak to you again.'

'There's worse things than babies,' said Nan. 'They're nice, babies are.'

'Damn you both,' said Mum.

*   *   *

THERE'S worse things than babies, dear God in heaven there are.

It was all drinkin' i' th' owden days, an' feights all t' time. The children used come runnin' across the fields shoutin', 'Harry Carter's feightin' again,' an' we'd all go an' watch. He lived at t' top o' t' brow, an' he were allus after the women even though he was married. His little lads would be pushin' through t' crowds an' shoutin', 'Don't feight, Daddy,' but he never took any notice. He was forever askin' Herbert Harrison's wife for t' go wi' him, an' she'd allus tell her husband on him, it were like a game. They just wanted an excuse. One time I was stood wi' a big crowd watchin' them stagger about the street and Dr Liptrot came up alongside me. He didn't see me, though, he were glued to th' action. Finally Herbert Harrison knocked Harry Carter down, then he turned an' walked off. Harry got up, rubbed his chin an' stumbled towards us. I ducked away, but as he drew level Dr Liptrot patted him on the shoulder and said, 'Now, then, let that be a lesson. Feightin' dogs come limpin' whoam.' Harry stopped for a second, looked at the doctor, then hit him so hard he knocked out both his front top teeth.

It weren't just the men who drank, neither. My

150

grandmother Florrie used to have a big oak sideboard with a long dark patch on the top. Once she caught me an' Jimmy playin' wi' matches outside on the flags and she dragged us in and pushed us reight up again' the drawers of this sideboard. 'Do you know what made that mark?' she said. I shook my head; I'd only have been about seven and she could be very fierce. 'A neighbour set herself afire with an oil lamp,' she told us. 'She were dead drunk, an' she came running out into t' yard and staggered in here, all i' flames. She laid her arm along this sideboard, an that's why there's a mark.' She put her face close to ours. 'So think on.' 'Did she die?' Jimmy asked. 'Of course she did,' said my grandmother, and she clipped us both hard round the ear.

I never saw it happen myself, but as soon as I knew the story it was in every dream I had for months. Jimmy never said owt, but I know he dreamt it too.

There was a lot of drunkenness in them days. My grand-father was allus on t' spree, my mother said. He used to knock his beer ovver and lap it up off table top like a dog, he were terrible. And when he'd spent up he'd go and stand outside the pub and wait for people to treat him, he had no shame. Even as a little girl my mother was sent wi' a jug to t' Waggon an' Horses for him, when he was too idle to get his own ale.

His friends laughed an' called him a 'character', but Florrie had another word for it. At his funeral do, when they'd had a bit, some of 'em were singin';

'Me father was an 'ero
'Is brav'ry med me blush

They were givin' free beer up at Bogle
An' me father got killed i' t' crush.'

My mother said it was disgustin', an' they were all tarred wi' t' same brush.

Then after, two of his mates from t' colliery were tellin' tales about him, how he'd gone to t' pictures once to see a Charlie Chaplin. He'd not been gone above an hour an' he was back in t' pub, an' they said, 'What's up, Peter, were it not a good show?' An' he said, 'They turned all t' lights out, so I got up an' came whoam.' They were all two-double laughin'.

'Aye,' said another man, 'an' there were a time when we went to see the Minstrels at Southport, an' a chap came on and sang "Danny Boy" an' he were really good, so all th' audience started shouting, "Encore! Encore!". An' Peter called out at t' top of his voice, "Never mind bloody Encore, let bloody man sing again!" '

Someone else said they remembered Peter Marsh coming out of the polling booth once, very pleased because he'd said to himself, 'Well I'm not voting for 'IM'—an' put a great big cross next to t' candidate's name. Was he soft i' th' head, or was it just the drink? No one seemed to care, it didn't matter, 'cause he was such a Character.

Florrie wasn't laughing, though. She had twenty-two years of his meanness wi' money and his not bothering about the babies she'd lost. She never married again; I think she'd had enough of men. So she lived with her daughter Polly, and then me when I came along, and it became my dad who had us all on a piece of string wi' his antics.

There were times as Jimmy hated his father,

hated his comings and goings and the fact he would never marry our mother. 'He loves you, in his own way,' Mam used say. 'He gave you his name.' 'That just meks it worse!' said Jimmy. She had no answer to that, 'cause it was true. I think she felt it was her fault she couldn't keep him.

So as he got older Jimmy started to go wanderin', all ovver t' fields an' down by t' canal. He'd walk an' walk, as if he were lookin' for summat. An' he ran errands for people an' made a bit o' money that way. He used to see a lot of Mrs Crooks at Hayfield House; she was a widow and had never had children of her own. 'I'll pay thee Friday,' she'd say to him, an' she allus did. Then one day, he should have been at school, Harry Poxon saw him at t' side of t' canal, leanin' ovver wi' a stick. 'Tha'll faw in,' he said. That were t' last time he were seen alive. They were five days wi' a grapplin' hook before they found him, under t' bridge at Ambley. Mrs Crooks sent forget-me-nots for his coffin and all the school lined up an' sang 'There's a Friend for Little Children'.

He were only ten when he died.

*   *   *

THREE O'CLOCK in the morning and there's somebody standing at the bedroom door.

'I can't sleep. The baby's kicking.'

'Go back to bed, Charlotte,' I mumble, still only half out of a dream.

But it isn't Charlotte, it's Nan.

CHAPTER SEVEN

All night I'd been dreaming I was drowning; now I'd wakened to the image of the baby lying face up, motionless, under water, and a terrible chill of knowing it was somehow my fault.

Then as my head cleared I thought about how its body was actually floating inside me now, this very minute, hair flowing round its huge head, and how everything would all gush out—

I couldn't face school. I lay in bed till eleven staring at the ceiling.

'I'll tell them I've had flu,' I said to Mum when I finally made it downstairs.

'Say what you damn well please,' she replied.

So I walked out through the front door, down Brown Moss Road, Gunners Lane and out onto the Wigan road. I was going to walk until I dropped off the edge of the world.

By the Cock Inn I turned right and started down the public footpath to Ambley, past the golf course and Hayfield House behind its screen of trees. I didn't know where I was going, didn't care. Rooks cawed overhead and sparrows flirted in the dust on the rutted track. Elder-flower and dog roses were still thick among the hedgerows; you could smell the fertility in the warm air.

I turned off the track, scrambled down the canal bank and began to make my way along the towpath. A barge chugged past, castles and roses round the door, Jack Russell perched on the roof. The middle-aged woman steering smiled and nodded. Now there was an idea; I could always go and live on a boat, sail off up the Man-chester Ship Canal and start a new life. A blackbird ran across my path chuck-chucking, and the baby fluttered. You daft tart, I told myself. That's exactly why you're in this mess now, starting a New Life.

As I drew level with the Fly and Tackle I realized I was thirsty. I fished in my pocket to see if I had any money and extracted £3.30 in loose change. I climbed up the worn stone steps onto road level, checked for traffic and crossed over.

After the brightness outside, the interior of the pub was dark and I had to blink a few times before I could get my bearings. I'd passed the place enough times on the bus, but I'd not been in before; it was a bit of an old gimmers' place, popular for Sunday lunches and real ale. Squinting, I made out movement behind the bar. A fat bald man was drying glasses and singing 'Born in the USA' over the jukebox. There were sweat stains under the armpits of his shirt.

'Have you got a telephone?' I asked, hovering by the door.

He pointed to an annexe by the ladies' and carried on being Bruce.

Inside the booth I checked my watch and dialled Daniel's mobile number. 'Please have it switched on,' I prayed. There was a click.

'*Hell*-o.'

'Daniel! It's me! Hey!—What's that moaning sound?'

'Hey. Just a minute, I'll move somewhere a bit quieter. That's better. They're doing some sort of charity karaoke at one end of the common room. Just what you need after a hard morning's physics, some boil-ridden Year 10 apeing Noel Gallagher at

155

top volume. Are you all right? I saw you weren't in registration this morning—'

'Yeah, I'm fine, just not feeling very schooly today. Look, have you got any frees this afternoon?'

'Surely you mean *Study Periods*? Actually I have one genuine, and one by default because Mr Chisnall's away at a conference so he's set us work to do in the library. I do hope you're not going to suggest bunking off.'

'Too right I am. Can you get away at all?'

'What, now?'

'Yes, please. It's a bit of a crisis. Another one. Sorry.'

'No problem, I'm on my way. Are you at home?'

'God, no. Do you know the Fly and Tackle?'

'At Ambley? We went there two Sundays ago for my mum's birthday. Nice line in pies, dire jukebox. OK, I'll be with you in . . . twenty minutes. Don't do anything foolish.'

He rang off. I got two halves of cider and went outside to wait.

I sat at one of the wooden tables and watched the glinting cars hunching over the little stone bridge, and the water sliding under it. The banks were lush and the trees bent low with green fruits. Two swans glided past sending a V of ripples behind them that broke the reflec-tion of a perfect sky. If only I'd had a camera. The scene was idyllic, something like the picture on the front of Nan's old toffee tin she uses for storing buttons. I'd come back here, I promised myself, and take a picture of this place; maybe even do a painting, and give it to Nan. She'd like that.

At last Daniel's shiny red Ka, last term's present

for passing his driving test, bobbed over the bridge and disappeared into the car park. Thirty seconds later he emerged through the back door into the beer garden, blinking. If only he'd do something about his hair, I thought meanly.

'There's a man in there auditioning for *Stars in their Eyes*,' he said lifting his long legs over the bench and laying his jacket down carefully.

'I know. *Nuts in their Head*, more like. They'd have to strap him into some corset to get him to look like Bruce Springsteen. And put a paper bag over his face. Here.' I slid his glass over.

'Cheers.' He took a long drink. 'Now, this crisis. You've not changed your mind again?'

'God, no. I still want the baby.'

'Thank Christ for that. I cancelled the clinic when you phoned, and anyway, being realistic, you're probably too late.'

'I know. I've done it now, haven't I?'

'Yep. So, I brought you this.' He reached into his jacket pocket and pulled out a banana.

'What is it with you and fruit? I've had two apples today already. You're turning into a food fascist.'

'No, it's not to eat, well you can if you want, I suppose. This is your baby.'

We both looked at it, lying on the table. It was mottled brown and there was a fingernail scar at the stalk end.

'I hope to God it's not.'

'I don't mean it's banana *shaped*, I mean it's about that size. I looked it up on the Internet.'

'Oh, my God, really?' I put out a hand and stroked the clammy skin, then picked it up and held it against my stomach. 'Wow, weird.'

157

'You still don't look particularly pregnant, you know,' said Daniel peering at my bump. 'A bit fat, maybe. I wouldn't guess, just seeing you.'

'Yes, well, that's why I wanted to talk to you. I want to, now I've decided, there's no point in hiding any more, I want to tell them at school. And I'm terrified, and I don't know how to go about it. I mean, I could just walk in wearing my T-shirt, that'd be a dead giveaway, you know, no fleece or anything to cover it. They all think I'm mental still wearing winter stuff anyway, I'm nearly passing out with heat exhaustion in some lessons and I have to keep saying I'm cold. Or I could take Julia aside and ask her to tell everyone, she'd love that, all the drama. Then I'd be waiting for the summons, Mrs Lever poking her head round the classroom door, lips pursed, asking ever so politely if I could pop along to the Head's office, while everyone looks at each other and whispers. *Or* I could go straight to the Head, or some other teacher maybe, and ask them to handle things. They could have, you know, a special assembly on it and I could be shuffling about outside the hall listening. Oh, God, either way is going to be completely awful.' I put my head in my hands. 'What am I going to *do*, Daniel? How, *how* am I going to cope with all the fallout?'

'You will. You're that sort,' he said confidently.

'What do you mean?' I asked through my fingers.

'Well, ahm . . .' His hands fluttered. 'Hmm . . . OK, have you ever smoked?'

'No. Never even tried a cigarette.'

'Why?'

I took my hands away from my face and considered. 'Well, I weighed up the pros and cons.

158

Stinky breath, needless expense, appalling health risks, grief from adults, looking like a slag, versus maybe losing two pounds and joining in with everyone. I decided it wasn't worth it. Why d'you ask?'

He grinned and slapped the table top. 'Have you any idea how few people think that way? You are *so* unusual.'

'I am?'

'You know you are. Most people want to fit in at any cost, whatever the risks; you, you don't give a monkey's.'

I was staring at him.

'Can I be totally honest with you?' He looked straight into my eyes.

'Be my guest.' I wondered what the hell was coming.

'I think you're driven by bloody-mindedness.'

A vision of my mum flashed up, and for a second I thought I was furious. Then I started to laugh. 'Go on.'

'Well, you're incredibly self-contained, aren't you?'

'I—oh, I wouldn't say . . . In some respects maybe.'

'Oh, come off it, you know you are. You've got friends, yeah, but you don't care whether you sit with a group in the common room or on your own.'

'That's not true! You make me sound like some kind of freak-girl. Honestly, Daniel, I'm just a normal teenager—apart from being up the duff, obviously.'

'No, that's not it. What I mean is you're not afraid to swim against the tide. You're an *individual*. That's why—' He broke off and studied the canal for a while. 'Anyway, I'm not saying you're in for a picnic, but if anyone can cope with it, it's you.'

He really did know how to make you feel better.

'Damn you for being right.'

'My pleasure. Can I get you another drink?'

'Lemonade, I suppose. Have to think of the banana's welfare. Don't want the little thing pickled.'

When he came back I said, 'Don't suppose I'll have much time to be self-contained after the baby's born.'

'I don't suppose you will. Have you thought of any names yet? You could start talking to it, you know, it can hear you in there.'

'Honestly? God, that's so spooky.' I looked down at my stomach and spoke to the bump. 'Chiquita if it's a girl, Fyffes if it's a boy. What do you think of that, then?' No response. 'Too disgusted to reply. Oh, Daniel, it's so nice to be able to *talk* to someone about all this. Mum can't even bear to look at me; half-term was hell. Mind you, I did get a lot of revision done . . . Do you think I should tell a teacher, then?'

'If you can find one you like. Mrs Stokes?'

'Oh, ha ha. No, I was thinking of Mrs Carlisle, she was my form tutor in Year 10 and 11. She's a bit of an old hippy so she won't be too shocked. She always gave me nice pastoral reports.'

'She could even have a word with your mother,' suggested Daniel, under the impression that Mum was in a rational enough state to be spoken to.

'Well. Let's not get too carried away. One step at a time. Eh, Chiquita?'

'So you'll be in Tuesday?'

160

'I've an appointment at the hospital tomorrow, so it'll be Wednesday. God forbid I should miss the exams.'

'I'll have chocolate and Kleenex ready.'

He really got me thinking. Was I not normal?

I remember seeing Charlotte Church on telly last Sunday, hair shining with cleanliness. 'I'm just an ordinary teenager,' she kept saying. Yeah, right. So what's an Ordinary Teenager? I can't see she has a right lot in common with, for instance, Gary Whittle who I went to primary school with and who I remember once tied a firework to a cat's tail. He's in a Young Offenders' Institution now. And she's certainly nothing like me and my ever-expanding bulge of shame. The only thing I can see teenagers have in common is that they've waved twelve goodbye and they haven't reached twenty yet.

Imagine:

General Studies Paper 1: Section 1, Arts and Society

Q 1: How normal are you?

Intro: need for both individuals & society (esp media) to stereotype across age range, class, ethnic group, occupation etc; usually collection of negative characteristics; allows person to feel superior and in possession of all significant facts on basis of flimsiest evidence.

Para 1: teenagers pigeonholed by jealous middle-aged & elderly. Threatened not by teenagers themselves but by reminder of their

161

own mortality & wasted chances. Unflattering characteristics projected onto young include:

Para 2: moodiness. Unfair accusation; not confined to any specific age group. My Mother = Queen of the moods. If sulking an Olympic sport, she'd get row of perfect 10s. A grown woman who can out-strop any adolescent.

Para 3: materialism. Unfair again. Rife throughout society—Ikea on a Sunday! No point *my* being materialistic anyway as we have no money.

Para 4: vanity. Unfair. Self-obsession an insecurity thing, not age-related. In fact, older you get, more you focus on looks eg Grecian 2000, Playtex corsets, super-strength Dentu-fix etc. Teenagers aren't the ones spending £70 a pot on La Prairie face cream.

Para 5: habitual drunkenness. Inaccurate! 1/4 of our 6th form = Muslim for a start. Also Dave Harman = Jehovah's Witness & Alison Gill teetotal ∵ mother killed by drunk driver last yr. To judge by what staggers out of Working Men's every Sat night, worst offenders are 50+.

Para 6: spottiness. Even this boring old chestnut wrong. Supply teacher in Science labs this term has spots *and* wrinkles, must be at least 40 poor cow. I only get them on my back & shoulders, so doesn't count.

Conc: can't stereotype teenagers way you can old people. No such thing as typical teenager.

∴ if no such creature, I can't be judged as either normal or abnormal. QED.

*   *   *

I WAS SITTING IN a council office overlooking the Town Hall Square, sulking. Across the desk sat Mrs Joyce Fitton, my social worker; I'd already written her off as a waste of time.

'What have you found out?' I'd asked as soon as I'd sat down.

'Nothing yet. That's not why you're here. This is a counselling session. So we can be sure of where you want to go.' Mrs Fitton wore glasses on a chain and had a big motherly bust. She talked slowly and kept stopping to smile. I wanted to smack her.

'This place could do with a good clean. Those Venetian blinds are thick with dust,' I said rudely. I was so disappointed.

'I can see you're very angry, Karen. With your birth parents?'

No, with you, you daft old bat. I took a deep breath.

'I just can't cope with all these delays. I thought today you'd have some information for me.' I thought today you'd have found my mother and solved my life for me. I imagined you handing over a big thick file containing photos of my real mum, a résumé of her life so far (including the empty hole I left in it), pictures of her lovely house (polished wood floor, French windows, field with ponies at the bottom of the garden) and a beautifully written letter on Basildon Bond saying how much she wanted to see me.

'You need to have a clear idea of what you hope to get out of any contact you might make. And be sure you can handle the possibility of rejection and disappointment.'

'Oh, I'm good on those.' God, I sounded bitter.

Mrs Fitton took her glasses off and gave me a long look.

'Of course we may decide, after careful discussion, that you don't in fact want to find your birth parents,' she said. 'Some of these situations are potentially quite damaging, you know. I would say,' she put her glasses back on and began to sort pieces of paper on the desk, 'that unless you have the right, ahm, approach, you're laying yourself open to a lot of harm. Not that I want to be negative.'

I took the hint.

'Yes, absolutely. You're just doing your job. So, do you think you can find her?'

'I think there's a very good chance, yes. And your father, if you want.'

'To be honest, I haven't really thought that much about him. It's my mum I feel drawn to.'

She smiled again. 'That's usually the case, Karen. Even with men. There's something very special about the person who carried you for nine months, then went through labour for you. Most people assume there's going to be a special bond.'

'Isn't there always?'

'Usually. Now, have you discussed this issue with other members of your family?'

'Oh, yes.'

'And what have their reactions been?'

'Everyone's totally behind me. I have a very close relationship with my adopted mother, we can

164

talk about anything.' So long as it's bollocks. 'And my daughter and I are more like friends, sisters, sort of thing.'

'So you anticipate them welcoming your birth mother into their circle?'

'Oh, absolutely.' I won't let them anywhere near her.

Mrs Fitton wrote some notes in a small hand.

'And what do you expect to get out of finding your birth mother, Karen?'

Ah ha, I'd been expecting this question somewhere along the line, and I was ready.

'I just want to ask her about her experiences, tell her about mine. Talk to her as one woman to another. I'm not trying to, ha ha, replace my own mum, God forbid. I'm not looking to her to solve my problems or anything mad like that.' I rolled my eyes. Crazy idea.

'Have you got problems at the moment, then?'

Damn and blast.

'No, nothing to speak of, you know. Only ordinary, everyday, little problems, like everybody has. The washing machine breaking down, the bin men not coming, that sort of thing.'

She nodded sympathetically. 'Someone keeps taking our wheeliebin, would you credit it? We've had to paint our number on the side.'

I tutted.

'Well, you sound as if you've given this whole business a lot of thought.'

'Oh, yes.' That bit was true, at any rate.

'Are you happy then if I go ahead and contact the mother and baby home on your birth certificate?'

'They've closed down.' It slipped out. 'I, I tried

there first, phoning, but it's a business school now.'

She didn't even blink. 'Yes, they relocated. We've dealt with them before. They should have all your records. Then we can make another appointment and go over the papers, and see where we go from there. Maybe think about your dad too.'

'How long will that take?'

'Couple of weeks, not long.' She smiled once more. 'You seem like a level-headed young woman, Karen. I'm sure you'll cope with whatever we turn up.'

Level-headed? Didn't these people take psychology exams? Gullible old trout. Still, I wasn't going to own up to being a bag of neuroses. I watched her fill in a Post-it note and stick it onto her computer, next to a small orange gonk with goggle eyes. Fancy getting to that age and still believing the best of people. Bloody odd.

We shook hands and as I was going out I said, 'I'm sorry I was so rude about your blinds.'

Mrs Fitton smiled.

'We get a lot worse than that here, believe you me,' she said.

*   *   *

I'd have liked Nan to go with me to the hospital only she wasn't fit. I could just imagine the consultation with the midwife: 'So, Charlotte, how many weeks pregnant are you?'

Nan: 'Do *you* believe they've sent a man to the moon? Load o' rubbish.'

I'd have liked to take Daniel, but it was too much of an imposition. The potential for embarrassment was colossal ('No, this isn't actually the father, he's only come along to hold my urine sample') and besides, he had a Maths exam that day.

I suppose I could have taken Mum, if she wasn't still a quivering mass of rage. We nearly came to blows last week when she gatecrashed my doctor's appointment.

'Folic acid? Never mind bloody vitamin pills, tell her what a stupid girl she's been. Tell her, Doctor. Did you know she was supposed to be going to university?'

Fortunately Mum's fairly scared of health professionals so when he told her to shut up, she did. In fact she hasn't spoken to me since.

The midwife I saw at the hospital was really nice. Dead young, not much older than me I think, and that helped. The first thing I asked her was: 'How can you have a period and still be pregnant?'

She sketched me a little womb on a notepad and a little egg implanting itself.

'As the egg burrows in it sometimes breaks a few blood vessels. That'll be what you had. Not much blood, just spotting, is that right?'

I nodded glumly. The things grown women keep quiet!

'I bet you didn't know whether you were coming or going,' she smiled. I think she must have guessed, looking at my birth date and the absence of a partner, but she didn't say anything at first. It came out when she was strapping the black Velcro sleeve round my arm to take my blood pressure.

'My mum's on the way,' I lied. 'She must have been held up.'

'And your partner?'

The sleeve tightened and the blood pulsed in my fingers.

'Is a grade-A bastard. He's history.'

There was a hiss as the air seeped out and the sleeve went slack.

'I see. We do get a few of those.' She unstrapped me briskly. 'Do we know anything about this bastard's health? His blood group, any serious illnesses in the family, that kind of thing? I only ask because of this form we have to fill in.'

'Nope.'

'OK, then, not to worry.'

Like I said, she was really nice.

After she'd filled in pages and pages on my diet and progress, we listened to the baby's heartbeat, *pyow-pyow-pyow-pyow* through a special microphone. Then it was time to go and drink a pint of water and wait for the scan.

The scan. Night after night I'd had that scan, and always there was something wrong. The baby had no head, or it looked like an octopus, or it was too small—

Outside in the waiting room were a whole lot of bloated women. Some of them were reading magazines, some were trying to amuse hyperactive toddlers; nearly all of them were with someone. I sat down near a lone black lady with a football-up-the-jumper type profile and tried to catch her eye. She smiled when she noticed me, that secret club smile pregnant women pass round between themselves.

'Have you been waiting long?' I said.

'About half an hour.'

'How far are you on?'

168

'Thirty-seven weeks. The baby's turned the wrong way round, they're going to see if they can persuade him to do a somersault. Otherwise I might have to have—'

She broke off as a tall man in a suit came and sat down next to her. He put a hot drink down on the table, kissed her cheek, then reached over and patted her stomach. I edged away, feeling miserable. It was important not to think about the nightmares.

I rooted in my bag for the funky little paperback I'd been given by the doctor; *Emma's Diary*, a week-by-week guide to pregnancy. I wanted to see what it said about birth defects. As I pulled the book out a scrap of paper fluttered down onto the tiles. I got down on my hands and knees to pick it up, and recognized Nan's swirly writing.

> *Don't think you're of little importance*
> *You're somebody, somebody fine*
> *However you tumble, and get up and stumble*
> *You're part of a vision Divine*

A vision Divine. My eyes blurred with tears and I scrambled back onto my seat. Oh, Nan.

Forty minutes later, just as my bladder had passed from painful to critical, a little grey-haired nurse called me into a dim room, hoisted me onto a table, and pulled my shirt up and my leggings down to my pubic bone. I stared down at the slightly flattened bump as she squirted cold gel on my skin and then stood back for the doctor to get in there with his probe thing.

'Look at the screen,' whispered the nurse, beaming.

And there, in flickering white profile, was a head

169

and an arm.

'It's sucking its thumb,' she said.

My God. So there was a baby in there after all. It was all true. The foetus squirmed about as the doctor pressed hard into my flesh for what seemed like ages.

'Don't hurt it!' I called out in alarm.

'It's fine,' he murmured and carried on methodically, taking down measurements every time the machine went *beep*. 'Sorry, when was the date of your last period?'

'I told the midwife, I don't know.' Who keeps track of these things?

He moved the probe around and two waving legs came into view. 'And you haven't had a dating scan . . . Well . . .'

The image froze.

'What's the matter?' I felt panic rise. Next to my hip the machine made a sinister whirring noise.

The nurse leaned over. 'It's OK, he's just taking a nice picture for your notes. You can take a copy home if you want.'

'Is there something wrong, though? Is my baby all right?'

The doctor flicked a switch and the screen froze again, then the overhead lights came on. 'You're fine, your baby's fine. I'd say you were about—' he glanced over at my notes—'about twenty-six weeks. So I'm going to put your due date down as the sixteenth of October.'

'Oh my God, that's my Nan's birthday!'

The nurse grinned and helped me up off the table, but the doctor was busy writing on my file.

'Can I ask a question?'

'Sure,' he said without turning round.

170

'Can you tell whether it's a boy or a girl? I'd really like to know. For the names and stuff.'

He glanced over his shoulder at me.

'It's not hospital policy to disclose the sex,' he said briefly, and turned back again. I wondered how he could be so unmoved by the miracle he'd just revealed.

'You'll have to knit lots of lovely white things,' twittered the nurse, squeezing my arm. I'd have liked her as a mother, I decided. 'Now, I'll bet you're desperate for a pee. I'll show you where the toilet is.'

And then I was on the bus going home, the grainy flimsy photo clutched in my hands. There was another universe-upside-down moment, when for the duration of that ride I and my baby were at the centre of creation, and the feeling that we two were all evolution had been working towards for millions of years overwhelmed me. Nobody on the 416 seemed to notice my fantastic revelation, but that's the way the world works, isn't it? We miss amazing things every day, right under our noses. Maybe it's for the best. If we went round being amazed all the time we'd never get anything done.

I bounced into the house and went in search of Nan, but there was only Mrs Crowther from Crossroads reading last night's *Bolton Evening News*. 'She's having a nap in her room,' she told me. 'At long last. She's been up and down like I don't know what. Something's mitherin' her.'

I shrugged and went to find something to eat. In the kitchen I smoothed out the little picture again and drank in the detail. Just its top half, the face in profile, a big forehead. I wondered who it looked like and a pang of memory, Paul's shining face and

171

floppy hair, skewered me where I stood. Would he not like, would he not want to see . . . ? But that was not Paul I remembered, not the real Paul, who was scum. This baby didn't need a fantasy father.

I wanted to phone Daniel, but a glance at my watch told me he'd still be doing his sums so I made a giant cheese sandwich and went upstairs to do some more thinking.

When I opened the door and saw what was on the bed I couldn't believe my eyes.

*   *   *

ONE OF THE THINGS that's bothering me most about this baby business is that it means I'm on my way to being old. Thirty-four, it's no age is it? You see TV presenters older than me (occasionally). I want to throw out my jumpers and leggings and start again, wear spaghetti straps and combat trousers and little butterfly clips in my hair. Would I really look like mutton? How *can* I be a grandma? Yet once this baby's born I'll feel as if I've started down the slippery slope which ends with Werther's Originals, *The People's Friend* and Death. I didn't think I was even middle-aged really, but look, here I am, Grannie Karen. So even less chance of finding a man. I mean, it's not exactly an alluring chat-up gambit: Why don't you come back and see my grandchild? I bet Charlotte never thought of that, did she. How did I ever manage to produce such a selfish daughter?

*   *   *

Laid neatly across the bed were three blouses, a

pair of jeans and a long floaty skirt. I went over and had a closer look. *MUM-2B* said all the labels. It was maternity wear! My first set of decent clothes for six months. I tore off the saggy size-16 leggings I'd bought off Wigan market and pulled on the jeans. They were really clever, sort of stretchy round the top and then skinny on the legs like real jeans. It was brilliant to have something that felt comfortable again. I struggled out of the T-shirt and put on the nicest blouse, a floral job, and all right, I looked a bit mumsy, but what could you expect in the circumstances? The point was everything fitted in the right places and didn't feel like it was going to fall down or cut me in half. Next I tried the skirt, also brilliant, with the same blouse then another, then the third, then I took off the skirt and put the jeans back on and it was then that the front door went and I heard Mum's voice in the hall.

'Mum!' I shouted down.

'Just a minute,' she called back. I heard her talking to Mrs Crowther, then the door going again. Finally her footsteps on the stairs, and she was in my room.

'Well?' She sounded sharp and I faltered.

'All these clothes . . .'

'Yes?'

'Did you buy them?'

'How else do you think they got there?'

'Oh, Mum, thanks so much—'

She cut me short. 'I ordered them from the catalogue. If you don't like them, don't pull the labels out and I'll return them. You can pay me back in instalments, we'll have to work it out.'

Even the news that they weren't a gift didn't dampen my gratitude.

'It's so nice of you . . .'

'Well, let's be honest, you were beginning to look a complete sight in that other stuff.' She turned to go and I stepped forward and grabbed her arm.

'Oh, Mum, I've got to show you something—' I picked up the scan photo from the pillow and held it out shyly.

She took one glance and then her eyes flicked away. She wrenched her arm free and walked out, slamming the door.

*   *   *

SOMETIMES it's hard to see what a woman sees in a feller. I loved my dad 'cause he were my dad; we didn't see him so often, but when we did he were grand wi' us. He made Jimmy a boat out of wood wi' a mousetrap inside it, so's when you pressed a button at t' side it flew apart. We used play wi' it for hours out on t' flags at t' back. For me he made a little chair—I have it now—wi' spindles an' turned legs. When I got too big for it, it did for my dolls. An' although he could be sharp-tongued, he only twice laid a finger on me an' that was for sayin' 'Good shuttons' to the milkman—I didn't know it was rude—and for mouthin' 'What a face our cat's got' at my mother; she saw me in the mirror. He would never have touched our Jimmy, he thought the sun shone out of him; we all did. He had his father's charm wi' none of the arrogance.

But when I grew up, an' especially when I got married, I began to see what a terrible time he'd given my mother. Grandma Florrie hated him;

174

hated the way he'd turn up at the house an' expect to stop the night, but she never said no because Polly'd be beside herself wantin' him to stay and so would we. Sometimes his mother, Grandma Fenton, would come round an' the two owd women would sit on the horsehair sofa and moan about his behaviour.

We felt sorry for Grandma Fenton. Fancy havin' produced a son who hated women. She'd been in service when she got caught and she'd never say who the father was, although it was pretty obvious it was the chap who employed her; he wouldn't have owt to do wi' it, I suppose. So when Harold was young she had a poor time of it, no benefits in them days, of course. She used have a stall again' the Victoria where she sold nettle beer, brandy snaps and treacle toffee. An' she were a nice woman, it was a shame. She'd have done anything for Polly. She never got much love from her son.

I know I've been lucky. Bill were a wonderful husband and father. And the more I see of the world, the more I think there aren't so many on 'em about.

*   *   *

I'D BEEN putting it off—frankly I'd rather have driven six-inch nails into my kneecaps—but it had to be done. Steve had got to be told about the situation.

I wouldn't say we were on bad terms; he's too bone-idle to harbour a grudge. For him the past is the past, he's not fussed about the way our marriage turned out. He always seems quite pleased to see me (which is about once a year) and quite pleased when I leave.

He lives in Harrop, at the bottom of the Brow; you could walk it, but it'd be a heck of a climb back up. I took the Metro and parked it up the entry at the end of the terrace.

'Hey up.'

He'd seen the car and was standing at the door in his stocking feet. He'd grown a moustache since I'd last seen him and it made him look older. Still as lean as a whippet, though, still that sharp-featured face and the cheeky grin.

I walked up the overgrown path and went through the dark hall, picking my way past cardboard boxes, to the back sitting room.

'Have a seat. Kettle's just boiled.'

There were more boxes and some bundles of news-paper on the floor, lots of used crockery dotted about, a pair of jeans folded over a wire maiden by the unlit gas fire. When we'd first split up I'd been appalled at the way he lived, but now I just left him to it. A bit of peeling wallpaper border never hurt anyone, I suppose. As long as it wasn't in my house, obviously.

'So what's this all about? You sounded a bit rattled on the phone. Is it summat to do with Charlotte?' He handed me a mug with a picture of Linda Lusardi on it and sat down opposite.

'Yeah. God, there's no easy way to say it. She's got herself into trouble.'

'Wha', at school? I thought she were a gold-star pupil.'

'No, you great lummox, *into trouble*. She's pregnant.'

'Oh, bleedin' 'ell.' Steve put his cup down on the carpet and shot me a twisted grin. 'Not our Charlie.

176

I thought she had more sense.'

'Apparently not.'

Steve shook his head. 'I can't believe it. Not our Charlie. She's such a clever girl. Cleverer than us, anyroad, I thought. What did she think she were doin'?'

I shrugged and lay back against the sofa wearily. 'It's not like I haven't warned her a thousand times. But you know what she's like, so deep. So difficult to talk to. I wasn't even absolutely sure she had a boyfriend for ages, she's so secretive. And she's well on, it's too late for an abortion. She hid it from everyone.' It wasn't my fault, I wanted to add, but then Steve would never have thought like that anyway. I was justifying to myself, not him.

'An' this lad, what's he got to say about it all?' Unconsciously he drew himself up and squared his jaw.

There was a pause.

'I've not really pursued that line,' I said awkwardly.

'What do you mean? Haven't you been round to his house, had a talk with his parents? Because it seems to me he's got some explaining to do.'

I couldn't tell him I'd been too wrapped up in blaming Charlotte and my own inadequacies to dream of doing anything other than getting rid of the pregnancy. When this plan had failed I was so drunk with fury I couldn't think straight. I couldn't even bring myself to say good morning to Charlotte, let alone have a rational discussion about the role of the baby's father. In any case, I secretly didn't blame him, I blamed her, because whatever they say, there'll never be equality of the sexes till men can get pregnant; she was bright enough to know she'd be the one to get caught, so she ought to have sorted it. Men'll just try for what they can get where sex is concerned, they don't think it through; that's for us women to do. So as far as I was concerned it was her fault.

But Steve had scented a villain and his blue eyes were bright.

'What's this little bugger's name and where's he live?'

'Paul. Paul Bentham. He lives round the corner, off Barrow Road, apparently. He used to go to school with Charlotte when she was in the juniors. Cocky so and so. He dumped her about three months ago, and that's why I thought she was so moody, still pining for him. I never dreamt . . .'

'Well, I'm going to pay this Paul Bentham a visit and tell him exactly what the state of play is. He can't just walk away; I didn't, did I? You've got to face up to your responsibilities even at that age. Little shit.' He thumped the arm of the chair. 'Upsetting our Charlie like that and then doing a runner. Poor lass. Is she all right?'

What about me? I wanted to shout. I'm not all right! I want to jump on the next bus to Manchester airport and flee the country, except the whole house would collapse without me. Christ, I can't even pop down the shops without checking Nan's bag or Charlotte's sanity; I feel like that Greek bloke who had to hold the world up on his shoulders.

But I hadn't come round to moan. There's no point with Steve, he blocks it out, which is partly why we used to have such God-awful rows. He never understood that women like to complain for the sake of it, to get things off their chest, and they

178

don't *want* to be fobbed off with practical solutions and courses of action. They just want sympathetic attention, and lots of it.

So I said, 'She's fine. I'm not worried about her at the moment, she's—' a bitter laugh escaped— 'really into the pregnancy now and pretty up-beat. Though I think it'll all go pear-shaped when the baby's born.'

'Well, it does, dun't it?'

'Exactly.'

There was a silence while we both remembered the unholy fuck-up we'd made of the post-natal months.

'Well, she's got you to look after her,' said Steve and a big spear of guilt ran through me. 'So what d'you want me to do? I'm no good at talking to her . . . She scares me a bit, if you want to know.' He laughed sheepishly. 'She's so bloody clever, and she's taller than me an' all . . .' He ran his hand through his hair. 'I don't know her well enough.'

I could have made a nasty remark here but I was too conscious that the feelings Steve was trying to articulate were basically my own. In any case, I needed more aggro like I needed a hole in the head.

'I could probably find some extra cash,' he continued. He gestured vaguely at the cardboard boxes. 'I'm looking after some stuff for a chap at work, and there'll be a few quid in it at the end for me. I don't mind passing it Charlotte's way.'

'I can't pretend it wouldn't be welcome. Money doesn't buy you happiness—'

'But at least you can be miserable in comfort,' he finished and we grinned briefly together. 'Right-oh. 'S not a problem.'

'I didn't come round here to scrounge, though.'

'I know you didn't.'

'I thought you needed putting in the picture. She might—she might still want to come round and talk it over with you.'

A look of panic crossed Steve's face. 'Oh, bloody hell. Look, I'll tell you what I'll do. I'll go round to see this lad and I'll see if I can sort summat out. I mean, I can't make things any worse, can I?'

I gazed at my cup and considered. Linda Lusardi simpered out at me from under a film of tannin.

'Probably not. Just make sure you don't lose your temper,' I said.

*   *   *

I bottled it, the big school revelation. At four o'clock Scan Tuesday I phoned Mrs Carlisle and told her the whole sorry story. She said to give her half an hour to have a think, then she rang back and said what they'd do was let me sit my exams up in Mrs Duke's office, out of the way, and I could come and go during lesson time so nobody would see me. So that's what I did, sloping in and out of the building like a bulky shadow. For the external papers I had to have a teacher sit in with me, but for the internal ones I was just left alone to get on with it; me, a bottle of Evian, a packet of Polos and my little curly photo. I've never felt so focused.

At the end of the last exam Mrs Carlisle came and had a long chat with me. She'd brought me a syrupy mug of real coffee, unaware that even the smell of instant made me heave. Still, it was something to do with my hands while she went on about deferred university places and childcare

180

options for next year. She'd done a lot of research. 'You mustn't let go of your dreams,' she said, twice. I didn't even know what my dreams were any more.

On the last day of term she gathered the lower sixth girls together and told them the score. I'd had every intention of going in and saying goodbye; Daniel thought I should. But when it came to it I couldn't face the glare of publicity and spent the morning down the canal bank at Ambley again, throwing leaves in the water and watching them float off to freedom.

That was on the Wednesday; on Thursday I had a phone call from Julia asking me to meet her in town for lunch and I thought I owed it to her, so I went.

The thing about Julia is that she's brimming with social aplomb. She must get it from her mother, a girlish woman with a bright, lipsticked smile who can talk to anyone. I remember last Open Day there was a woman with no hair, I think she must have had cancer, and Julia's mum just breezed up to her and started chatting away. I was on the refreshment stall and I'd been dreading this woman coming over in case I said something like, 'Do you need a wig?' instead of 'Do you need a tray?' So, I have to admit, if the boot had been on the other foot and it was Julia who'd been pregnant, I'd have been struck dumb with embarrassment.

No such problems for Julia. She came rushing over to my table and gave me an enormous hug round my neck and then said, 'Look at *you*! You look *amazing*! Your hair's really glossy and your skin's absolutely *glowing*! Fantastic!'

She sat down and ordered, then produced a plastic bag containing a fluffy toy from Anya, a card

181

signed by the sixth-form girls, and a book on pregnancy month by month from Mrs Carlisle. I was completely overwhelmed.

'Anya wanted to come too, but we thought it might outface you seeing us both together. But she says she'll ring you next week. We'd have been in touch before but Mrs Carlisle told us when you were first off you'd got suspected glandular fever and didn't want to get out of bed. But, wow, you're doing great. Everyone's really excited, and they all send their best wishes.' She sat Anya's little fluffy rabbit-thing up on its hind paws. 'Sweet! So, how you doing?'

I'd been feeling not too bad until the presents, but the unexpected kindness slew me. My face went red and my voice strangled with the effort of not crying.

'It's really nice—' was all I managed.

'Say no more.' Julia was brisk. The drinks arrived and a plate of cakes. 'God, don't you just *love* these chocolate muffins? I could literally eat them till all my buttons popped off. Fantastic. Oh, you missed some major gossip over the last few weeks. Did you know Denny's been suspended for selling funny cigarettes to Year 9s? One of them nearly set fire to the toilets, apparently, trying to light one of his home-made fags. God knows what was in them, because it wasn't tobacco. Martin Ainsworth reckons it was dried seaweed. Some of the kiddies lost their voices, that's how the teachers knew something was going on, they'd all come back in after break croaking like frogs. Anyway, at least it wasn't proper dope because he'd have been out on his ear, you know how twitchy the Head is over drugs.'

182

It was relaxing to have her rattle on like this. It made me pretend I could be normal again, with the usual teenage concerns and excitements. She made me laugh in spite of myself, and the baby inside me jumped and squirmed.

'. . . So then Jimbo told Simon that he'd seen Abby and Dom eating each other's faces in Fatty Arbuckle's, and Simon went absolutely ballistic and told Abby she was a tart in front of everyone in the dinner queue, so Dom jumped on him and there was this huge fight, tables everywhere, and Mr Barry had to drag them apart and make them go to separate rooms to cool off and their parents were called in. It was really hectic.' Julia stopped to draw breath. 'So you can see you've missed loads. I don't know how anyone's got any work done. I certainly didn't. My report was a disaster. Like I really care.' She took a big bite of cake and winked at me.

'Mine was brilliant,' I said gloomily. Mum had been in a terrible temper when it came through the post. It was one of those no-win situations, like every year when the GCSE results improve and the press go, 'Oh, standards must be slipping.' But if ever the results were down on last year's, it would be, 'Oh, we see standards are slipping,' and the *Daily Telegraph* would commission a special shock report on how thick today's teenagers truly are. So if my exam marks had been bad Mum would have been beside herself because I was throwing away my chances. The fact that they were better than I could ever have expected made the pregnancy even more of a disaster because I was clearly destined for great things. Or would have been.

'Julia,' I said, 'what happened when Mrs Carlisle told you about me?'

183

She paused for a fraction of a second only. 'Well, we were all really surprised, and a few people looked at me because they must've thought I knew about it—'

'You can understand why I couldn't say anything?'

'Yeah, yeah, of course. A big thing like that, you need to get your own head round it before it becomes public property. Then the twins asked if they could send you a card and Mrs Carlisle said she thought that'd be very nice. That was it, to be honest. Oh, a few people have asked me whether you'll be around next year. Will you?'

'I dunno. I don't know what it's like having a baby around. If it's not too much hassle I could put it in a crèche or something and come back in January. Maybe sooner. I don't want to have to repeat the year, not with all those bozos from Year 11 coming up. The teachers could send me work and I could get Special Consideration for the exams. Oh, I don't know. It goes round and round in my mind. We'll have to see.'

Julia was nodding, then she said, 'And of course, somebody asked me who the father was . . . I told them I didn't know, but I don't know if they believed me. Obviously you don't have to say anything if you don't want to.'

I could tell she'd been burning to get this question out. Well, she'd been pretty good with me so far. It would be a relief to say something at last.

'I don't think it's anyone you'd know. A lad I used to go to school with years ago. Paul. But we're not together any more. He didn't want anything to do with me once he'd found out. I got it *so* wrong. You'd think, if you'd . . . if you'd slept with someone—that you'd know them pretty well. That's what I'd thought anyway, more fool me. I hope—I hope he gets run over by a lorry, very slowly, so his ribs crack one by one and you can hear his screams all the way to Blackpool. I hope he moves to the other side of the world and I never see him again. Oh—'

A pain shot through my groin.

Julia was on her feet at once.

'Charlotte! Are you all right? Do you want me to get someone? Shall I phone for a doctor?'

I shifted on the chair. 'It's OK, stop flapping. I think it was a one-off. Ooh!' This twinge bent me over and made me gasp.

'Stay where you are, I'll get an ambulance.'

'Come back!' I shouted as Julia shoved her chair out of the way and prepared to do a mercy dash. 'I'm not going into labour. At least, I don't think I am. The pain's in the wrong place. It's down here. Ow.'

Heads were beginning to turn and the panic that always overtakes me if I inadvertently become the centre of attention began to well up. There was another twinge. I had to get out, and quickly.

'I need to go home,' I said. 'Can you walk me to the bus stop?'

'To the bus stop? You must be kidding. I'm driving you home. But don't you dare give birth on my mother's new seat covers, we'd never hear the last of it.'

Julia drove me back from town with exaggerated care, glancing over at me continually. Was the seat belt too tight? Were the pains coming every three minutes? Did I want her to turn the car round and go to the Royal Bolton? I kept saying no and

185

gradually the pains went off. She began telling me about her holiday plans and her new bedroom, and then we were pulling into Brown Moss Road, both of us heaving a sigh of relief.

She stopped the car. 'You gave me a fright, missus. Are you OK now?'

I nodded.

'You're not just saying that?'

'No. Honestly. Thanks.'

'Do you want me to walk you to the door?'

'No, really. I feel fine now, it must just have been . . .'

We both caught sight of him at the same time. Julia turned to me puzzled.

'Who's that man bleeding onto your doorstep?'

'Oh God,' I said. 'Oh God oh God. This is why I never bring anyone home.'

CHAPTER EIGHT

'Id wed a bid wrog,' my dad said through his hanky. 'I'b sorry, Charlie.' Mum had got him sitting on the sofa leaning forwards and pinching his nose; she has to deal with nosebleeds all the time at school.

'Don't keep swallowing,' snapped Mum, 'it'll make you sick. Spit into this if you have to.' She thrust a Pyrex bowl under his chin.

'I can't believe you went round there. Why didn't you say anything to me first? What was he like? Was he really angry?'

Part of me was horrified that Dad had crashed my private life like this, after years of sitting on the

186

sidelines. But part of me was grateful that someone should finally have thought to give Paul a good bollocking, it was about time. If that's what had happened. It didn't look too promising.

'Aggry? He were brickid hisself when he realized who I was. I told hib the score. Dobody walks away from subbat like that. Be a ban, I said. Face up to your responsibilities.'

'Is that when he hit you?' said my mum. I knew what she was thinking because I was thinking it too. He looked pathetic, with his red hanky and his head bowed, a button hanging off his shirt. Beaten up by a seventeen-year-old, nice going, Dad.

Through the muffles of clotting blood we finally got the tale, though how much he'd brushed it up I wouldn't like to say.

He'd gone round late afternoon when he knew Paul would probably be in (and I guess hoping his old man wouldn't). A 'little lad' opened the door and then shouted for Paul who came down the stairs unsuspecting. Dad started his speech which quickly turned into a slanging match, during which Paul maintained first that the baby wasn't his, and then that since it was my decision to keep it against his wishes, he couldn't be called to account. (I broke in to argue at this point but my mother shut me up.) After a few minutes of hurling insults at each other, Paul had turned to go back upstairs and my dad had completely lost it, lunged forward and grabbed Paul round his legs. Paul fell face-first onto the step—'He'll have a beltin' black eye tomorrow'—and in the struggle to get away kicked out, making contact with Dad's nose—'it were nowt, a lucky blow'. At this point Mr Bentham appeared on the landing, bleary with sleep and taking out his earplugs—'though he soon looked sharp when he saw me'. He ran down and hoisted Paul upright, checked him over briefly and propped him against the banisters. Meanwhile Dad had been shouting the odds about his son's behaviour, and despite Paul's denials, the finer details of the situation had begun to dawn on Mr Bentham. He'd apparently turned to take a swipe, seen Dad's berserk blue eyes and his bloody nostrils and let his arm drop to his side. (I suspect this bit is true. Mr Bentham goes in for a quiet life.) Then he'd told Dad to get out of his house and if he wanted to take it further to get a blood test done. 'I will, don't worry. We'll have the CSA on you. An' you want to see that lad of yours gets a good hidin',' my dad had told him, and stormed out.

'So, full of sound and fury and signifying nothing,' I muttered. My mother leaned over and cuffed me round the ear.

'Less of that, madam. A thank you would be nice, after what your dad's been through. Even if it was a waste of time.'

Dad shot us a despairing glance and I immediately felt sorry. A proper daughter would have got up off her backside and given him a hug, but of course that was impos-sible, so I just gave him a thin smile instead. 'Thanks, anyway. Hope your nose doesn't hurt too much.'

He took the hanky away experimentally.

'I was trying to help.'

'I know you were. He's a total git.'

'Well, I must admit, I don't know what you ever saw in him, love. I thought he were an arrogant little gob-shite.'

The baby elbowed me sharply and I thought,

188

You poor bugger, that's your father we're talking about. What an inheritance.

'Do you mind if I go upstairs and have a lie-down?'

Mum and Dad shook their heads and I dragged myself up to my room. Next door Nan was snoring and mumbling. I flopped onto the bed. The baby kicked on.

'It's probably something called "round ligament pain",' said Dr Gale. 'Nothing to worry about. Your muscles are having to hold up a tremendous weight, it's not surprising they're putting up a bit of a protest.' We were in the back garden of Daniel's enormous house enjoying the sunshine. They'd installed me in a sun-lounger in the shade of a beech tree; later on, under that same beech tree, Daniel would try to kiss me and I would refuse, so spoiling a perfect day.

'That's what the midwife reckoned. All the joints are under such pressure I'm bound to get some aches and pains. It was really scary, though. My friend thought I was about to give birth.'

'You'll be fine,' smiled Mr Gale. 'You look perfectly healthy to me, anyway.'

He was nice, Daniel's father. Tall, like his son, but more assured, quite distinguished. Lovely newsreader accent. I bet all his menopausal women patients harboured fanta-sies about him. He made me feel relaxed despite the fact that I'd never met him before and I was seven months pregnant and I didn't know what he'd been told about me. I suppose he sees all sorts in his surgery. The sun shone warm on us both and bees crooned among the lavender at our feet.

Inside I could hear Mrs Gale and Daniel preparing the evening meal. I'd have called it tea, but here it was dinner and it happened at seven not five. I remembered Mum trying that one out on us a few years ago; Nan was nearly eating the tablecloth in frustration, and I kept sneaking Custard Creams so by the time the food was on the table I didn't want it. 'Eeh, I can't be doin' with this caper every night,' Nan had said. Big row.

I wondered what Mum would make of the Gales' Edwardian villa. Actually she'd be struck dumb with envy and inadequacy as she ticked off their Minton floor, the polished staircase, the quality art prints on the walls. By the time we reached the dream kitchen her jaw would be on the floor, as mine was. Kitchens aren't my thing, I tend just to breeze through on the scrounge, but even I could see this one was like a show-home. It was huge, for a start, with a quarry-tiled floor and immaculate units and—yes, Mum would have died—an Aga *and* a conventional high-tech built-in oven. Then there were all those little tasteful touches that I've seen on the front of Mum's house magazines; bunches of dried herbs hanging from the ceiling, gleaming copper pans, a hotchpotch of Victorian tiles along the back wall.

'Mum does cake decorating for weddings and parties,' said Daniel dismissively. 'She works for Relate too.'

He'd taken me out through French windows into the lovely garden and introduced me to his father, brought us drinks, then left us alone to have a chat.

'So, have I set your mind at rest?' asked Dr Gale. 'You don't want to be brooding and worrying just now, especially over something that's perfectly

190

normal. Try to keep yourself calm. Calm mums-to-be make calm babies, so the research has it.'

'Really?'

'Oh, yes. You think about it. There are all sorts of chemicals passing between you, including all the ones your body releases when you're under stress. In the later stages of pregnancy it could have an effect on the foetus's eventual personality. And at this point, well, you've got a viable baby in there now.'

'What do you mean?'

'I mean that if you went into labour tomorrow there'd be a good chance the baby would survive. Provided it got immediate and proper care. It'd be a skinny little chap but it would have all its parts, more or less.'

I laughed and stroked my bump. 'It's certainly pretty active.'

'Good.' Dr Gale took a sip of his drink and looked out over the lawn.

I wish I could move in here with you for the next three months, I thought.

Dinner was grilled trout and salad and, guess what, Mrs Gale had grown all the parsley and dill herself. I thought of Mum's Herb Garden two summers ago, a row of pots along the back windowsill. Most of the herbs grew fantastically tall and then fell over; some of them didn't grow at all. Nan kept putting her used teabags in the pot nearest the drainer, which didn't help.

'Daniel tells me you're hoping to read English at university,' said Mrs Gale pleasantly. I say pleasantly, but really she was gritting her teeth to stay nice. I had some sympathy. There was her precious son bringing home some pregnant slapper who clearly didn't know which knife to use and, having wrecked her own life, was hatching God knows what plan to wreck his.

'I'd like to go to Oxford,' I said through a mouthful of fish.

'We wanted Tasha to apply, but she had her head set on Birmingham, for some reason.' Grimace. 'Still. Daniel'll probably apply to Lincoln. David went there.' Mrs Gale nodded at her husband.

'Smashing. Is that a nice university, then? Isn't it very hilly?'

Dr Gale coughed politely. 'I think you've misunderstood. I went to Lincoln *College*, Oxford.'

How we all laughed. I gave up the battle with the fish and put my cutlery down. I'd begun to feel sick if I ate too much at one go.

'Gillian went to St Hilda's. We met at a May Ball.'

'How romantic,' I said, meaning it. These were people who'd got everything right, done their lives in the right order.

'Yes, she was with a chap I detested. Ended up punching him in the mouth.' He smiled at his wife and raised his glass. 'Marvellous days.'

'And you were with Elise Osborne, owner of the most irritating laugh in Oxford,' replied Mrs Gale smartly. 'Finished with that plate, Charlotte?'

I helped clear away and we finished with fruit, which is also something which never makes an appearance in our house due to it generally sitting in a bowl till it goes mouldy and then getting thrown out. Poor Mum. She'd love to do this: Italian bread, wine, five cheeses, grapes. She used to try us with different foods but she's given up

192

now. Nan's preferred dish is belly pork, two disgusting bow-shaped pieces of meat covered in a thick layer of fat which Nan eats with her fingers; she'd have it for breakfast, dinner and tea if Mum'd let her. Alternatives are a nice bit of tripe, Fray Bentos steak pudding, Greenhalgh's whist pies or potted shrimps. Oh, and tinned salmon. Should Mum ever be foolish enough to serve up something mad like rice or pasta, it ends up in the bin, untouched. How Nan got through the war I'll never know.

I'm a grazer and don't like sitting down to meals. I eat yoghurts by piercing the lid with my thumbnail and drinking them down in the light of the fridge door. Makes no mess, you see. You'd think Mum would be grateful for this low-maintenance approach, but no. If I want a biscuit I have to go through all the palaver of extracting a plate from under a tower of cups or bowls—quite often I'll have scoffed the biscuit by the time I've got the plate down—and then there's the washing up and putting away again for what would have been a twenty-second eating experience. As if a few crumbs mattered. If she had a life, then they wouldn't.

So we all sat round and ate fruit nicely. And apart from a few sly looks from elegant Mrs Gale, the meal was great.

'Coffee?' she asked at the end.

'Not for Charlotte, she's gone off it.'

'It's true.' I didn't tell her what I'd told Daniel, though, that I thought it tasted of piss. 'I'll have another grape juice, though, if that's OK.'

Daniel moved round to pull my chair out for me. 'And I'll have some more of that wine. We'll take it

193

outside.'

It was still nearly as light as day but cooler out on the patio. I breathed in the evening and felt rejuvenated. Banana-baby rolled and wriggled inside me, making strange shapes I could feel under my palms. The greens of the lawn seemed to glow under the evening sky and my eyes fixed and unfocused on a cloud of midges swaying over the pond near the hedge. It must be so much less stressful being this far up the social scale, to have the space and the cash and the knowledge about the world. I thought of Mum and wished I didn't have to go back home.

'It's a lovely garden. God, that heady scent . . . Makes me think of Keats: *I cannot see what flowers are at my feet*. Although presumably that wasn't because he was straining to see over an enormous bloated belly.' Baby heaved, a blackbird began singing near us and for a moment I felt as though I was on a film set. 'You're so lucky, you know.'

Daniel helped lower me onto the steps and sat down beside me. 'Yeah, I suppose so.'

'No supposing about it.' I wondered whether to count his blessings for him—nuclear family, pots of money, social poise—but decided it might be in bad taste. In the end I said: 'Your house is incredibly calm.'

'Is it?'

I looked at him but he was gazing at the horizon.

'Oh, yeah, amazingly. Well, compared with my place, it is. So is Beirut, probably.' The bird finished singing and flew away, a cut-out black shape across the streaky sky. 'Don't you like it here?'

'Not much.' He rested his chin in his hand.

'Actually I was quite happy in Guildford.'

'Why did you move?'

He sighed. 'Dad got an offer he couldn't refuse from an old university chum. He wanted to start up a practice with my dad as a partner. Dad said it was Fate and went off to see, and liked the place. So we all upped sticks and followed. If it had been one year earlier or later we probably wouldn't have gone, they wouldn't have wanted to disrupt my education, but I'd just finished GCSEs. Conveniently.' There was a bitter note to his voice. 'I'd chosen my options for Year 12 and I was looking forward to a great year dossing with my mates—I had some, down there. Miles and Toby. We used to have some great laughs. And they weren't like those geeks I sit with in the common room; God, they're so boring they even bore themselves.'

I moved away slightly and stared at him.

'I had no idea you were so fed up.'

'We email each other, but Miles has got a girlfriend now so I don't expect I'll be hearing much from him for a while. Anyway, it's not the same.'

'Maybe you'll move back there,' I said, 'if your dad's job doesn't work out.'

'I don't think so.' He picked up a piece of gravel and flicked it out over the grass. 'You see my mum was having an affair, so we won't ever go back.'

I drew in my breath. 'God.'

'He was one of her Relate clients. She broke every rule in the book. She'd have been chucked out pronto, but luckily for her everyone involved decided to keep their mouths shut. He went back to his wife. We had a family conference about what to do, not that anyone was very interested in what I wanted. Then this job offer came up. Dad reckoned it was the only way to keep the family together. But he's still really angry, and so's she, for different reasons. Mad! In some ways it might have been better if they'd split up. I don't know. It hacks me off the way we pretend, like this evening.'

It was shocking to see him like this. I'd not thought of him having his own problems, he was just someone who supported me through mine. I edged nearer again and put my arm round his shoulders.

'It's the wine talking. No, it's not the wine talking, it's me.'

'Oh, Daniel.'

'You're the only thing that keeps me sane, I think,' he said, and in a swift movement turned his head and kissed me on the mouth.

I didn't stop to consider, it wasn't a conscious decision, but I pushed him away and put the back of my hand to my lips. The sour tang of wine and guilt. He jerked backwards and stared, then dropped his head down so I couldn't see his face.

'Sorry, sorry, sorry. Stupid—'

I couldn't make out the rest.

'No, I'm sorry, Daniel. I really am. Sorry.'

Behind us the French windows slid open, then we heard the click of his mother's heels on the patio. A chill breeze passed over my shoulders and at the end of the garden the leaves of the beech tree stirred suddenly.

'Have you two finished with your glasses?'

'Oh, yes,' said Daniel. 'We've definitely finished.'

*　　*　　*

THEY PHONED ME at work, on the last day of term. The kids were all high as kites, clearing display boards and turning out drawers. Year 6 were running round the building trying to find drawing pins to prise off the walls because Mr F had promised a Mars Bar to the child who brought him the most.

Sylv took the message, so she was beside herself with importance by the time I hit the office at morning break.

'Social services have been on. They want you to make an appointment to see a Joyce Fitton as soon as you can. Here's the number. Is it about your adoption?'

'Yes,' I said. I didn't have the energy to lie.

'Oh, Mr Fairbrother, Karen's found her birth mother.'

Mr F, who had just popped his head round the door to ask for the stapler, looked at me in surprise.

'No,' I corrected. 'Sylv's a little ahead of herself. I've got an appointment with social services, that's all. They might have some information, then again they might not. A lot of it's talking, you know, assessing.'

'Assessing what?' asked Sylv.

'Can I break in here and ask you to find a file on the computer?' said Mr F. 'Only it's quite urgent. See you later, Karen.'

I backed out gratefully and went to ring from the staff room.

I HADN'T SPOKEN TO Joyce on the phone, it was another woman who took down my name in the

197

diary, so I didn't know what she'd found out. Surely, this time, she'd have the address of my mother. The desk was a sea of papers and there was a plastic carrot stuck on the computer next to the gonk. It didn't look very professional to me. Some-one had had a go at the blinds, though.

Joyce put her glasses on and opened a cardboard folder with my name on the front.

'I'm not able to disclose the address of your birth mother today, Karen,' she began.

'Fucking hell! What do we pay our fucking taxes for?' I felt like shouting. Fucking social workers! What do you do all day, sit round and drink coffee? 'Cause you don't do any fucking work, that's obvious.

'What's the delay?' I managed.

'Are you disappointed?' Joyce inclined her head sympathetically.

'I seem to have been waiting for ever.'

'It's hard, isn't it. Well, what I can give you now is a contact for your mother, someone who does know where she is and, if you like, can act as an intermediary.'

'Why? Doesn't she want to be found?'

'It's a little complicated.' Joyce put the file down and leaned forward, elbows on the desk, hands clasped. 'After she left the mother and baby home she went to stay with this lady, who was like a kind of foster-carer. She offered the girls who didn't have any support in the area a halfway house, until they'd got themselves set up with a job and lodgings, or decided to go back home. When your mother left she kept in touch over the years—I don't believe she had anything more to do with her own family back in Wigan. She settled in London and, er, changed her name.'

'You mean she married?'

'You need to speak to our contact, Mrs Beattie, Mary Beattie. She's expecting you to call and arrange something.'

'Right, well. You'd better give me her address.'

Joyce handed over a sheet of paper.

'What you can do, as I said, is use her simply as an intermediary; you don't have to meet your mother at all if you don't want to. You could just exchange letters through Mary without giving your own address.'

'Why would I want to do that?'

'I'm only telling you your options, Karen.' Joyce folded her hands over the closed file. 'And obviously I'm here if you feel you want to talk it through afterwards.'

All this bloody mystery, what a fuss over nothing. They make a job for themselves, social workers. Still, at least I could sort things out myself now, and we'd get on a damn sight faster too.

'Thanks,' I said, standing up and putting the paper in my handbag. 'I'll have to run, I've got a date.'

'Good luck,' said Joyce.

I walked out under a grey sky and hurried off to the municipal gallery to meet Mr F.

It was a collection called Dogs In Art.

'I like paintings to look like something recognizable, not a chaos of splodges. I don't know if that makes me old-fashioned.' Mr F, Leo-Since-We're-Not-At-Work, was standing in front of a large picture featuring a woman in a white nightie holding a cocker spaniel. 'I don't particularly care,

199

either. Have you seen this little fellow? We used to have a spaniel when I was a boy.'

'What was it called?'

'Kipling. My father named him.'

'We had a black cat called Chalkie. My dad named him too. The funny thing was, he went missing the week my dad went into hospital for the last time. Neither of them came back. Chalkie wouldn't have known what to do with himself without my dad for company anyway; he used to sit on the workbench while Dad tinkered about in the shed. Dad used to say he was teaching him how to hold a nail in his paws.'

'He sounds like a nice man.'

'Oh, he was. He really was.'

We walked on in silence and saw a dachshund on a riverbank and a gundog lying next to a pile of pheasants.

'And how did the interview with social services go? If you want to talk about it.'

'Oh, yeah, there's no problem. Well, at least I think there's no problem. They're being a bit cloak-and-dagger about making actual contact, but I've got the address of a woman who knows her so it's up to me now.'

'So you'll be off down to London?'

'Ah, well . . .'

We walked on past a St Bernard standing silhouetted on a mountain ridge and a medieval whippet sitting at the feet of a knight.

'It's weird, but I feel . . . almost scared now the end's in sight. No, maybe not *scared*, but kind of reluctant to take that final step. I keep thinking about my childhood; memories I thought I'd forgotten have started popping into my head, some of them in dreams. Nan on a picnic with a caterpillar stuck to her tights. The time she helped me win the Easter bonnet competition at school. I wonder if—if I'm kind of rejecting all that by looking for my real mother. Because they weren't all unhappy times.' We stopped in front of a Great Dane standing over a tiny baby. 'In fact, the more I think about it, I actually had quite a nice childhood. Before Dad became ill, the most frightening event I experienced was Dr Who fighting the Sea-devils. The only betrayal I can remember was finding out the label on my teddy bear's blanket said Pure New Wool and not Mr Fuzzy's. It only went sour between me and Mum after Dad died. And some of that was probably my fault. See, within her limitations she's been a good mother. We just weren't matched, that's all.'

'Are you feeling disloyal?'

'Yes.'

'Come and have a cup of tea and a bun.'

Leo led me out of the gallery—'Unashamedly populist but very enjoyable nevertheless,' he told the woman at the desk—and across the road to the Octagon.

'This is something I remember.' I stirred the sugar round in the bowl with a teaspoon. 'Did you believe in sugar stealers when you were little?'

'I'm not sure what you mean.'

I started to smooth out the granules with the back of the spoon. 'Those floaty seeds—dandelion clocks and such—we all thought at primary school that they were insects, or something, and they lived on sugar. I was always find-ing them in our larder. I really thought it was true for ages.'

Leo laughed. 'No, I can't say I've heard that one.

Tell me another.'

I chopped patterns in the smoothed-out grains while I thought.

'OK, what about those green glass chips you get on graves.'

'What about them?'

'Well, if you take even one of them home with you, the ghost of the person whose grave it is will come and haunt you in your bedroom until you put it back.'

'Did you ever try it?'

'No way. Too scary. But a boy in our class did and he swore he was woken in the night by an evil old woman. He lived with his grandma, though, so that was probably it.'

Leo was chuckling and wiping his eyes. 'Stop, stop. You'll have me choking on my bun.'

'And there was a big craze for giving yourself love bites on the arm, of course we were only eight, we didn't know what they were. Some lads had completely purple forearms. I'm amazed nobody contacted the NSPCC. Then a girl called Sharon Dawes said her mother had caught her doing it and told her it would give her cancer, so we all stopped overnight. Except for Christopher Flint, but he was mad. He got sent to a special school in Little Lever.'

We were both giggling now.

'Sounds like Gavin Crossley,' said Leo. 'I can't see him being with us much longer, the rate he's going.'

'Oh, he was much worse than that. He pushed a wardrobe on top of his brother once, and fired an airgun at Mrs Porter from the newsagent's when she refused to give him a paper round.'

'Village characters.'

'Happy times.'

'So do you think you'll go to London or not?'

'God knows. I'll toss a coin. No, I won't; I'll count the currants in my bun. Evens says I go, odds I stay.' I took a knife and began to saw. 'I can always change my mind later.'

$$* \qquad * \qquad *$$

I NEVER had no new clothes when I was a girl except for the lace-up shoes I wore on a Sunday, it was all hand-me-downs. So at Field Days, Walkin' Days they're called now, I used have to go at t' back o' t' line even though the only time I ever missed church was when I broke my arm. I'll tell you who allus walked under the banner, it was Annie Catterall in her fancy white frock, an' she never went to Sunday school nor nothin'. It was only 'cause her parents could afford to kit her out. One time my friend Lily Alker was on a ribbon off a banner, I don't know how she managed it 'cause her father was an invalid. She'd perhaps lent a frock off someone. Anyroad, they were gettin' to th' end of the procession and this ribbon broke. Annie pocketed it, took it home an' made hair braids out of it. When she got found out she was stripped and sent to bed, besides gettin' a good hidin'. So perhaps I was best off marchin' at the back.

The worst whippin' I ever got was when I took all my mother's buttons to play in t' street. We used make a circle in t' dirt an' try an' flirt these buttons in, an' if you got a button inside you could have your pick of all the others. I got in a row many a

203

time for it, but you don't think when you're young. They used play piggy too, an' cock-on-big-or-little. Piggy were t' best, though I don't think they play it now. You used put your piggy, which were a fat peg of wood with a whittled end, on a brick on t' floor so as snout was hangin' ovver th' end. Then you got a stick and you walloped it so it flew i' th' air. Some big lads could mek it go right along t' street. They used guess how many strides away it was. Sometimes the Co-Op held races down the Chantry, but I never won owt. I could never run, me. I got a doll once, but that was only 'cause everyone did; I still finished last.

But they were poor days. When times were good Grandma Florrie made parkin an' barm cakes, steak puddings and cow heel with a crust on top. A tripe man used come round t' streets too, shoutin'. But in the years after the war, when I was still only little, my mother had to go to the church for charity loaves, you could have two a week. An' there were allus people singin' in the streets, beggin', an' miners squattin' at street corners 'cause they had no work.

My mother was marvellous, now I think about it, because me an' Jimmy never felt it, all that poverty, not really. I wish I could have known her longer.

*   *   *

Anya had phoned up to say she was going into school for her module results and did I want to meet her there.

'The twins are going for a picnic in the park after, if it's not raining. They're dying to see you. So am I. Come on, shift yourself.'

204

I thought I was too miserable to lift my head off the pillow, but I went in the end. Missing Daniel was like a pain; worse than splitting up with Paul, which had been a series of stabs to the chest. This feeling was a deep, dull ache all over, as if I was about to come down with flu.

I wondered if I was going to bump into him at the office. Theoretically students come between 10 and 12 to pick up their slips, but in practice there's a seething crowd of hysterical teenagers round the front door by 9.50 and a mad rush when the head of sixth comes down to open it. I slid in with the general melee at 10.03 so I didn't have to wait around being gawped at. Generally the students who come later are the ones who know they've either done really well or really badly. A lot of posturing goes on, class jokers pretending to be amazed they didn't do even worse; huddles of girls patting and hugging tearful friends in an agony of embarrassment at their own success. The teachers stand around and offer congratulations where appropriate, and avoid eye contact where it's not. The air is electric. I hated it last year, hated it again now.

For those few minutes my pregnancy was completely forgotten. Anya and I stood in isolated pools of agony, tearing open the slips, gazing, absorbing, then shrieking at each other, at anyone who'd listen.

'I got an A!'

'Oh my God, so did I!'

Anya put her arm round me, no mean feat, and we tottered out onto the drive like two drunks. Mrs Carlisle hurried after us.

'Well done, both of you. Looking forward to

next year.' She smiled at me. 'This is for you, my home phone number. You can call me at any time and we can get together to talk about how things stand.' She passed me a sealed envelope. 'Don't let it fall into the wrong hands. I don't want obscene calls all summer!'

'She is *so* nice,' said Anya as we walked slowly out of the gates towards the park. We passed the twins on their way in, mad with nerves, but there was still no sign of Daniel. It occurred to me he might be away or have arranged for them to be posted. But I couldn't stop scanning the faces as one car after another drove past us over the ramp and crawled round the quad.

'Do you want to talk about the baby?' asked Anya unexpectedly. 'Now, I mean, before the twins come out. Because we weren't sure whether you'd like to or not, and we didn't want to get it wrong.'

Poor Anya. It must have cost her an effort to say that.

I shook my head. 'Thanks. No, I don't, not this afternoon. I think I'd like to just be me, not Mrs Pregnant. Do you mind?'

'No, not at all.' There was relief in her voice. I wished then, so keenly, that I could have shed the pregnancy for a few hours, unstrapped the bulge and hung it up in the wardrobe. I wanted a break, time off for good behaviour, one last good laugh with the girls and then I'd be ready to go back to it in the evening. It was so *part of me*. I looked awful now and felt breathless most of the time, couldn't bend down, constantly needed to pee . . . You're a big parasite, I'd told the baby in the bath. Let it hear, I didn't care.

When the twins caught up ('two Cs') we strolled

to the park and sat round the sunken garden, eating. And although there was this great black hole in the conversation, everyone including me trying to avoid the topic that was screaming in our faces, it was good because there were so many other things to talk about. Teenage things, trivia, plans, gossip. I couldn't exactly join in, but I could listen and laugh and tease.

An ice-cream van rolled up and Anya and I went to get 99s for us all. The sun was pretty hot now and there was a shimmer over the grass. As I cast my eyes over the red and white flower beds sloping up to the entrance I spotted Daniel walking quickly towards us. I didn't know what to do, and anyway I had an ice-cream cone in each hand so I was a bit restricted. I smiled, then looked away in case that was too much. One of the ice-creams began to melt and drip over my fingers, so I twisted my hand round and tried to lick it off. Daniel broke into a run.

'No!' he shouted.

'What's up with him?' I turned to Anya but she only shrugged.

Without losing speed he charged at me and, like a jousting knight, knocked the 99 from my grasp. It splatted onto the floor, cone upended, and began to merge with the gravel.

He overshot, blasted through a flower bed and staggered to a halt several metres away, panting. Anya pulled a Loony face at me.

'What the bloody hell do you think you're doing?' I asked. This was some bizarre revenge for rejecting him.

He came up to us, wild haired and grinning.

'That was a close one. Didn't your midwife tell

you about listeria?'

'Yeah. Deadly bug. It's in blue cheese and pâté and I don't like either. So?'

'And in soft ice-cream from vans, if you're unlucky. Can't be too careful. Can I treat you to a choc ice?'

'Jesus.' I turned to Anya with a despairing look. What would you do with him?

'I'll leave you to it,' she said, sniggering, and joined the goggle-eyed twins back on the bench.

What could I do? 'I'll have a Zoom,' I said grimly.

We must have made an odd couple from a distance, me like a barrel on legs and him a tall streak of nothing. When he gave me my lolly he flourished his hand and bowed. I could have kicked him.

'Listen, Prince Charming, do you want me to stick this up your nose?' I hissed.

We went over and joined the others but there were a lot of meaningful looks going on behind our backs and stifled giggles. I'll give them the benefit of the doubt and say they were still a bit hysterical from the exam results.

'Well,' said Anya after about thirty seconds, 'we must be off if we're going to hit the shops. Are you coming into town with us?'

'Not a lot of point me trailing round the Arndale at the moment. I'll have to be getting back soon, anyway.'

I knew they couldn't wait to be on their own. They'd probably phone Julia from town and give her a blow-by-blow account of the Madman in Queen's Park.

We said goodbye with lots of hugging and

promises to ring and good lucks, then they scarpered. Daniel was lying along a bench chewing his lolly stick.

'Waiting for the E numbers to kick in,' he said.

'I think they already have. Did you take your Ritalin today?'

'The only problem I've got is Grade Deficit Disorder,' he said sitting up and shading his eyes.

'Really? What did you get?'

'B and a C. My parents will be scandalized. Still, serves them right for moving me at a critical period of my development.'

I went and sat at the other end of the bench.

'B C isn't too bad. They're only modules. You can retake, can't you?'

'Yeah, yeah. It's OK, I've got all the spiel worked out in my head for when I get home. You got an A, didn't you?'

'More trouble at home; my mother'll make me wear it round my neck like the albatross. How did you know?'

'Lucky guess. Well done. My dad'll be delighted, he thinks you're wonderful.'

'It was nice of him to drive me back last week.'

'No problem. He enjoyed talking to you. He says you're intelligent. I got a bollocking though for being too pissed to drive you myself.'

'Were you? Pissed?'

'Oh, yes.' He inspected his lolly stick and read out the joke. 'What zooms along the river bed at 100 m.p.h. ?'

'I dunno.'

'A motor pike and a side carp. Nice one.' He pocketed the stick and got up. 'I'll give you a lift back now, if you want.'

'I won't say no.'

And so, just like that, we fell back into step as if nothing had happened. Maybe both of us had too much to lose.

'Do you mind if I don't ask you in? Only I'm dead tired, I really need to lie down.'

'I've got to get home myself. Face the music.' Daniel grimaced. 'Bloody parents, they're a liability. See you!'

He bibbed his horn and I trailed up the front path feeling suddenly depressed. Reaction, I suppose. I struggled with the door, tossed the results slip on the table and collapsed on the sofa. Nan came out of the kitchen, beaming.

'Eeh, it's our Charlotte. You're looking bonny, love. Get your feet up and Debbie'll make you a cup of tea. She's brought a little present for you.'

I blew her a kiss.

'I do love you, Nan,' I said.

*   *   *

WHEN I GOT IN Milady was lying on the sofa admiring a tiny sleepsuit, Nan was massaging Charlotte's feet and Debbie the cleaner was holding a needle and thread over her tummy.

'I can't tell whether it's swinging in a circle or not,' Debbie was saying. 'And I can't remember which way round it is, anyway. Can you, Nan? Is it a circle for a boy and a straight line for a girl?'

'Perhaps it's a hermaphrodite,' quipped Charlotte. I know for a fact neither of them know what that is, but they both laughed.

I picked up the scrap of paper on the table and winced. It was the report fiasco all over again. Shame she didn't get an A in Doing as you're Damn Well Told.

'You do know you're throwing your life away,' I snapped as I went past. She never even turned her head.

'Ooh, I just saw the baby move!' exclaimed Debbie. 'Bless it.'

'Can I have a feel?' said Nan.

THREE DAYS later I walked out.

CHAPTER NINE

THE DAY STARTED as per usual, with Nan wandering in and announcing it was morning. Up with the lark, that's my mother. Back in her bedroom I changed her bag then she stumped downstairs and had a wash. Meanwhile I threw on leggings and shirt. Nan returned to her room to get dressed and I trailed down to the kitchen to make breakfast. It's a kind of ballet sequence we've refined over the years, and the only one who ever throws a spanner in the works is Charlotte, rising unexpectedly early or locking herself in the bathroom for a pre-school hair crisis.

But this morning I'd finished my toast and Nan still hadn't made an appearance, so I went back upstairs to see what the matter was. She was sitting on the bed in her underslip glowering at the chair.

'What's up now?' I asked. 'Your Weetabix is going cold.'

'I'm not wearing that.' She pointed to the dress slung over the chair back.

'Why ever not?'

'It's not red.'

'Oh, for God's sake. It's a lovely frock, Mum. You wore it last week.'

She glared at me.

'I tell you what, why don't you put that little maroon cardigan over the top? That's reddish.'

No answer.

'Well, you can't go to church in your underslip. Maud and Ivy'll be here soon, you don't want to hold them up.' I opened the wardrobe door and rifled through her clothes. 'Wait a minute, what about this?' I pulled out a grey dress with scarlet flowers on the skirt. 'This is a nice one.'

'It's not red enough.'

With enormous control I put the grey dress back and walked out onto the landing to check the laundry basket. Maybe her red wool two-piece could be redeemed with a squirt of Febreze and a good shake. I rooted about and found it, but there was a soup stain down the front. I flung it back in and stood there thinking. I had four choices. I could throw myself over the banisters now, this very minute. Then they'd all be sorry. I could burst into noisy tears which no one would take any notice of. I could go into Mum's room and slap her across the face—oh, I know it's a terrible thought, I'm supposed to be her carer and it's not her fault etc. etc., but believe me, there are times when I come so close I have to walk away and count ten. Or, and this was the plan resolving itself before my eyes as being the most reasonable course of action under the circumstances, I could run away.

I went back into Mum's room and pulled out all the spare bags and tape she needs for changing and put them on the dressing table. Then I got out the little scissors from her jewellery box and cut the right size openings in the top of every bag.

'I'm old enough to do as I like,' she snapped suddenly.

'No, Mum, you're not old *enough*, you're *too* old, that's the point.'

I got the overnight case from the top of her wardrobe and took it into my room. (*We're off! We're off!*) My head started to sing a stupid song of Nan's to the rhythm of my breathing. I packed a smart suit and a pair of courts, two pairs of leggings and assorted tops, knickers, travel wash, make-up and curling tongs. (*We're off in a motor car!*) Walking past Mum's bedroom I could see she'd lain down on the bed and closed her eyes. I carried straight on downstairs to the bathroom where I topped up my sponge bag, then in the hall I checked my handbag and address book. (*Sixty bobbies are after us and we don't know where we are!*) Finally I scribbled a note to Charlotte saying I'd gone to stay with a friend for a few days but I'd give her a ring that evening and if she needed help to contact her dad or social services. It was completely irresponsible of me. I imagined the expressions of horror when Charlotte finally roused herself to let Maud and Ivy in and they discovered the truth together. Well, they'd just have to sort it out.

I slammed the Metro door so hard the hinges all but fell off, then stuck a Madonna tape on full blast. All the way to Manchester I justified myself to the music. 'Rescue Me'. 'Secret'. 'Bad Girl'. I couldn't believe what I'd done.

Then, as I drew into the half-empty car park, the tape came to an end and a man on the radio said Princess Diana was dead.

I sat in the car for a few minutes, listening; a car crash, France, early hours of the morning, a high-speed chase. 'The phone lines are open now for your calls,' the presenter said. 'Please do dial and let us know how you're feeling about this terribly sad, this shocking tragedy; hello, Gemma from Radcliffe.' Gemma, quavering: 'I just can't believe it, she was so young—' I switched the radio off and got quietly out of the car.

I walked up to the station, past the screaming headlines on the newspaper stand, past a huge chalk heart someone had scrawled on the wall near the cafe, *R.I.P. DI*. Unreal. I bought my ticket on autopilot and went to stand on the platform where a little group was talking to each other animatedly. Tight-faced fifty-something woman, nasty claw-shaped brooch on her coat; very thin man freezing in shirt sleeves; young lass in salwar kameez and anorak, towing meek child: normally they'd all be busy maintaining personal space. But this morning was different.

'In a tunnel,' claw woman was saying, 'awful.' 'Those boys,' murmured the young mum, shaking her head while her tiny daughter stood with her face upturned, watching pigeons fly between the metal rafters above our heads. The thin man balled his fists: 'Bloody journalists. They want locking up. They've no bloody scruples.'

'It said in our paper she was just Very Badly Injured,' claw woman piped up, 'I thought she was still alive till I put the telly on. I can't believe it.'

214

Thin man saw me staring at his *Observer* and handed it to me without a word. I held it up, saw the pictures and read the words, so it was true.

Then the train to Euston slid in.

As the coach lurched out of the station I sat alone in my corner by the window and thought about Diana, and about me. I remembered all the royal wedding celebrations, all that hope and happiness in the midst of my own messed-up life, her lovely smiling face and that rumpled fairytale dress. Everyone had seemed united, you'd felt like the whole nation was with you as you sat in front of the telly watching that balcony kiss. I'd kept the souvenir issue of the *Radio Times* and even copied the haircut, briefly. I thought she was charmed, then it turned out she'd been duped just like the rest of us. Confessing and crying on prime-time TV; I'd squirmed for her. And now after so much unhappiness she was dead, shocking proof that money and elegance and class and beauty, none of them mean anything in the face of Fate.

Sadness tightened on my chest, and guilt. If she couldn't get it right, what chance had the rest of us? Then my own failings and inadequacies seemed to rise up like a cold mist around me so that I suddenly found myself in tears and had to stare out of the window at the blurred countryside. I didn't even know her, I thought, so why am I crying?

*   *   *

It was turning into a surreal kind of day. No Mum, Dad in the kitchen unloading frozen ready-meals and tins of Nan food, and all the TV stations awash with the Diana story, whichever channel you

215

flicked to.

'I know it's a shame, but I don't know why there's all these women in tears,' I muttered. 'You'd think she'd been personal best friend to a hundred thousand people. I reckon they're putting it on for the cameras.'

'I got you six of these mini pizzas 'cause they were on special offer,' said Dad. He was well pissed off, you could tell. 'What a flamin' carry-on. I have to be at work tomorrow, you know. I've had that much time off the boss has given me a warning. But Ivy Seddon says they're organizing a rota at the Over Seventies', and I've been on the phone to social services and there's a nurse coming round every morning for an hour. That Crossroads woman's here tomorrow and then there's that cleaner you have. It'll be like Paddy's market. You certainly won't be on your own, love. I'll come round every evening after I've had my tea. Anyroad, your mum might not be away so long, she could be back in a day or two.'

'I'm not bothered, Dad.' I wasn't either. In some ways it was a relief to have her out the house. 'She's done it before, remember. That time she found a lump in her breast and took herself off to Fleetwood for a long weekend.'

'Aye. And it were nowt in t' finish. Do you think she really has gone to stay with a friend?'

'I wouldn't have thought so. She doesn't have any.'

'It's norra man, then?'

'Nah.'

'I just wondered.'

'She's been horrible about the baby, you know. She wanted me to get rid of it.'

216

Dad became very busy stacking the freezer compartment.

'Well, she was only thinking of you. She thought it would be for t' best. You know, your education and that.'

'I don't think I'll ever forgive her.'

Nan wandered in.

'Where's our Karen?'

Dad and I exchanged glances.

'She's had to pop out for a while. Do you fancy a brew?' Dad unplugged the kettle and held it under the cold tap.

'I need my bag changing,' she sighed.

'Over to you,' said Dad.

*　　　*　　　*

AS SOON AS I got off the train I found a mobile phone place, threw my credit card at the assistant and emerged with a Nokia, a charger and twenty quid's worth of vouchers. 'You've one blob left on your battery,' the smart lad in the shop had said. 'You're telling me,' I joked, but he'd lost interest. Then I went outside onto a grass verge, away from all the bustle, and read the instruction booklet. At last I felt ready to dial.

Unluckily it was Steve who answered, so the first few seconds were him calling me every name under the sun. When I could get a word in edgeways, I told him my number and got him to write it down and read it back; it's not that he's thick, far from it, but he's careless. I asked after Charlotte and Nan and got another mouthful of abuse, then I heard Charlotte's voice in the background asking to speak to me. I knew if I let her I'd fall apart; I'd turn straight back to the station and climb on the next available train home. So I said quickly, 'Tell her I'll be home in a day or two. Battery's flat. Got to go.' Then I pressed *End* and switched off for half an hour. If I was going to do this right I needed to clear my head.

I retraced my steps into the station, bought a street map off a stall and went down the escalator to the Underground. I stood in front of the Tube map for ages, trying to work it out while people barged into me and sighed with impatience over the top of my head. I reached forward and tried to trace the route with my finger, like a slow reader. Northern line, change at King's Cross to the Piccadilly. That was OK. But which *zone* was I in and how much would that make the ticket? There was a massive queue at the ticket office so I spent ages studying one of the machines to a background of irritated tuttings from the woman behind me. At last I pressed the right button and a bit of card dropped into my palm. Now, which escalator? I stood like a rock in the middle of a swirling river. An oriental man with a briefcase stood on my foot. 'Sorry,' I said. He disappeared into the crowds without looking back.

I made my decision, glided down past the adverts for theatres and museums, and found myself in a windy tunnel that smelt of burning rubber. Did I want platform 1 or 2? How should I bloody know? A quick check of my pocket diary and down the tiled walkway, then finally out onto a platform with a lot of bored-looking people. Almost instantly there was a terrific noise and the train shot out and slowed to a halt in front of us. The doors hissed open. I stood back politely and was nearly knocked over in the rush to get on.

The last time I was in London was a school trip to coincide with the Silver Jubilee. We'd worn school uniform and our commemorative badges because, our form mistress had said, that's what the Queen would want, not jeans and Kickers. We'd gone to stand outside Buckingham Palace and someone had said the Queen was definitely in because of the way the flag was flying, so she might have looked out of the window and seen us.

The train came into King's Cross, where there was a teenage girl begging with a baby on her hip. I thought of Charlotte and pulled out my purse. The girl's top lip was covered in sores, but her eyes were pretty. Where was *her* mum, I wondered.

'What's his name?' I asked smiling at the round-eyed snotty baby.

'Ellie,' she said and pocketed the note neatly.

I thought about her all the way to Arnos Grove.

At last I came up the steps into the sunlight, feeling bruised. I pulled out my street map and started walking. I was looking for Hemmington Grove and Mrs Mary Beattie.

*   *   *

Actually it's no big deal, changing Nan (after all, I'll be doing nappies soon). It used to freak me out at first, but now it just makes me sad. Nan lies meekly on the bed with a towel under her, her dress pulled up and her knickers and tights round her thighs. There are poor little white hairs between her legs and the skin is loose round her belly. You peel off the old micropore tape and the used bag and put them in something like a nappy sack. Then you wipe round the weird, amazingly clean hole in Nan's flesh with a sterile tissue. You take the backing strip off the new bag, stick it down with the opening against Nan's stomach, and Mum likes to make extra sure with some tape on top. Sometimes, if the skin's red, we use Nivea but you have to be careful not to get it under the tape or nothing sticks and it's a disaster. Nan remains glassy-eyed throughout, then switches back into life the minute you pull her dress back down. So there you are. Nothing to it.

I was heading towards the bin after the lunchtime change when the doorbell rang. Dad was right, it was like Paddy's market. I thought it was another of Ivy's volunteers, but it turned out to be Daniel clutching a Moses basket.

'One of my father's patients asked if he could find a home for it. It needs a new mattress but it's got a stand and some frilly gubbins to go round the sides.'

'Brilliant.' I took it off him and laid it on the sofa while he went to get the rest from the car. Maud and Nan crowded round to see.

'Eeh, in't it lovely?' said Nan.

'Better than a drawer,' said Maud, peering inside. 'That's where me mother put me when I were born.'

'Well, they did in them days,' said Nan. 'In't it lovely, though.'

'Where's it going to go?' asked Maud.

Nan shrugged.

'It can come in my room,' I said. 'It'll have to. Be easier, anyway, if I'm getting up at night.' I glanced out of the window and saw Daniel struggling with a stack of books and a froth of broderie anglaise.

'Hang on.'

I waddled down the path and opened the gate for him.

'Come here, you daft 'aporth. Let me have some of the books, at least.'

'They're from Mrs Carlise. She thought you could be doing some reading before term starts. Don't take too many now, just these from the top.'

'Oh, God, I must phone her. I've been meaning—' I broke off with a cry and the paperbacks fell on the pavement.

'What's the matter?' Daniel threw his stuff back on the seat and put his arm round me.

'Get me in. Get me in, Dan.'

We staggered inside and I sat down breathlessly.

'What is it, Charlotte? Have you got a pain?'

Nan and Maud were hovering anxiously.

'Shall I make her a cup of tea?' asked Maud.

'Yes, that would be excellent. Thank you.' Daniel came and sat next to me and fluttered his hands. 'What is it, Charlotte?'

I groaned. 'It was Paul. Across the road, you didn't see him. He was walking past with a Spar bag. He saw me—' Oh Christ, the humiliation. He'd seen me and stared, then deliberately looked the other way till he was round the corner. He'd have run if he could. Bastard.

'Paul.'

'Yes.'

'Dirty bugger,' said Nan miming a spit. 'He'll come to his cake and milk.'

'I'm not terrifically good at that sort of thing, but I'll go after him and hit him if it would make you feel better,' said Daniel. 'All you have to do is tell me where he lives.'

Even in the midst of my personal hell I couldn't help but smile at the image. 'Excuse me,' Daniel would probably say first, 'do you mind if I punch you in the mouth?' Then Paul would knock seven bells out of him.

'No, it's OK. My dad's tried that one. Silly sod.'

Daniel let out a sigh of relief and Maud came in with the tea.

'Look, are you definitely all right? Do I need to get you to a doctor?'

'No, really, I'm fine. Just mortified, that's all.' I took a sip of tea. 'Thanks, Mrs Eckersley. I could do with a lie-down, though.'

'Good idea. Get your feet up.' Daniel rose to his feet. 'I must be going, anyway.'

'Please stay,' I said. 'Come up to my room so we can talk.'

Maud gave me a funny look and I nearly said to her, 'For God's sake, I can't get any *more* pregnant, can I?'

'I'm sorry the room's so small,' I said as Daniel folded himself into the beanbag chair.

'What are you smiling at?'

'Nothing. It seems strange you being here, that's all.' I was reclining on the bed with Nan's V-shaped pillow behind my head, trying to find the right way to lie. 'The trouble with being this size is you can never get comfortable.'

'I suspect you're going to get even bigger before you've finished.'

'It's all right for you, Slim-Jim.' I lay back.

'Shall I put some music on?'

'Yeah, will you? The tapes are on that shelf by your head. Pick what you like, so long as it's chilled.

222

Actually, that one on the top is good, it's what Julia did for me. Supposed to be my labour tape. Soundtrack to my agony.'

'Everything's very . . . to hand in this room.' Daniel switched on the cassette player by leaning to one side and stretching across the shelf. The music started and we listened for a few minutes without speaking.

> *What sense does love make?*
> *Your brain's turned inside out*
> *A chemical illusion*
> *That makes you want to shout*

It was me who began. 'The thing about Paul is, I hate him but in a way I still love him. No, not *him*, but the person I thought he was. He seemed great at first because he was so happy-go-lucky and I'm so serious; I actually thought he was *good for me*. Mad. Even now I can't totally shake off the promise of those initial few weeks. My brain still hasn't caught up with recent events. I *know* he's a shit but he's the baby's father too.'

'Not if he doesn't want to be. You can't force him to have anything to do with the child if he doesn't want to. You might be able to extract a few quid out of him after the birth, but that's about all.'

'I know. But biologically . . .'

'Biology's nothing. Inserting your knob at an opportune moment.'

We both blushed. The song finished and another one began.

> *You are the star–sun–moon that guides me*
> *My lightship in the storm*
> *You keep me safe from harm*

Safe and warm
Through the storm

'The other problem is he's practically on the doorstep, as demonstrated today. We'll always be bumping into each other, it'll be awful.'

Daniel chewed his fingernail. 'All the more reason to get your university place sorted, you can always defer it. Put that wanker behind you and get on with your life.'

'I know, I know. You are right.' I heaved myself up slightly and grinned feebly at him. 'Actually, now I think about it, he was a wanker at primary school. He was one of those lads who used to set up trouble and then walk away. It was never him who got shouted at. But he was funny and good at football so he had a lot of mates. He knew all these rude songs.'

'"My Uncle Billy had a three foot willy", that sort of thing?'

I smirked. 'It was four foot round here. You were obviously suffering from shrinkage down south.'

'Huh,' said Daniel.

'Then there was the classic: "Ooh, aah, I lost my bra, I left my knickers in my boyfriend's car", and "Jesus Christ superstar, wears plastic knickers and a Playtex bra", "All the girls in Spain wash their knickers in the rain". It was all underwear.'

'The knickers-knackers-knockers school of comedy.'

'If you say so. He had this joke too; he'd go up to you and he'd say, "Are you a PLP?" If you said no, he'd say, "Are you not a Proper Living Person, then?" If you said yes he'd go, "You're a Public

Leaning Post, then," and barge into you.'

'Sounds like a genius.'

'And once we had this student teacher in, a really nice bloke, actually. He was always changing in and out of his tracksuit like Superman or something, and one time when he left his shoes in the classroom Paul wrote WAN KER on the bottoms with Tipp-Ex. Or at least, that's what he meant to write. But he got the shoes mixed up, so when this teacher sat on the floor with us at storytime with his legs out in front of him and his feet together, it actually said KERWAN on his soles. Everyone still thought it was dead funny, though.'

'I suspect there's a lot of inbreeding in this village,' said Daniel.

*　　　*　　　*

NUMBER 80 was a neat Edwardian semi with white-painted sills, a black front door and two giant terracotta pots on either side of the step. I could see swagged Sanderson curtains at the bay window and a fern in a Wedgwood planter. I must have stood for ten minutes just staring; I suppose I was hoping someone would come out, but no one did. Eventually I picked up my case and carried on down the road, swinging my head from right to left as I searched for B & B signs. I turned right at the bottom of the road into a street where the houses were smaller and terraced and found a bed and breakfast place at once.

The hall smelt of elderly dog and the wallpaper was grubby but I wasn't too fussed. It was only a base. The wheezing old lady who led me up to my room asked lots of questions but then didn't give me any time to answer, which suited me. I shut the door on her and took off my shoes; it was time to phone Mrs Beattie. Where was my mobile?

I psyched myself up to press the on button, but this time the battery really was flat. Now that was Fate. I threw the phone down on the bed in relief. Then I had second thoughts and put it on to charge while I unpacked and had a wash in the poky little sink. Looking at myself in the mirror I wondered what my mother would make of me after all this time. I wanted her to be impressed, to think I'd grown up to be a stylish, together sort of woman. I wasn't in bad nick, on the whole. My skin was quite good for my age—a few lines round the mouth, that was all—and my hair was in between cuts which is when it looks its best. I'd wear my suit and courts, and paint my nails if I had time. I lay back down on the bed and caught my breath with the enormity of it all.

My mother.

After an hour I tried the phone again. The screen lit up; it was time.

A posh woman answered.

'Am I speaking to Mrs Mary Beattie?'

'Yes, you are. Can I help you?' She sounded cool and professional, like a consultant's receptionist: I'm sorry I can't give you your test results over the phone.

'Er, my name's Karen Cooper. Mrs Fitton from Bolton Social Services might have rung about me. I think—she said you might be able to—can you help me find my birth mother? Her name was Jessie Pilkington. She stayed with you once, a long time ago.'

'Yes, yes . . . Joyce Fitton did ring.' She paused

226

and I could hear my own breathing in the receiver. 'Yes, well, what we thought you could do was come down and see me sometime and I'd talk you through—'

'I'm here.'

'Are you actually in London?'

'Yeah. I'm staying with a friend. I'd like to, if it's not too much trouble, I'd like to come and see you.'

'Let me check my diary,' she said.

I wandered over to the window and gazed down at the back yard. It wasn't so different from a two-up, two-down in Wigan. It was more the *feel* of the place; it had to be London, somehow. It just didn't feel northern.

'Right.' She was back on. 'Can you manage tomorrow morning? Say, ten? Or is that too early? Where are you coming from?'

'Ten's fine. I'll be there.'

'I'll look forward to seeing you,' she said, and my heart dropped like a stone with terror.

*   *   *

That night it was antenatal class. I plonked myself at the back and tried to look older than I was, also as if I'd just left my loving husband at home instead of an angry dad and a mad grannie.

The midwife held up a plastic pelvis and forced a doll's head through it. I sat there, thirty-four weeks pregnant and still thinking: *This isn't me, this is not going to happen to me. I'm not ready. I can't do it.*

'Burned your bridges now, girl, haven't you?' I heard my mother's voice say.

I SAT ON the chaise longue, waiting for Mrs Beattie to make tea, feeling exhausted. All night long I'd been running after trains. One was going to America and I said to John Noakes (because he was with me), 'How can it go across the sea?' and he said, 'Oh, anything's possible.' I got up far too early, felt cold, got back in bed again and painted my fingernails. I turned on the radio but it was all still Diana's death. I had a little weep—half of it was nerves—and then went down to breakfast which I couldn't eat. My landlady was clearly a big Elvis fan and all through the meal I kept my eyes fixed on the Love Me Tender wall clock whose hour hand was the neck of a guitar. Time moved so slowly I thought the thing was broken. Then I got dressed and was all ready to go by nine twenty, so I had to walk up and down the road several times. Even though Mrs Beattie wasn't my mother I'd put on the suit.

'Here we are,' she said, passing me a china cup and saucer. I looked in vain for a safe place to put it down. If I spilt tea over this nice chintz! I perched the cup on my lap and took in the room.

'This is such a lovely house,' I said. It was too. Everything I'd seen, I wanted.

'It's rather big for me now I'm on my own. The stairs are becoming difficult too.'

I wondered how old she was. Seventy? Very elegant, though. Nothing like Mum. 'You could get one of those stairlifts.'

'It might come to that.'

We sipped our tea. What was she thinking? Inscrutable, that's what she was.

228

'Well, about my birth mother,' I announced.

She pressed her lips together and put down the cup on the slate hearth. 'Yes. There are some documents on the bureau, if you'd like to fetch them over. Bring the side table and we can have it between us. I need to take you through this.'

My heart thumped as she separated the sheets of paper one by one.

'Do I take it you know nothing about your mother at all?'

'Only that she was very young and she wasn't married. Oh, I knew she'd stayed in London. Probably couldn't wait to escape!' I squeaked with nervous laughter. My voice was too loud in that quiet room.

'Right,' said Mrs Beattie carefully. She pushed a piece of photocopied paper towards me. 'I want you to read this.'

It was a newspaper report dated April 1971. A man and a woman living in Croydon had been charged with manslaughter after a child had died in their care. The six-year-old's body showed signs of serious malnourishment and was covered in bruises and sores. She—it was a little girl—was described as looking like a child two years younger because of her small frame. Neighbours had become suspicious after seeing the girl foraging in dustbins and reported what they had seen to social services, but somehow the messages hadn't got through. School noticed nothing because she was never there. She hadn't even been on the At Risk register when she died.

The little girl's name was Emma and Jessie Pilkington had been her mother.

I read it and read it and read it and it still didn't

make sense. Mrs Beattie reached out and took my hand. I was shaking.

'Would she have been my sister?' I whispered.

'Half-sister.'

'Oh, God. My little sister.' I started to cry. Mrs Beattie sat back and let me, patting my hand. The clock ticked and traffic swooshed past the window; I wasn't aware of anything else. We stayed like that for a long time.

At last she said, 'I have a photograph, but you may not want to see it.'

I wiped my eyes. 'Of Emma?'

'Of all of them. Taken from a newspaper.'

'I think it might break my heart.'

She put her arms round me and I felt like I was a child again, Nan holding me the first time we knew Dad was ill. There was a ticking clock then as well, and the radio in the kitchen playing 'Bridge Over Troubled Water'.

I'm on your side.

'Did Mrs Fitton know all this?'

'Yes.' Mrs Beattie wiped her eyes. 'But because I'm a trained counsellor and I used to work for social services she thought I'd be the most suitable person to talk to you about it. And, of course, I knew your mother.'

'How could she do something so *awful*? I mean, your *own child*?' Charlotte, baby Charlotte crying in her cot, toddler Charlotte throwing porridge on the floor, wetting the bed; beautiful Charlotte.

'She became involved with a violent man, as a lot of women do, you'd be surprised by how many, all walks of life. She was a very . . . needy person, not at all able to stand up for herself, despite the big talk. So she stayed with this man even after he

230

began to abuse her daughter—it wasn't his child, she'd got pregnant by another man, which didn't help matters. She always maintained she never actually hurt Emma herself. I don't know if that was true or not. There certainly wasn't enough evidence to convict her of direct cruelty; her defence claimed the only reason she hadn't acted to save her daughter was that she was frightened he might start beating her as well. It may have been true. She got four years; he got fifteen, but he died of cancer before he was released.'

'Good.'

'Then when Jessie came out of prison she changed her name and moved. There was terribly bad feeling towards her from the public, as there always is in these cases, though I don't think the press was as intrusive then as it is now. She'd had hate mail, death threats, so she tried to walk away from what she'd done and reinvent herself. By and large she succeeded.'

I put my hands to my temples. 'I still can't take it in.'

'It must be a great shock for you. Can I get you anything, a glass of brandy?'

'No. I'll take a couple of paracetamol, I've some in my handbag.' But I knew paracetamol would never take away the cold clamping sensation in my heart, or stop me reliving those horrific phrases from the report.

Mrs Beattie went off to get a glass of water and I found myself opening the file again, scanning for those pictures. Don't do it! part of me was screaming, but I had to know. And there she was, a fine-featured little girl in a check dress and a cardigan, smiling away and looking as if she didn't

231

have a care in the world. I closed the file quickly. My heart felt as if it was going to burst with grief and fury.

'So my m— Jessie Pilkington's still alive?' I asked when Mrs Beattie came back.

'Yes, she is. I have a contact address for her, even though I haven't spoken to her for many years now. She sends a card at Christmas, that's all.'

How could a child-killer send Christmas cards? 'Don't you hate her?'

'It's difficult . . . I hate what she did, certainly, but there are other factors. She's been punished, of course, she's served her time. You have to remember too that she was a victim herself in many ways. Her own father . . .'

I put my hands over my ears. 'Stop. Oh, please stop.'

Mrs Beattie took the file and slid it under her chair. I wished I could have done that with the new knowledge in my head.

'I feel like a different person,' I said. 'Nothing will ever be the same again.' She nodded. 'I need to go away now and think about this. Can I have Jessie Pilkington's address?'

'I have no right to withhold it from you.'

'But you don't believe I should have it?'

Mrs Beattie pulled her cuff straight and smoothed her skirt. 'I'm not sure you could do anything very constructive.'

'All the same.'

She went back into the file and pulled out an envelope. 'It's in there. Think carefully about how you want to handle this situation tonight, and come and see me tomorrow. We'll talk it over together.' She clasped my hand again. 'You've been very brave. Whatever your life has been like, it's made you a strong person.'

'I don't feel strong.'

'Well, you are.'

Then she hugged me again and I left.

I DON'T KNOW why I did it. I should have gone straight home but I knew I'd never settle till I'd seen Jessie Pilkington, or whatever her name was, and talked to her face to face. I trailed back to the B & B, collected my stuff and set off for the Underground.

Back on the Tube everything seemed squalid and threatening. People looked at each other out of the corner of their eyes; hardly anyone spoke. Even the beautiful young couple strap-hanging seemed like they were mocking the rest of us when they laughed together. The diversity was frightening too; every race, language, class and sub-class seemed to be on our train and it made my head spin. I unfolded the envelope and checked the address for the umpteenth time. Lewisham. What was that like, then? You hear the names of these London boroughs they don't mean a right lot. Certain ones have memory-tags attached—Brixton (riots), Peckham (Del Boy), Lambeth (Walk)—but mostly it's all pretty vague. Well, how many Londoners know the difference between Worsley and Whalley Range?

Maybe she'd make it all right. She might say something that would explain and make it not so bad. It couldn't be any worse. In any case it was what I needed to do.

It didn't take me long to suss out that Lewisham

233

isn't a top-class area full of millionaires. There were a lot of boarded-up windows, for one thing, and metal grilles on some of the shops. Big difference to Hemmington Grove. I got the feeling terracotta pots wouldn't survive that long here. A filthy man with a droopy eye came up to me as I stood turning my street map round, and shouted something in my face. I put my head down and started walking.

It took me nearly twenty minutes to find her street, Bewely Road, and it was grubby and depressing. I followed the numbers down until I came to a sixties block of flats, two storeys high, with coloured panels, orange and blue, stuck to the bricks under the windows. There are some flats like that in Wigan, just as you get near the town centre. They smack to me of desperate mothers caged up with screaming toddlers, and teenagers pissing in the stairwells. Maybe I was being a snob; your house doesn't make you who you are, I should know that. But I didn't feel sure of anything much any more.

She lived on the ground floor. I rang the bell— by now I was so nauseous and swimmy I had to lean against the jamb—and waited. The plain front door swung open and there she was.

It was the toes I noticed first; she was wearing sandals and her toenails were painted red, but dirty underneath. Leggings, a baggy T-shirt, much like I knock about in when I'm at home, and a face that was mine but old and twisted with sourness.

'I know who you are,' she snapped in an accent that was still northern. 'Mary phoned me. She warned me you might turn up.'

'Can I come in?' My mouth was very dry and the

234

words sounded odd as I said them. 'I've come a long way.' Behind her I could hear a television going but I couldn't see past her into the hall.

'I don't care how far you've come. You've to go away. I never asked to see you. What do you want to come rooting round and stirring up trouble for? Haven't you got a life of your own?'

'That's what I wanted to talk to you about, tell you what I've done with myself over the years. I thought you'd like to know. There's things I need to ask you.'

She pushed her greying hair behind her ears and lowered her voice. 'Look, I just want you to sod off. If I didn't want you when you were a sweet little baby I'm hardly likely to want you now you're a bitter-faced thirty-year-old, am I? For God's sake. I owe you nothing.'

'I'm thirty-four, actually.'

She made to shut the door.

'Wait!' I wedged my shoulder painfully into the gap and forced it open again. A smell of chip pan floated out. 'Tell me about my dad at least. He might want to see me even if you don't.'

'You'll have a job. He's dead.' She laughed meanly. 'And a bloody good job an' all.'

'Well, who was he? I've a right to know.'

'Oh, *Rights*, is it? We've all got Rights, love. Well, I'll tell you, since you're burning to hear the truth. He was an evil bastard. He just wanted rid of you. He'd have done it hisself if I'd let him, he did it to another lass. D'you get me?' I must have looked blank. '*With a—*' her face screwed up and she made a kind of clawing movement with her hand—'*coat hanger.*'

I clapped my palm to my mouth and took a step

235

back, and she slammed the door. I noticed my suit had a black mark all the way down the front.

*   *   *

Daniel had come round again and we were watching children's TV prior to our frozen pizzas. It was so relaxing without Mum there.

'You won't believe this but I need to pee *again*,' I said heaving myself up off the sofa. There was a sudden rush of water between my legs. 'Oh, my God.' We both stared at the dark stain spreading over my skirt. 'I think I've wet myself.'

'That's not wee,' said Daniel.

*   *   *

I WAS STANDING on the platform at Euston when my mobile rang. I nearly had kittens when it went off.

'Hello?' I was expecting another ear-bashing from Steve.

'Hello,' said a polite young man. 'I don't believe we've ever met, but I'm just ringing to tell you your daughter's in labour.'

CHAPTER TEN

'Shall I phone the hospital or your father first?' Daniel asked as I struggled with the bath towel he'd brought me to mop up the mess.

'God, *I* don't know,' I snapped. I was really frightened.

236

'OK. I'm going to ring for an ambulance. Lie down and try to relax.'

I stretched out on the sofa and willed the baby to keep moving. 'My antenatal notes are on the sideboard. You might need to give them some details.'

'Fine.'

Daniel disappeared into the hall. I started to pray.

When he came back he looked cheerful. 'They'll be here in ten minutes. Now, what do you need to take?'

'There's a sports bag upstairs. I'll come with you.' I started to haul myself up.

'No. Stay horizontal. I'll sort it.'

'There are some extra things written on a Post-it note stuck to the handle,' I shouted after him. 'Don't forget my Walkman. And try not to wake Nan. I can't cope with her as well.'

I lay there for about ten seconds, then got up. 'Oh, little banana, hang on,' I whispered. I shuffled to the phone, still holding the towel between my legs, and dialled Dad's number. Thank Christ; he was back.

'Yep?' he said with his mouth full.

'Dad? Can you come over right now? I've got to go to hospital.'

'Charlotte? Are y'awreet, love? What's up?'

'We think the baby's coming.'

There was a choking noise followed by coughing. 'I thought it weren't due till October.'

I started to cry.

'I'll be round straight away,' he said. 'Damn and blast your mother.' He hung up.

'Get back on that sofa,' hissed Daniel over the

237

banisters.

When the ambulance came I wanted Daniel to come with me.

'No, Charlotte, that doesn't make sense. I'll stay till your dad arrives, then I'll follow in the car. That way I can come and go from the hospital; otherwise my car'll be stranded here and I'll have no transport.'

I started to sob even though we were standing in the road with all the curtains twitching. '*Don't* make me go on my own. *Please* come. I'm so *scared*.' I grabbed his hand and squeezed the fingers desperately.

'Has your father got a key?'

'Yeah,' I sniffed.

'Fuck it, then. Come on, let's get this show on the road.' And he lifted his long legs and climbed into the back of the ambulance.

*   *   *

'I'm going to strap this round your tummy so we can hear your baby's heartbeat,' said the Irish midwife. 'You'll need to lie fairly still. Do you think you're having contractions?'

They'd met me with a wheelchair, which was pretty freaky—did they think the baby might drop out if I walked up to the ward?—and pushed me along the shiny corridors at speed, Daniel trotting alongside. Now he was lurking at the foot of the bed. I wouldn't let him out of my sight. Mum was on her way; he'd telephoned her from the hospital foyer, but she thought it would be about another five hours.

I didn't know if I was having contractions or not.

'There's a funny feeling low down every so often but it doesn't hurt.'

The nurse nodded and pointed to a slip of paper hanging out of the monitor like a long white tongue. 'This will tell us if you're in the early stages of labour,' she said. There was a black wavy line drawn along the centre.

'It looks like a lie detector,' said Daniel.

Pyow-pyow-pyow-pyow went the baby. The midwife left the room.

'Your mother thought I was Paul.' Daniel grinned.

'Oh, God, what did you say?'

' "I certainly am not." Then she decided I must be a doctor.'

'It's the posh accent. My mum's a sucker for BBC English.'

'Look, I could wheel the telephone in here, there's one outside, if you want to speak to her. She sounded fairly frantic. She said she'd never have gone if she'd realized, but that first babies usually came late.' He fished in his jeans pocket. 'I've got about a pound in silver.'

'Put it away,' I said grimly. He didn't ask again.

Ten minutes later a doctor arrived to Do An Internal.

'I'll pop outside,' said Daniel and slunk away. Poor bugger, neither fish nor flesh nor good red herring.

'My name is Dr Battyani,' said the smily gentleman in the white coat. 'I will try not to hurt you. Now, will you put your heels down, your ankles together and let your knees fall apart.' He poked about for a minute or so while I stared up at the air vents in the ceiling, and it did hurt, quite a

239

lot. 'You are only two centimetres dilated,' he announced, pulling the sheet back over my shame. 'But I can see from the monitor you are having mild contractions. Although your baby is early we will not try to stop your labour because of the risk of infection. What we might do is administer a steroid injection to help your baby's lungs cope better.'

My heart cringed with fear. 'Will my baby be all right?'

'You are in the best place,' he said, and left.

The contractions started properly about half an hour later.

'It hurts but it's not too bad,' I said to Daniel, who was reading out the *Times* crossword to me. 'I have to say, so far labour's been quite boring.'

'I wouldn't complain, if I were you,' he muttered, chewing his biro thoughtfully. 'Whenever I've seen women on TV giving birth it always looks grim. Loads of gripping onto brass bedsteads and rolling about screaming. Maybe you've got a high pain threshold. Now, what about "seed pod", five letters?'

But an hour later, when the midwife was examining me again, I was sick as a dog. Daniel melted away again as I retched into a kidney basin and moaned. 'It's really hurting now. Can I have something for the pain?'

'Well, you're getting there. Six centimetres.' She pointed to the chart by the bed which showed circles of increasing diameter. The biggest one was like a fucking dinner plate. I was never going to make it to ten, that was just plain ridiculous; what the bloody hell did they think I was made of, latex?

'Ohhhhhhhhhhhhhhhhhh HHHHHHHHHHHhh hhhhhhhhhhhhhhhh,' I panted miserably, overtaken by a wave of agony. My God, it was wonderful when it stopped, but it was like being in the eye of the hurricane. You knew it was only a temporary respite.

'We can give you some gas and air. But you need to try and work with the pain.' She was all happy and brisk, I hated her.

'What do you mean?' Why did they talk such bollocks? I really couldn't be doing with it.

'Keep on top of your breathing. Deep, controlled breath *as soon* as you feel a contraction coming on, then *slowly* out with the pain. Hum if it helps.'

'But what about the drugs? I want drugs.'

'Well, pethidine isn't a good idea with you being a wee bit prem, it can make the baby a little woozy and we need him nice and alert. I'll sort you out with the gas and air.'

'I want an epidural. It says so on my birth plan— ohhhhhhhhhhhhhhh HHHHHHHHHHHHHHHHHHH HHHHhhhhhhhhhhhhhhhhhhhhhhhhh. Jesus. Oh, I can't do this. I can't.'

She gave my hand a squeeze. 'Of course you can. You're doing great.'

Fucking five-star liar.

'The epidural!'

'Ah, the anaesthetist's with another lady at the moment. We'll bring him in as soon as he's free.' She nipped out sharpish.

My wail brought Daniel scuttling back in. 'Charlotte, what is it?'

'What's the good of writing a *fucking* birth plan if nobody takes any *fucking* notice of it?' I shouted at the top of my voice. Let the evil bitch hear. Far off someone else was yelling too.

'Medieval women used to chew willow bark, I gather. Contains natural aspirin. Sorry. I'll shut up.' He dabbed at my neck and forehead with a cold flannel. His expression, wide nervous eyes and fixed mouth, made me think of a cod trying to smile. I could nearly have laughed.

Mrs Happy trundled the tank of nitrous oxide in and invited me to bite on the mouthpiece. 'Like the breathing, start inhaling the second you feel the pain beginning.'

I took a huge great lungful and nearly fainted. Another contraction hit me.

'Is it any good?' asked Daniel, trying to read the writing on the side of the container.

'Bloody rubbish,' I said when I'd stopped groaning.

* * *

IT WAS LIKE being in prison, sitting on that train. All I had with me was my own thoughts, one dreadful memory after another layering themselves on top of each other, and uppermost, fear. There was no relief. Wherever I turned my gaze there was an awful image imprinted on my mind's eye, like the mad stain on your vision after you've looked too long at a lightbulb. The pictures, some of them from the past, some from the future, blotted out the placid faces and the countryside around me. As we neared Manchester night was falling and all I could see when I stared out of the window was my own scared white face.

'I want to get up,' I raved.

'We need to keep the monitor pads round your tum. Concentrate on your breathing now. Not much longer.' The midwife wrote some notes and checked her watch.

'Well, I need to take this off, then.' I'd managed to get myself all tangled up in the T-shirt I'd brought. Why was it so fucking hot in here?

'Er.' Daniel was hovering at the edge of my vision. 'Look, Charlotte, would this be a good time to go? My dad's here and he's going to drive me back to get the car. But I'll stay if you want me to. You know I won't leave if you need me.' He reached out for my hand just as another contraction swept over me.

'Charlotte? Charlotte?'

'It's fine,' I managed to gasp. 'Yeah, go.' I needed to concentrate on the rhythm of the pain. I could see now why animals crept off on their own to have their litters in bushes. I couldn't cope with his concern, his anxious questions, that bloody flannel.

'Sure?'

I closed my eyes; perhaps he'd think I'd fainted.

'I'd go if I were you,' whispered the midwife. 'You can come back tomorrow, bring her a nice big bunch of flowers.' I saw her wink at him.

'He's not the father, you knowoooooooo-WWWWWWW WWWWWWWWWWooooooooooo,' I howled. Her smile never slipped.

'See you then,' he muttered and waved limply. It felt better when he'd gone.

*   *   *

'THE 10.05 TO BOLTON is running . . .' The TV screen over my head flickered for a second . . . 'thirty-five minutes late. We apologize for any inconvenience.'

'But I NEED to get to my daughter!' I shouted up at it, my voice echoing slightly under the iron rafters. No one on the platform took much notice; after all, there are a lot of nutters around these days.

*   *   *

'Now, Charlotte, I need you to listen to me.' The voice was coming as if from under water. 'Charlotte, I can see the top of the baby's head when you push. Lots of lovely dark hair. What I need you to do is to push as hard as you can with each contraction. Yes? Tuck your chin down and push through your bottom.'

I was beyond speaking now but I tried to do as I was told. There aren't the words to describe the sensations, I was only a heaving mass of muscle and pain, all control gone.

'Keep on top of it now. Down through your bottom.'

I pushed with all my might but I was getting exhausted. 'I can't do it,' I managed to gasp.

'Yes, you can. Come on now. You want to get this baby out, don't you?'

Stupid fucking question.

I pushed till I thought my eyes would pop but we didn't seem to be making much progress. I thought of all the women in history who'd had babies. Why

244

did you never hear what it was really like? Had it been this bad for all of them? Some women had loads. Mrs Shankland at the post office had *seven*; had she been through this every time?

'Charlotte.' This was a man's voice. 'It's Dr Battyani again. How are you doing?' Sensibly he didn't wait for a reply. 'I've had a little look at you and I think we need to make a small cut.' He didn't say where, but I knew. We'd done it at antenatal class and I thought then, Whatever happens, I do *not* want one of those, no way. 'It's OK,' he consulted his clipboard, 'we will numb the area with an anaesthetic first.'

Oh, so you've *got* fucking anaesthetics *now*, have you? I thought. 'Nyerhhhhhh,' I managed. He took this as a yes; well maybe it was. I was so desperate to get the baby out by now they could have threatened to use a blow-torch and I'd have agreed.

The next part is confused because I was waiting for the cut, and an Irish voice said, 'There's somebody here to see you,' and 'Come in round this side and hold her hand.' Then a huge wave came over me and I began to push again. 'That's it, Charlotte, you're doing so well, the head's nearly out.' There was somebody crying near my face and when I opened my eyes it was my mum, my mum, and she held my hand tight then the head was out, and with a great slither and a gush the whole baby plopped onto the bed in a slimy mess. I was sobbing and panting and my mum looked like she'd been dragged through a hedge backwards with tears running down her cheeks.

I collapsed against her while they took the baby and checked it over. 'Time of birth, 23.42,' I heard a woman's voice say. The baby squalled when they

245

put it on the cold scales.

'Bless it,' choked Mum. 'I've no hanky.' She wiped her eyes on her coat sleeve leaving a smudge of mascara on the beige cuff.

The midwife brought the baby over and laid it on my chest where it squirmed and hiccupped.

'You've got a little boy, five pounds ten,' she beamed.

'Oh, a boy. I thought it would be a girl.' I stared down at it, him, in bewilderment, with his matted black hair and his screwed-up, puffy eyes. I'd made that. He was mine.

Everything was quiet for a moment; somehow I'd expected a fanfare of trumpets or exploding fireworks, but there was nothing except the sounds of the midwife clearing away. Dr Battyani leant over me and lifted the purple baby up in his large brown hands.

'We need to check him over again,' he said and took him over to a table on the other side of the room.

Mum hugged me and kissed my hair while a new midwife appeared and began fiddling about down below. 'I'm just after your placenta,' she said cheerfully. 'Then we're all done and dusted.'

Together Mum and the first midwife tidied me up and put my nightie on from out of the case, combed my hair and sponged me down.

'Can I have my baby now?' I asked, still feeling like I was floating.

'He needs to pop down to the SCBU to have a spot of oxygen,' said Dr Battyani. 'Just to help his breathing.'

Mum and I looked at each other in horror.

'Is he going to die?'

Dr Battyani tutted and shook his head. 'He is a strong healthy baby for thirty-four weeks. But he will be more comfortable during the night if we give his lungs a little assistance. Have you got a name for him so we can write it on his tag?'

'No.' I thought briefly of Fyffes. 'Oh, God, Mum, I've no name for him . . .'

'Do not panic. We can put your name on.' The doctor came over to my bed and spoke to Mum. 'She needs to get a good night's rest. You can stay with her for a little while.'

My limbs began to tremble with fatigue. I closed my eyes and snuggled against her, something I hadn't done since I was tiny. 'Oh, Mum, I'm so glad you're here.'

She leant over me, stroking my arm.

'My father and I just wanted to say well done,' said Daniel emerging from the shadows.

'Are you a hallucination?' I asked reasonably. He laughed. Mr Gale stood behind him. I could see Mum eyeing them up and down. 'I thought you were going home?'

'Dad said I could hang around till midnight. And you got there in the nick of time.'

'Didn't we all,' muttered Mum.

*   *   *

HOW OFTEN DO PARENTS say sorry? (Well, most of them don't listen, for a start, so they never even realize they've done anything wrong.) In the struggle to take on the mantle of parenthood, and it is like a mantle, a big padded-shouldered superhero costume, you fall into this trap of arrogance. It starts early on when you're outside a supermarket and your toddler is screaming for something totally unsuitable they've spotted on the shelves and taken a fancy to, e.g. a box of After Eights. You have to be firm, obviously. You have to look as though you know what you're doing because there's always this fear that if you don't some passing shopper will spot your deficiencies and report you as a fraud, someone who's only playing at being a parent. Then your children will be taken into care and your life will be in ruins.

Also you have to convince your child that you're in charge, because this is what kids are supposed to like, firm boundaries and what have you. But listen, I don't believe they ever do think you're in charge. They know all along that what you're doing is simply steam-rollering your opinions through because you're bigger and can smack harder and shout louder, and that's not really the same thing as being in charge. But you're so caught up in the role you convince yourself that whatever the situation, you're right and if your child disagrees they must there-fore be wrong: the After Eights come to symbolize your superior understanding of the way the world works. And this is true up to the point where you die, so that there are even now seventy-year-olds being berated by parents in their nineties for being wasteful with money, deficient in visiting duties, slatternly round the house, etc.

Larkin wrote that famous poem about your mum and dad fucking you up; notice he didn't go on to say, 'And afterwards, when you're all mature adults, they can appreciate all their mistakes and apologize wholeheartedly over drinks on the patio.'

I was going to break the mould. I was going to tell Charlotte I was sorry, and watch the sky crack

248

and the earth split apart.

'I THINK THEY'VE forgotten about us,' she murmured, resting her head on my arm. 'They were pretty busy earlier on. I'm not bothered. It's nice, this, just us two. Do I look a right state?'

'You've just given birth, it doesn't matter what you look like. Was that your new boyfriend, the lad with all the hair?'

'No. He's a friend . . . from school.'

'Some friend to come with you and hold your hand like that. He deserves a medal.' I shifted round on the bed and gazed at her damp hair and her red eyes. She seemed so young, as if she'd woken up from a bad dream and sneaked into my room for a cuddle like she used to after Steve left. 'Oh Charlotte . . .'

She let out a huge yawn. 'What, Mum?'

'I'm so sorry.'

Her blue eyes flicked onto me and her brow furrowed. 'What for? You were here, weren't you, in the end. I was all right. You know, they reckon that gas and air is only a temporary effect but I think it stays in your system. I could rise off this bed and drift round the ceiling.' She stared up at the dirty tiles as if they were the most beautiful things she'd ever seen.

'No, I didn't mean going away. I shouldn't have done that either—'

'Where did you go?'

'Lyme Regis,' I blurted out. *The French Lieutenant's Woman* had been on Granada last week.

'Mmm. Dig up any skeletons?'

'What do you mean?'

249

'Any old fossils. Ammonites, that sort of stuff. I know I'm talking rubbish, ignore me.' She closed her eyes again.

'Oh, I see. No, it was very quiet, really. I had to do some thinking. But I should never have walked out like that, without any warning. It wasn't fair. Sometimes I feel like I've been following some sort of manual, *The Guide to Being a Bad Mother*; actually there've been times when I feel I could have *written* it.'

'God, Mum, there are plenty worse than you.'

I pictured for a moment a door slamming in my face and, further back, a little shabby figure cowering in a corner, nobody there to protect her. Tears spilled over my cheeks again.

'I've been rotten to you over this pregnancy,' I sniffed. 'I only wanted you to have a happy life.'

'I know, Mum. But let's not argue all the time from now on, eh? I hate it when we argue, the air turns all . . . spiky. Nan hates it too.' She stretched and tried to roll onto her side. 'You know, I used to be jealous of Nan when I was younger, 'cause of all the time you spent looking after her. You once said to me, "Love isn't a cake, you can't divide it up into slices." And I said, "No, but time is. A clock even looks like a cake." Do you remember?'

'No.' God, I had got it wrong. 'I'm sorry for that as well, if you felt neglected.'

'It was my problem, selfish adolescent; you were just trying to do your best. I can see that now. I can see a lot of things. I really love her, you know.' She sighed and there was a long pause. I thought she'd dropped off to sleep and I was wondering about slipping over and dimming the lights over on the other side of the room. Suddenly she said, 'Tell me

250

what it was like when you had me. I've never asked.'

I settled back against the metal bars.

'Well, some of it's still very clear. It was the best and worst day of my life, I think. I remember, I was in labour for nearly twenty-seven hours and they had to use forceps, which is why you've got that tiny dent over your left cheekbone. The midwife was absolutely horrible. When I told her how much agony I was in she said, "You should have thought of that before you got yourself into this mess." Honestly. You'd report them today. Steve wasn't with me because he said he couldn't face seeing me in pain, lame excuse. And Nan was beside herself with worry; she was terrified of losing me, or you, because she hadn't long been a widow, so by the time you were born she was like a wet rag. She held you first—I think she may even have cut the cord, I'll have to ask her—and then she put you in my arms. All the nurses commented on your blue eyes, and you fixed me with this fierce gaze, as if to say, You're *mine*; don't even think about giving me away. It made my insides melt, because it was the first time in all the pregnancy that I'd realized you were an actual person.'

I glanced down, proud of my speech, but Charlotte was fast asleep with her thumb in her mouth.

*　　　*　　　*

I woke with a shock when the breakfast trolley rattled past the door. My first thought was, The baby's died in the night and they daren't tell me. I pressed the buzzer and a young nurse came in

251

carrying some charts.

'How's my baby?'

'Oh, he had a very good night. You're both going up to the ward today. You can have a shower first, make you feel more human; I expect you'll be feeling a bit bruised and battered, but that soon passes. I just need to do your obs while I'm here.'

She took my temperature and blood pressure and all the time I was trying to get my head round the fact that I had a baby, I was a mother. Surely it was all a mistake. I couldn't really have a baby, not *really*.

Up on the ward there were lots of real mothers all with their babies next to them in clear plastic cribs. The space by my bed was empty. I lay there, the biggest fraud in the world, while the woman opposite picked her child up, put her hand inside her nightdress and fished out a breast. Then she clamped the baby to her nipple and started to flick through a magazine with her free hand. It was pretty impressive. To my right a girl about the same age as me was changing a nappy, like she knew what she was doing. I tried to peer over her shoulder but it looked a bloody complicated arrangement and the baby kept wriggling. When she'd parcelled up its tiny bottom she put its sleepsuit back on, bending the minute limbs carefully, poking inside the sleeve openings with her finger to extract the curled fists. Finally she picked it up, her hand behind its floppy head, and called the nurse who brought a bottle which the baby drank with its eyes closed. I knew for certain I'd never be able to do any of this. I'd drop him, sure as eggs is eggs, or break his arm trying to dress him. I'd better tell them now I wasn't fit to be a mum.

Just then they wheeled him in.

'Here we are,' said the nurse parking him expertly and flipping on the brake. 'Here's your mummy.' There was no response from the swaddled heap. 'He's still asleep.' She leant over the side of the crib and touched his head. 'What a lot of lovely hair.'

'Is that normal, to sleep so long?' I could feel myself panicking again.

'Oh, yes. Labour's a very tiring experience and not just for the mum. He'll wake up when he's ready. My goodness, you'll be praying for him to go to sleep before he's much older!'

I leant over and watched his crumpled face. There was absolutely no movement. I looked for signs of breathing but there were too many blankets round him so I gingerly swung my legs out of bed *ow ow ow ow* and started to unwrap his body. At last his chest was uncovered and I could see it rising and falling. Thank God. I got back into bed and lay there watching that small movement, up and down, because if I didn't it might stop.

He didn't wake properly until after dinner and by then I was convinced he was going to starve to death. 'Help me feed him,' I said to the nurse pathetically.

I'd just got my boobs out when Mum walked in.

'Oh, Christ, you've not brought anyone with you? Imagine if my dad saw me like this, or Daniel!'

Mum rolled her eyes and drew the curtains round. 'How are you getting on?'

'I can't seem to make him open his mouth wide enough.' I looked down at the feeble scrap rooting

253

about blindly. 'See, he hasn't a clue. I thought it was instinct.'

The midwife manoeuvred him around and pushed another pillow under my arm. 'Stroke his cheek, that makes him open his mouth.' She took hold of my breast and sort of stuffed it between the baby's lips. It was a shock having another woman touch me like that.

I shivered. 'I don't like this. It feels funny.' The baby tugged at my nipple and broke away. He started to cry at a pitch that went right through you.

'I don't think you're going to be able to do this, Charlotte, it's very difficult you know. You might be better off bottle-feeding,' said Mum.

I pulled my head up, annoyed. 'Give me a chance. We've not been at it two minutes. Anyway, what did you do with me?'

Mum looked smug. 'Oh, you were entirely breastfed for four months.'

I frowned. 'Well, so's he going to be. Come on, matey. Put some effort into it.' I pulled his face against me and again felt that questing mouth on my skin.

'Here,' said the midwife. She pulled my shoulder forward and turned his head. He shifted in my arms, latched himself on and relaxed. 'That's right.' She stood back to admire the composition. 'Now, can you see him swallowing? That's what you need to watch for. It's a slightly tricky technique at first, you need to persevere, that's all. Give me a shout if you need me again.' Mum gave her a wink and I knew I'd been had. I didn't care.

I sat up like a queen, like a mummy, while he suckled on. 'Well,' I said after we'd sat in reverent silence for a while, 'pigs can do it, and cows and sheep.'

'Dogs and cats.'

'Mice and rats.'

And we both started to laugh.

*   *   *

IT WAS THE first time in all the pregnancy I'd realized you were an actual person, and although you'd got your dad's blue eyes, the expression behind them was mine. Stubborn. Perhaps that's why we've argued so much, being so alike. I knew you'd be trouble though, even then, but there was nothing at all I could do about it because I'd just fallen down a big well of love.

*   *   *

Baby Jesus had the Three Wise Men: I had Dad, Daniel and Nan. Dad came first, shuffling in as if he had a poker up his bum.

'What's up with you?' I asked, amused.

'I 'ate hospitals, me. Brrrrrrr. Even the smell of 'em makes the hairs on my neck prickle.' He sat down in the easy chair by the bed but kept his back straight, alert for any sign of attack. 'How are we, then? Oh, I see him. He's a grand little chap, in't he? Very nice. Well done.'

'How have you been getting on? What did you do about Nan's bag?'

He grinned. 'Oh, I phoned that woman from Crossroads and pleaded with her to send someone, I said it were an emergency, like. I told her to send a nice young nurse, preferably a blonde.'

'And did she?'

'Aye. His name were Simon.'

I sniggered. 'Serves you right.'

'P'raps it does. Hey, before I forget I brought you a book. I know you can't get enough on 'em.' He pulled out a carrier bag from under the chair and extracted a Penguin Classic. 'There you are. I looked at the cover an' I thought, That'll be right up our Charlotte's street. I got it off a bloke at work, he has whole van full of 'em.'

I picked it up off the bedspread. *Tess of the D'Urbervilles,* I read. 'Oh, Dad, you are priceless!' I gave him a hug.

'What's up? You've not read it, have you? I dunno what it's about but it looks like the sort of thing you like.'

I muffled my laughter on his shoulder.

He didn't stop long but before he went he gave me something else.

'Come here an' I'll tell you summat you'll bless me for over the next few weeks. It'll be t' best piece of advice anyone gives you. Come closer, I'll have to whisper it.'

I moved closer, intrigued.

'When that baby of yours cries you'll want to run to it right away. And that's fine, most o' t' time. But there'll be some days as you can't cope and he's screaming away and you think you might throw him out the window. Well, at times like that you change his nappy, try him with a bottle, get him burped and then you leave him. You close the door, go downstairs and have a cup of tea. Nobody phones the police, God dun't strike you dead with a thunderbolt; you give yourself five minutes and then you go back. And if you're really lucky, little

256

bugger'll have gone to sleep.'

'Thanks, Dad.'

'No problem.'

Next came Daniel, bearing a huge bunch of flowers. There was also a book on babycare by Miriam Stoppard.

'I don't know if you've got this already, but my father says it's a definitive work.' He tossed it on the bed and lounged in the chair. 'I can't believe how normal you look after all that trauma.'

'Get away, I look like a dog. And I feel as I'd been run over. Just as well he's so good.' I nodded at the cot.

Daniel rose and peered across. 'Skinny little chap, isn't he? Dad says he wouldn't have had a chance to lay down all his fat stores but that he's a good weight for his age.' He poked the baby experimentally but it didn't stir. 'Does he do any tricks?'

'None at all. Very disappointing. Oh, yeah, he does black poo.'

'Lovely.' He sat back down again. 'Decided what to call him yet?'

'Nope. I was going to have a chat with Mum about it. She might know some family names I could use.' I looked across at the cot again and got another electric shock of disbelief. 'It feels so weird having him here.'

'Yeah, I know what you mean.' Daniel took his glasses off and began to clean them on his shirt. 'I'm sorry I was so crap towards the end.'

I turned to him in surprise. 'You weren't. You were great. I'd never have got through the first few hours on my own.'

257

'Yeah, but when you started having those terrible pains . . . I didn't know what to do, and it was awful watching you like that and not being able to do anything. Plus, I think in retrospect I should have worn a placard round my neck saying NO, I'M NOT THE FATHER. There were one or two embarrassing moments with nursing staff. One of them asked me whether . . .' He gave an awkward laugh. 'I'll tell you some other time. Hey, did you ever actually use Julia's birthing tape?'

'Oh, that. No, I forgot all about it. Actually being strapped to the monitor was bad enough, I couldn't have coped with headphones as well.'

'You can listen to it now; it might help you relax.'

'Good idea,' I said. But even as he was digging in my suitcase I realized that I couldn't put my phones on *and* listen for the baby. It was going to be a very long time before I wore my Walkman again.

Nan came in the evening. She looked smart, as if she was going to church, in a red two-piece and pearls. You could tell she was worked up, though.

'Where's little thing,' she quavered. Mum guided her round to the cot and she gazed at the baby in total adoration. 'Eeh, little lamb. It's like our Jimmy, safe and sound. In't he beautiful? Eeh. How can they hurt 'em, honest? Oh, Charlotte love, he's beautiful.' She gave me a perfumy kiss and Mum installed her in the best chair. Her whole attention was focused on the cot. 'They're all as matters really, babies. Han't he got a lot of hair? He does favour our Jimmy.'

'Who's Jimmy? He can't favour anyone, can he?' I mouthed at Mum.

'No,' she whispered, 'but don't say anything.'

258

I watched Mum watch Nan and I thought she seemed different with her, somehow. Nothing I could put my finger on, but sort of calmer towards her. I might have been imagining it of course; I was brimming with hormones.

'Can I hold him?' asked Nan, her face shining.

I glanced at Mum. 'Will she be all right?'

'She'll be fine. I'll keep my arm round him. Let her, Charlotte, it'll mean such a lot.'

Mum scooped him up and laid him gently across Nan's lap so that his head was cradled in the crook of her elbow. He was coming round and his blue eyes were peeping. Nan sat stiffly as if she hardly dared breathe.

'Have you got any further with names yet?' asked Mum.

'No. I keep thinking, who does he look like, but then getting depressed . . . I don't *think* he looks like Paul, do you?'

'I only ever saw him twice, if you remember, and that was nearly a year ago. But it doesn't matter, even if he does. Who you are is the way you were brought up, it's nothing to do with your genes. I'm sure of that.' She pulled a strange expression.

'If you say so. But you'd better tell the scientists so they don't waste any more time on research. Anyway, I hope to God he isn't like Paul, I hope he's a nicer person than that.'

'We'll bring him up right,' said Mum. 'He'll know the difference between right and wrong.'

'And if he doesn't we'll smack his bottom.'

'No, we won't,' said Mum quickly. 'We'll find other ways. You shouldn't hit children, not for any reason.'

It took a second for this revelation to sink in.

'Bloody hell, Mum,' I said outraged, 'I wish you'd thought like that when I was small. You never had any problem slapping *my* legs. My God, there was that time in Stead and Simpson's . . .'

'I know, I know. I'm sorry.' Her mouth had gone all funny, as if she was going to cry, so I left it. Maybe these hormones were infectious.

Nan began to sing to the baby in a wobbly voice.

'How can I be poor
When there's gold in your darling curls?
How can I be poor
When your dear little teeth are like so many pearls?
Your lips to me are rubies
Your eyes are diamonds rare
So while I have you, my baby,
I'm as rich as a millionaire.'

'Oh, Nan, that's lovely. He hasn't got golden curls, though.'

'He hasn't got teeth, either, but I don't suppose he's going to put in a complaint.'

'What should we call him, Nan?'

'Eeh, tha'll soon be spittin' in t' fire,' she told the baby. 'Tha will. Yes tha will.' He stared up with round unfocused eyes as she waggled her head at him.

Mum opened her handbag and pulled out her diary. 'I made a note of some family names for you.' She flicked through the gilt-edged pages to find the scrap of ribbon. 'Here we are. There's Bill, of course; William if you like. It'd make Nan's day if you called him that.' She smiled over at Nan but got no response; Nan was too wrapped up in a baby bubble to notice. 'Harold; you could shorten that to

Harry; that was Nan's father's name. Jimmy, or James of course; that was Nan's little brother.'

'I didn't know she had a brother.'

'Oh, he died very young. I think he was knocked down by a tram. Or that might have been her dad, I'm not sure. She's had a tragic life, really, because her mum died when Nan was only in her thirties, and she lost her father when she was a teenager.'

'Like you.'

'Yes, like me. He'd have loved that baby, you know.' I saw her eyes flick over Nan's pink-and-white head and over the tiny black-haired scalp inches below. The baby's skin was still dark purply-mottled; Nan's was pale and blue-veined and liver-spotted. Mum heaved a great sigh which turned into a yawn. 'Sorry, love, I'm done in.'

'*You* are?'

'I know, I know, I remember what it's like.' She peered in the diary again. 'Oh and then there's Peter, that was her grandad, so your great-great-grandad.'

I shifted my bra strap and winced.

'They're a bit like icebergs, families; all that hidden history.'

'I don't think icebergs are anything like as hazardous, though,' said Mum closing the book.

*   *   *

MY VERY first memory is rocking our Jimmy in his cradle by the fire and gazing into that terrible red glow deep down in the coals, while Grandma Marsh sang to lull 'im to sleep.

'Th' art welcome little Bonny Brid

261

But shouldn't ha' come just when tha did.'

She allus called him Bonny Brid; well he were, a little angel. I were never jealous; I just couldn't wait for 'im to grow up so's we could play together. By eight he were t' best in our street at spittin'; he'd fortify himself wi' pop beforehand then give t' others monkey nuts, casual like, so when it came to it they were dried out; he won all sorts that way. An' if I were feeling down he'd sing 'Tickle me Timothy, Tickle me do' till I cheered up; he were allus full o' fun. That time he got under t' table playin' Pirates and pulled t' leg so th' end dropped down, I told me mother it was me even though her best cup were broken. An' I ought to have tekken more care of him. If I'd been with him that day down by the canal—

*   *   *

Out of the corner of my eye I became aware of movement. 'Nan?'

Nan was slowly slumping forward, the baby sliding down her lap. My heart thumped with fright but Mum made a grab for him and caught him as he began to roll. I saw a thread of saliva hang from the corner of Nan's mouth and stain her red top.

'Quick, Charlotte,' said Mum, dropping the baby back in his cot and rushing to Nan's side. 'Press that buzzer of yours and get a nurse.' I hesitated for a second, stunned at the sight of Nan deflating like a balloon. 'Do it!' she shouted. 'I think Nan's having a stroke.'

?

THEY SAY as it's a tunnel wi' a light at th' end, but I found mysen on t' canal bank at Ambley, wi' Jimmy.

'Awreet?' he says, big grin on his face.

'You're looking well,' I say, 'considering.' He just laughs and puts his arm through mine.

He tugs me over in the direction of the bridge— it's a beautiful day, all reflections in the water, very peaceful, and as we get near I can see all sorts of folk sitting on the opposite bank having a picnic. They've a blanket and some bottles of ale, a basket full of barm cakes and pies and things. There's a lot of babies lying on t' ground, waving their legs in the air or sitting up and patting the grass round them, chuckling to themselves the way babies do—and the queer thing is, there's not one on 'em skrikin'. One's crawled ovver an' cadged itssen a barm cake and it's chewin' away, must have a tooth coming. There's a little girl laid out on her front in a summer frock and cardigan, blowing bubbles at them out of a basin of soapy water, she's got a bit of wire bent in a loop. Jimmy's arm tightens on mine and I squeeze back, all warm. I'm dying, I think, and it's lovely.

'Look,' says Jimmy, pointing under the trees, and it's Grandma Marsh and Grandma Fenton; Grandma Marsh is holding up a skein of red wool while Grandma Fenton winds it into a ball. They're nattering so much neither of them take me on. Jimmy digs me in the ribs and makes a face, so I give him a hug.

'You han't changed,' I tell him. He shrugs. I want to ask him about our mum and dad but something tells me to wait.

There's a tenor horn starts up and I know it's

264

Bill before I spot him. He's at the water's edge standing very still and straight. He doesn't wave, never takes the horn away from his lips, but he's playing for me. 'Stranger in Paradise'; the notes dance across the water like light, like a language. There's such love in the air, you could get drunk on it. There's no rush. He'll wait for me.

We're nearly at the bridge.

'Come on,' says Jimmy, 'only a cock-stride now.' He pulls me along by the hand and his eyes are shining. I want to run, because suddenly I've all this energy, maybe I could just jump the canal, but as I put my fingers on the coping stones darkness comes up round the side of my vision and everything falls away. And while I watch, there is a pin-point of light, tiny, getting bigger. It's coming towards me very fast, very fast.

CHAPTER ELEVEN

'MRS HESKETH! Nancy! Can you hear us?'

You've to go away. It's hurting my eyes. I'm dead.

*   *   *

I sat in that hospital corridor for hours. Might as well have moved in, the amount of time I was spending there. One floor up in another wing I'd sat with Charlotte while she gave birth; now I was waiting to see whether my mother was dying. Sorrow and joy a few hundred yards from each other. Turn left, up the stairs and through the double doors.

Over my head the strip light hummed. My eyes were sore with lack of sleep. Even when I'd managed to snatch a few hours it had all been trains again, exhausting, only this time I'd known where I was headed; I was trying to get back home. I would have done too if that bloody platform hadn't turned into Chorley market.

I kept having to blink to stop the reflections in the night-sky window from flickering. Every time a trolley went past it felt like the rubber wheels were trundling right over my heart, the rattling and clanking dislodging bits of my brain. I wondered whether Emma had been to hospital, sat in Casualty while nurses tended broken bones and exchanged glances over bruises. *Why* hadn't anyone done anything? Why hadn't *Jessie*? Every time I tried to think about that a gulf of incomprehension opened up in my mind and instead I saw again her face, hard, sour, in the crack of the door. It was fear in her eyes at the end, not anger; she'd been afraid of me. She'd always be running away from the past, there'd be no rest. Nor should there be.

I wondered if he'd suffered at the end, that man. I hoped he had. I hoped he'd had terrible pain for a long time, and then gone to hell. I could understand now these stories of ordinary people hiring hitmen. In the face of such evil, what else is there to do but wipe it off the face of the earth?

You try not to think about life's darkest things, but sometimes they just flood into your head and you can't stop them. In a place like this, in this no-man's-land of time, you've no chance. Because bcing in a hospital reminds you how every second sees someone off or ushers someone in, souls squeezing in from the dark or flitting out into it. There are supposed to be ten ghosts behind every living person, aren't there? And what about the ones waiting to be conceived, baby-ghosts of the future? If they knew what pain was waiting for them, how many would choose not to be born? Awful images were flying into my mind one after another. War reports on the news, Diana in a hospice with a little bald lad, NSPCC posters, even that mocked-up TV ad for immunizations where the tiny baby rolls about on the edge of a cliff. Curtains closing on Dad's coffin. A strange sea in front of Buckingham Palace.

The hospital clock ticked on taking lives with it and the dead queued up to be remembered. I'd been waiting for ever. I ached to hold Emma and make it all right; she was there, surely, just by me, I could feel her; and behind Emma all those other children who cry at night from fear or pain or loneliness crowded round and reached out little hands to me until I thought I was going to scream—

'Could I have a word?' The doctor was a young Indian woman, very pretty, slightly beaky nose. I looked up at her gormlessly and struggled to my feet. My handbag dropped down my arm onto the floor but I was too tired to bother. We stood facing each other and I searched her expression, trying to guess. There was a lash on her cheek and a stray hair coming down over her forehead. I wondered if she ever wore one of those red spots on her brow. All this in a fraction of a second. Make eye contact, I pleaded, because if you don't, I'll know it's bad news.

Nan was in a room off the main ward on her own when we went. I wondered if that was a bad sign. She certainly had enough wires and tubes coming out of her.

'They won't know what damage has been done to her brain until she comes round,' Mum had told me. 'But she might be able to hear us, they say it's the last sense to go. So watch what you say. She's no teeth in so she looks a bit grim, anyway.'

I'd forgotten she was so small. There didn't seem to be anything of her under the covers, and her hands resting on top were like little turkey claws.

'Mum?' I whimpered, but she shushed me and patted me forwards.

'Let's get his lordship installed first.' She hoisted the baby's car seat onto a chair—he was sparko from the journey—and drew one up for me. Then she sat down herself and started unpacking all the goodies people had sent. 'I thought I'd tell her about them even if she couldn't see them, something might filter through, and she'd be so pleased everyone was thinking about her. Now. Mum?' She leaned over the bed and raised her voice. 'Mum, Charlotte and the baby are here, they've come to see you. And I've brought some presents and cards. They're all asking at church after you, your name was read out for special prayers, apparently. The vicar sends his love.' She fished in a Morrison's carrier bag. 'I've all sorts in here for you, shall I put them on the bed? No, best not, they might interfere with one of these tubes.

268

Anyway, Ivy's given you some lemon-scented tissues, they'll be useful.' She plonked them on the bedside table. 'I've brought a stack of *Woman's Weeklies* from Maud, and a cologne stick. Mrs Waters from the library's sent you a big bag of Mintoes, here, and Reenie's given me a pot of honeysuckle hand cream for you. I could put a bit on for you now if you like.'

There was absolutely no response, it was awful, but Mum just chattered on.

'There's all sorts of cards too, I'll read them out in a minute. Oh, there's a bottle of Lucozade from Debbie, and Nina from Greenhalgh's brought round a tin of Uncle Joe's Mintballs . . .'

I sniggered with nerves.

'What?'

'Sorry. It's the name. It always makes me laugh.'

'What, Uncle Joe's Mintballs?'

'Yeah.' I was fighting giggles; it was that or tears.

Mum smirked; I think she was on the verge too. 'Well, you know what they say about Uncle Joe's Mintballs, don't you?'

'No.'

Mum lowered her voice. *'Uncle Joe's Mintballs keep you all aglow, Give 'em to your granny and watch the bugger go.'*

We stared at each other for a second and then burst into hysterics. I laughed until my ribs hurt, we laughed so much Mum went red and I got hiccups, then she knocked the tin off her lap and it rolled all the way to the door, which was hilarious, and the baby woke up and Mum tried to pick him up but she couldn't undo the straps which was also incredibly funny.

And then Nan opened her eyes and said, 'Blast

269

id.'

*   *   *

I SCREWED my eyes up tight. If I didn't open them happen I could get back. I could almost feel that warm stone under my palm still. When I'd looked down at Jimmy he'd got dandelion seeds stuck in his fringe and I wanted to brush them out with my fingers and feel his bonny hair again. But a wall of black had come up between us and I knew he was gone, Bill was gone, all of 'em. I'd missed the boat. I couldn't stand it.

*   *   *

'Wake up, Nan, and give my little boy a name. We're waiting on you to christen him. We can't go on calling him Banana-baby for ever, he'll get teased at school.' I chafed her small cold fingers under their tape while Mum went to call for a nurse. My mouth was dry as I watched her eyelids flicker and wince. 'Nan? Nan!' She sighed deeply but made no other movement. If she dies now they might think it's my fault, I thought. 'Come on,' I hissed. The baby suddenly sneezed twice and I felt Nan's body twitch. I put my face close to hers on the pillow and saw the lashes flutter and a huge tear roll out and pause, then spread into the wrinkles of her cheek. Her lips pursed and I could see she was trying to say something. The lines round her mouth deepened.

'What, Nan, what?'

The breath came out of her in little pants but no words. I dropped her hand and ran for Mum.

270

*   *   *

LET ME get back, I wanted to say. Give me summat, quick, while I still remember how to get there. If I can just go to sleep and if they'd just turn this blasted light out. I tried and tried but I couldn't make my mouth work.

*   *   *

'What's she saying?' Mum asked me as the nurse held Nan's wrist, counting.

'I couldn't tell. Her teeth . . .'

The nurse adjusted some machines and wiggled tubes, then unhooked the chart at the end of the bed and made some notes. Nan snorted a little and moaned. The nurse put down the chart and bent lower, putting her ear to Nan's lips, frowning. We waited. She straightened up.

'Apparently she's won a holiday. For two. I'll just fetch the doctor.'

*   *   *

THAT wasn't what I wanted to say at all.

*   *   *

It was baby's naming day and Nan's birthday. The nurses stood round the bed clapping while I took a photo with one of those disposable cameras; Nan in a new bed-jacket holding a cake on her lap. The walking frame was just visible in the corner but to cut it out of the picture I'd have had to chop Nan's

271

arm off. I told her this.

'Might as well chop it off, all the use it is,' was her comment. 'Do you know why they clap when someone old says their age? It's because you're not dead yet, that's all.'

'I see it hasn't affected her speech, then,' muttered Dad to me.

'No. She's been lucky, really. If you call not being able to walk properly or feed herself without stuff going everywhere "lucky". She's getting very frustrated though, stuck in bed. She used to be so active. How many eighty-one-year-olds do you know who can still touch their toes?'

'Aye, well, she's short. She dun't have so far to bend down.'

'Stop it. I think she's really depressed.'

Dad looked chastened. To be fair, he's not good at tragedy. He only came because Mum put the screws on, how it might be her last birthday and she'd always thought so much of him.

'So how's she going to go on when they turf her out of here? I mean, Karen's got her hands full with you and the baby, never mind hauling miniature pensioners about. What's she going to do?'

'It were t' best place for her t' 'ave a stroke,' said Ivy loudly, grasping Dad's arm. She nodded at Nan. 'I were sayin', it were t' best place for you. You've some beautiful flowers.'

'Blood and bandages.' Nan pulled a face at a vase of red and white carnations. 'They're bad luck. I've told the nurses but they don't do owt.'

'Let's have one of you, William and me on the bed with her,' said Mum. 'Steve,' she handed him the camera, 'if you'll do the honours.' Mum and I

272

settled on the metal-framed bed either side of Nan, with Will like a fat white grub on her lap. 'Ready.'

'Right-oh. Say Hard Cheese.'

'Eh, it's a poor do,' said Nan closing her eyes.

*   *   *

IF THE TIMES had been different I'd have felt completely disorientated by Nan's uncharacteristic gloominess, but you've got to be realistic. It was chaos in our house, and you can only take on board so much at a time. I was going all out to be a Better Mother in the most trying of circumstances, I mean the house looked like several bombs had hit it. Nan was out of the way for the time being, true, but I was trailing off to visit nearly every day and Charlotte had me going up and down those stairs like a demented yo-yo.

—Mum, Mum, my jeans still won't do up!

—That's because you had a baby six weeks ago. Your figure'll come back, give it time. Dry your eyes and we'll have a cup of tea.

—Mum, Mum, his stump's fallen off!

—Well, they do. Wipe round his tummy carefully and watch you don't catch it when you're changing his nappy.

—Mum, Mum, there's all bits in his poo!

—That's normal. Come on now, Charlotte, stop worrying about *every little thing*.

—Mum, Mum! *Mum!* I've forgotten how to bath him!

—Oh, for Christ's sake, Charlotte, just have a go! His head's not going to drop off! Five minutes' bloody peace with the *Bolton Evening News*, that's all I wanted.

Etc.

I can't believe how she's changed; she used to be so damned independent and now she's on my back all the time. Secretly, though, it's quite nice. I like being able to tell her what to do and have her listen for once. She hangs on every word, asks me constantly about when she was a baby. We talk like we haven't done for years. When the baby blues hit she went down like a rag doll, completely useless. He'd got jaundice, and I *told* her it was very common and not serious but she kept yammering on about him turning into a banana; I thought she was going mental. Then she came out of it and two days after we were joking about the size of her boobs. 'Look at this, Mum,' she said, holding up one of her old bras against her massive chest. 'It's like a fairy bra.' We were two double laughing. She's doing ever so well, really. There'll always be rows, the habit's too ingrained, but I really do feel as if I'd been given a second chance with her.

*   *   *

People think I'm coping but I'm not.

All these secrets women keep. Actually, I can understand why; after you've given birth you feel as if your body's been turned inside out and left hanging on the line for a week. If word got out what it was really like, nobody would get pregnant ever again. I'm certainly not up for it a second time, no way, Will'll have to resign himself to being an only child. I'm such a mess down there it's horrific. I can feel these knobbly stitches; they're supposed to dissolve on their own but I'm not convinced. I touch myself in the bath and it's not

274

my body any more.

My breasts aren't mine. They've changed into tender, meaty bags of milk and they go knobbly too if Will sleeps through a feed. Then I have to go and milk myself into the bathroom sink like a big cow. It sprays out in tiny jets, it's just weird.

The baby's weird, too. He's got pathetic scrunched-up little legs and a huge tummy now, and eyes that scan your face as if they're going right inside your head; I hope to God they're not. His willy's funny, a tiny soft teapot-spout of a thing. When you're cleaning the poo off it you think it's impossible that one day it'll be this huge hard veiny stalk with wiry hairs all round it. Mum says he's a good baby to what I was, he only wakes once or twice in the night and goes back down after a feed, but it's killing me getting up to him at all hours. How do people manage without sleep? Sometimes I lie awake in the dark, waiting for him to cry, and I wonder if he can read my thoughts and whether that starts him off.

Once, and I haven't told anyone this, he was crying and crying in his cot and it was half-past three in the morning. He had wind but I didn't know, I thought he was doing it to spite me. I picked him up and he carried on screaming into my ear and my whole body started to tremble because of the urge to shake him hard. A good shake will show him, make him stop, I thought. Then I came out of it and remembered what Dad had said, but as I went to put Will back down he let out a huge burp and stopped crying immediately. I went down and had a cup of tea anyway.

He is a sweet baby. I call him Will, Mum calls him William, to Nan he's Bill or sometimes 'Bonny

Brid'. Dad refers to him as 't' little belter'. I can change his nappy now no problem, I sing him songs by Oasis; he's gaining weight and he might have smiled for the first time today. Mum said it was a smile, anyway.

But I'm still a fraud. I put him to the breast and look down at his fragile skull and I think: I don't love you yet. I wouldn't want any harm to come to you, I'd fight off a tiger with my bare hands if you were in danger. And yet there's a gap inside me where I'm sure I should be feeling something more. You shouldn't just be *fond* of your baby, should you?

What have I done?

*   *   *

THE HOUSE is full of cards and people troop up the path almost daily with bits and pieces for the baby. Mr F sent a book of lullabies from around the world; Debbie's sister brought a bag of clothes, 3–6 months, she'd finished with. All Mum's friends from the Over Seventies' have given something, knitted cardigans and teddies and what have you. Mrs Katechi from the Spar gave us a scrapbook entitled 'Baby's First Year'; Pauline came with a bag of gifts from the staff and kids, even a couple of parents had chipped in. A lot of it's second-hand but that doesn't matter, William's not going to complain, is he?

Charlotte wanted to know why everyone was being so nice.

'I don't know half these people. Why have they bought me presents?'

I was writing thank-you notes at the table but I

276

stopped and put my pen down. 'Do you know, it's funny, I remember thinking exactly the same, but I can understand it now. It's because a new baby's a blank sheet, it's not made any mistakes like an adult has. People want to get in on that innocence and celebrate it while it's there. It's very attractive, that unspoilt life, sort of magical. It gives us all hope. The baby's got a chance of getting it right where we've failed.'

Charlotte snickered. 'Steady on, Mum. Isn't it just that babies are cute?'

William, who was lying naked on his changing mat with his chubby legs kicking, snorted and sneezed.

'Maybe. That's only my take on it. Hey, you'd best put his nappy on before he wees. It goes a long way with boys, I've discovered.'

'I know, it's like a fountain.' Charlotte knelt— she's getting so capable with him—and started to strap him up. 'Yeah, I can understand people being nice with *him*, who wouldn't be? But I thought some of them might be a bit off with me, you know, not being married and that. The older ones, anyway.'

'Oh, love, there probably isn't a woman alive who doesn't think, There but for the Grace of God. The older ones especially, I shouldn't be surprised, because when they were young it was a lot easier to get caught.'

Charlotte snapped the last popper on William's suit. 'Oh, God, imagine, Mum, imagine Ivy Seddon . . . and Maud Eckersley . . . on their backs, in the grass!'

'Stop that now, madam, you've a nasty mind. I've got to give them both a lift to the hospital this afternoon. I think all those hormones must have affected your head. Hell's teeth, what an image, though.'

'But they must have been young once. They must have courted and that . . .'

I put the last card in its envelope.

'Oh, I don't think so. Sex wasn't invented until the 1960s, you know. Before that everybody behaved themselves.'

'Did they? Did they really?'

'What do you think?'

*   *   *

When Mum asked me what I wanted for my birthday I said, 'Sleep.' It was true. Key of the door or not, all I wanted was to get my head down for a few hours. You could stick your parties and your presents. I thought she'd roll her eyes and suggest a gold locket, but she only said, 'You'd best get expressing some milk, then.'

So on the morning of my eighteenth birthday the fairies came and spirited Will away and I slept on in a tangle of sheets. I slept till noon, woke up and went back out again. This second time, though, I started to have a very strange dream. I was on the London Underground and a dwarf with a black beard was crushed up next to me. He kept looking at me and licking his lips so I tried to move away but the crowd was packed too tight. Then he reached up and started squeezing my breasts hard. Harder and harder he squeezed until it really hurt, then I woke up.

I was lying in a pool of my own milk. It had soaked right through my bra, my T-shirt and the

278

bottom sheet. My breasts were so hard I could have lain on top of them and been a foot off the mattress. 'Bloody hell,' I said, in some pain, and stumbled out of bed. I staggered to the landing, blinking in the light, desperate to find my baby and have him relieve some of the pressure before I exploded.

'God, Mum!' I shouted as I reached the bottom of the stairs. 'Where's Will? I've got to give him a feed, my boobs are like two rocks. And I've got milk all down me.'

I opened the door to the lounge and in my thickheadedness took in a small crowd: Daniel, Julia, Anya, Mum, Ivy and Maud, Mum's boss (?), Debbie, Dad, a banner, balloons, cocktail sausages. 'Happy birthday,' I heard Daniel say weakly.

I turned and fled upstairs, locking the bedroom door behind me. Ten seconds later Daniel knocked.

'Come on, Charlotte, I'm sorry, we're sorry, let me in.'

'Go away!' I shouted. 'I want Mum.'

She came, with fat-chops Will slumped against her shoulder. 'Here you are.' She handed him over and he started rooting immediately. 'Get yourself settled first.' He latched himself on and began to gulp. 'He's missed his mummy, haven't you? He's been fine, though, good as gold all morning,' she added hastily. 'Now, are you all right? I'm *ever* so sorry—'

'What do *you* think? Standing there like I'm in a wet T-shirt competition in front of all and sundry, no make-up on, my hair like a bird's nest, how would you like it? God, Mum, how *could* you?'

'It was meant to be a surprise.'

279

'Yes, well, it was that all right. Stop smiling! It's not funny, it's *not*. Christ Almighty. *Why* didn't you come up and warn me? It was awful. I don't think I'll ever set foot outside this bedroom again. I'll get agoraphobia and it'll be totally your fault.'

Mum patted my knee. 'Come on, nobody minds. I did keep coming up to check on you, every fifteen minutes. I was going to let you come round then say Daniel was here, so you could get your lipstick on. But last time I looked in on you, you seemed to be sound asleep and it didn't seem fair to wake you, then Maud wanted to know how long to put the vol-au-vents in for and I got waylaid. We only caught a glimpse, for Heaven's sake. Nobody minds, honestly.'

'I do.'

'I was trying to do something nice for you, Charlotte; give me a break.' Mum looked weary suddenly. 'I get tired too, you know. In fact, with having to take care of miladdo here all morning *and* sort out a buffet, I'm absolutely jiggered. But I wanted it to be nice for you because it's your eighteenth, it's special. I think I'll take your present back to Argos, you don't deserve it.'

'What is it?'

'You'll have to come downstairs and find out.'

Will put his palm on my bare chest and spread his fingers ecstatically. I put my hand out to meet his and he caught and gripped my thumb. His hair was still thick and dark and none of it had dropped out as Maud had predicted.

'You funny monkey,' I said to him. 'You don't care what state I'm in, do you? You haven't a clue. Oh, hell. All right, I give in.'

'Don't put yourself out or anything! Honestly!

280

Everybody in that room just wants to wish you a happy birthday, stop being so horrible.' She took wriggling Will off me while I hunted around for clean clothes.

'It's not my fault I'm bad-tempered, you know, it's the hormones.'

'Rubbish. You can't go on using that excuse for ever. Now, I've brought you up your toothbrush and I've even filled Nan's jug and basin next door for you so you don't have to trail through the lounge to the bathroom, you can make yourself decent up here.'

'Am I a miserable cow?'

'At times.'

'Why can't we have an upstairs bathroom like normal people?'

'When we win the lottery. Now get a move on.'

Actually it was Daniel who gave me the best birthday present, although Mum's was pretty amazing.

She wheeled it in on the hostess trolley. 'We thought you'd had enough things for the baby. This is just for you.'

'For your studies,' said Dad shyly.

'It's a good package.' Daniel handed me the scissors and I started to undo the Sellotape. 'Though you might want to upgrade at some point.'

So I knew it was a computer before I'd got all the paper off. 'Oh, God, how did you . . . ?'

'Your Dad put some money towards it, and Nan. We don't want you to forget your plans for the future.'

I circled the huge boxes in awe. 'But you already got me the car seat. I don't deserve this.'

'Yes, you do,' said Dad and Daniel in unison:

'No, you don't,' said Mum.

'Where's it going to go?' I thought of my room, the tiny desk, the two square metres of floor space.

'We can maybe move the display cabinet out of that corner. We'll have a chat about it later.' Mum went into the kitchen and came back with a bin liner. 'Help me get that polystyrene into here before it goes all over.'

'When's this cake going to get etten, then?' asked Dad.

Julia and Anya (box of goodies from The Body Shop) stayed till Dad left for his next shift, then Debbie (photo album) had to catch the bus. Maud and Ivy (book token and arnica cream) tottered off to an evening service at church which left Mr Fairbrother (*The Little Book of Calm*) and Daniel (nothing as yet). Mum started to ferry crockery through to the kitchen and Daniel jumped out of his chair as if he'd been stung by a wasp.

'I'll do that, Mrs Cooper, you sit down.'

Mum flushed with pleasure. 'Well, that would be very nice. Just leave everything out on the drainer and I'll put it away tomorrow.'

'I'll pour us all some wine,' said Mr Fairbrother.

I sat in the kitchen to keep Daniel company and rocked Will, who went to sleep.

'I wonder if everybody's life turns so weird after having a baby, or if it's just mine. I feel as if all the things I was certain of before have been blown away.'

'Such as?' Daniel groped in the water for the dishcloth.

'Mum; she's almost human these days, that break must have done her some good. Nan not

282

being around, that's *really* strange, I mean she's *always* been there. Part of me misses her like mad and part of me's dreading her coming home. I mean, a two-month-old baby *and* Nan under the same roof. Chaos. Mum'll go all ratty again, it's a shame, and there's every chance Nan'll get ratty back now she's on this new medication.' Will mewed unexpectedly, then settled again. 'Then there's Dad being around so often, that's pretty unnerving. He doesn't change though, he's still charming and useless. And this bloke, Mr Fairbrother—'

'He wants us to call him Leo, he said earlier.'

'Leo, then. What's he doing buzzing about the place? He's too old for Mum, surely. Not her sort at all.'

'I thought he seemed OK. I don't think your dad liked him, though.'

'No, well, they're like chalk and cheese. And then Julia and Anya coming; I was really touched. Did you arrange that?'

Daniel tried to push his glasses up and got foam on his nose. 'Might have done.' He blew the bubbles off and they floated down like snow to settle on the tiles. 'I was going to take you out to Pizza Hut and ask them to come along, then your mum phoned and told me about this—'

'She phoned your house?'

'She was chatting to my dad for ages before he put me on.'

'Oh, God. I am sorry.'

Daniel shrugged. 'I wouldn't worry, he's a natural flirt, it doesn't mean anything. My mother calls it his Bedside Manner.' He emptied the bowl and filled it up again ready for the pans. 'She'd like this Belfast sink. Thirties, isn't it? She'd probably kill for these original black and white tiles too.'

'She wouldn't like having to traipse through the kitchen to have a bath, though.'

'I was wondering about that. I suppose the bathroom was added on after the house was built.'

'I know Nan and Grandad moved in here just before the war but I don't know if they used a tin bath and the outside privy or whether the council had updated it by then. I'll have to ask her. Mum remembers there being a range in the front room, where the gas fire is now, but that went in the seventies.'

'It's full of character, your house. Full of history.'

'Get away. You can say that because you don't have to live here. I'd swap you any day.'

Call-me-Leo appeared in the doorway holding two glasses. 'Are you having your wine in here?'

'Stick it on top of the fridge for now.' I got up carefully; Will was totally out. I carried him through into the living room and laid him in his bouncy chair. With his head thrown back and his turned-up nose he looked like a piglet in a Babygro.

'Bless him,' said Mum. I could see the bottle of wine was well down.

'Can you look after him for a bit longer? Birthday treat?'

She nodded. I went back to the kitchen and picked up my glass. 'Leave that now, Daniel. Come on.'

'I was hoping you'd say that,' he smiled.

Up in my room he turned all serious. 'I've been waiting to give you this,' he said, putting his hand in his jacket pocket. 'I didn't want to do it in front of

284

everyone.' He pulled out a small black cube, about the size of, well, a ring box. Oh, hell, I thought. 'Take it,' he said, placing it in the palm of my hand. Any minute now he was going to sink to his knees and ruin everything. I swallowed and opened the lid.

'Oh, Daniel.'

'They're your birthstones. You have got pierced ears, haven't you? I forgot to check.'

I was laughing with relief. 'Oh, they're lovely. Brilliant. I'll put them in now.' I stood in front of the wardrobe and fitted the tiny pins through my lobes. The blue gems glittered as they swung in the light. 'I like my ears. One part of me that hasn't changed shape recently.'

Behind me Daniel glowed with pride. 'You look fantastic,' he said.

I turned round and since we were standing so close together it wasn't much of a stretch to reach over and kiss him. He put his arms round me and we fused together, lips, hips and toes. If this was a film, I thought, music would be swelling and the camera would be circling us in a long close-up. He kissed really well, surprisingly well. Maybe he'd left more than friends behind in Guildford; I'd never thought to ask.

'Come and lie on the bed,' I said quietly.

'If you're absolutely sure.' He looked into my eyes. 'Are you?'

'Yes.'

We lay for a long time snogging and writhing against each other. He ran his fingers down my back and neck, seemed to know instinctively not to touch my breasts. His kisses on my skin were light and shivery, but he scrupulously avoided contact below my waist, even though I was grinding my hips against his crotch like a complete floozy. Suddenly I wanted him to touch me, really touch me. I didn't care about the flab or what the stitches looked like, I just needed his fingers. I guided his hand down, past the waistband of my skirt, under the hem of my knickers, an electric path. I thought I was going to die with lust.

All the time he was gazing into my eyes and moving his hand really gently, so gently. I knew I was soaking wet; I knew too that the sensation was better than anything I'd ever felt with Paul. No thrusting or stabbing, no jagged nails, just his feathery fingertips slicking over and over the exact spot it felt most good. The pleasure got more and more intense, became a different feeling altogether, he had to keep going, he mustn't stop, I closed my eyes and came, came, came on his hand, in waves of the most exquisite, fantastic, glorious—

'Are you all right?'

I opened my eyes. 'Oh my God. That was unbelievable. I never knew what it was like. Oh, God.' I collapsed back onto the pillow. 'You're brilliant. You knew exactly what to do.'

'I've been reading up on it,' he said modestly.

I buried my face in his chest. 'You and your bloody Internet.'

'Ashley Carter, actually, historical novelist. One of my mother's dodgy paperbacks. She keeps them in the bottom of the wardrobe; she thinks I don't know. It might all be crinolines and fans on the front but it's hot stuff between the covers, I can tell you. They've been quite an education to me over the years.' His face was pink and he'd taken his glasses off which made him look different and

286

vulnerable. I had a sort of leap of love for him then and reached over to snog him again. I felt the hardness at his crotch against my belly.

'Is there, is there anything I can do for you?' I asked.

'I should think *so*,' he sighed, lying back as I unzipped his trousers.

*   *   *

I HAVEN'T DREAMT about the London visit at all, and I was expecting nightmares. Maybe it's because I think about it all the time so there's no need for my subconscious to drag it out at night. Emma haunts me like a little ghost, her big eyes, her wispy hair. I see her everywhere, as a child in the kids at school, as the adult she never had a chance to be. There's a weathergirl on GMTV who reminds me of her for some reason, something about the arch of her brows. My heart does a stupid jump when Judy Finnegan announces her.

What can I do, Emma? I ask her, but she just looks sad and frightened. She's become my imaginary friend; any day now I'll find myself setting a place for her at the table. And sometimes in the night my heart bulges against the mattress with emotion, and I feel as if the love in me could flow out like a huge sea and bathe all those children no one wants, their little limbs, if only I could get to them. What can I do?

As for *her*, she's a bad sensation that crawls over my memory from time to time, often unexpectedly. The gaps between flashbacks are getting longer though. Maybe, some time in the future, a whole day will go past and I won't picture her at all. Did

Nan ever actually know Jessie Pilkington? It seems impossible; such goodness meeting such evil. In any case, I found my real mother. Surprise, surprise, she turned out to be Nan after all.

I was thinking through all this again while I sat in the consultant's waiting room, ready for him to deliver her long-term assessment. I was all set up for an argument: *Don't you dismiss my mother as a bed-blocker! She's paid her National Insurance contributions all her life, she's only asking for what she's entitled to. If it takes her a long time to recuperate, then so be it, you'll just have to make arrangements. Don't we care about old people in this country any more?* No consultant was going to walk all over me.

And yet, when I met him, Mr Hammond turned out to be perfectly reasonable.

'Take a seat. Now, Mrs Coper.'

I laughed out loud. 'Oh, I wish! It's *Cooper*, actually.'

'Oh, dear, that wasn't a very good start, was it?' He amended his notes. 'I see you've been looking after your mother, Mrs Hesketh, for thirteen years, is it?'

'Yes, I suppose it will be . . . Although to be honest, she looked after me for a while. I suffered from mild post-natal depression, then it came back when I got divorced so when I moved into Mum's I was a bit of a mess. She was marvellous with my daughter, got her in clean clothes every day, made her her packed lunch for school when I couldn't manage; it's not a time I like to think about, I'm not very proud of myself.'

Sudden mental image of me sitting at the table with tears running down my face and Charlotte's paintbrush in my hand. Nan's patting my shoulder and saying, 'Nay, they don't put children into care just because their mother's done a bit of painting.' From upstairs we can both hear Charlotte thumping about, furious with me because during the night when I had more energy than I knew what to do with, I've filled in every damn page of that magic painting book I bought her, she's not even got to do one tiny bit. 'I couldn't stop myself,' I keep saying, 'it was like a compulsion.' And Nan keeps patting, and Charlotte keeps thumping. Oh, I did weirder stuff than that; don't know why that incident popped into my head.

When I came back to myself Mr Hammond's eyebrows were raised above the steel frame of his glasses and I realized my mouth was open, God knows what he thought of me. I pulled myself together and carried on.

'So it's only in the last, oh, I don't know, five or six years she's been bad. It's difficult to pin down exactly when the balance tipped from caring to being cared for. For ages she was just forgetful; we put it down to old age. I can't really leave her on her own now in case she sets the grill pan on fire or floods the sink, but then again some days you wouldn't credit it, she's as right as rain and you wouldn't guess there was anything wrong with her. I gather that's pretty normal, is it, with dementia?'

Mr Hammond gave a slight nod. 'It can be.'

'Weird, isn't it? You never know which side of her you're going to get, is she putting it on or not; sometimes, you know, I could—' I clenched my fists in front of my face, then laughed to show it was just a joke. Wonder if he was fooled? I suppose he's seen enough carers to know the score. He kept nodding anyway, didn't call the police. 'But I've been able to manage because she's been so independent physically. She can get in and out of a bath no trouble, climb the stairs, dress herself; marvellous, really.'

Mr Hammond clasped his hands and looked sympathetic. 'I'm afraid things are on a different footing now,' he said.

'I guessed so.'

'You have to understand that for the foreseeable future Mrs Hesketh is going to be significantly disabled. At the moment nurses are helping to feed, dress and toilet her. She's going to need a lot of care.'

There was a silence while I took this in.

'What about physiotherapy?'

'That may have some long-term benefits, but it isn't going to work miracles.'

'Will she be able to climb the stairs?'

Mr Hammond shook his head. 'She won't be able to *walk* without assistance. She was quite severely affected by the stroke. So what we have to decide, together, is how to provide the level of care that your mother needs to achieve the best possible quality of life.'

So this was my penance for rejecting her and trying to find something better. I was going to have to fireman's lift her every time she needed a wee, for the rest of her life; spoon-feed William with one hand and her with the other. My heart sank to my boots.

'She wants to come home. She'll have to come home eventually, but can you not keep her another month or two? My daughter had a baby eight weeks ago and the house is upside down, as you can imagine, and we're going to need more help from social services . . . Can you see to that for me or do I have to contact them myself?'

'I'm still not sure you understand the full picture,' he said gently. 'I don't see how you can cope on your own. Your mum will need a *lot* of care.'

I thought of her bedroom, of carrying her downstairs to the toilet in the night, or of trying to fit a bed in the living room, then where would the table go, where would we eat? Maybe if we shifted the sideboard—but where? Could we make Nan's room into a study-cum-dining room for Charlotte to work in? It would be funny eating upstairs, and taking food all the way from the kitchen and then the dishes back again . . .

'Do you work?' asked Mr Hammond.

'Part time. Why?'

But he didn't have to say anything. My life was telescoping before my eyes.

'I think you should consider a nursing home,' he said.

'Oh, I'm sorry, that's out of the question. We'll find a way of managing,' I replied. I knew that however grim the situation was, there was no way I could hurt Nan any more than she was already. It was an impossible idea, Nan not being around.

As I got up to leave an idea I'd been trying to suppress for a long time rose to the surface. Mr Hammond seemed a kind man. 'Can I ask you something?'

'Go ahead.'

'Do you think my getting divorced all those years back might have triggered the dementia? She was really cut up about it; family's everything to her.'

291

'No.'

'Oh. Thank you.' I got as far as the door. 'And, er, is there any chance that her stroke might have happened because I had a few days away on holiday the week before?'

'No.'

'Oh. I thought I'd ask.'

'Goodbye, Mrs *Coper*,' I heard him say as I closed the door. I didn't know what to make of that.

I walked through the hospital building, past the maternity unit with its soft colours and posters of happy breastfeeders, past the children's ward with its giant Tigger mural, to the shop where I bought a family size bar of chocolate. I wolfed it down unhappily, then I went to see Nan. She was trying to turn over a page of *Woman's Weekly*, licking her thumb and index finger and fiddling with the corner. 'Damn useless,' she was muttering. But her face lit up when she saw me, and that was something. 'Eh, it's our Karen. You look bonny. Have you brought that baby today? He's so lovely, little thing.'

'No, Mum, I'll bring him tomorrow.'

She looked vacant for a second, then she was back again.

'Ooh, it is lovely to see you, I can't be doing with hospitals, everyone talks rubbish. And you look bonny; have you a new frock on?'

'No, Mum. It's C&A, I got it when we went to Chester that time. Do you remember? It poured down so all we did was go in shops.'

'Aye. No, not really. Have you brought that little baby, then?'

AFTER THAT I went back to Steve's and accidentally slept with him.

'You're full of surprises, you.' Steve shifted so he was leaning up on his elbow. 'I'd have changed t' sheets if I'd known.'

'Oh God.' I closed my eyes in irritation. 'Why do you have to be so disgusting! You're never any different.'

'It's part of me charm.'

When I left the hospital I was too upset to go home so I went shopping. After an hour wandering round Debenhams I still didn't feel like going back, so I stopped off at his house. I was hoping for a cup of tea and half an hour to get my head round things before I talked to Charlotte. What I got was Steve fresh out the bath, clean shaven again and slightly tipsy still from the night before. 'I'd best sober up, I'm back at work in two hours. I hate these evening shifts. I could do wi' workin' part time.'

'You could do with packing up altogether,' I laughed. 'I've never known anyone as lazy.'

He scratched his head amiably. 'Aye, well, life's too short. So, what can I do you for? Everything all right with our little belter?'

I told him about the consultant. 'You see, Nan's so trusting, she's like a baby herself. I couldn't put her in a home, it would be cruel.'

Steve pulled at the belt of his dressing gown. 'Aye, it's a poser. Can social services not sort summat out for you?'

'I don't know. They'll have to, won't they? Oh, the thought of having to go through all those different departments again and fill in all those assessments.' I didn't want to have to go near their offices again either in case I bumped into Joyce

Fitton and had to face the look of pity in her eyes. 'It's been one thing after another this year. I must have broken a mirror or run over a black cat.'

'I've been thinking,' said Steve (and he moved chairs to sit next to me), 'this in't the drink talking, you know, this has been on my mind for a while.'

'What has?'

'All it is, I've enjoyed helping out a bit more, you know, being around, involved. It's nice to see more of Charlotte now she's not so hoity-toity all the time, it's done her good to roll her sleeves up and change a few nappies. I'm not much of a one for babies—'

'You can say that again.'

'No, fair enough, but the lad'll need someone to play footie with him as he grows up and I'd quite like to be, well, around.'

'You are. You've been quite helpful at times. What are you trying to say, Steve?' I was aware of his arm pressing against mine and the smell of his aftershave.

'Are you seeing that feller?'

'Who? Leo Fairbrother?'

'Yeah, th' headmaster.' He rubbed his lip where the moustache had been. 'Is he your boyfriend?'

'No.' This was true; absolutely nothing had happened between us and it didn't look as though anything was ever going to. I had no idea what Leo was up to, but it didn't seem as though a great seduction was on the horizon. I'd more or less given up. 'What about you? What about that woman from Turton, that one who ran the London Marathon?'

'Oh, her? She were nowt.'

'Nowt as in Nothing or Nowt as in Bad-tempered?'

'Both, really. She wanted me to go jogging, can you imagine? I said, the only way you'll get me to jog is to put a pub at t' finishing line. She weren't amused.'

'What are you like.' I nudged him good-humouredly, he nudged me back and it turned into a clumsy embrace. His face loomed into mine, his lips hit my cheek then my mouth, and my face went into shock. 'Bloody hell, Steve, what are we doing?'

He stopped. 'Why? Do you not like it?' He had a point; it was very nice. I'd not slept with anyone for over a year; some of the men at the Over Seventies were beginning to look pretty tasty. 'No strings, come on. It'll do us both good.'

'I can't sleep with you, don't be ridiculous.'

'You know your trouble?' said Steve kissing my neck where he knew I liked it. 'You look for problems. Sometimes you just have to go with the moment. Stop analysing everything.' His hand dipped under my collar and eased down my bra strap, making my nipples tingle with anticipation. His dressing gown fell open. 'You don't know what you do to me.'

'I've a fair idea,' I mumbled as he unbuttoned my top.

CHAPTER TWELVE

'Does this mean I'm back in, then?' Steve pulled his jeans on and fastened them round his skinny waist.

'Back in where? Have you seen my tights?'

'They're here, stuck on this lampshade.' He threw them over. 'Back in the bosom of me family.'

I wriggled my hand down inside each leg to turn the tights right-side out. 'Get off. It's not like you live in Australia, is it? You are part of the family, whether I like it or not; you're Charlotte's dad and she needs you around at the moment.'

'I were thinking, though.' He sat down on the edge of the bed. 'We could have another go, couldn't we? I don't mean move back or anything mad like that, but we could meet up for a drink sometimes and, and . . .'

I located my shoes, slipped them on and stood looking down at him. 'No, Steve, no way. It would be too complicated.'

'Complicated? I'm about the least complicated chap you could have. There's nowt complicated about me, now is there? Go on, admit it.'

I sighed. 'That's not what I meant. The answer's no.'

'Ahwww. I've got you a smashin' Christmas present, an' all.'

'Bribery won't get you anywhere. We haven't bought each other Christmas presents for thirteen years. I'm not going to start now.' I picked up his mucky hairbrush and tried to smooth my hair without actually touching the bristles. 'Let's quit while we're ahead, eh? You can come round when you want, but no more of this malarky.'

He put his face under mine and grinned. 'It were good though, weren't it?'

*   *   *

The first place we went to was at the bottom of the village: Bishop House. The air had been freezing, the sky looked like tracing paper and the tarmac drive was slippery under the pram wheels. The light was failing too, even though it was only mid-afternoon. As far as I was concerned Bishop House had just been a big Victorian pile behind some conker trees on the bus route to Bolton, but now there was every chance it could be Nan's new home.

'You see,' Mum had said over breakfast, 'I'm not sure I can give her the care she needs. She's been really poorly and she's never going to get completely better. That's what the doctors say. She needs qualified nurses round her twenty-four hours a day.'

I stared out of the window trying to take in the news. The Ribble bus went past and I remembered the trips with Nan to Wigan on the top deck, and the Pick 'n' Mix from Woolworth's we always used to choose together. I really enjoyed going shopping with Nan as a child because there was never a row *and* I got my own way and a bag to put it in. She loved my company, and I loved hers, simple. Then, as I got older, things changed; I changed. For all those hours she'd spent cutting pictures out of catalogues for me and helping me make pastry animals, suddenly I never had the time for her any more. God, I'd let her down.

'I could help out. Can we not get the council to put in one of those stairlifts Thora Hird's always chuntering on about? They do walk-in baths too, I've seen them advertised during *Countdown*. If the two of us work together . . .'

Mum shook her head. 'You've more than

enough on your plate. It's all you can do at the moment to wash your armpits in a morning and put your sweater on right-side out. Well, isn't it? You don't understand the level of attention she'll need, *I* didn't at first. You're thinking of the old Nan, Nan as she was. She's a different person now.' She was speaking in a slow, sort of rehearsed way that made me think she'd been over the arguments again and again.

'I feel as if she'd died, it's horrible, Mum.'

'You mustn't think like that, Charlotte.' Mum stirred her coffee rapidly, but she didn't elaborate.

We sat in gloomy silence while Will watched us seriously from the hearthrug. I tried to get some cornflakes down but they stuck in my throat. I'd really thought, once Nan was out of danger, it was simply a matter of time and she'd be out of hospital, back home and making a nuisance of herself. I mean, here we were on the verge of the twenty-first century, they could send cameras to Jupiter and Saturn, so why couldn't medical science sort out her wayward limbs? It was unbelievable that Nan wasn't coming home.

'We'll find somewhere nice with some young male nurses she can flirt with. Everyone'll love her, she'll be happy as Larry once she settles in.'

I was still wondering about this as the huge front door of Bishop House opened and a smell of pee hit us. I noticed Mum had got baby sick all down the back of her sleeve, but I knew she was so keyed up it was probably better not to mention it. We pushed Will up the wheelchair ramp and parked him in the hall while the young girl who had let us in went to fetch the Matron.

'God, it's hot in here,' said Mum, unwinding her

298

scarf. 'You'd better unwrap William before he cooks.'

As I was fiddling with the baby's blankets a tiny old man came out of the TV lounge and moved shakily towards us. He fixed on my mother and snapped: 'I need to go to the toilet!'

Mum raised her eyebrows at me. 'I'll see if I can find a nurse.'

'You don't understand, I need to go *now*.' His eyes were watery and desperate; he made me want to throw up.

'Hang on, Mum.' I popped Will back down and ran along the hall, round the corner (only four old ladies playing cards in a side room), doubled back and checked up the stairs to the landing, but there were no staff in sight. 'Nurse!' I shouted. 'Nu-urse!' a white-haired biddy in a blue dressing gown sang back at me cheerfully. She waved at me over the banisters till I got to the bottom. 'You'd think they'd have a bell or something . . .' I called as I stalked crossly back to the pram, but Mum and the old man had vanished. I hoisted Will out again and went to sit on the stairs to wait. Finally she reappeared, frowning.

'Honestly! That poor man.'

'You didn't—?'

'Well, of course I did, once we'd found where the toilet actually was. He was terribly upset. Did you manage to find a nurse?'

'Nope. So, did you have to, *wipe his bum*?' I couldn't believe what she'd just done. I was full of appalled respect.

'*No*, only his willy.' Mum checked her watch. 'What can that woman be doing? Don't look so funny, it's only what I have to do at school sometimes only on a bigger scale, Reception are forever having toilet incidents. If it had been Nan you'd have wanted someone to help her, wouldn't you?'

That shut me up. We waited for another five minutes under the feeble Christmas decorations stuck to the light fittings, then the young girl came back.

'Mrs Street says she's very sorry but she's been delayed.' She lowered her voice. 'A resident passed away this morning and she's with the daughter now. But I can be showing you around till she's free.'

We walked along behind the girl whose hair needed washing. It was a sad route. Every door opened like a blighted Advent calendar: a lady on her own, slumped in an easy chair, watching *Bodger and Badger* on children's TV; three old women all asleep where they sat, sticks laid on the floor; a bald, hunched man sitting looking out of a bay window at the gathering dark. The furniture was cheap and nasty, house-clearance stuff in white melamine or black ash and the carpet was that rough, corded type; some of it was stained. In one room we passed a lady was lying in her bed shouting, 'Help! Help!'

'Do you not need to go in to her?' asked Mum.

The girl smiled. 'No, she's all right, our Mrs Wallis. She always does that, then when you go in and ask her what's up she says, "Was I shouting?" She's fine, really.' She shut the door on Mrs Wallis' cries. 'It's a lovely place for them, they get their meals laid on and their own rooms, and there's always company for them. We do bingo and concerts too. The children are coming from St Peter's next week to do carols in the dining room.

It's a nice home, this one.'

I searched for irony in her face but there was none. I grasped Will to me and he rooted against my shoulder and whimpered.

By the time we got outside we were nearly hysterical with the horror of it all. I could see the relief on my mum's face in the security floodlights. Her breath came out in a frosty cloud.

'We can't send her there!'

'Oh, thank God, Mum. It was *awful*. The thought of her in with that lot . . .'

'I know. And yet, do you know, I think the staff were trying their best. It's just so sad . . .' She shook her head. 'That commode, though!' She started to giggle.

'Well, *I* didn't know what it was, I thought it was just a seat. I was tired; you try carting Fatso here round for forty minutes, I thought my legs were going to give way.'

'It wouldn't have been so bad if it had been empty . . . Your face!'

'All right.' I was laughing too, it was the nerves. 'But we're not sending Nan there, are we?'

'No.'

'Good. Merry Christmas.'

'Merry Christmas, Charlotte. Incidentally, did you know you've got baby sick on your shoulder?'

From inside the depths of the pram, Will's eyes glittered.

'You little soiler,' I told him.

*   *   *

I'D MADE UP my mind, to be honest, or at least I thought I had; come hell or high water there was no way my mother was going in a home. But it was Leo who said, 'Have you investigated Mayfield?' Apparently his father had had a couple of weeks' respite care there and they'd both been impressed. 'More like your four-star hotel,' he told me in the Octagon bar after we'd been to see *An Inspector Calls*. 'Very upbeat, not at all depressing even though some of the residents are pretty laid-up. I know it's further away than you'd want, ideally, but you've always got the car, it's only fifteen minutes or so. Worth a recce, anyway, I'd have thought. I'll come with you if you like.'

So I took his advice but went with Charlotte. It was a family thing, after all.

Mayfield was modern orange brick and overlooked a superstore, but inside it was clean and airy. The only detectable smells were furniture polish and dog. *Blossom Where Ye Are Planted* proclaimed a tapestry over the vestibule door.

'Mum, have you seen this?' Charlotte pointed to a six-foot-high cage full of budgies all going berserk because a tortoiseshell cat was lounging across the top and dangling a paw over the side.

'They're the best of friends, really,' said the Matron, a smart woman in navy who met us in the hall. 'They just enjoy scolding her, but she's too well-fed and lazy to do any harm, even if she could get at them. Aren't you, madam?' The cat flicked an ear at her but otherwise made no movement. 'Oh, and there's Bertie as well.' Bertie was a yellow Labrador who came up to the pram and laid his head on William's blanket. 'Everyone loves Bertie.' Matron patted his flank. 'I have such a job trying to stop our guests from over-feeding him.'

Charlotte stroked the dog and it wagged its tail

302

so hard its back end nearly went over. 'Nan would like him,' she mouthed at me.

I don't know what it was, whether the paint they used was brighter or the windows were bigger, or perhaps it was because we were seeing the place in the morning rather than at dusk, but it was a different world to Bishop House. There were still some very poorly old people there but there seemed to be more activity. Even the television watchers were arguing amongst themselves. How Old is Too Old to Give Birth?

'We like Mr Kilroy in here, don't we?' said Matron. 'What is it today? "I Had A Baby At 60"? Good God. What do you think about that, Enid?'

'I reckon she's mental,' said a lady in a pink cardigan. 'I put the flags out when I had my last one, and I were only twenty-six. Teks me all my time t' look after mysen, never mind a babby.'

They all went mad over William, though. Enid wanted him on her bony knee.

'See the doggy? Can you see that nice doggy? That's my Bella, that is.'

Bertie trotted up to each outstretched hand in turn before exiting.

'Off on his rounds again,' said Matron. 'He's everyone's pal. So, what else can I show you?'

Mum put out her hand to shake Matron's. 'I think we've seen enough, haven't we, Charlotte? Thanks for the tour, we're very grateful. And you do have a place available?'

'At the moment.' She touched Mum's arm gently. 'These decisions are never easy, but sometimes it really is for the best. Have a think and get back to me.'

Bertie raced past us pursued by a woman with a

303

zimmer frame.

'Honey! Honey! Come back here!' she was shouting. 'Damn dog's got my paper,' she complained as she passed Matron.

'Never mind, Irene, gets you your daily exercise, doesn't it?'

She let us out and we stood on the porch for a while looking out over Morrison's.

'What do you think?' Charlotte asked me.

'I think . . . it wouldn't be so bad,' I said. We walked slowly down the path onto the main road to where the Metro was parked. 'I only hope Nan agrees.'

You wait for years to overtake your parents and then when you do it's no kind of victory. When I was little and being told off, I'd think, Just you wait, when I'm grown up I'll show you. Sometimes Dad used to pull rank on me, *Because I Say So*, and I hated it. But nothing prepares you for the day when you realize your parents are weaker than you. It's like having the ground fall away from under your feet.

I sat by Mum's bed holding her hand for a long time before I spoke. I was talking to her, though.

Mum, I said, *I wanted to tell you something, a secret you should know.* She breathed evenly in her sleep. *It's something I've only just found out.* The funny thing was, in profile she did look a bit like me. We had some of the same lines and wrinkles, anyway. *Listen, Mum, you know when I got pregnant? I think*—the idea formed itself properly into actual words—*it might have been Freudian.* The way she was lying made her skin smooth out and she seemed years younger lying there next to my face. *Do you understand what that means? What I'm trying to say is, deep down, part of me was too scared to take exams and go off to university, start a new life away from everything I'd ever known. I didn't know it then, it wasn't conscious, but I can see quite clearly now. I think falling pregnant was a way of avoiding all that risk. So I would never have got rid of Charlotte, for all I moaned on at the time. And I don't blame you. I don't blame anyone. It's the way life works out.*

When she woke up I was going to tell her about Mayfield.

* * *

There were little yellow chicks all over the house suddenly.

'What're these in aid of?' I asked Mum, who was producing them at fantastic speed. 'I didn't even know you could knit.'

'Nan taught me years ago, you don't forget. You can knock these off in an hour. Ivy showed me. Then they fit over a Cadbury's Creme Egg, can you see?' She put her fingers inside the chick's body and filled it out. 'If you're not doing anything you could sew some eyes on those two over there. There's black wool in the basket.'

'I've got to change Will, he stinks. Anyway, what are you making them for?'

'The NSPCC. I talked it over with Leo, we're going to have a big drive at school next term and see how much we can raise with lots of different events. I thought we could have an Easter fair and sell these, say, a pound a time? Or could we get away with charging more, what do you think?'

'I think you're bonkers,' I said, hoisting Will

onto his plastic mat and undoing his poppers. 'We're in the middle of Christmas, never mind Easter. I don't know how you've got the time.' I undid the nappy. 'Oh, God, look at that. It's gone up his back.'

'Well, I thought if I did two or three a week from now till March, and buy a couple of eggs every time we go shopping . . .'

Will chortled with delight as I wiped him down. 'It's not funny and it's not clever,' I told him. He grabbed his genitals and grinned. 'Perv,' I said and strapped him back up.

'Then I was wondering about a duck race on the canal at Ambley, and a sponsored walk, and maybe cake sales every Friday by the back doors, because if we have them outside then the cleaners won't complain about crumbs . . .' Mum's needles clicked busily.

'You're turning into Nan, you are,' I joked.

'Don't even think it,' she said.

I presume it's her way of coping. Apparently it was really hard to get through to Nan about not coming back here, and whenever Mum thought she'd finally broken the awful truth, Nan would gaze up at her and say something like, 'I can't wait to get home to that baby.' In the end she gave up.

Oh, another funny thing I found: talk about turning into Nan, she left some papers on the cistern, of all places; a pack from the DFEE about Returning to Education. I wonder what's going on there, and if Leo Fairbrother put her up to it. He seems to be behind a lot of stuff these days. I won't say anything, though, I don't think I was meant to see it. I left the pack where it was and it was gone next time I looked, anyway.

On Christmas Eve Daniel came round to have A Talk.

'What's going on here?' he said, surveying the chaos in my bedroom. 'Is this really the best time for a major clear-out?'

'Mum's idea. She wanted me to move into Nan's room, but I don't want to, so we're setting it up as a study-cum-nursery type thing. If you think it's bad in here you should see next door. Come and have a look, it's so weird.'

Mum had pushed Nan's wardrobe against the chest of drawers to clear a wall, and the bed was piled high with old-lady underclothes and spare bedding. The carpet was darker in an oblong where the wardrobe had been and there were some spectacular cobwebs across the newly revealed wallpaper. God knows what kind of tarantula hybrid had been sharing Nan's room for the last few years.

'The desk's going along there, and the bookcase. And Will's moving in the New Year, I thought he could have his cot under the window.' I squeezed round the bed and looked out over the frosted Working Men's. It would have been nearly beautiful, but for the fact that two lads were going from one vehicle to another inscribing rude messages on the sparkling windscreens. I opened the window catch and shouted down, 'There's two Gs in BUGGER, you know. What's Santa Claus bringing you? Lobotomies?' They whipped their heads up, saw me and gave me the finger. I gave it back and shut the window again. 'Nice to see community spirit's alive and well. Christ, it's bloody

307

freezing out.' I pulled the curtains shut quickly and hugged myself warm. 'Don't know what's going to happen to the bed, though. It seems really disrespectful to start messing about with Nan's stuff when she doesn't even know she's not coming back. Like she was dead, only she's not.'

'Maybe your mum could put it in storage.'

'Maybe.' I perched on one side of the mattress and Daniel perched on the other. 'It's what we're doing to Nan, after all.'

He reached across and squeezed my hand. 'Hey up,' he grinned, in a pathetic attempt at a northern accent.

'Watch it, you.'

'By 'eck.'

'Bugger *off.*'

He pursed his lips and fluttered his eyelashes. 'Ooh, Mr 'Igginbottom, is that a ferret down your trousers or are you just pleased to see me?'

I picked up some big ecru knickers and threw them at him. 'Stop it, will you? I want to be miserable for a minute. You don't understand, Nan's always been here.'

'You said.'

He held out his arms and I crawled across the bedspread to him. He pulled me against his chest and I found I was shivering.

'Well, she has. And I never really took her on. I thought she was a nuisance half the time. It's too late.' I sagged my shoulders and exhaled slowly. 'I've been a rubbish granddaughter. Why don't we ever say the things we should to the people we care about?'

'Like you said, she's not dead yet. Sort it out, if that's the way you feel. Look, I'm not trying to be unsympathetic, but simply by producing Will you've probably done as much for her as any doctor. Go and see her. Talk to her.' He gave me a squeeze, then took my face between his hands. 'And listen, there's one thing you should know that's more important than anything else right now.'

I searched his eyes. 'What?'

'That there's a damn great spider on your shoulder.'

I yelped and shot off the bed, pulling at my jumper and staggering into the wall.

'Hold it!' shouted Daniel and launched forward, clapping his hand over the dark shape that squatted between the tufts of the candlewick bedspread. 'Gotcha!' He held it up as if for inspection. 'Oh no, it's got away!' he yelled as the black blob leapt out of his hands and at my feet. I screamed at the top of my voice and threw myself against the wardrobe. The hairy mass flopped onto the floor. And lay still.

'You total bastard,' I said, and picked it up.

Mum appeared in the doorway, the old cross expression back on her face, like it had never been away. She wears it well.

'Will you two make a bit less noise? I've just this minute got the baby down—' She wiped her brow with the back of hand like a poor woman in a Victorian melodrama.

'Sorry—'

'Sorry, Mrs Cooper.' Daniel cocked his head on one side and raised his eyebrows earnestly; it made him look about twelve.

Mum huffed.

'It's all my fault I'm afraid, Mrs Cooper, I was being very immature.' Daniel's neck craned into an even more humble posture.

'Yeah, he was, Mum, actually, it was his fault, he threw this—God, it's not funny!—fake moustache at me.' I held it up for her to see. 'What's it doing in here? I don't remember having any pirate costumes as a kid.'

'Let me see.' She held out her hand and I placed it in her palm. 'Oh.' She smiled, turning the moustache over in her fingers so it was tape-up. 'You'd never believe it, this was Nan's.'

Daniel's eyebrows shot up. I snorted. 'Get away.'

'No, honestly. She used to do a lot of plays for the Mothers' Union, comedy ones, in dialect. She was always the man, for some reason.'

'But she's such a midget!'

'I think that was part of the joke. She'd be paired up with some hefty woman as the wife; hen-pecked husband, that sort of thing. Seaside postcard couple. They used to perform over at the Working Men's, in the days when it wasn't quite so seedy.'

'God, really? Did you ever see her?' It was fascinating, this Nan I never knew.

'Oh, no; it was only when I was very little. Apparently she was very good, though. Had the audience in tears a time or two, with laughter. Ask Maud, she'll remember.' She passed the moustache back to Daniel like she was offering him a canape. 'Here you go, lad, try it for size.'

Daniel took it politely and pressed it against his lip. 'What do you think?' he tried to say, turning to me, but the moustache fell off and dropped down between his legs in a spider-type action. I half expected it to scuttle off across the rug.

'Gerrross! You look like the love-child of Professor Winston and Cher. Don't *ever* grow one

310

of your own, promise?' I bent double and fished it off the floor. 'If you do, you're dumped, OK?' I put the moustache to my lip; it smelt of must. 'Imagine Nan dressed as a man, though.'

'Wherever did it come from?' asked Mum, stepping forward to shift some of the ancient pillowcases and sheets. Some of them still had the cellophane wrappers on. 'Did it drop out of these? Oh, wait a minute, what's this?'

She lifted some linen and nestled in between the layers was a pink raffia knitting bag with wooden handles. It had been squashed under the sheets so long it had left its shape imprinted in them, top and bottom, like a fossil. A ginger moustache was sticking out of the top, and as Mum picked the bag up, a thick wooden peg fell out and rolled against my thigh.

'And this is?'

Mum frowned. 'A piggy, probably.'

'You what?'

'Some game they used to play in the olden days.' The ghosts of Nan's past crowded round to see.

'I wonder what they did with it,' said Daniel, attempting to spin it on the bedspread.

'Hit it with a bat and ran after it, I think.' Mum rummaged in the bag and brought out a little plaster figure with a flat white triangle where its nose should have been. She held it out for us to see.

'They called these kewpie dolls, with their pot-bellies and moulded hair. This'll be old, you know.'

'Worth anything?'

'Wouldn't have thought so. Seen better days, haven't you, love? Never mind, so have we all.' Mum put the doll on the bed and emptied the bag

311

carefully between me and Daniel, then she knelt down so she was on a level with it all. Papers, cards, odds and ends had spilled out. A pair of pink baby bootees caught my eye.

'Oh, sweet! Were these mine?'

'No. They were mine. And the lamb rattle.' Mum looked sad as she touched them.

'These must be from World War One,' said Daniel flicking carefully through a bundle of postcards with embroidered fronts. 'Amazing. This is real social history.'

Mum handed me a letter to Santa she'd written when she was about six or seven.

'Purple felt tip? Bit sloppy, that. And what's that zombie-thing in the corner?'

'Zombie?' Mum imitated outrage. 'That's a drawing of Barbie. My whole happiness hung on that doll, you know, I thought it would complete my life. Even though it was in the days before she had all these poseable limbs and bum-length hair, what have you. It's all gone completely mad now, of course; they do Barbie Penthouse Apartments and camper vans, and beauty salons, discos . . . Takes all the fun out of it. I used to cut up shoe boxes and line them with wallpaper, stop sniggering, Charlotte. And you couldn't get Ken outside the States, nobody would import him, so I made do with an Action Man I got from a jumble sale. His gripping hands came in useful many a time.' Mum smoothed out the letter wistfully. 'Tell you what, though, I wish I'd kept that doll, it would have been really collectable. Nothing like those interchangeable pink-and-blonde bimbos you had when you were tiny. This one had black hair cut in a fringe and an op-art dress, à la Mary Quant.

312

Quite scary, actually, but it could have been an heirloom.'

'Cool,' I said, then laughed. 'God, Mum, how sad are we?'

'Do you realize, these cards have seen actual bloodshed,' Daniel broke in. 'This thumb-print here, it might even be blood. Wow. You should take them into school, Mrs Carlisle would love it.' He turned one over and started to read it.

'No.' Mum took it gently out of his hand. 'Sorry. I want to look through them first. They might be personal. Nan's grandad was killed out there, you know.'

The light in the room shifted and the air in the chimney sighed. Daniel gazed at his knees in embarrassment, so to make him feel better I undid the safety pin on the crepe bandage I'd found and began to wind it round his wrist. He didn't seem to object so I carried on up his arm, tying a neat knot at the shoulder. After a minute he shook himself out of his mood and started a retaliatory action with a bobbin of thin pink ribbon. His fingers wove the satin in and out between my fingers, his long bony fingers mixed up with my thin girly ones, and I thought, I love you, you daft sod.

*   *   *

AND THEN EMMA was leaning into me, I could almost hear her breathing at my shoulder. So I reached under the papers and there was a New Testament with a black cover, very plain, but with a gap in the gold edged pages like a half-closed eye. I opened it up a fraction and caught a glimpse of a pink slip of paper, *Certified copy of an entry . . .*

313

General Register Office . . . caution. My adoption certificate. They didn't see anything, the pair on the bed; too busy mucking about with ribbons. Well, let them. It didn't matter anyway. I closed the book and pushed it back in the bag. Next to me, Emma sighed again.

*   *   *

Mum came over all moony suddenly and said she wanted to be on her own for a while, so I took Daniel back to my bedroom. There was even less space than usual but he managed to wedge himself into the corner nearest the door; I didn't tell him that at the bottom of the bin bag by his elbow was all the memorabilia from six months with Paul. I'd squirted hair mousse over the handful of cards, notes, photos and tickets before dumping them; now the room smelt like a cheap salon—The First Cut, perhaps. Daniel's nose wrinkled but he didn't say anything. I picked up a dog-eared magazine article entitled 'Perfect 10: Nails to Die For'. 'God, look at this! Imagine having *time* to paint your fingernails!' I dropped it in the plastic sack. 'A lot of this seems totally out of date now. From another era.'

'I can see what you mean. Oh, this is no good; if I don't move soon I'll seize up.' Daniel uncurled himself awkwardly and picked his way over the mess on the floor to install himself on the bed. He lay down and put his hands behind his head, very at home. 'So, now the dust has settled, what are you going to do with your life?'

I shrugged. 'There's only so much dust *can* settle with a baby. Mum still wants me to go off to uni but

314

it seems impossible at the moment. Mrs Carlisle thinks I should have a year out to retake the modules I missed; she has this idea that she can send me assignments through the post and I could just come in for a few lessons a week. Apparently the Head's OK with that.'

'And you?'

'I really want those As. I worked hard enough for them. But it's going to be a bloody funny year.' He caught my rueful gaze and held out his hand. I stepped over and sat next to him.

'Come here.' He pulled me down, wrapped me in his long arms and kissed my hair. 'Listen. I won't go, I've decided. I'm not leaving you, Charlotte.'

'Don't be daft,' I mumbled into his chest. 'You had your heart set on Oxford.'

He snorted. 'Some chance. With an offer of three As it's not very likely. Dad can pull all the strings he wants, it's not going to get me in unless my papers get mixed up with some other poor sod's. Anyway, that's not important any more. You and Will are what matter.'

I moved away and touched his face. 'It *is*, Daniel. If you don't get into Oxford, somewhere else'll take you, you're too bloody clever. I bet Durham or Manchester accept you. You've got to go and get that degree. *I'd* go if it was the other way round.'

'Would you?' He looked surprised.

'Oh, I don't know.' Faintly from downstairs we heard Will begin to cry. I tensed to go to him, but then he stopped; Mum must have nipped down and picked him up. I let my muscles relax again, but my mind was racing. 'It's all too difficult. My brain's not what it used to be.'

315

'How about I defer my place and take a year out? I might be able to swing some sort of job at the engineering works; could your dad put in a good word for me?'

I laughed. 'My dad? That really would blight your chances. No, don't. We'd still have to part at the end of the year, unless I got in at the same uni and there's no guarantee of that.' Daniel looked mournful. 'Come on, it's only what happens to thousands of couples every year. And in the end they either make it or they don't—'

'We will.'

'Yes.'

'I don't want to leave you.'

This was getting out of hand, I felt.

'Daniel!' I shook him by the shoulders, pushed him against the mattress and climbed astride him. His eyes were wide and miserable. I blew in his face but he only turned away. 'Right, you!' I growled, putting my mouth close to his ear, 'Stop being such a silly bugger. It's not till next September, anyway! You might meet some fancy piece and run off with her long before then. Snap out of it! Lighten up! Because if you don't I'm going to have to take your trousers down and interfere with you.'

There was a pause.

'Did I tell you how depressed I've been?' he said.

Afterwards we lay quietly and I combed his hair with my fingers.

'You really should get this chopped, you know.'

'Do you think? I've always thought of it as my finest feature.'

'Get off.' I ruffled his mop. 'You look like Young

316

Einstein.'

He gripped my wrist and kissed it. 'I know you think I was being over the top before, but this is the first time in my life, well certainly the first time since I left Guildford, that I feel like I belong with someone. Does that sound mad?'

'No, 'cause I think I feel like that too. It's . . . trying to find out where you fit in. I've never felt very good at that. Mind you, this household hasn't been exactly conducive to forming settled relationships. It's been such a battleground, and with the three of us it was always two against one, different combinations. You won't have had that with there being four of you.'

'No, but I know what you mean about the rows.' We shuffled into spoons and he put his arm across me and talked into the back of my neck. 'About a year before we left Surrey there were shouting matches every night, and actually there were just the three of us then because my sister had left home. Then, after the rows came the freezing silences and the "Tell your mother that I won't be in for dinner" and "Tell your father that he'll have to cook his own, then" routine, with me in the middle. I never want to go through that again. If they ever start up I shall leave, I'm old enough now.'

'Move in here. See how the other half live.' I reached back and dug him in the ribs.

He sighed. 'All us damaged adolescents, all over the country, trying to create our own families. I hope to God we succeed.'

*   *   *

317

THE FEELING hit quite suddenly; perhaps post-natal depression's catching. I'd spent a long time going through Nan's bag, although I didn't look at the certificate again. There were four suspender ends, and seven Robinson's Golly vouchers bulldog-clipped together, and an empty cotton reel with nails hammered in for French knitting (Nan had drawn a smiley face in biro on the side); an award for long service at the paper mill with my dad's name on it; there was a Temperance Society newsletter dated 1899, God knows whose that was; there was my first baby tooth folded in greaseproof paper in a BunnyBons tin; and a scraggy binker mat I'd made in the juniors, all lumpy knots underneath.

I thought of Nan as a young woman, a girl, then as she was now. The present didn't wipe out the past, she had been those other, young, people.

Then Will began to cry again so I gathered it all together and took the bag downstairs with me. And as I hoisted him up and held his squirmy bulk to my chest, it seemed to me that time split clearly down the middle and I realized what I'd so nearly done.

Once, when I was about seven, I'd found a sparrow's nest in one of the bust-up garages on the edge of the estate. There were three blue eggs, perfect as a painting, against some white fluff and grey-brown feathers. The mother bird was going frantic, chip-chipping at me from the rafters above, so at first I just looked, but finally the urge to cradle the smooth warm shells against my palm became too much and I picked them up. They felt precious and thrilling. I carried them carefully back home and took them straight to Dad. I assumed he'd be as excited as I was.

His face went angry, then sad when he saw what I had. Deep lines came from his nose to the corners of his mouth; it was much, much worse than if he'd shouted at me. He marched me back in silence to the nest and made me roll them gently back in, then we stood for a while waiting to see if the mother bird would come. 'You see,' he'd whispered, 'she might be able to smell you on 'em, then she'd be too frittened to come near.'

'Does that mean the babies'll die?' It had only just dawned on me that that's what the eggs were; I mean, you buy eggs in the supermarket like a packet of biscuits, don't you? Then when you eat them it's yellow and white goo inside, not tiny birds. I felt terrible. Dad nodded almost imperceptibly and I burst into tears. We waited a good thirty minutes but no mummy bird appeared.

'Don't give up hope,' he said comfortingly, as he took my hand to lead me home, but I wasn't daft. I knew eggs had to be kept warm. I knew what I'd done.

'Thing is,' he explained as we got past the church, 'if you take even one egg you're not killing one bird, you're killing millions.'

'How come?' I'd been wiping my nose on my cardigan sleeve all the way but he didn't tell me off for it.

'Because that bird would have had babies, and those babies babies of their own, and so on and so on, down the generations. Ad in-fin-i-tum.'

It wasn't like him to heap coals of fire on my head, so I knew he thought it was serious. All the rest of that summer I trailed back and forth to the garage in the hope that I could deliver some good news and wipe the slate clean, but each visit the

319

eggs were still there, proof of my guilt. At the beginning of autumn the whole nest disappeared, I don't know whether it was lads or gales or a fox maybe; do they eat rotten eggs? I stopped going, anyway.

To make it up, Dad bought me a pair of binoculars for my birthday the next year and took me up the Pike to see if we could spot the albino jackdaw (we did!), only the effort of climbing winded him and it took us a long, long time to stagger back down again. I think maybe that was the very beginning of him getting ill. I can still remember Nan's face as he finally tottered in through the front door. So all things considered, I never really got into birdwatching.

But baby Will lying so trusting in my arms, delicate flaring nostrils, little screwed-up yawn; I so nearly destroyed you. I was so nearly *such* a bad mother. I can't believe what I almost did with your life and your mother's. Every time I look at you, I'll feel the weight of what might have happened; all that future wiped out. Your first tooth, your first step, your first word, your first day at school. And so I should. I'll make it up to you, Will; I'll be such a good grandma, I really shall, really.

*   *   *

Strange thing: I heard Mum crying in the night when I got up to do Will's feed. She was sobbing and it sounded like she was talking to herself too. Anyway, I didn't go in. I was knackered, and I wouldn't have known what else to say. She'll just have to work the Nan thing through.

320

*   *   *

I'VE KEPT thinking of summat the vicar said at Bill's funeral: the Door is Always Open. It is Never Closed. I wish I'd asked him what he meant but he's dead now, Mr Speakman.

What did he mean?

*   *   *

IT TURNED OUT to be a weird Christmas, all right, even though it started off fairly normal. It was the first Christmas with Emma, for a start. Throughout the morning she hung at my elbow, round-eyed. 'You're never going away, are you?' I asked her silently, and she shook her head.

Nan came home for Christmas dinner, thank God, or I'd have spent the day under a cloud of guilt. I cut the food up for her while the plate was still in the kitchen; Matron had tipped me off about that. Then I chopped Charlotte's up too, so she could eat with grizzly Will on her knee. So we got through that all right, although pulling the crackers proved to be a bit of a challenge and the snaps made Will bawl. He worked himself into such a foul temper Charlotte finally took him upstairs where he went to sleep at once. Then Steve arrived with his Brilliant Present.

'I'm not stoppin', my sister's expectin' me. I wanted to drop these off, though.'

There were some CD-Roms for Charlotte, a bottle of dodgy perfume for Nan, a ridiculously large teddy for William and a spiral-bound notebook for me.

'What's this?' I asked, turning it over and finding

321

only a W. H. Smiths price label on the back. True, it had a nice picture of Lake Windermere on the front but I didn't see that was anything to get excited about.

'Take a look inside. There's twenty of 'em. Took me ages.'

I flipped a few pages over.

1 voucher for
1 hours babysitting
signed
Steve

'Good, in't it? A chap at work saw it on Oprah Winfrey an' he said it had gone down a treat.' He stood back and waited for the applause.

'Thanks. Really, that's a great present. I appreciate it.'

Steve beamed. 'I thought so. Only don't make it a Saturday afternoon 'cause of the footie. An' I'm out Tuesday and Thursday evenings. Fridays can be tricky, too. But apart from that . . . I'm all yours! Hey by the way, how much did you pay for that tree? 'Cause I know a chap at work selling 'em for a pound a foot. He gets 'em off motorway reservations, digs 'em up at night, 's not like it's stealing or anything. I'll sort you one out next year.'

When he'd gone Charlotte wanted to know what the deal was.

'It's just a way of getting back in with me, I know what he's up to. But don't look a gift horse in the mouth, eh? I don't suppose he knows what he's letting himself in for.' We looked at each other and sniggered. 'I'd like to be a fly on the wall when he has to change one of William's demon nappies.'

'Or when Will pukes all down Dad's back.'

'Quite.'

'This scent smells of toilet cleaner,' said Nan. 'Put it under t' sink wi' t' Vim.'

Daniel arrived shortly afterwards like some kind of rogue Santa, bringing with him an entirely new future.

I could tell he was on pins from the word go.

'I got all these for Will,' he said breathlessly, unpacking a stack of garish toys from the Early Learning Centre. 'Dad says a baby's brain carries on developing for months after birth, so he needs plenty to stimulate him.' He pressed a plastic cow in the stomach and it mooed. 'That'll get those neurons sparking.'

'Have you been running?' I asked.

He only gave a nervous giggle and handed me a huge poinsettia. 'For your table,' he explained. 'Although I have to say it looks extremely nice already.'

We all turned to the scene of devastation that was the remains of the turkey dinner. A trail of gravy bisected the white cloth, and Nan had wiped her hands on her paper hat and screwed it up in the sauce boat. Dead jokes lay curled next to a set of jacks, a metal puzzle and a fish key-ring.

'Yeah, right,' said Charlotte. 'We did have a centrepiece but I set it alight and melted the robin.'

'Jolly good. Now, take these; I haven't finished yet,' said Daniel producing more parcels with the flourish of a conjurer. I began to wonder if he was drunk.

There was talc for Nan and a snakeskin belt for Charlotte to match some boots she had. She was made up.

'Are you taking your coat off or what?' I

laughed.

'Yeah, sit down, for God's sake, Fidget Britches,' said Charlotte. 'And while you're here you can settle a debate.' She pointed at the silver tinsel tree with folding arms we bring out every year. 'Is that or is that not a Middle-Class Christmas tree?'

'Be quiet,' I said without much hope. 'I've got to go and strip the turkey.'

'Hang on a minute. What do you say, Dan?'

He shuffled himself backwards into the settee and shrugged. 'I'm not entirely sure what you mean.'

'Well,' said Miss Clever, 'Mum thinks we should start having a real tree because it's posher, even though it's loads more hassle.'

'I *like* them,' I said. 'I like the smell, it's atmospheric. We'd have had one this year but what with one thing and another I never got round to it.'

'Only,' she went on, 'I told her that in real Middle-Class homes they care about the environment too much to cut down trees on a whim, so it's actually cooler to have an artificial one.'

'I think they're both rather fun,' he said, 'if you have to have a pagan anachronism in your front room.'

'Well, what sort of tree do your parents have, Daniel?' I asked, rising to tackle the mess on the table.

'Norway spruce. But my father has a synthetic one at the surgery, I don't know if that counts.'

'See,' said Charlotte, but actually I thought *I'd* won that one.

*   *   *

'**What was** all that about trees?' asked Daniel when Mum was in the kitchen sawing the last bits off the turkey.

'You're a bonny lad,' said Nan attempting to lean over and pat his knee. 'I'm nearly ninety, you know.'

'Splendid.'

'They think as 'cause you're owd you're not so gradely reet.' Nan sat back with a satisfied look on her face.

'Do they? Do they really?' He turned to me.

'Oh, yeah, well, I was winding her up. She's such a daft bat at times. Listen.'

> '*While shepherds washed their socks by night*
> *All watching ITV*
> *The angel of the Lord came down*
> *And switched to BBC,*'

sang Mum over the noise of the radio, then, '*Bugger bugger bugger!*' Evidently the turkey was putting up a fight this year.

'Have a toffee,' said Nan brightly. But I knew she couldn't open her handbag so I got down on the rug, fished some out for her and began unwrapping the cellophane.

'It's Mum's fixation about being Middle Class. It's stupid, I keep telling her we're probably all Middle Class these days.'

'I wouldn't have thought it mattered.'

'Ah, well, that's because you're Real Middle Class. It's the half-and-halves, caught in between, who obsess about it. Nan knew where she was, working in the mill and proud of it; I'll probably go

325

off and get my degree—eventually—and earn my twenty-thousand-plus a year, so I'll be all right.' Daniel's eyebrows moved up and down rapidly. 'Yeah, well, if everything goes to plan, that is. Sorry, didn't mean to sound so smug. But Mum's in the land of the class-dispossessed; part-time school assistant living in an ex-council house. She's Aspirant Something, but I don't know what.'

Daniel squirmed and opened his mouth to say something, then changed his mind.

'The irony is, she's become Middle Class and she doesn't even know it.' I placed the naked Mintoes on Nan's lap and clambered back on the sofa. 'Shall I tell you why?'

'I'm utterly intrigued.'

'It's the fact that, instead of spending her energy moaning about things, she's now getting up and actually doing something to make them better. As long as I can remember she's droned on about how life ought to be different and I always thought, "Well, why not see if you can change it, then?" And I never had a satisfactory answer, unless you count, "We don't do that kind of thing", "That's the way it is", "We put our heads down and slog on". But your Middle-Class person says, I'm going to write to my MP, organize a rota, lobby the council, hold a meeting. Middle-Class people *act*, they don't suffer.'

'Too much of a generalization,' said Daniel hugging himself like a man who's been accidentally shut in a freezer. 'I know plenty of whinging Middle-Class. Half my father's patients probably fall into that category.'

'Huh. It's my theory and I'm sticking to it.'

'Mrs Waters is fed up 'cause she's having a hip

op,' Nan piped up.

'No. She said she's fed up with her son playing hip-hop.' I sniggered, then felt mean when she looked confused. 'He plays his music loud,' I explained.

'Well, they do, young 'uns. You do.'

'I don't—'

There was an extra loud clatter and a yelp from the kitchen. I got up to investigate.

'Do you think your mother's going to be long in there? Because there's something I want you all to hear,' he blurted out. 'Together. I think.'

Radar Ears was back in like a shot.

*　　　*　　　*

IT WAS LIKE an old-fashioned film. 'Mrs Cooper, may I have the honour of asking Charlotte to be my bride?' A shock, but quite a nice one. I mean, a doctor's son. I came through wiping my bleeding thumb on my apron, all ready to play Understanding Mother.

*　　　*　　　*

He stood up as soon as Mum walked in.

'Eeh, are you going?' mumbled Nan through a mouthful of toffee. 'You'll want a coat on, it's bitter out.'

He shook his head, embarrassed, and moved so that his back was to the fire. Me and Mum sat in front of him like an interview panel while he straightened his fingers, spread them out and put his palms together. Then his hands dropped to his sides and I thought, Oh God, what's coming now?

Because I really hadn't a clue. He raised his head and began.

'I should have said this earlier, when I first came, but I didn't know how—I have something I need to tell you both. At least, I think I should tell you—I mean, there's no question whether I should tell you, it's whether I should tell you both together, or just you, Mrs Cooper, or maybe you, Charlotte, and get you to speak to your mother.'

'Maureen Tickle had a broken ankle for six weeks before they X-rayed it,' said Nan. 'She'd been walking on it an' all. Exercise, the doctor told her, honest to God.' Her lips snapped shut and she stared at Daniel's knees.

'Go on,' Mum prompted him. She was gripping her thumb so tightly the tip had gone white.

'Right, well. The thing is, I may have been out of order, acting behind your back, in fact I probably was, and you're going to be very cross. My father will be furious with me when he finds out, he'll say I did it all wrong.'

'*What*, for Heaven's sake?' I tried to catch his eye but he was looking over the tops of our heads.

'They've a new woman at the Post Office, great big teeth like a rabbit.'

'Shut up, Nan, just a sec.'

'It was meant to be a surprise. I've been doing some research on the Internet. I thought you had a right to know—' Daniel pulled out an envelope from his jeans pocket and made as if to offer it to Mum, then pulled it back and held it to his chest. 'But I can see now I should have gone to you first because it was to do with your family, no business of mine—'

'Please, Daniel, tell us.' I rose from the settee

328

and he let me take the envelope out of his hands. I started to unfold the contents, a printout from some website or other, an envelope paper-clipped to the back, and for a moment I thought, Christ, he's found Mum's birth mother, bloody hell what a can of worms that'd be. I sat back down quickly, not sure what to do. But then my eyes focused properly. www.nationalsavings.co.uk, the footer read. A photo of a smiling woman with her arms in the air, over the legend *Congratulations!*.

Mum leaned against my arm, scanning the page. 'Is it Ernie?' she asked, and swallowed. She undid the paper clip.

'Don't get too excited, chaps.' Daniel grimaced with emotion. 'It's not the jackpot. But it's better than a poke in the eye with a blunt stick. Tax-free, as well.' He was rocking on his feet; I think he'd have liked to run for the door and take off down the street.

'I'm sorry to disappoint you, Daniel, but I don't think we have any premium bonds. You must have typed in the wrong letters or something.' Mum's voice was quavering because, like me, she'd spotted the line where it said *£10,000!*. 'This is somebody else's prize.'

'Lucky bastards,' I said with a feeble laugh.

'No, no. That's what I was trying to tell you. It was absolutely the wrong thing to do, to go behind your back. When I spotted the bonds I should have handed them straight to you—'

'What bonds?' Mum's hand was really shaking as she undid the flap of the envelope.

'The ones out of that old bag. In Charlotte's grandma's room. It was in with all those silk postcards.' Daniel's face was flaming, his hair

329

spectacularly on end where he'd pushed his fingers through it over and over again. 'Oh, hell, I can't believe I behaved so crassly; I should have just handed them over at once. I had this idea it would make a nice surprise.'

'Is there a James Bond on this afternoon?' asked Nan. 'He's a swanky chap.' Everyone ignored her and she closed her eyes. Mum spread the yellowed bonds out on the sofa between us. *Issued by the Lords Commissioners of HM Treasury*, the one nearest me said. *£1.*

'So Nan's won £10,000?' I laughed. It was a hysterical thought. 'My God, she'll be able to buy cartloads of belly pork!'

Nan opened her eyes and started to giggle too, though I don't think she had a clue what was going on.

'No, hang on a minute,' said Mum waving the page and breathing hard.

'What now?'

Mum frowned. 'Well, there's no name on the bonds themselves . . . but it says Miss *Karen* Hesketh on the card that's with them. Does that mean . . .'

'Oh, my God! I bet Nan and Grandad bought you these when you were a baby! How many are there?'

Nan was smiling broadly.

'Twenty pounds' worth. That would have been a fortune in those days.' Mum got up slowly and knelt in front of Nan, holding up the scraps of paper under her nose in a fan. They looked a bit like bank notes. 'Did you? Did you buy these for me when I was born?' Nan carried on smiling but said nothing. 'It's very important, Mother. Do you

330

understand me? Did you buy these—for *me*?'

'They're dated-stamped April 1963, if that's any help,' murmured Daniel politely.

Mum put the bonds into the dip of Nan's skirt and took Nan's hands in hers. 'Oh . . .'

Nan patted her daughter's head absently, sighed, then closed her eyes again. 'It were a good big turkey,' she muttered. Her lips parted and she was asleep immediately, head lolling onto the antimacassar. How do they do that, old people, just drop straight off? Mum rocked back onto her haunches and Daniel helped her to her feet.

'OK, Mrs Cooper?'

She looked him in the eye. 'Are you absolutely sure this money's ours? Because I don't think I could stand it now, you know, if you were wrong.'

He stared right back. 'Mrs Cooper, I wouldn't have said a word till I was one hundred per cent positive.'

'No, you wouldn't, would you?'

'No.'

So Mum cracked open a foul bottle of wine one of the kids at school had given her at the end of term, and Daniel had one glass and then went because he said we had a lot to talk about. After I closed the door on him I went back into the room and Mum and I looked at each other and burst out laughing. 'Oh, my God,' Mum kept saying. 'Oh, my God.'

*   *   *

I KNEW CHARLOTTE had in her mind a huge shopping spree; she'd have blown the whole lot on clothes *easily*, might have taken a few months but

331

she'd have done it. But it was my money. I told her that straight off. Her face fell.

'Well, can we at least have the bathroom done, then? You said you would.'

I shook my head.

'Well, *what,* then?' She was brewing a strop, it was quite funny to watch. Well, all that tension had to go somewhere. 'You're not going to stick it all in the bank for a "rainy day", surely? Come on, Mum, life's too short.'

Emma nodded at me.

'I will share this money with you. In fact I'll split it down the middle, fifty-fifty.' Her eyes lit up. £5,000 to spend in Top Shop! 'But listen, we need this money to do something very important.'

'What?'

'It's going to get us both through university.'

You could see the cogs going round.

'Both? Are you . . . ? D'you know, I *thought* there was something going on with you and college. Bloody hell.' She was shaking her head. 'Will they take people so . . . people like you?'

'Get away.' I made to give her a kick. 'I'll be a mature student. Yes, all right, stop pulling faces, it's not that funny. There are thousands like me, apparently, I've been looking into it. I just never thought it was really on, what with the cost. But as soon as Daniel told us. . . . Oh, Charlotte! I still can't believe . . . There are debts to be sorted, quite a few of those, store cards, catalogues . . .'

'My computer.'

'Your computer. But the rest is going to pay for a teacher training course for me at Manchester Metropolitan, and your English degree, wherever you decide to do it. Because you must go on and do

332

it now, Charlotte.'

I felt so full of energy, like I really was ready to step into this new millennium everyone kept going on about.

'I never had any intention of not applying,' she said, a bit haughty. 'But I can always get a loan.'

'I could throw this glass of wine over you. Don't be so daft! Why get in hock when there's a big lump of cash sitting there for the purpose? *And* it'll help fund a place for Will at the best nursery we can find. If you're all right with that.'

'Course it is; God, don't ask me. You'll be lumbered with the little star while I'm away, it's for you to decide.' She combed her fingers through her hair and sighed. 'Bloody hell, Mum, it sounds mental, but £10,000's hardly going to be enough, is it?'

I took a swig of wine. 'It won't cover everything, no, but it'll give us a damn good start.'

'You going to tell Dad? He gave us some out of that bogus compensation claim that time.'

'He didn't, actually. Although it wasn't his fault; he was supposed to get thousands but the claims company took most of it in fees. Serves him right, painting on bruises with eyeshadow. So, no, I think we'll keep quiet for now. Not that he'd begrudge it going on your education, he really wouldn't. He's proud of you.' Even if he does find you scary.

She kicked off her mules, stretched out on the sofa and put her feet in my lap like she used to do when she was very young. It was such an ordinary, intimate gesture, but she'd never have done that six months ago; when we hated each other. I looked down at her neat young toes and for a second remembered her as a baby, a startling memory of fat feet pressing into my naked thighs as I held her up, giggling, by her baby armpits. All that clean, innocent skin, this little piggy.

I came out of the dream and tuned back in.

'What I don't understand, though,' she was saying, 'is why the Premium Bond people didn't contact us. Is it like the lottery, it's up to you to check your numbers?'

I took her toes between my palms and she squeaked and wriggled; what a shock that we could be like this again. I was overwhelmed with the desire to bend right over and give her an enormous hug, thank her for having once been such a beautiful baby, but she'd have thought I was unhinged. Instead I just said; 'Yes, I was thinking about that. They're supposed to write. We should have had at least one letter the October, November before last. I wonder what happened to it.'

From the armchair, Nan smacked her lips and muttered. Charlotte turned her head round to look, then made a despairing face at me.

'Oh, God. She could have done anything with it, Mum. Toasted it, pushed it under a carpet, stuck it behind a pic—' She gave a funny sort of giggle. 'Well, who knows. They could have sent us a whole load of *Congratulations!* and she'd have snaffled them one after the other. Like having a vicious dog lurking behind the letter box. Who knows *what* vital communications we've lost over the last couple of years. But then, you'd think they'd have used the telephone . . .'

'Which she won't ever answer.'

Charlotte clapped her hand to her brow. 'And if we were tied up and missed the call . . .'

'They don't keep trying for ever. There are

thousands in unclaimed prizes, apparently, Daniel said.'

'Thousands of people with grannies who eat the post?'

'Maybe.' I thought of what the New Year was to bring, the bed waiting for Nan at Mayfield. Remembering was like having a family Bible settle on your chest. 'Anyway, that's one problem we won't have to deal with any more.'

LEO CAME in the evening, after Nan had gone back. I told him about the money; I wasn't going to at first, but then it just came out. He was delighted for us, as I knew he would be. He *is* a nice man.

                    *   *   *

There are a lot of things money can't touch, of course.

It was so weird leaving Nan in that home. We got her set up in her room—a pleasant one with a bay window and a tree outside that hid most of the car park—put her slippers by the bed, her underclothes in the drawers, her knick-knacks out on the shelves. She didn't have much with her. Big photo of Will on one side of the bed, Mum's wedding on the other, but pride of place went to a blown-up print of her and Grandad sitting on a form, they look about twenty, having a cuddle. She's got white stockings on and black shoes with a bar across and her hair is straight and shoulder-length. She's looking into the camera, only half-smiling, as if she has something on her mind. He's looking at her, his arms tight round her shoulders, shy grin. His legs are out in front of him and you

335

can see four little studs at the front of each sole. They are so *young*.

'You'll be able to watch the birds, Mum.'

'Aye.'

When we walked away she was sitting on the bed like a lost child. Matron was chatting away to her but she wasn't taking much notice.

'I don't think I can stand it,' said Mum clinging to the door jamb.

'Come on. Quick, before you bottle it. If she's really unhappy after a few weeks, you can think again, but you've got to give it a try. The doctor said it was the best place.' I took Mum's sleeve and pulled her away, down the corridor. Bertie trotted past us, tail beating. I watched with my fingers crossed, and he disappeared into Nan's room.

'I need a drink,' said Mum.

'Do we not need to get back for Debbie?'

'I told her half three and it's not half two yet. She's got my mobile if William plays up.'

So we found a wine bar, and sat there for nearly an hour, just two women sharing a bottle of Chardonnay.

*   *   *

CHARLOTTE HAD BEEN moth-eating me about filling in the family tree at the front of William's Baby Record book. I'd drawn a blank after three generations, so I told her to ask Nan. 'Take those old photos in the shoe box while you're at it, I've been meaning to get them labelled up for ages. And leave William here with me or you'll never get anything done.'

When she came back she was bubbling with

336

excitement.

'God, it was mad, Mum! They had a full-scale emergency on when I got there because this old biddy reckoned she'd seen her friend eat a bit off a firelighter. They had an ambulance out, the doctor, everyone running round looking for the First Aid book, do you induce vomiting or not. Then in the end it turned out to be a chunk off a Thornton's nougat casket. Matron had to have a sit down after. Never a dull moment at Mayfield, she says.'

'And how was Nan?'

Charlotte started unpacking the carrier bag of photos. 'Amazing. It was like switching a light on, Mum; she just came to life. We talked for hours and it was dead interesting.'

She pulled some photos out of an envelope and laid them on the table. I stuck William under his baby gym and came to see.

'That one's their wedding day.'

'I guessed that.'

'Yeah, but check out that hat! You can hardly see her face. Is that the locket she still wears?'

'Probably. Gosh, doesn't my dad look dapper with his buttonhole . . . He was no age when he died, it was such a shame.' I picked up the picture and held it to the light. The dad I'd known had always been tired and short of breath; here was a young, happy, vigorous man starting out in life.

'And did you know he'd been engaged to someone else when she met him?'

I put the photo back down, surprised. 'No. She never said anything.'

'Yes, really. She snaffled him! Can you imagine Nan doing something like that? I reckon she was a bit of a minx when she was a girl.' Charlotte shook her head in mock disapproval.

'She must have really been in love.' I thought of my own wedding album, stuck underneath the wardrobe in shame. 'And she was right too, they were devoted to each other for over forty years.'

'My God, that's fantastic.' Charlotte picked out another; Nan in a gaberdine-type coat and a group of young girls in pinafores. They were standing, along with a big, stern man wearing a watch and chain, in front of a vintage bus. 'Nan said that was a charabanc. They called it Whistling Rufus and they went on trips to Blackpool and Southport in it. She couldn't remember who those people were, though.'

'Looks like a school party. Unless, no, she's about eighteen there so she'd have left school. It must be mill workers. She always said she had some good times at Jarrod's, but they don't seem so happy there, do they? Maybe good times are relative . . .'

But Charlotte wasn't listening. 'Have you seen this one, Mum?' In her hand was a very faded, creased and yellow photograph of four people: from left to right, a little girl, standing, with ringlets, hands folded in front of her; sitting, a grim old lady in black silk and wearing clogs with their curved-up soles; a boy, younger than the girl, standing awkwardly in a dark outfit with a large white collar, something like a sailor suit; and a pretty, anxious woman in her twenties, perched on a straight-backed chair, an oval locket against her white blouse. 'Do you know who they are?'

We huddled together and gazed at the four solemn faces. Only the boy was smiling, as if he couldn't keep his energy and youth from spilling

338

out.

'Well, that's Nan,' I said, pointing to the girl. 'And that'll be her grandma next to her.'

'Florrie Marsh, that's right. I've written it on the back. She looks a right old battle-axe, doesn't she? The other woman's Nan's mother, Polly. She's sad there because Nan's father kept leaving them, apparently, then coming back again. He was living with some trollop in Chorley when that picture was taken.'

I thought Polly looked tired to death. 'Poor thing. Awful not to know where you stand, so humiliating. Especially in those days. Nan would never tell me much about it, too ashamed, but I knew there was something funny about the set-up. Well, well.' I put my finger gently to the boy. 'I can guess who he is, what a little angel.' His dark suit was spoilt by a white crease in the paper running the length of his body. 'Terrible to die so young.'

'Nan's brother Jimmy. Aww, see, one of his socks is coming down.'

'Did she say anything about him?'

'He drowned in the canal.'

'Really? Poor lamb.'

'She cried when she told me, I think they were pretty close. But she was all right after,' she added hastily. 'I started telling her about Will puking into Ivy's shopping bag and she cheered right up.'

We shuffled the pictures together and Charlotte slid them back in their envelope.

'I tell you what, Mum,' she said as she put the lid back on the shoe box, 'I'm going to take that portable tape deck and record some of Nan's stories because they're really interesting, How We Used to Live and all that. I could keep the cassettes

339

for Will when he's older, his family history.'

(My family history, I thought.)

'It's like . . .' Charlotte put the box at the bottom of the stairs and came back in. 'You know when the TV's on but you're recording a different channel to the one you're watching? It's like that with Nan. What you see on the surface isn't what's going on inside. We think she's mad half the time, but it's just that she sort of lives in a different dimension to the rest of us.' She rescued Will from where he had wedged himself against the hearth and held his face up to hers. He laughed and tried to swipe at her hair. 'Well, her time frame's different, anyway. Nan's past *is* her present. I mean, there's not much this decade has to offer her, is there? You know, if someone in their twenties was widowed and then disabled, everyone would be going on about how tragic it was, but because Nan's old she'd expected to get on with it. She's a really amazing woman actually. I reckon there's more going on with Nan than anyone ever realized.'

*　　　*　　　*

I was listening to Radio 4 and they were interviewing Kate Adie about what it was like to report on the conflict in Bosnia. She said what made it difficult sometimes was that the people there had no concept of an incident being the result of a single moment's action; when something happened it was because of an accumulation of events, sometimes stretching back for decades. She was sent to cover a massacre that had taken place in a small town near the main fighting.

'What happened here yesterday?' she asked an

eye-witness.

'In 1943 . . .' the man began.

Everyone's history is the product of someone else's; what we think of as our own experience is only what's been bestowed on us by others and you can't walk away from that.

And why should you?

SNAPSHOTS FROM THE FUTURE

Will stands up on his own for the first time, falls over and bangs his head on the marble hearth. For ten seconds I think he might be dead, and in that gulf of horror I realize then that I do love him after all. It must have sneaked up on me when I wasn't looking.

Mum comes home from school with the news that Leo Fairbrother's getting married, shock announcement. Some well-to-do fifty-something he's met in Italy, Maria Callas lookalike, though she actually comes from Oldham. How will Mum take this terrible blow? To be honest she seems fine about it; maybe they were only ever good friends. In the event Mrs F provides Mum with twice the social life (teaches her bridge, invites her to wine-tastings) and passes on her old Aquascutum and Jacques Vert, all contributions gratefully received. Now they go to the Octagon as a threesome (though I think it stops there).

I come in quietly through the back door. It's Reading Week at university, and no one's expecting me. I can hear voices before I get inside.

Mum is sitting on the toilet with the door open, blowing up a balloon, while Will rushes around the kitchen shrieking. 'Mummee!' he yells when he sees me.

'Good God, is there no privacy in this place?' she moans, her voice echoing off the tiles.

I put my bags on top of the fridge and lie down

342

on the floor so that my son can climb all over me, giggling. It's good to be home, but only because I don't live here. Maybe I'm a bad mother for not being around all the time, but, hey, I'm doing the best I can. What more can any of us do?

It's a Friday teatime in November and I'm phoning home as usual.

'Shall I put Nan on?' asks Mum. 'She's been to a funeral today so I brought her back for tea.'

'Go on, then.'

There's a scuffling and someone says, 'Bloody hell fire,' then the sound of heavy breathing.

'Hello? Hello?' ('There's nobody there,' she tells Mum. 'Yes, there is,' snaps Mum, 'have some patience, for God's sake.')

'HELLO, NAN.'

'It's dark here. Is it dark where you are?'

'YES. I'M ONLY IN YORK.'

'They've a big bonfire at the Working Men's. Are you having a bonfire?'

'WE'VE GOT SOME FIREWORKS FOR LATER.'

'Are they?'

'NAN?'

'It were a beautiful sermon.'

'NAN.'

'What?'

'I LOVE YOU.'

'I love you too.' ('Here, Karen, I've got myself fast with this wire all round me.')